Social Forces in
of Cross-Strait

MW01503567

Adopting a critical political economy perspective this book sheds new light on the social and political struggles that shaped the political dynamics of Taiwan-China relations and cross-Strait rapprochement between 2008 and 2014.

Presenting a careful analysis of primary sources and interviews, the book reconstructs the historical, political and socio-economic factors that shaped Taiwan's path to the Sunflower Movement of 2014, reinterpreting this process as a struggle over Taiwan's role in the global economy. It challenges received wisdoms regarding the rise and fall of the rapprochement: First, the study argues that the rapprochement was not primarily driven by political elites but by capitalist conglomerates within Taiwan, which sought a normalisation of economic relations across the Taiwan Strait. Second, it finds that Taiwan's social movements during that period were not homogeneous but rather struggled to find a common vision that could unite the critics of the rapprochement.

The insights provided not only offer a deeper understanding of Taiwan's protest cycle between 2008 and 2014, but also serve to recontextualise the political dynamics in post-Sunflower Taiwan. As such it will appeal to students and scholars of Taiwan Studies, East Asian Politics and Social Movement Studies.

André Beckershoff received his PhD from the University of Tübingen, Germany. He specialises in international political economy and social movements. His recent publications include *Assessing the Presidency of Ma Ying-jiu in Taiwan: Hopeful Beginning, Hopeless End?* (co-edited by Gunter Schubert, Routledge, 2018).

Routledge Research on Taiwan Series

Series Editor: Dafydd Fell

SOAS, UK

The *Routledge Research on Taiwan Series* seeks to publish quality research on all aspects of Taiwan studies. Taking an interdisciplinary approach, the books will cover topics such as politics, economic development, culture, society, anthropology and history.

This new book series will include the best possible scholarship from the social sciences and the humanities and welcomes submissions from established authors in the field as well as from younger authors. In addition to research monographs and edited volumes general works or textbooks with a broader appeal will be considered.

The Series is advised by an international Editorial Board and edited by *Dafydd Fell* of the Centre of Taiwan Studies at the School of Oriental and African Studies.

For more information about this series, please visit: https://www.routledge.com/Routledge-Research-on-Taiwan-Series/book-series/RRTAIWAN

Social Forces in the Re-Making of Cross-Strait Relations

Hegemony and Social Movements in Taiwan

André Beckershoff

Routledge
Taylor & Francis Group

LONDON AND NEW YORK

First published 2024
by Routledge
4 Park Square, Milton Park, Abingdon, Oxon OX14 4RN

and by Routledge
605 Third Avenue, New York, NY 10158

Routledge is an imprint of the Taylor & Francis Group, an informa business

© 2024 André Beckershoff

The right of André Beckershoff to be identified as author of this work has been asserted in accordance with sections 77 and 78 of the Copyright, Designs and Patents Act 1988.

All rights reserved. No part of this book may be reprinted or reproduced or utilised in any form or by any electronic, mechanical, or other means, now known or hereafter invented, including photocopying and recording, or in any information storage or retrieval system, without permission in writing from the publishers.

Trademark notice: Product or corporate names may be trademarks or registered trademarks, and are used only for identification and explanation without intent to infringe.

British Library Cataloguing-in-Publication Data
A catalogue record for this book is available from the British Library

ISBN: 978-1-032-49800-3 (hbk)
ISBN: 978-1-032-49804-1 (pbk)
ISBN: 978-1-003-39554-6 (ebk)

DOI: 10.4324/9781003395546

Typeset in Times New Roman
by KnowledgeWorks Global Ltd.

Contents

Figures

Tables

Acknowledgements

This book would not have been possible without the encouragement and support of family, friends and colleagues. First and foremost, I am deeply indebted to my supervisors Professor Gunter Schubert and Professor Hans-Jürgen Bieling for their relentless support, guidance and encouragement. I am also grateful to all participants of their research seminars for their constructive criticism.

I gratefully acknowledge the funding sources that made my research possible. The ERCCT Research Fellowship granted by the ERCCT and financed by the Ministry of Education of the Republic of China (Taiwan) funded the early stages of this project including my research in Taiwan. I am thankful to Professor Tang Ching-Ping, who hosted me at the National Chengchi University and whose assistance greatly benefited my fieldwork. My second field trip was funded by the Centre d'études français sur la Chine contemporaine (CEFC) in Taipei, and I thank Professor Stéphane Corcuff for hosting me.

I also wish to thank R.O. Arling (né Müllan), Stefan Braig, Stephan Engelkamp, Ulrich Hamenstädt, Igor Rogelja and Elisa Tamburo for their comments, advice and encouragement.

Finally, I would like to express my deep and sincere gratitude to my parents for their continuous and unparalleled support.

Note on Romanisation

Where known, I have used the romanisation preferred by the individuals or the commonly used romanisation for public figures, organisations or place names. In all remaining cases, Hanyu Pinyin is used.

Abbreviations

ACE	Alliance against the Commodification of Education
AID	Agency for International Development
AMM	Anti-Media Monopoly Movement
AMMA	Anti-Media Monster Alliance
APROC	Asia-Pacific Regional Operations Center
ARATS	Association for Relations Across the Taiwan Straits
ART	Alliance of Referendum for Taiwan
ATJ	Association of Taiwan Journalists
AU	Asia University
BIY	Black Island Nation Youth Front
CCP	Chinese Communist Party
CCU	National Chung Cheng University
CDFFA	Credit departments of farmers' and fishermen's associations
CEPD	Council for Economic Planning and Development
CER	Committee for Economic Reform
CFL	Chinese Federation of Labor
CGU	Chang Gung University
CMR	Campaign for Media Reform
CNAIC	Chinese National Association of Industry and Commerce
CNFI	Chinese National Federation of Industries
CNS	China Network Systems
COA	Council of Agriculture
CSAW	Cross-Strait Agreement Watch
CSCMF	Cross-Strait Common Market Foundation
CSSTA	Cross-Strait Service Trade Agreement
CTEA	Cross-Strait Tourism Exchange Association
DFCSTSA	Democratic Front Against the Cross-Strait Trade in Services Agreement
DPP	Democratic Progressive Party
ECFA	Economic Cooperation Framework Agreement
EDAC	Economic Development Advisory Conference
EOI	Export-Oriented Industrialisation
EPZ	Export processing zone

ESB	Economic Stabilisation Board
FA	Farmers' Association
FJU	Fu Jen Catholic University
GATT	General Agreement on Tariffs and Trade
GDP	Gross Domestic Product
GNP	Gross National Product
GSP	Generalized System of Preferences
ILO	International Labour Organization
INPR	Institute for National Policy Research
ISI	Import substitution industrialisation
ITRI	Industrial Technology and Research Institute
IYF	Independent Youth Front
JRF	Judicial Reform Foundation
KMT	Kuomintang
MAC	Mainland Affairs Council
MoEA	Ministry of Economic Affairs
MOTC	Ministry of Transportation and Communications
NASME	National Association of Small and Medium Enterprises
NAWCF	National Alliance for Workers of Closed Factories
NCC	National Communications Commission
NCCU	National Chengchi University
NCKU	National Cheng Kung University
NCTU	National Chiao Tung University
NDHU	National Dong Hwa University
NGO	Non-governmental Organisation
NHBP	No Haste Be Patient
NKNU	National Kaohsiung Normal University
NPF	National Policy Foundation
NPP	New Power Party
NSBP	New Southbound Policy
NSC	National Security Council
NSYSU	National Sun Yat-sen University
NTD	New Taiwan Dollar
NTHU	National Tsing Hua University
NTNU	National Taiwan Normal University
NTPU	National Taipei University
NTU	National Taiwan University
NUK	National University of Kaohsiung
NYMU	National Yang-Ming University
ODM	Original design manufacturer
OEM	Original equipment manufacturer
PFP	People First Party
PRC	People's Republic of China
R.O.C.	Republic of China
ROCCOC	General Chamber of Commerce of the Republic of China

SCS	Solidarity of Communication Students Taiwan
SCU	Soochow University
SDP	Social Democratic Party
SEF	Straits Exchange Foundation
SFM	Sunflower Movement
SME	Small and Medium Enterprise
SOE	State-owned enterprise
TAHR	Taiwan Association for Human Rights
TAITRA	Taiwan External Trade Development Council
TAO	Taiwan Affairs Office
TAUP	Taiwan Association of University Professors
TAVUR	Taiwan Alliance for Victims of Urban Renewal
TBA	Taiwan Business Association
TDW	Taiwan Democracy Watch
TEEMA	Taiwan Electrical and Electronic Manufacturers' Association
TFI	Taiwan Federation of Industries
THEU	Taiwan Higher Education Union
THU	Tunghai University
TIWA	Taiwan International Workers Association
TLF	Taiwan Labor Front
TPP	Trans-Pacific Partnership
TRF	Taiwan Rural Front
TSMC	Taiwan Semiconductor Manufacturing Company
TSTA	Taiwan Strait Tourism Association
TSU	Taiwan Solidarity Union
TWC	Third Wednesday Club
UMC	United Microelectronics Corporation
US	United States
WHA	World Health Assembly
WHO	World Health Organization
WLM	Wild Lily Movement
WSM	Wild Strawberry Movement
WTO	World Trade Organization
YAMM	Youth Alliance against Media Monsters
YLU	Youth Labor Union 95

1 Introduction

When Ma Ying-jeou became president of the Republic of China (ROC) in May 2008, he announced the dawn of a new era in cross-Strait relations. For over two decades, Taiwan had struggled with the growing social and economic interactions with its former adversary, the People's Republic of China (PRC). Ma's predecessors Lee Teng-hui and Chen Shui-bian had – arguably unsuccessfully – attempted to curb economic exchanges with China to minimise Taiwan's economic dependence. By 2008, the PRC had not only become Taiwan's largest trading partner but also the projection screen for the hopes and desires of an increasing number of Taiwanese who sought educational or employment opportunities in China. Ma Ying-jeou, seeking to acknowledge rather than repress these developments, paved the way for the resumption of quasi-official talks between China and Taiwan for the first time in over a decade, resulting in several technical agreements said to facilitate the economic and social interactions across the Taiwan Strait.

After several years of steady but substantial progress, this rapprochement came to an abrupt halt. On 18 March 2014, between 200 and 300 students rushed into Taiwan's parliament, the Legislative Yuan, overwhelmed security forces and began an occupation that would last for 24 days. The immediate trigger for what is now referred to as the Sunflower Movement (SFM) was the impending ratification of the Cross-Strait Service Trade Agreement (CSSTA), a trade pact negotiated between Taiwan and China that was the most ambitious initiative of the Ma Ying-jeou government to date. The SFM not only stalled the ratification of the trade agreement but also nurtured doubts about the government's pursuit of closer economic and political relations with China. Ultimately, the CSSTA was never ratified, and the SFM heralded the demise of Ma Ying-jeou's political vision of a rapprochement with China.

Why did the cross-Strait rapprochement, which seemed to have inspired "a period of expectation and hope" (Gramsci 1971: 120) that was the foundation of Ma's electoral successes in 2008 and 2012, metamorphose into a source of collective disillusionment that prompted a severe political crisis within the span of only a few years? The purpose of this study is to investigate this reversal of fortunes by looking at the role social groups in Taiwan played in both the rise and the fall of the cross-Strait rapprochement. Only by looking beyond the political arena, is it

DOI: 10.4324/9781003395546-1

possible to comprehend why the rapprochement that was once portrayed as beneficial to all Taiwanese came to be seen as profiting only a small circle of economic
and political elites.

Explaining the Cross-Strait Rapprochement

Throughout most of the 1990s and early 2000s, scholars were puzzled by the
state of cross-Strait relations, which was characterised by the apparent paradox
of "political conflict and economic interdependence" (Kastner 2009). When the
rapprochement finally seemed to erode this exceptional situation, scholars of the
realist school of international relations attributed this shift to the "rise of China".
In their view, the gravitational pull of the Chinese economy was driving an inevitable trend of economic integration that translated into ever-increasing political
leverage of the Chinese Communist Party (CCP) over the smaller economies and
polities drawn into its economic sphere. This perspective prompted predictions that
portrayed a deepening of economic interdependence and political dialogue as essentially irreversible. As Shambaugh wrote in 2010:

> [C]ross-strait relations have now developed to such an extent that the 'Taiwan
> issue' has essentially been resolved. Game over. The ultimate form of union
> between the island and the mainland is still undetermined, but it will be more
> a question of form than substance. The essential interdependence that is be-
> ing built will be enduring.
>
> (Shambaugh 2010: 224)

This "game over"-hypothesis was shared by others. Only weeks before the SFM
initiated the reversal of political relations across the Taiwan Strait, Mearsheimer
(2014: 39) wrote that "if China continues its impressive rise, Taiwan appears destined to become part of China". This distinctly undialectical approach, which is
only capable of imagining future developments as a linear continuation of present
trends, is unsatisfying on many levels. A purely structuralist view based on the
"rise of China" is not equipped with the theoretical tools that are necessary to grasp
the manifold social and political contradictions, which shape the political, social
and economic relations across the Strait.

Another strand of literature thus emphasises the dimension of agency to account
for the dynamics of cross-Strait relations. The rise of China becomes the backdrop
against which governments on both sides of the Taiwan Strait attempt to shape
cross-Strait interactions "to either take advantage of or try to offset the 'spillover'
effect from economics to politics" (Keng and Lin 2013: 169). The rapprochement
is then usually attributed to policy changes made by Hu Jintao, who became General Secretary of the CCP in 2002. On the one hand, Hu is seen as having succeeded
in increasing Taiwan's economic reliance on China (ibid.: 176). On the other hand,
he is credited with having adopted a more flexible and conciliatory approach to
Taiwan after the coercive approach against Lee Teng-hui and Chen Shui-bian had
been deemed a failure (Chen 2012). Rather than having abandoned the ultimate

goal of unification, the PRC merely adjusted the means of achieving it. This new approach is said to have paved the way for the dialogue between the CCP and the Kuomintang (KMT) (Wu and Dittmer 2013: 26–27), and changes in Taiwan's domestic politics are ultimately seen as a consequence of this development (Chang and Chao 2009: 112–113). Unlike the realist perspective, these agency-centred approaches do not assume a deterministic view of cross-Strait relations. Hu (2012: 953; 2013: 226–233) sees potential stumbling blocks in the form of Taiwan's political status, which might result in disputes over its participation in international organisations, and a potential for growing impatience on the Chinese side. Wu and Dittmer (2013: 47), considering domestic and international politics as well as economic factors, also provide a more nuanced view, concluding that "there is no assurance that the current rapprochement will continue". The question of whether the rapprochement across the Strait would progress or stagnate, however, is only considered with regard to political – i.e., intergovernmental – factors.

The approach of 'linkage communities' takes the role of social groups in shaping the cross-Strait rapprochement into account (Wei 1997). It explores how the increasing social contacts across the Taiwan Strait shape the interests of these social groups, which may then act as advocacy groups vis-à-vis the Chinese and Taiwanese governments to drive the integration "from below" (Keng and Lin 2011). It thereby seeks to breathe life into the assumptions of the previously discussed approaches. The most-studied group is that of Taiwanese businesspeople based in China, or *taishang* (Keng and Schubert 2010). These studies assess the direct influence of taishang towards the Chinese (Lee 2008) and Taiwanese (Schubert 2013) governments. Lee (2008: 162) shows that Taiwanese businesspeople based in China were successful in achieving significant influence with *local* governments in China as the central government recognised their strategic value.[1] With regard to the influence of taishang on policymaking in Taiwan, Schubert (2013: 53) examines their impact on elections through voting and the sponsoring of political parties and their candidates. While the impact of these direct attempts to shaping Taiwan's cross-Strait policies is seen as rather limited, individual tycoons have been successful through informal political lobbying and by shaping public opinion through the acquisition of media outlets (Schubert and Keng 2012: 148–152). Although these studies provide crucial insights into the impact of Taiwanese businesspeople on policymaking, they need to be complemented by a look at the more indirect ways through which particular social interests shape the conditions under which political processes unfold.

In recent years, several publications have attempted to synthesise the factors discussed above. Scholars have attributed the rapprochement to the emergence of a "united front" (Kaeding 2014: 126; Wu 2017: 440), a "cross-Strait elite" (Matsuda 2015: 32) or a "cross-Strait plutocracy" (Cheung 2010: 21). Sharing similar theoretical premises and arguments, these perspectives can be grouped under the "China Factor" approach.[2] The central premise is that the rise of China has endowed the CCP with the necessary financial resources to broaden its strategy of "using business to steer politics" (Wu 2017: 426–427). "The quintessential feature of Beijing's influence operations", Wu (2021: 25) writes, "is providing material incentives to local collaborators (or co-operators) in return for political ends, often in the guise of innocuous commercial exchanges". Through these incentives, the CCP is said to have forged a united front that comprises "a cooperative KMT, local political figures, and Taishang" (Wu 2019: 220). "These notables and celebrities have become an army of reservists for the China lobby, beating the drum for the 'China opportunity'" (Wu 2021: 28), allowing China "to penetrate into all spheres of commercial, social, and cultural activities" in Taiwan (Wu 2017: 431).

While the China Factor approach has produced valuable research on mechanisms that shape the rapprochement, in particular with regard to Taiwan's media sector (Huang 2017; Lin and Lee 2017), its explanatory power is constrained by a number of considerable theoretical flaws. First, it overemphasises the authorship of the CCP, which is seen as "utiliz[ing] its huge financial capacity to 'buy Taiwan'" (Wu 2017: 431), while the KMT is cast in the role of a compliant junior partner. This reduces, second, the role of Taiwan's bourgeoisie to that of "local collaborators" (ibid.: 430) for China, neglecting the fact that the bourgeoisie is capable of articulating and pursuing their own interests and has the capacity to shape the terrain on which political processes unfold. Conceiving of the rapprochement as "mainly driven by top-down policies from both governments" (Cheung 2010: 26) thus sees social forces only at the receiving end of the rapprochement, not as devising, organising and moulding it. Finally, subaltern groups are conceived of as being passive. Farmers or "naïve" students (Kaeding 2014: 128) are portrayed as groups that are "tak[en] advantage of", while "the media are increasing [sic] manipulated" (ibid.: 127–128) by the CCP. This view fails to acknowledge that the involvement of students, farmers and other subaltern groups in the cross-Strait rapprochement is not the result of simple manipulation. These subaltern groups are aware of opportunities in China, and in certain ways, these interests are addressed by improved relations between China and Taiwan.[3] These flaws of the China Factor approach are also reflected in research on social movements in Taiwan informed by this perspective, so we will return to these questions below.

Approaches to Cross-Strait-Related Social Movements in Taiwan

Prior to the SFM, social movements that are now considered episodes of the protest cycle related to the cross-Strait rapprochement received little systematic attention. The dominant paradigm for the study of social movements in Taiwan was primarily informed by the country's democratic transition (Ho 2010; Hsiao 2011; Fan 2019). In 2013, publications on social movements in Taiwan declined to a low level after plateauing throughout the 2000s (Ho et al. 2018: 121), a fact that can be partly accounted for by the decline of social movements under the Chen Shui-bian government (Ho 2005).

The SFM changed this. Several publications shed light on the SFM itself (Ho 2015; Rowen 2015; Beckershoff 2017), and the events of 2014 not only reinvigorated Taiwan's society but also the academic interest in the study of social movements. Movements that had received little attention before were now cast in a new light, leading scholars to reconsider the Wild Strawberry Movement (Hsiao 2017), the Anti-Media Monopoly Movement (Ebsworth 2017; Wong and Wright 2018) and various local movements (Chen 2017; Cole 2017) that were now understood to have been related to Taiwan's China-focused accumulation strategy. As a result, the object of inquiry was no longer the individual movement, but a protest cycle related to cross-Strait relations as a whole (Wei 2016; Hsu 2017; Ho 2018b; Wu 2019).

The shift towards interpreting these movements as responses to the China Factor (Kaeding 2015: 210–212; Wu 2017: 426, 436–437; Hsu 2020), however, comes with the cost of retrospectively imposing a homogeneity on the protest cycle for which there is no empirical basis. Forced into the epistemological straitjacket of the China Factor, the protest cycle appears as a more or less linear evolution from the Wild Strawberry Movement (WSM) to the Anti-Media Monopoly Movement (AMM) and the cycle's point of culmination, the SFM. As the reconstruction of these movements below will show, however, each episode of contestation was characterised not only by a rich complexity of grievances but also by tensions and internal struggles among currents that resulted from the various trajectories of groups that participated in the movements. This study will by no means argue that China is not a major factor in social mobilisation between 2008 and 2014. Neglecting these internal contradictions, however, obscures the potential alternative paths that were open to the movement at various junctures, and if China ultimately prevailed as the principal motif of the movement's self-conception, an empirical analysis is necessary to explore why this path was chosen among the various alternatives that were considered at different times.

The tendency to interpret the protest cycle from the China Factor perspective was cemented after the emergence of Hong Kong's Umbrella Movement in late 2014 invited comparisons between the two cases. While there is ample reason for such a comparison, it comes with the pitfall of overemphasising the common factors in these movements. In the case of the Umbrella and Sunflower Movements, this common element was found in the China Factor (Kaeding 2014, 2015; Yuen 2014; Ho 2019a; Wu 2019), and various publications emphasised how China-related factors such as identity (Kwan 2016; Au 2017a,b) affected these movements. This perspective further reinforced the view that the SFM and the movements preceding it are best understood as a response to China's attempt to incorporate Taiwan. Consequently, the multiplicity of grievances that informed the protest cycle in Taiwan is excluded, considerably limiting the potential of comparative approaches. It not only consolidated the epistemological homogenisation of the protest cycle in Taiwan but also removed it as a case for comparative research with similar movements elsewhere around the globe, such as the Occupy or Gezi Park movements.

By shedding light on the factors that contributed to protest in Taiwan beyond the China Factor, this study will argue that the comparison with Hong Kong should be complemented by comparisons to social movements that go beyond the China Factor as a common element. South Korea, for instance, suggests itself not only due to its similar socio-economic and political trajectory as an East Asian newly industrialised economy that is significantly shaped by its adherence to neoliberal developmentalism (Cho and Jessop 2001) but also because it experienced similar social movements (Lee 2014b), including movements against agricultural imports from the US (Ho and Hong 2012), rising tuition fees (Shin et al. 2014; Wei 2016: 155–160; Della Porta et al. 2020: 17) and youth unemployment (Sohn 2019).

Two further strands of literature are of note. The first of these explores the role of social media in Taiwan's protest cycle. Scholars have studied the impact of social media on local (Tsatsou and Zhao 2016; Hsiao 2018) and international mobilisation (Chen et al. 2015) as well as the implications of "online-only" participants (Hsiao and Yang 2018). In addition to commonly known social media, Taiwan's own PTT platform has received attention (Cader 2017; Hsiao 2017). The authors generally agree that social media are a helpful tool to maintain and activate networks, to support the coordination of mobilisation processes and to channel political ideologies (Au 2016). It is, however, doubtful that social media can replace the "offline" structures that are the result of long and arduous processes of day-to-day organising (Hsu 2009: 103–104). It is therefore necessary to carefully reconstruct the emergence of social networks that were then activated during social movements. In addition to looking at how movements made use of existing social media platforms, scholars have highlighted how Taiwan's activists established their own platforms to live-stream from the Legislative Yuan, launch crowdfunding initiatives or establish platforms to coordinate tasks during the occupation (Cheng 2015; Lee 2015; Liao et al. 2020). The authors largely praise the positive effects of these innovations. Lee (2015), however, also shows how the self-imposed around-the-clock media presence constrained the movement and contributed to the containment of radical demands. This promising avenue will be further explored in this study.

A final body of literature emerging from the academic engagement with the cycle of social contestation in Taiwan is concerned with its effects on Taiwan's political system. Authors have studied how the emergence of new political parties in the aftermath of the SFM affected Taiwan's political spectrum (Fell 2018; Ho 2018a) and how extant parties have recruited SFM activists (Ho 2019b) or allowed them to run as candidates (Wang 2020). While these studies have shown that the SFM has introduced new issues into Taiwan's domestic political discourse and has the potential to upset the dominance of the country's two major parties, the relation between activists and political parties still demands further clarification. While Brading (2017: 161), for instance, argues that "the DPP, with its Taiwanese roots and swift decision to recast its political stance through a change to its leadership, became better placed to win the 'hearts and minds' of young Taiwanese", Nachman (2018) finds significant tensions between SFM activists and the Democratic Progressive Party (DPP) and suggests the DPP received activist votes out of strategic anti-KMT considerations rather than a correspondence of political visions. By shedding light on the particular internal dynamics of the protest cycle itself, this study can provide further context to these questions and contribute to an assessment of whether the institutionalisation of Sunflower activism has to be seen as reinvigorating party politics or as a weakening of movement activism.

The Rapprochement as a Contested Hegemonic Project

The discussion above has identified several shortcomings of the extant approaches that have been proposed to explain the dynamics of cross-Strait relations. In essence, these shortcomings can be attributed to the inadequate ways in which these approaches conceptualise the role of social groups. The neglect of how social forces *within* Taiwan have contributed to driving the rapprochement results in an overemphasis of the authorship of the CCP, reducing Taiwan's bourgeoisie to the role of compradors and conceiving of the subaltern as groups that have merely been manipulated into supporting the process. The social contestation of the rapprochement is then portrayed as the resistance of a homogeneous civil society against the increasing influence of China over Taiwan, obscuring the degree to which other factors have contributed to grievances and thus social mobilisation. The predominance of the 'China vs. Taiwan' and 'state vs. civil society' angles limits the explanatory power of these approaches.

The aim of the present study is to shed light on the social struggle over Taiwan's relationship with the PRC that unfolded within Taiwan. To this end, we will here adopt an analytical perspective that allows us to reinterpret the cross-Strait rapprochement as a contested hegemonic project, that is, the attempt by Taiwan's bourgeoisie to organise consent to a normalisation of economic relations across the Taiwan Strait. The major argument, which will be substantiated over the following six chapters, can be summed up as follows: As Taiwan's previous social formation – characterised by a developmental state growth regime – reached exhaustion both in terms of economic success and domestic as well as international legitimacy, its internal contradictions contributed to the relocation of industrial production to China. From this reorganisation of production from the late 1980s onwards emerged social forces, which increasingly depend on the access to global markets, especially China. Facing political obstacles to achieve closer economic ties with China, Taiwan's bourgeoisie organised a common project that relied on key organic intellectuals and business groups to articulate and disseminate a narrative that portrayed closer economic ties with China as natural, normal and necessary, and universalise their particular interests by offering ideological and material concessions to subaltern groups in Taiwan. This raises the question under which conditions the subaltern groups consented to this process and when they rejected it. To achieve a critical understanding of this dynamic, this study reconstructs the strategies and mechanisms through which the forces that constitute the hegemonic project operate. The analytical emphasis lies on understanding how these initiatives managed to include or marginalise subaltern forces and where, by contrast, attempts to secure consent from broader strata of Taiwan's society were met with resistance.

To this end, Chapter 2 reconceptualises the cross-Strait rapprochement as a contested hegemonic project. The Gramscian notion of hegemony allows us to shift the analytical attention to social forces that seek to secure the consent to Taiwan's neoliberal developmentalist accumulation strategy. Drawing on the works of Rosa Luxemburg and Henri Lefebvre, the chapter then sets out to provide methodological pointers for a process analysis of hegemonic contestation as the struggle over social forms of everyday life.

Chapter 3 discusses the historical and structural origins of the hegemonic project that attempts to secure consent for neoliberal developmentalism in Taiwan. These dynamics are mainly conditioned by the ways in which the contradictions of the developmental state were resolved. The neo-mercantilist accumulation strategy paired extraversion with protectionism. Although the liberalisation of the 1990s and 2000s saw an increasing erosion of internal and external barriers to accumulation, trade relations with the PRC were exempted from this for political reasons. The emergence and politicisation of Taiwan's bourgeoisie set into motion the implementation of a neoliberal developmentalist project that relies on the "normalisation" of trade relations with the PRC.

The following three chapters will then provide a process analysis of hegemonic contestation in Taiwan. Three phases can be distinguished. The first of these phases, which will be discussed in Chapter 4, is characterised by the hegemonic project's attempt to de-politicise the rapprochement by portraying it as the technocratic management of technical issues arising from a quasi-natural trend towards economic integration. The analysis will expound on how this narrative was promoted by a network of civil society organisations representing the interests of Taiwan's bourgeoisie. Although the WSM emerged in response to hegemonic interventions, its reconstruction will shed light on the ideological and material constraints that prevented a more effective social mobilisation.

Chapter 5 explores the hegemonic project's response to this social challenge. It reconstructs a shift from a narrative of technocratic management to one that attempts to naturalise closer relations across the Taiwan Strait by emphasising cultural proximity. This shift relied on the establishment of a broad network of civil society organisations to integrate subaltern groups like students or workers. This process will be illustrated by the case of increased cross-Strait cooperation in the media sector, a hegemonic initiative that in turn prompted the emergence of several centres of contestation. A detailed analysis will show how these currents were forged into the AMM.

Chapter 6 then reconstructs how the hegemonic initiatives designed to restore Taiwan's global competitiveness were experienced in the everyday lives of Taiwan's students, farmers and workers, contributing to an accumulation of grievances that resulted in the adoption of radical forms of ideology and practice. The signing of a trade agreement between China and Taiwan acted as a catalyst for the 2014 SFM. Against extant analyses, this study will argue that the SFM was characterised by a struggle over the adequate forms of politicisation that accounts for the fragmentation of movement currents during and after the movement.

The concluding chapter, finally, will discuss the implications of this analysis for our understanding of social and political dynamics in post-Sunflower Taiwan.

Limitations and Contributions of the Study

Although this research design will allow us to gain a deeper understanding of the dynamics of cross-Strait relations under Ma Ying-jeou, a few notes are in order. A first limitation resulting from the research design is the empirical focus on Taiwan's society. Even though the processes examined here are necessarily related to the PRC, this study is mainly concerned with how social forces *in Taiwan* attempt to universalise their particular interests or contest the attempted universalisation of the interests of other groups. Due to the scope of this study, the interest formation and potential social contestation in China is not considered. This should, however, not affect the validity of the findings presented here, as the CCP enjoys a relative autonomy from civil society and its political goals and the means it has employed to achieve these have remained constant over the period examined here.

A second drawback arising from the analytical perspective adopted here is that the mode of presentation does not follow a uniform structure across the various chapters. While each episode of hegemonic contestation was studied following the same mode of inquiry, the mode of presentation differs as the structure of each chapter is dictated by the need to depict and explain the particular dynamics that conditioned each episode. Furthermore, the presentation of findings does not follow a strict chronological order. Drawing on a distinction proposed by Jessop (2003: 4), the aim is not to provide a *chronology* of hegemonic contestation in Taiwan, but rather a *periodisation*, which privileges the reconstruction of the underlying factors that characterise each distinct phase, at times resulting in "intersecting and overlapping time horizons" (ibid.). In particular, the analyses presented in chapters five and six overlap chronologically, as the trajectory of certain groups, currents and movements can only be distinguished on a methodological level.

The analytical precedence the cycle of hegemonic contestation takes over individual episodes means that, third, this study does not seek to provide an exhaustive account covering all features of each of the social movements considered here. While competing imaginations and potential alternate paths will be explored, in many cases more could have been said on various aspects of each movement. An exhaustive account of the AMM, for example, would need to discuss the movement's transition into parliamentary politics, covering the political debate on anti-monopoly legislation. Conversely, there were hegemonic initiatives that could have been discussed at further length. One example is the Economic Cooperation Framework Agreement (ECFA). The limited protest against the ECFA, however, did not spill over into an episode of generalised social contestation. Given the limitations of space, these aspects will therefore not be fully explored.

The contributions of this research project are twofold. Empirically, this study sheds light on the involvement of social forces driving the rapprochement from within Taiwan. The analysis illustrates the degree to which Taiwan's bourgeoisie has been instrumental in setting up networks of civil society organisations that sought to organise consent for closer economic relations across the Taiwan Strait. Furthermore, the detailed analysis of the social contestation related to the rapprochement results in a more nuanced understanding of social movements in Taiwan. Rather than assuming a homogeneous civil society in Taiwan, the following chapters illuminate how these movements were fraught with internal tensions that were the result of an intense and highly contradictory process of organisation. Both of these insights will serve to contextualise the competing visions that will shape Taiwan's political and social dynamics for years to come. Theoretically, this study exhibits how the analytical perspective of hegemonic contestation is able to bridge domination- and resistance-focused approaches. These theoretical contributions will be discussed at length in the following chapter.

Notes

1 Lee (2010: 66; 2014a: 68–69) later suggests, however, that the privileges and influence enjoyed by Taiwanese businesspeople in China declined as the political rapprochement reduced their strategic value to the central government while the increased competition from foreign and Chinese businesses reduced the local governments' dependence on Taiwanese investments.
2 In an attempt to generalise the findings of China's relation with Taiwan and Hong Kong and make the approach applicable to more cases, the China Factor approach has recently been merged into the debate on China's 'sharp power' (see Fulda 2020).
3 Clark and Tan (2016: 339), for instance, note that even after the SFM, one third of young Taiwanese want to pursue employment opportunities in China.

Bibliography

Au, Anson (2016). "Reconceptualizing Online Free Spaces. A Case Study of the Sunflower Movement". In: *Journal of Contemporary Eastern Asia* 15.2, 145–161.

——— (2017a). "Collective Identity, Organization, and Public Reaction in Protests. A Qualitative Case Study of Hong Kong and Taiwan". In: *Social Sciences* 6.4, 1–17.

——— (2017b). "The Sunflower Movement and the Taiwanese National Identity. Building an Anti-Sinoist Civic Nationalism". In: *Berkeley Journal of Sociology* 27. http://berkeleyjournal.org/2017/04/the-sunflower-movement-and-the-taiwanese-national-identity-building-an-anti-sinoist-civic-nationalism/ (last accessed on 26/11/2020).

Beckershoff, André (2017). "The Sunflower Movement. Origins, structures, and strategies of Taiwan's resistance against the 'Black Box'". In: *Taiwan's Social Movements under Ma Ying-jeou. From the Wild Strawberries to the Sunflowers*. Ed. by Dafydd Fell. London and New York: Routledge, 113–133.

Brading, Ryan (2017). "Taiwan's Millennial Generation. Interests in Polity and Party Politics". In: *Journal of Current Chinese Affairs* 46.1, 131–166.

Cader, Joshua (2017). "From (anti-mainland) Sinophobia and shibboleths to mobilisation on a Taiwanese message board". In: *Chinese Social Media. Social, Cultural, and Political Implications*. Ed. by Mike Kent, Katie Ellis and Jian Xu. London and New York: Routledge, 163–174.

Chang, Wu-ueh and Chien-min Chao (2009). "Managing Stability in the Taiwan Strait. Non-Military Policy Towards Taiwan under Hu Jintao". In: *Journal of Current Chinese Affairs* 38.3, 99–118.

Chen, Chien-Kai (2012). "Comparing Jiang Zemin's Impatience with Hu Jintao's Patience Regarding the Taiwan Issue, 1989–2012". In: *Journal of Contemporary China* 21.78, 955–972.

Chen, Hsuan-Ting, Sun Ping and Gan Chen (2015). "Far from Reach but Near at Hand. The Role of Social media for Cross-National Mobilization". In: *Computers in Human Behavior* 53, 443–451.

Chen, Ketty W. (2017). "This land is your land? This land is MY land. Land expropriation during the Ma Ying-jeou administration and implications for social movements". In: *Taiwan's Social Movements under Ma Ying-jeou. From the Wild Strawberries to the Sunflowers*. Ed. by Dafydd Fell. London and New York: Routledge, 92–112.

Cheng, Tracey (2015). "Taiwan's sunflower protest. Digital anatomy of a movement". In: *Digital Activism in Asia Reader*. Ed. by Nishant Shah, Puthiya Purayil Sneha and Sumandro Chattapadhyay. Milton Keynes: Meson Press, 87–97.

Cheung, Gordon C.K. (2010). "New Approaches to Cross-Strait Integration and its Impacts on Taiwan's Domestic Economy. An Emerging 'Chaiwan'?". In: *Journal of Current Chinese Affairs* 39.1, 11–36.

Cho, Hee-Yeon and Bob Jessop (2001). "The Listian Warfare State and Authoritarian Developmental Mobilization Regime in the East Asian Anticommunist Regimented Society". *Conference paper prepared for the workshop "In Search of East Asian Modes of Development: Regulationist Approaches"*. Tunghai University, Taichung, 19–20 April, 2001.

Clark, Cal and Alexander C. Tan (2016). "Identity and Integration as Conflicting Forces Stimulating the Sunflower Movement and the Kuomintang's Loss in the 2014 Elections". In: *Contemporary Chinese Political Economy and Strategic Relations. An International Journal* 2.1, 313–349.

Cole, J. Michael (2017). "Civic activism and protests in Taiwan. Why size doesn't (always) matter". In: *Taiwan's Social Movements under Ma Ying-jeou. From the Wild Strawberries to the Sunflowers*. Ed. by Dafydd Fell. London and New York: Routledge, 18–33.

Della Porta, Donatella, Lorenzo Cini and César Guzmán-Concha (2020). *Contesting Higher Education. Student Movements Against Neoliberal Universities*. Bristol: Bristol University Press.

Ebsworth, Rowena (2017). "Not wanting Want. The anti-media monopoly movement in Taiwan". In: *Taiwan's Social Movements under Ma Ying-jeou. From the Wild Strawberries to the Sunflowers*. Ed. by Dafydd Fell. London and New York: Routledge, 71–91.

Fan, Yun (2019). *Social Movements in Taiwan's Democratic Transition. Linking Activists to the Changing Political Environment*. London and New York: Routledge.

Fell, Dafydd (2018). "Taiwan's political parties in the aftermath of the 2016 elections". In: *A New Era in Democratic Taiwan. Trajectories and Turning Points in Politics and Cross-Strait Relations*. Ed. by Jonathan Sullivan and Chun-Yi Lee. London and New York: Routledge, 63–82.

Fulda, Andreas (2020). *The Struggle for Democracy in Mainland China, Taiwan and Hong Kong. Sharp Power and its Discontents*. London and New York: Routledge.

Gramsci, Antonio (1971). *Selections from the Prison Notebooks*. Ed. by Quintin Hoare and Geoffrey Nowell-Smith. London: Lawrence and Wishart.

Ho, Ming-sho (2005). "Taiwan's State and Social Movements under the DPP Government, 2000–2004". In: *Journal of East Asian Studies* 5.3, 401–425.

——— (2010). "Understanding the Trajectory of Social Movements in Taiwan (1980–2010)". In: *Journal of Current Chinese Affairs* 39.3, 3–22.

——— (2015). "Occupy Congress in Taiwan. Political Opportunity, Threat, and the Sunflower Movement". In: *Journal of East Asian Studies* 15.1, 69–97.

——— (2018a). "From protest to electioneering. Electoral and party politics after the Sunflower Movement". In: *A New Era in Democratic Taiwan. Trajectories and Turning Points in Politics and Cross-Strait Relations*. Ed. by Jonathan Sullivan and Chun-Yi Lee. London and New York: Routledge, 83–103.

——— (2018b). "The rise of civil society activism in the Ma Ying-jiu era. The genesis and outcome of the Sunflower Movement". In: *Assessing the Presidency of Ma Ying-jiu. Hopeful Beginning, Hopeless End?* Ed. by André Beckershoff and Gunter Schubert. London and New York: Routledge, 109–131.

——— (2019a). *Challenging Beijing's Mandate of Heaven. Taiwan's Sunflower Movement and Hong Kong's Umbrella Movement*. Philadelphia, PA: Temple University Press.

———— (2019b). "The road to mainstream politics. How Taiwan's Sunflower Movement activists became politicians". In: *After Protest. Pathways Beyond Mass Mobilisation*. Ed. by Richard Youngs. Washington, DC: Carnegie Endowment for International Peace, 61–67.

Ho, Ming-sho and Chen-Shuo Hong (2012). "Challenging New Conservative Regimes in South Korea and Taiwan". In: *Asian Survey* 52.4, 643–665.

Ho, Ming-sho, Chun-hao Huang and Chun-ta Juan (2018). "The Institutionalisation of Social Movement Study in Taiwan". In: *International Journal of Taiwan Studies* 1.1, 115–140.

Hsiao, Hsin-Huang Michael (2011). "Social movements in Taiwan. A typological analysis". In: *East Asian Social Movements. Power, Protest, and Change in a Dynamic Region*. Ed. by Jeffrey Broadbent and Vicky Brockman. New York, Dordrecht, Heidelberg, London: Springer, 237–254.

Hsiao, Yuan (2017). "Virtual ecologies, mobilization and democratic groups without leaders. Impacts of Internet media on the Wild Strawberry Movement". In: *Taiwan's Social Movements under Ma Ying-jeou. From the Wild Strawberries to the Sunflowers*. Ed. by Dafydd Fell. London and New York: Routledge, 34–53.

———— (2018). "Understanding Digital Natives in Contentious Politics. Explaining the Effect of Social Media on Protest Participation Through Psychological Incentives". In: *New media & Society* 20.9, 3457–3478.

Hsiao, Yuan and Yunkang Yang (2018). "Commitment in the Cloud? Social Media Participation in the Sunflower Movement". In: *Information, Communication & Society* 21.7, 996–1013.

Hsu, Jenshuo (2020). "From Martial Law to Sunflower. The Evolution of Taiwan's Student Movement". In: *Asian Education and Development Studies* 10.4, 555–564.

Hsu, Julia Chiung-wen (2009). "Internet et les nouveaux mouvements sociaux à Taïwan". In: *Hermès, La Revue* 55, 97–105.

Hsu, Szu-chien (2017). "The China factor and Taiwan's civil society organizations in the Sunflower Movement. The case of the Democratic Front Against the Cross-Strait Service Trade Agreement". In: *Taiwan's Social Movements under Ma Ying-jeou. From the Wild Strawberries to the Sunflowers*. Ed. by Dafydd Fell. London and New York: Routledge, 134–153.

Hu, Weixing (2012). "Explaining Change and Stability in Cross-Strait Relations. A Punctuated Equilibrium Model". In: *Journal of Contemporary China* 21.78, 933–953.

———— (2013). "Prospects of cross-Taiwan strait relations. Toward an involutional process?" In: *New Dynamics in Cross-Taiwan Strait Relations. How Far Can the Rapprochement Go?* Ed. by Weixing Hu. London and New York: Routledge, 218–234.

Huang, Jaw-Nian (2017). "The China Factor in Taiwan's Media. Outsourcing Chinese Censorship Abroad". In: *China Perspectives* (3/2017), 27–36.

Jessop, Bob (2003). *The Political Scene and the Politics of Representation. Periodizing Class Struggle and the State in The Eighteenth Brumaire*. https://www.lancaster.ac.uk/fass/resources/sociology-online-papers/papers/jessop-political-scene.pdf (last accessed on 28/11/2019).

Kaeding, Malte Philipp (2014). "Challenging Hongkongisation. The Role of Taiwan's Social Movements and Perceptions of Post-Handover Hong Kong". In: *Taiwan in Comparative Perspective* 5.July, 120–133.

———— (2015). "Resisting China's Influence. Social Movements in Hong Kong and Taiwan". In: *Current History* 114.773, 210–216.

Kastner, Scott L. (2009). *Political Conflict and Economic Interdependence Across the Taiwan Strait and Beyond*. Stanford, CA: Stanford University Press.

Keng, Shu and Ruihua Lin (2011). "Integrating from below. Observing the 'linkage communities' across the Taiwan strait". In: *China's Quiet Rise. Peace Through Integration*. Ed. by Baogang Guo and Chung-chian Teng. Plymouth: Lexington Books, 139–156.

——— (2013). "Bidding for Taiwanese hearts. The achievements and limitations of China's strategy to engage Taiwan". In: *New Dynamics in Cross-Taiwan Strait Relations. How Far Can the Rapprochement Go?* Ed. by Weixing Hu. London and New York: Routledge, 169–189.

Keng, Shu and Gunter Schubert (2010). "Agents of Taiwan-China Unification? The Political Roles of Taiwanese Business People in the Process of Cross-Strait Integration". In: *Asian Survey* 50.2, 287–310.

Kwan, Justin P. (2016). "The Rise of Civic Nationalism. Shifting Identities in Hong Kong and Taiwan". In: *Contemporary Chinese Political Economy and Strategic Relations. An International Journal* 2.2, 941–973.

Lee, Chun-Yi (2008). "When Private Capital Becomes a Security Asset. Challenging Conventional Government/Business Interaction". In: *East Asia* 25, 145–165.

——— (2010). "Between Dependency and Autonomy. Taiwanese Entrepreneurs and Local Chinese Governments". In: *Journal of Current Chinese Affairs* 39.1, 37–71.

——— (2014a). "From being privileged to being localized? Taiwanese businessmen in China". In: *Migration to and from Taiwan*. Ed. by Kuei-fen Chiu, Dafydd Fell and Lin Ping. London and New York: Routledge, 57–72.

Lee, Mei-chun (2015). "Occupy on Air. Transparency and Surveillance in Taiwan's Sunflower Movement". In: *Anthropology Now* 7.3, 32–41.

Lee, Yoonkyung (2014b). "Diverging Patterns of Democratic Representation in Korea and Taiwan. Political Parties and Social Movements". In: *Asian Survey* 54.3, 419–444.

Liao, Da-chi, Hsin-Che Wu and Boyu Chen (2020). "Social Movements in Taiwan and Hong Kong. The Logic of Communitive Action". In: *Asian Survey* 60.2, 265–289.

Lin, Lihyun and Chun-Yi Lee (2017). "When Business Met Politics. The Case of Want Want, a Different Type of Media Capital in Taiwan". In: *China Perspectives* (2/2017), 37–46.

Matsuda, Yasuhiro (2015). "Cross-Strait Relations Under the Ma Ying-jeou Administration. From Economic to Political Dependence?". In: *Journal of Contemporary East Asia Studies* 4.2, 3–35.

Mearsheimer, John J. (2014). "Taiwan's Dire Straits". In: *The National Interest* 130 (March-April), 29–39.

Nachman, Lev (2018). "Misalignment between Social Movements and Political Parties in Taiwan's 2016 Election. Not All Grass Roots Are Green". In: *Asian Survey* 58.5, 874–897.

Rowen, Ian (2015). "Inside Taiwan's Sunflower Movement: Twenty-Four Days in a Student-Occupied Parliament, and the Future of the Region". In: *The Journal of Asian Studies* 74 (01 Feb), 5–21.

Schubert, Gunter (2013). "Assessing Political Agency Across the Taiwan Strait. The Case of the Taishang". In: *China Information* 27.1, 51–79.

Schubert, Gunter and Shu Keng (2012). "Taishang as a factor shaping Taiwan's domestic politics. Politics, economics, society and culture". In: *The Vitality of Taiwan*. Ed. by Steve Tsang. Basingstoke and New York: Palgrave Macmillan, 139–163.

Shambaugh, David (2010). "A New China Requires a New US Strategy". In: *Current History* 109.728, 219–226.

Shin, Jung Cheol, Hoon-Ho Kim and Hong-Sam Choi (2014). "The Evolution of Student Activism and Its Influence on Tuition Fees in South Korean Universities". In: *Studies in Higher Education* 39.3, 441–454.

Sohn, Injoo (2019). "The Contentious Politics of Youth Unemployment. Comparing Korea and Taiwan". In: *The Korean Journal of International Studies* 17.1, 55–77.

Tsatsou, Panayiota and Yupei Zhao (2016). "A 'Two-Level Social Capital Analysis' of the Role of Online Communication in Civic Activism. Lessons from the Role of Facebook in the Sunflower Movement". In: *Social Media + Society* (October-December), 1–16.

Wang, Austin Horng-En (2020). "Do Social Movements Encourage Young People to Run for Office? Evidence from the 2014 Sunflower Movement in Taiwan". In: *Journal of Asian and African Studies* 55.3, 317–329.

Wei, Yang (2016). "The Restless Decade before Sunflower Movement. The Emergence and Practices of Networks of Social Movement Youth Activists (2007–2016)". (In Chinese). Unpublished Master Thesis. National Tsinghua University. https://hdl.handle.net/11296/6t7myw (last accessed on 09/12/2019).

Wei, Yung (1997). "From 'Multi-System Nations' to 'Linkage Communities'. A New Conceptual Scheme for the Integration of Divided Nations". In: *Issues & Studies* 33.10, 1–19.

Wong, Shiau Ching and Scott Wright (2018). "Generating a Voice Among 'Media Monsters'. Hybrid Media Practices of Taiwan's Anti-Media Monopoly Movement". In: *Australian Journal of Political Science* 53.1, 89–102.

Wu, Jieh-min (2017). "The China Factor in Taiwan. Impact and response". In: *Routledge Handbook of Contemporary Taiwan*. Ed. by Gunter Schubert. London and New York: Routledge, 426–446.

――― (2019). "Taiwan's Sunflower occupy movement as a transformative resistance to the 'China Factor'". In: *Take Back Our Future. An Eventful Sociology of the Hong Kong Umbrella Movement*. Ed. by Ching Kwan Lee and Ming Sing. Ithaca and London: Cornell University Press, 215–240.

――― (2021). "More than sharp power. Chinese influence operations in Taiwan, Hong Kong and beyond". In: *China's Influence and the Center-Periphery Tug of War in Hong Kong, Taiwan and Indo-Pacific*. Ed. by Brian C.H. Fong, Jieh-min Wu and Andrew J. Nathan. London and New York: Routledge, 24–44.

Wu, Yu-Shan and Lowell Dittmer (2013). "What drives the cross-strait rapprochement? Political competition, globalization, and the strategic triangle". In: *Mobile Horizons. Dynamics Across the Taiwan Strait*. Ed. by Wen-hsin Yeh. Berkeley: Institute of East Asian Studies, 25–48.

Yuen, Samson (2014). "Under the Shadow of China. Beijing's Policy Towards Hong Kong and Taiwan in Comparative Perspective". In: *China Perspectives* (2/2014), 69–76.

2 Theoretical Approach

The Cross-Strait Rapprochement as a
Contested Hegemonic Project

The writings of Antonio Gramsci have inspired countless empirical research projects and theoretical debates, the survey of which is far beyond the scope of this chapter. Rather than attempting to reconstruct the depth of how his thought has been applied to current issues, the following sections will interrogate his thought with the aim of outlining a conceptual apparatus that can help us decipher the cross-Strait rapprochement as a contested project. To this end, the chapter will bridge two approaches within Gramscian-inspired research: the domination-focused and the resistance-focused approaches (Huke et al. 2015). In a way, these two currents are already present in Gramsci's work. Living the dialectical unity of theory and practice, Gramsci was as much a *student of* the historical and political factors that shaped the terrain of inter-war Italy as he was an *activist on* that terrain. And while Gramsci's political ambition was to construct an emancipatory project by and for Italy's working class, his political activities were inseparable from his comparative analysis of the successful and failed attempts by the bourgeois class to organise its hegemony. Within Gramsci's writings, therefore, we have two moments that are dialectically linked: the moment of analysing how dominant classes produce and reproduce their supremacy on the one hand, and the moment of studying past and present forms of resistance in order to point out the potential for constructing a progressive movement on the other.

To some degree, it is therefore surprising that this unity, while often invoked, is rarely realised in research (see criticisms by Drainville 2004: 29; Winter 2011: 152–153; Huke et al. 2015; Shields 2015: 671). Since a selection of notes from Gramsci's *Prison Notebooks* was published in English in 1971, a large body of literature has emerged on the question of the reproduction of bourgeois rule. Only more recently, Gramscian ideas have received systematic treatment in the study of resistance movements.[1] Nevertheless, there seems to be little constructive dialogue between both sides – on the contrary, the relationship between the two camps seems to be marked by mutual criticism (Shields 2015: 671). This is all the more puzzling if one considers that the origin of the division into opposing (or to put it in a more conciliatory way: complementary) strands in contemporary research is not so much theoretical as it is epistemic: While both strands agree on the basic theoretical arguments advanced by Gramsci, it is their specific research interest that

DOI: 10.4324/9781003395546-2

leads them to privilege either the reproduction of domination or the formation of protest and resistance movements.

This bifurcation into opposing research foci and methods conceals the degree to which domination and resistance are mutually constitutive. To overcome this opposition of empirical perspectives, this chapter aims to shift the emphasis on the dialectical (i.e. relational and process-based) aspects that can already be found within Gramsci's own writings. The following sections propose a praxeological rearticulation of Gramscian concepts, arguing that ultimately both perspectives condense in a process that will be called *hegemonic contestation*: the struggle over forms of everyday life. This point, where domination and resistance are fused into one real and observable process, is consequently privileged as the empirical point of departure.

To arrive at this rearticulation, the first section introduces Gramsci's central concepts as well as the set of questions around which they emerged. It builds on criticisms within Gramscian literature to reconstruct the dialectical dimensions that are inherent to the notion of hegemony and thereby overcome the domination-resistance dichotomy. The second section argues that such a dialectical conception of hegemonic struggle necessitates a turn towards everyday life as the empirically relevant site of struggle, as the forms of everyday practice are both object and medium of contestation. This praxeological rearticulation of hegemony, however, demands new tools to guide the empirical inquiry. Section three therefore combines these arguments into an outline of a dialectical process analysis, providing three concepts that can guide the empirical analysis.

From Hegemony to the Contestation of Hegemonic Projects

The political thought of Antonio Gramsci (1881–1937) emerged at a historical juncture that shaped his analyses in a profound way. Imprisoned under Benito Mussolini's fascist rule in Italy, he spent the last years of his life making sense of the social and political developments in Italy by analysing and conceptualising similar conjunctures in Italian and European history and history of thought. The thread that holds together his writings from this period, which later became known as the *Prison Notebooks*, is the question of revolutionary practice. Gramsci, who had been the leader of the Communist Party of Italy, asked why a socialist revolution had been possible in underdeveloped Czarist Russia but not in the capitalist core countries of Western Europe, where the workers' movements had arguably been much stronger. His tentative answers emerged through a series of theoretical criticisms and arguments as well as historical analyses, the conclusion of which is condensed in the following passage:

> In Russia, the State was everything, civil society was primordial and gelatinous; in the West, there was a proper relation between State and civil society, and when the State trembled a sturdy structure of civil society was at once revealed. The State was only an outer ditch, behind which there stood a powerful system of fortresses and earthworks[.]
>
> (Gramsci 1971: 238)

While the Russian state collapsed first with the overthrow of the Romanovs and then with the capture of the Winter Palace, Gramsci argues that in capitalist social formations the state is supported by the "formidable complex of trenches and fortifications of the dominant class" (Gramsci 2012: 390), which is analytically distinct from the state apparatus. Social reproduction was safeguarded not only through the repressive institutions of the state but through a social process that aimed at the continuous organisation of consent to this form of rule. From this crucial insight, Gramsci developed his notion of *hegemony* as a form of political rule that is primarily based on the consent of the masses and where force and coercion become secondary.

To become hegemonic, a social group has to complement domination with leadership (Gramsci 1971: 57) "by presenting itself as ethico-political, [i.e.,] as the representative of universal moral values and as the carrier of rational and objective principles independent of narrow socio-economic and socio-cultural interests" (Fontana 2008: 92). In other words, the key to organising consent is to universalise the leading group's particular interest, portraying it as the "motor force of a universal expansion, of a development of all the 'national' energies" (Gramsci 1971: 182) and "have the conditions for [a class's] existence and development … accepted as a universal principle" (Gramsci 1995: 353). As will be discussed in more detail below, this comprises the articulation and diffusion of an inclusive ideology, the implementation of a corresponding and comprehensive mode of living, but also the active integration of the interests of subordinate groups. With regard to empirical research, hegemony directs our attention to the specific mechanisms of universalisation and the organisation of consent, or in Gramsci's (1971: 59) words: "In what forms, and by what means, did [these groups] succeed in establishing the apparatus (mechanism) of their intellectual, moral and political hegemony?"

The terrain on which the process of organising hegemony unfolds is *civil society*, which encompasses "the ensemble of organisms commonly called 'private'" (ibid.: 12). Gramsci here specifically lists the press and publishing houses, newspapers and journals, libraries, groups and clubs (Gramsci 1995: 155), the church, trade unions and schools (Gramsci 1994: 67), as well as capitalist firms (Gramsci 1971: 261). The power of the leading groups rests on and permeates this molecular web of institutions, each of which contributes to organising consent to this rule – often against resistance from the subaltern classes (Overbeek 2004: 125). Civil society in the Gramscian sense is therefore not an idealised realm beyond class relations and class struggle, nor can it be understood as a realm that is in opposition to the state (Buttigieg 2005). Rather, it is the terrain on which the struggle for hegemony among the various groups of society takes place (Gramsci 1971: 235–239).

A key role in this struggle for hegemony belongs to a group that Gramsci calls *organic intellectuals*. They are defined not by the "intrinsic nature of intellectual activities" (ibid.: 8) but by the function they take in the process of organising hegemony (ibid.: 12). This function has two aspects: On the one hand, these organising activities are aimed at rivalling or subaltern groups in civil society, where organic intellectuals "create the conditions most favourable to the expansion of their own class" (ibid.: 5–6). On the other hand, organic intellectuals also have a function vis-à-vis their own social group, "giv[ing] it homogeneity and an aware-ness of its own function not only in the economic but also in the social and political fields" (ibid.: 5). Both aspects rely on the capacity to articulate coherent ideologies and disseminate them through civil society. In other words, an intellectual in the Gramscian sense "must be an organiser of masses of men" (ibid.), a "permanent persuader" (ibid.: 10) who furthers the hegemony of a specific social group. It is this organic relation to "a fundamental social group" (ibid.: 12), or class, that makes these organisers *organic* intellectuals (ibid: 5).

This understanding of civil society as the site of struggle between social groups led Gramsci to an innovative understanding of the state. If civil society is not a social realm independent of or – even less so – in opposition to the state but rather complements the state apparatus in the exercise of power of the dominant classes, it is an analytical imperative to understand "the organic relations between State or political society and 'civil society'" (ibid.: 52). Civil society, therefore, is best un-derstood as an aspect of the state. What Gramsci calls the *integral state*, in contrast to the "everyday concept of the State" (ibid.: 260), then encompasses

> the entire complex of practical and theoretical activities with which the rul-ing class not only justifies and maintains its dominance, but manages to win the active consent of those over whom it rules[.]
>
> (Gramsci 1971: 244)

These activities are "characterised by the combination of force and consent, which balance each other reciprocally, without force predominating excessively over consent" (ibid.: 80). Gramsci maintains the methodological distinction between political and civil society in order to be able to precisely analyse the ways in which consent and force operate in conjunction (ibid.: 160, 271; Gramsci 1995: 439). Opratko (2014: 189) points out that this distinction helps to analyse the *effect* of certain social processes rather than their *origin* in either civil or political society. Analytically, a Gramscian approach is therefore committed to studying social dom-ination from a "dual perspective" (Gramsci 1971: 169–170), examining the histori-cally specific combination of force and consent.

Due to his contributions to Marxist theory, Gramsci has been referred to as a "theoretician of the superstructures" (Bobbio 1979), that is, a theoretician of the po-litical, ideological and cultural forms of a given social formation. This is misleading insofar as for Gramsci (Gramsci 1995: 414), Marxism's strength lies in the fact that it analyses the development of structures and superstructures "as intimately bound together and necessarily interrelated and reciprocal." Through this formulation, he distances himself both from the idealism of Benedetto Croce as well as from econ-omistic and mechanistic interpretations of Marxism (Sassoon 1980: 120). While Gramsci rejects the latter for overestimating the role of mechanical effects from the structure at the expense of socio-political factors (Gramsci 1971: 178), he criticises Crocean idealism for detaching the social and political struggle from the structural conditions under which they take place, a methodological error that Gramsci insists will lead to "speculative history" (ibid.: 370–371, 436–437). In order to emphasise the dialectical relation of structures and superstructures, Gramsci conceptualises their relation as a *historical bloc*, "[t]hat is to say the complex, contradictory and discordant *ensemble* [of the superstructures] is the reflection of the *ensemble* of the social relations of production" (ibid.: 366). He therefore transcends the mechanistic and idealist conceptions of social change, returning to a key insight by Marx, which is neither structuralist nor voluntaristic:

> Men make their own history, but not of their own free will; not under circumstances they themselves have chosen but under the given and inherited circumstances with which they are directly confronted.
>
> (Marx 2010: 146)

The reasoning behind Gramsci's insistence on reading politics against structural transformations (and vice versa) is twofold. The first reason concerns the class character of *social forces*: While struggle among social groups takes place on the terrain of superstructures, these social forces cannot be reduced to their superstructural (i.e. cultural, political, ideological) determinations but must necessarily be understood in their relation to "[t]he level of development of the material forces of production [that] provides a basis for the emergence of the various social classes" (Gramsci 1971: 180). For Gramsci, it is against the background of social structures "that the problem of the formation of active political groups … must be posed" (ibid.: 432). Furthermore, social structures are a necessary factor in deciphering the struggle for hegemony among those forces: As social groups arise out of the relations of production, the dominant groups aim to secure the material base of the social formation or even expand it (ibid.: 5–6) by implementing a "political, moral and juridical superstructure" (ibid.: 410) that guarantees these relations of production and therefore the group's base. The central stake in the struggle for hegemony is therefore the creation of an organic cohesion between rulers and ruled, of a correspondence of structures and superstructures – in other words, a "historical bloc, in which there is a concrete correspondence of socio-economic content to ethico-political form" (Gramsci 1995: 360). This complex relationship between economic transformations, the superstructures that are supposed to guarantee these, and the articulation of a historical bloc by social forces is expressed in the following passage, in which Gramsci argues that

> ideological factors always lag behind mass economic phenomena, and that therefore, at certain moments, the automatic thrust due to the economic factor is slowed down, obstructed or even momentarily broken by traditional ideological elements – hence that there must be a conscious, planned struggle to ensure that the exigencies of the economic position of the masses, which may conflict with the traditional leadership's policies, are understood. *An appropriate political initiative is always necessary to liberate the economic thrust from the dead weight of traditional policies* – i.e. to change the political direction of certain forces which have to be absorbed if a new, homogeneous politico-economic historical bloc, without internal contradictions, is to be successfully formed.
>
> (Gramsci 1971: 168, my emphasis)

From a Gramscian perspective, the cross-Strait rapprochement can be understood in this sense, namely as the political initiative to bring Taiwan's superstructure back into correspondence with the transnational production that characterises the structures of accumulation in East Asia in general and across the Taiwan Strait in particular. What Gramsci here calls an "appropriate political initiative" is termed a *hegemonic project* in contemporary Gramscian research. This notion serves to overcome any static residuals implied by "hegemony", instead emphasising the continuous struggle that characterises the attempted organisation of consent. Emphasising the project character of social transformations precludes any reductionism of the rapprochement as a functionalist expression of changes in relations of power or production. A hegemonic project is the conceptualisation of Gramsci's (1971: 168) "appropriate political initiative" that is necessary to forge a new historical bloc. But as this concept has been employed by Gramscian perspectives with different accentuations (Kannankulam and Georgi 2012: 20–33; Bieling et al. 2013: 235), it is helpful to first assess the various uses of the term.

Bob Jessop proposes the notion "hegemonic project" to inject a strategic dimension into the process of capital accumulation and its extra-economic conditions of reproduction. Rather than seeing accumulation being determined solely by the logic of the capital circuit, he introduces the notion of accumulation strategies to analyse how the various capital fractions compete for a predominance within the economic realm (Jessop 1990: 198–199). An accumulation strategy here refers to "a specific economic 'growth model' complete with its various extra-economic preconditions" (ibid.: 198), and Jessop assumes that due to the differing preferences for the orientation of growth models by and the resulting competition among capital fractions, one capital fraction has to take a predominant position over the other fractions and successfully articulate an accumulation strategy in order to momentarily form a coherent growth model. What Jessop (ibid.: 199) terms "economic hegemony" then refers to the successful attempt by one capital fraction to have its articulation accepted by the other capital fractions. A hegemonic project, as distinguished from the accumulation strategy, goes beyond the realm of accumulation. It

> involves the mobilisation of support behind a concrete, national-popular program of action which asserts a general interest in the pursuit of objectives that explicitly or implicitly advance the long-term interests of the hegemonic class (fractions) and which also privileges particular 'economic-corporate' interests compatible with this programme.
>
> (Jessop 1990: 208)

While an accumulation strategy is articulated among the capital fractions, the attempt to organise consent from subordinate and subaltern groups then takes place in and through the integral state.

To increase the empirical precision of the term, Bieling and Steinhilber (2000: 106, my translation) propose to define hegemonic projects in a narrow way, understood as "concrete political initiatives that present themselves as solutions to urgent social, economic and political problems". In contrast to Jessop's economic-structural emphasis, this narrow conceptualisation shifts the attention towards the analysis of empirically observable processes. Bieling and Steinhilber (ibid.) also move beyond the mere coordination of interests among capital fractions. While hegemonic projects are necessarily the product of such a coordination among elite groups, their success depends on the capacity to forge "a myth of collective action or conduct ... that can electrify and inspire broad strata of society" (ibid.: 107, my translation). After the initial articulation by organic intellectuals, a hegemonic project has to go beyond the intra-elite process and address the general public – either by organising acceptance or by neutralising potential sceptics – not only through material concessions but also by offering affective imaginations that take the function of a "motivating myth" (ibid.: 108–109). The empirical analysis of this aspect is crucial if we wish to understand not only the degree to which a project emerges among elites of dominant groups, but also why (or why not) it is able to anchor itself in broad strata of society. While this shift in attention results in a substantial broadening of the concept into a direction that is crucial to the present study, the authors do not provide analytical tools for the empirical analysis to reconstruct the actual process of this anchoring.

The research group *Staatsprojekt Europa*, to some degree, reconciles the aforementioned positions. First of all, the authors associated with the research project build on the distinction between broader and narrower understandings of projects. Rather than seeing the macro-dimension of hegemonic projects and the narrow conceptualisation as competing interpretations of the same notion, they argue that in order to universalise its particular interest and thus achieve hegemony, a social group has to practically realise a number of smaller political projects that advance this goal (Buckel et al. 2014: 48). Every hegemonic project only exists insofar as it is realised in concrete and limited political projects, which on the one hand help to secure the economic and extra-economic conditions of accumulation, and on the other hand are also aimed at organising consent for this transformation. Second, the research group moves away from determining and differentiating hegemonic projects "objectively", that is, in relation to fractions within the circuit of capital accumulation (ibid.: 46). While they uphold the analytical necessity of relating various projects to class fractions (Kannankulam and Georgi 2012: 34), the strategies employed by various actors become the key criterion to identify and aggregate hegemonic projects (Buckel et al. 2014: 45–47). Methodologically, the research group *first* identifies clusters of strategies that further similar goals, and *then* attributes these to specific actors, before these actors are aggregated into hegemonic projects (ibid.: 46). Crucially, these agents do not need to be aware of the fact that their strategies, and the rationalities embedded within these strategies, link them to the same hegemonic project; rather, this is an analytical aggregation on behalf of the researcher (Kannankulam and Georgi 2012: 34). The *Staatsprojekt Europa*, however, remains committed to the analysis of the elite-based articulation of projects and the intra-elite competition among those projects. While the research group's authors (Buckel 2011: 640; Buckel et al. 2014: 46), similarly to Bieling and Steinhilber (2000), point out that hegemonic projects have to be anchored in practices of everyday life, the scope of the research ultimately does not necessitate the elaboration of concepts that can guide our empirical research.

From the discussions above, several points can be drawn. First, the work by Jessop sensitises us to the ways in which hegemonic projects are articulated among elites and helps us to pose questions concerning the material and ideological conditions under which certain articulations appear as more convincing than others. Second, following Bieling and Steinhilber, it becomes clear that the implementation of a hegemonic project rests on the success of smaller political projects that can consolidate the conditions of reproduction of the hegemonic project as a whole. To distinguish these smaller projects from large-scale hegemonic projects and to emphasise their *integral* (rather than strictly political) character, we will refer to these as *hegemonic initiatives*. Their organic relation (as instances of a common hegemonic project) makes it possible to analytically relate several limited initiatives under the conceptual umbrella of a hegemonic project, and by doing so it is possible to unearth organic relations between initiatives, which might appear as disparate and unrelated otherwise. The notion enables us, finally, to attribute these initiatives and their underlying rationalities (by way of observable strategies) to social groups that can be empirically identified and aggregated into a hegemonic project, in a manner similar to the approach taken by the *Staatsprojekt Europa*.

The authors discussed above agree that a hegemonic project can only be successful if it secures the active participation of the subaltern in the reproduction of relations of domination. Empirically, however, they pursue a domination-focused perspective. A full understanding of how and why hegemony functions within society (or, conversely, how and why it is eroded) cannot be reached by simply looking at the blueprint for hegemonic projects as they are conceived by the dominant groups. We have to put to the fore the process through which hegemony is anchored within the subordinate and subaltern strata of society. As this process is contested, hegemonic practices are shaped by practices of subversion, disruption and resistance.

This criticism is not new: For three decades, neo-Gramscian research practice has been criticised for its focus on domination (Burnham 1991), an argument that has since been renewed repeatedly.[2] This focus on the reproduction of domination, the argument goes, leads to a one-sided understanding of hegemony as a process orchestrated by elites. Hence, it fails to consider the role played by subaltern forces in social struggles. Even when Gramscian scholars do focus on resistance (e.g. Gill 2000; Robinson 2004), it is mostly understood on a structural level, thereby not only imposing a certain homogeneity upon the movements but also omitting the creative *praxis* of the subaltern. As these micro-processes are out of the conceptual reach of the notion of counter-hegemony, such a conceptualisation contributes to obscuring everyday acts of resistance (Huke et al. 2015: 728).

But while the general criticism of Gramscian research practice is not unfounded, we should be cautious of throwing the baby of Gramscian insights on hegemony out with the domination-focused bathwater. Rather than pursuing the formulation of "contrasting" or "complementary" approaches, as called for by Huke et al. (ibid.: 726, 731) – thereby consolidating the unfortunate division of labour within critical research between resistance- and domination-focused approaches – this section will argue that the dialectical potential lying dormant within Gramsci's notions has yet to be actualised. While Gramsci's thought is undeniably occupied with the production and reproduction of consent-based domination, it is not exhausted by it. On the contrary, Gramsci never grew tired of emphasising the dialectical nature of the struggle for hegemony and urged us to understand it as *one* "real dialectical process" (Gramsci 1971: 366).[3]

As has been mentioned above, it would be misleading to suggest that all Gramscian-inspired research is concerned with domination only, as in fact a large body of social movement literature based on Gramscian thought has emerged over the past decades. But while this development provides a necessary corrective to domination-focused approaches, it does not address the fundamental issue at stake: Despite the more refined conceptualisation of resistance, these approaches tend to reify domination in a similar way as domination-focused approaches reify resistance. By focusing *either* on the articulation of social movements *or* the strategies and methods pursued by elites to consolidate or transform the social formation, both strands of neo-Gramscian research tend to treat the opposite side as a pre-existing and unproblematic appendix (Shields 2015: 671). This does not only result in a conceptual split of one dialectical process into two processes – "hegemony from above" and "counter-hegemony from below" – that can supposedly be studied apart, but more often than not it also results in the "fixation" of the process that is considered epistemically secondary (Winter 2011: 154). Such a theoretical petrification ultimately obstructs our understanding of hegemony as a dialectical and continuous *struggle*.

Calls to transcend this epistemic division of labour have become louder (Cox and Schechter 2002: 42; Morton 2006; Nilsen 2009: 112; Holloway 2012: 516; Barker 2013: 43; Humphrys 2013: 374). Gramsci himself had already formulated a similar critique. Rather than substituting a one-sided focus on domination with an equally detrimental preoccupation with resistance, he demanded that "political science must … not only explain one side, the actions of one side, but also the other side, the action of the other side" (Gramsci 1995: 392). This passage shows that, for Gramsci, struggle is not only a crucial element that has to be carefully observed and studied; more importantly, our theoretical tools have to reflect the fact that domination and resistance are internally and dialectically linked to each other. The failure to conceptualise hegemony as anything other than a dialectical process will provide an incomplete or one-sided abstraction from the social processes under consideration. A Gramscian dialectic means that "struggle is not to be conceptualised as the simple clash of two unchanging social forces" (Humphrys 2013: 374). Rather, Gramsci (1971: 333) insists that is only through this continuous struggle that social groups progressively gain their particular self-conception.

Hegemonic projects therefore only exist in and can be studied as hegemony *qua* struggle (Buckel et al. 2014: 49; similarly, Rupert 2003: 185), as the reciprocal siege as which Gramsci (1971: 239) describes it. What drives the process is not simply a one-sided imposition by dominant groups. It is the "real dialectical process" that ultimately determines both the form a specific hegemonic project takes and the groups affected by it. If we want to understand the forms that the cross-Strait rapprochement has taken, as well as its transformations over the past decade, we have to understand them as both the means of struggle and the residues of struggle, as a succession of temporary equilibria between social forces. The following section will discuss the specific character of this contestation in more detail.

Towards a Praxeological Understanding of Hegemony

Proposing a praxeological understanding of hegemony – as hegemonic *contestation* – might strike as redundant or even absurd. It should be taken for granted that Gramsci's writings have human praxis as their central research interest, underlined by the fact that he conspicuously chose "philosophy of praxis" as the code word to refer to Marxism while he was imprisoned in fascist Italy.[4] For Marx (1992b: 423), the "materialist turn" is essentially a turn to human praxis, as he so unequivocally states in his eighth thesis on Feuerbach: "All social life is essentially practical."

And yet, it appears as if contemporary research practice has moved away from this central theme, particularly in the wake of post-structuralist interpretations of Gramsci. Although Laclau and Mouffe (2014: 93) state that ideology entails both discursive and non-discursive aspects, their approach to hegemony remains limited to the analysis of the *production of meaning*, omitting the *meaning of production* for the social formation. The conceptualisation of hegemony as the articulation of "chains of signification" and the fixation of meaning in discourse ultimately alienates their analysis from *actual* social phenomena. It is this postmodern detachment from practico-material life that persists in and dominates post-Marxist approaches within Postcolonial Studies and Cultural Studies, as well as in neighbouring fields. These authors, emphasising the seemingly post-materialist nature of identity-based movements, have uncoupled Gramsci's concern for the articulation of ideologies from his analyses of the material dimension of power, of the material-practical dimension of human life. Gramsci (1971: 377) himself vehemently opposed this reduction of class and class struggle to ideas (and vice versa), pointing out that "material forces would be inconceivable historically without form and the ideologies would be individual fancies without the material forces."

To a lesser degree, even within non-postmodern approaches guided by Gramscian concepts, research practice is regularly reduced to the analysis of conceptions of the world. However, the analysis of domination and explicitly articulated narratives of justification and inclusion can only partially grasp the actual effect of hegemony on the subaltern. The mere empirical passivity of the subaltern is then taken as an indication of the success of those conceptions. Resistance-focused approaches, conversely, focus on the common sense, the subaltern's conceptions of the world, as the decisive "battleground" (e.g. Chin and Mittelman 1997; Rupert 2003; Rehmann 2013). In both cases, research practice tends to concentrate on competing conceptions of the world as they are articulated by hegemonic projects, only indirectly relating these official ideologies to how they take effect on the ground. This conceptual detachment of ideologies from practice impedes an adequate conceptualisation of the link between hegemony on the one hand and the perception of concrete grievances as well as the articulation of resistance through collective action on the other. Crehan (2002: 172) refers to this idealist reduction of hegemony, which overlooks how hegemony shapes rationalities implicit in action, as "hegemony lite". But what is the precise relation between ideologies as conceived by organic intellectuals and the common sense that informs resistance by the subaltern? How does a hegemonic project attempt to anchor a particular vision of the world, and under which circumstances does it succeed or fail? In other words, what is at stake in hegemonic contestation?

Hegemony denotes a form of domination that is characterised by the organisation of consent rather than rule by coercion. A close reading of the *Prison Notebooks* suggests that Gramsci distinguishes two types of consent. First, hegemonic projects attempt to organise *active consent* by offering ideological or material concessions to subordinate and subaltern groups, so that the latter perceive the goals of the hegemonic project to be in their own interest. But Gramsci (1971: 12, 53) conceptualises a second, more subtle form of consent, which he calls *spontaneous* (or passive). Rather than being the outcome of a conscious decision to support the hegemonic project, this spontaneous consent is the result of "the moulding of one's personality" (ibid.: 323–324): "The State does have and request consent, *but it also 'educates' this consent*, by means of the political and syndical associations" (ibid.: 259, my emphasis). This process of "educating consent" therefore also takes place in "the domain of civil society … [that] operates without 'sanctions' or compulsory 'obligations', but nevertheless exerts a collective pressure and obtains objective results in the form of an evolution of customs, ways of thinking and acting, morality, etc." (ibid.: 242).

How does Gramsci conceive of the moulding of this spontaneous consent? From his writings, it becomes apparent that what appears as "spontaneity" on the surface is in fact the result of "a perfect preparation of the 'spontaneous' consent of the masses who must 'live' those directives, modifying their own habits, their own will, their own convictions to conform with those directives and with the objectives which they propose to achieve" (ibid.: 266).[5] Gramsci furthermore insists that the educative effort (the "perfect preparation") by the hegemonic project has as its aim the creation of a correspondence between the objectives of the ruling groups on the one hand and the "habits" of the masses on the other. It is this correspondence between the transformation of social structures and of ways of perceiving and thinking that results in "the belief about everything that exists, that it is 'natural' that it should exist, that it could not do otherwise than exist" (ibid.: 157). This naturalisation is the basis for "[t]he 'spontaneous' consent given by the great masses of the population to the general direction imposed on social life by the dominant fundamental group" (ibid.: 12). What Gramsci alludes to is the fact that this form of consent is the product of a hegemonic transformation of the ways of thinking and feeling, and therefore of classifying and judging relations of domination and exploitation (Femia 1975: 31).

It is here that Gramsci's praxeological understanding of ideology has to be addressed. He echoes Marx[6] by stating that people acquire consciousness of structural transformations and the conflicts arising out of this process through ideological forms (Gramsci 1971: 138, 365). Gramsci here introduces a distinction between implicit and explicit manifestations of ideology, which are grasped by two aspects of the everyday life of the subaltern: the common sense and norms of conduct. Common sense, one of Gramsci's key concepts, refers to the "conceptions of the world" (ibid.: 419) of the subaltern classes and can be seen as a shorthand for the historical and social conditions under which agents gain consciousness of their position in society. Unlike the official ideologies articulated by the dominant groups, the structure of the common sense is "ambiguous [and] contradictory" (ibid.: 423), because "the ensemble of social relations is contradictory" (Gramsci 2007: 321). These contradictory relations of everyday practice are the major source of the subaltern's common sense (Gramsci 1971: 420). The success of a hegemonic project depends on its ability to tie in with these experiences by providing the subaltern with ideological forms that attenuate the experience of these contradictions (Bieling and Steinhilber 2000: 107–108; Opratko 2014: 190). This process is facilitated by the fragmentary character of the common sense, which – far from being a coherent conception of the world – is a contradictory ensemble of lived reality, tradition and the residue of past ideologies. This makes it prone to the diffusion and absorption of parts of official ideologies through a process of "intellectual subordination" (Gramsci 1971: 327) that will be discussed below. Gramsci's notion of common sense therefore opens up the analysis of subaltern ideologies as an object or terrain of struggle.

But while ideological forms are partly actualised in the common sense, it is crucial to point out that they cannot be reduced to these explicit conceptions. Gramsci (1971: both 328) emphatically calls attention to the practice-bound nature of ideology, emphasising that it "is implicitly manifest … in all manifestations of individual and collective life" as an "implicit theoretical 'premiss'". The struggle over the subaltern's spontaneous consent therefore cannot be confined to the study of conceptions of the world. If social forms are the condensation of routine practice (Lefebvre 1968: 45–46), Nilsen (2009: 120) rightly shifts our attention to the "moulding of everyday routines". Intervening into routines of everyday life therefore shapes existing social forms or marginalises them. Conversely, the introduction of new everyday life routines entails the introduction of new rationalities. Gramsci calls these rationalities that are implicitly embedded in forms of practice "norms of conduct" (e.g. Gramsci 1971: 266, 326, 344, 369, 424) or "ways of thinking, feeling and acting" (e.g. Gramsci 1971: 242, 267, 302, 323; 1995: 277).

Norms of conduct and conceptions of the world are very closely related, and yet they are distinct: While a hegemonic project pursues the formation "of a unity of faith between a conception of the world and a corresponding norm of conduct" (Gramsci 1971: 326), Gramsci also discusses cases where both are not aligned. Most crucially, he describes a scenario in which the successful introduction of an implicit norm of conduct facilitates the introduction of the corresponding explicit conception (ibid.: 366). The implementation of everyday forms of practice therefore has to be analysed as a method to reinforce the common sense or provide a more fertile terrain for its moulding. Such a praxeological understanding leads to a far more complex picture of a Gramscian treatment of both everyday life and consent. If spontaneous consent does not require an active and conscious decision to endorse social structures, hegemony is not only about "winning the hearts and minds" of the people (active consent), but also about introducing new ways of act-ing, thinking and feeling, which bring about "spontaneous" or passive consent. It is in this way that Williams (1977: 109) argues that "[w]hat is decisive is not only the conscious system of ideas and beliefs, but the whole lived social process as practically organized". Understood in this sense, ideological forms are both the stake of the struggle and the medium through which struggle necessarily has to be articulated (see also Nilsen 2009: 112–115). Gramsci therefore follows Marx insofar as the latter analyses ideological forms "as both *material practices* and as *fields of social struggle* between classes, consequently designating their analysis as the central object of critical-materialist research and theory" (Demirović 2011: 40, my emphases).

If the organisation of spontaneous consent requires a naturalisation of relations of domination, and if this naturalisation depends on the ways of thinking and feel-ing, which are implicitly manifest in forms of practice, hegemonic interventions have to "change practical activity as a whole" if they are "to change, correct or perfect the conceptions of the world" (Gramsci 1971: 344). These changes are promoted through a "'diffused' and capillary form of indirect pressure" (ibid.: 110), which Gramsci describes as "molecular transformations" (ibid.: 344, similarly 109, 114). By this, Gramsci (1971: 60) refers to small interventions through "private" agents on the terrain of civil society. If "real hegemony disintegrates at the base, molecularly," (ibid.: 370) it is also true that hegemony is constructed molecularly at the base: Hegemony has to be anchored in practices of everyday life. These mo-lecular transformations amount to the "reprogramming of everyday life" (Lefebvre 2014: 702, 716), with the ultimate aim to achieve a correspondence between norms of conduct and objective social structures. As will be argued below, everyday life is as much the target of interventions as it is the place of origin of resistance to these interventions or the source of altogether new forms of practice.

If we conceive of everyday life as the site where hegemonic projects attempt to anchor by moulding everyday routines, we arrive at an understanding of hegemony that is profoundly *praxeological*: The success of a hegemonic project depends on the organisation of both active and spontaneous consent. To secure the latter, the hegemonic project attempts to shape not only the explicit conceptions of the world (the common sense), but also the ways of perceiving and thinking that are implicit in forms of everyday practice through molecular interventions. Hegemonic con-testation therefore has forms of practice as its target, but at the same time it can only occur in and through those very forms of practice that are at stake. To fulfil the potential of such a praxeological approach to hegemony, we need to develop empirical tools, which allow us to reconstruct both the mechanisms of molecular interventions into the implicit and explicit aspects of everyday life, and how resist-ance arises out of this attempt.

Resistance as Method

How then can a praxeological approach to hegemonic contestation guide our em-pirical research? This section will propose a method aimed at reconstructing the process of hegemonic contestation that relies on a systematic analysis of empirical data to understand how hegemony and resistance co-evolve in a dialectical fashion. The major focus of this method will be on relating various episodes of hegemonic struggle and its historical development by tracing the various social forms that shape how people make their own history under inherited circumstances. In other words, the aim of this section is to establish the methodological principles that will allow us to understand the laws of motion of hegemonic contestation: Why did the hegemonic project succeed in securing consent for certain initiatives but failed to do so for others, why did the struggle develop in this form rather than another, how did representatives of social forces experience the struggle, which narratives were adopted or created to express these experiences, and how did the material and ideological factors that shaped contestation emerge and evolve over time?

In addition to Gramsci's thoughts on the struggle for hegemony, this section will draw on two works by Henri Lefebvre and Rosa Luxemburg that can complement a Gramscian perspective by providing methodological pointers for empirical research. Both Lefebvre and Luxemburg were concerned with major social upheavals of their times: Luxemburg (2006) studied the mass strikes in Russia in the early twentieth century, while Lefebvre (1969) closely examined the events that unfolded in May 1968 in France. The concrete situation in Taiwan is not comparable to either of these events. What will be taken from the studies undertaken by Luxemburg and Lefebvre, rather, is their analytical perspective: Both attempted to shed light on how social movements emerged against the background of larger structural transformations and shifts in the constellations of social forces. Both authors emphasised how social struggles that emerged from seemingly accidental causes evolved into full-fledged systemic challenges, establishing new ways of thinking and acting over the course of protracted episodes of contestation. Crucially, the object of inquiry has to move beyond the observable moments of struggle to include the phases of apparent calm. Rather than understanding each social movement that will be studied in the following chapters on its own terms, the emphasis will be on what Luxemburg (2006: 134) calls the "law of motion" of the protest cycle as a whole, that is, the rhythm of social struggle and the change in its forms.

To make the argument that the various social movements studied here are organically related rather than being a succession of isolated protests, we have to establish a plausible empirical relation among them. On an immediate level, we can establish a direct lineage among the various movements, and the following chapters will identify individuals and organisations that played a role in several of the movements. Furthermore, they will trace the evolution of conceptions that were central to these groups. This analysis can support the claim that the various movements were related to each other. This study will, however, argue that there is also a deeper link that connects these movements. This link consists of their respective relation to the hegemonic project. As the hegemonic project attempts to secure active and passive consent, various points of resistance emerge to these hegemonic interventions. Although these various movements of resistance may not be aware that they emerged in response to a hegemonic project, it is possible to analytically reconstruct this relation.

To this end, the empirical analysis is guided by a second methodological princi-ple, the primacy of resistance. As the hegemonic process consists of a multitude of initiatives, it is necessary to focus on those initiatives that result in resistance. This principle is derived from Henri Lefebvre's observation that

> [c]ontestation is first of all a refusal to be integrated … Contestation is an all-inclusive, total rejection of experienced or anticipated forms of alienation. It is a deliberate refusal to be co-opted … Contestation thus brings to light its hidden origins; and it surges up from these depths to the political summits, which it also illuminates in rejecting them.
>
> (Lefebvre 1969: 67)

The methodological claim here is twofold. First, the empirically observable mo-ment of resistance provides an entry point into the analysis of resistance itself: It is a focal point for the various groups that have entered the terrain of struggle and therefore enables us to establish relations among these groups and to study their ideological position and their forms of practice. It also allows us to study the subjectivity of resistance: Why did these groups organise, and what did they perceive as the cause of their grievances? Second, and following Lefebvre, the em-pirically observable moment of resistance is a pathway to reconstruct hegemony, as it is the rejection of concrete hegemonic initiatives that "illuminates" the concrete mechanisms through which the hegemonic project attempts to secure consent. In-stead of studying the hegemonic project from the hegemonic centres outwards, this method consists of picking up the thread of hegemony where it is challenged to then unravel the hegemonic interventions by tracing the process backwards to the groups from which these processes emanate. This makes it possible to ultimately reconstruct the hegemonic project as an analytical aggregation. The method of in-quiry, working backwards from observable moments of resistance to reconstruct the hegemonic project, thus differs from the method of presentation in the follow-ing chapters, which proceeds in the opposite direction. Due to this difference, the hegemonic project "may appear as if we have before us an *a priori* construction", as Marx (1992a: 102) cautioned his readers in the postface to *Capital*, although this is only the result of a careful reconstruction.

Process Analysis of Hegemonic Contestation I: Identifying Points of Nucleation

Gramsci attributed the emergence of resistance to molecular transformations. Fol-lowing Lefebvre, these moments of resistance will provide the analytical entry point into the reconstruction of hegemonic contestation and thus the workings of hegemony itself. The first task is therefore to identify what can be referred to as the *point of nucleation*. In thermodynamics, nucleation refers to the conditions under which a reaction is set in motion that results in the transition of one thermodynamic state to another, often facilitated by impurities in the system. Common examples are how carbonised soda needs nucleation sites, such as rough or contaminated sites in a glass, in order for bubbles to appear or how dust particles allow for the formation of clouds or ice crystals. Transposed to the study of hegemonic contestation, it refers to a constellation of structural conditions and conjunctural factors that align in such a way that collective organisation occurs. Particular grievances might have been experienced before, at times for years, on an individual level, but nucleation is the moment where collective action is formed around these grievances. It is therefore necessary to identify the catalyst that is not only the objective cause for this particular grievance, but also to study the awareness, ideological constellations and the degree of organisation that contribute to a particular moment of nucleation.

In a section entitled "Americanism and Fordism", Gramsci (1971: 279–287) discusses the imposition of a new mode of living that corresponds to a new mode of production in the United States. It is in this passage that he describes the inherently contradictory character of hegemony:

> Problems arise from the various forms of resistance to this evolution encountered by the process of development. ... The fact that a progressive initiative [i.e., a *hegemonic project*] has been set in train by a particular social force is not without fundamental consequences: the 'subaltern' forces, which have to be 'manipulated' and rationalised to serve new ends, naturally put up a resistance.
>
> (Gramsci 1971: 279)

It is the attempt to organise consent itself that is at the same time the source of grievances and resistance. However, Gramsci is not wholly specific on what exactly drives resistance, under which conditions grievances experienced by individuals become the impetus for collective action. Luxemburg and Lefebvre acknowledge that the immediate and concrete catalyst for nucleation, while related to "a latent institutional crisis" (Lefebvre 1969: 68), might arise "from specific local accidental causes" (Luxemburg 2006: 136), from "subordinate" (ibid.: 132), "wholly accidental, even unimportant" (ibid.: 113) or "trivial" (ibid.: 118) causes that result in a "sudden extension" (Lefebvre 1969: 120) of the movement. It is therefore impossible to predict when and where the accumulation of grievances explodes into a movement.

Nevertheless, it is necessary to reconstruct the specific conditions of nucleation, as these tend to leave an imprint on the movement by shaping the "ideological forms in which men become conscious of this conflict and fight it out" (Marx 1992b: 426). A larger movement might emerge from the integration of various smaller movements or currents, each of which has been conditioned by specific local conditions of nucleation. Harvey (1996: 32–45), drawing on Raymond Williams, refers to these ideological forms that emerge in localised contexts as *militant particularisms*. As individuals organise and collectively act within a specific setting, developing ways of acting that are tailored to this setting, "[a] crucial aspect of the study of local rationalities is thus the unearthing not just of their content, but also of the form of its articulation and development" (Nilsen 2009: 125). Although various currents that together form a larger movement might be reacting to a related set of hegemonic interventions, the forms of struggle might have been conditioned by the particular circumstances of nucleation, leading to a discrepancy in experiences, analyses and outlooks that hinder the integration of these currents. Both Luxemburg (2006: 122) and Lefebvre (1969: 113–114) have therefore emphasised how the formation of larger movements and the attempt to integrate a variety of militant particularisms are characterised by the emergence of tensions and contradictions.

The empirical analysis of the process of nucleation proceeded in several steps. In a first step, publicly available media reports of social movements were analysed to determine the overall dynamics of mobilisation and to identify social groups participating in this process. At this point, the data was brought into a dialogue with already-identified hegemonic processes to investigate potential connections to the hegemonic project. If such a preliminary relation could be plausibly established, semi-structured interviews with representatives of these groups were conducted to reconstruct the various views and subjectivities that prompted these groups to organise collectively in a second step. In a third step, and only if a potential relation to hegemonic processes could be confirmed on the basis of the data collected in the interviews, primary sources (either obtained from these groups or publicly available) were brought in to allow for a more detailed reconstruction of the material and ideological circumstances of nucleation, with a particular focus on the debates both within and among the participating groups. Overall, the aim here is to identify and reconstruct the conceptions that informed the process of collective organisation, including the forms of practice that were put into action as well as alternatives that were considered but ultimately dismissed.

Process Analysis of Hegemonic Contestation II: Constellations

The hegemonic and counter-hegemonic groups found to have been involved in the process of nucleation will then provide the entry point into the systematic reconstruction of the constellation of social forces that characterised a given episode of hegemonic contestation. Gramsci proposes to analyse "the formation of a collective will ... in all its molecular phases", including how a group "is first set up [and] how its organisational strength and social influence are developed" (Gramsci 1971: 194). Similar to the dimensions proposed by Gramsci (see Gramsci 1971: 181), the social forces relevant to the study of hegemonic contestation will be assessed with regard to their conceptions, their forms of practices and their apparatus.

The first dimension relates to the *conceptions* that the various groups draw on to make sense of processes of contestation in which they are involved, including their analysis of the social conjuncture, their self-identity, their grievances and demands as well as proposed ways to meet these demands (Nilsen 2009: 124). As different groups tend to develop conceptions that are conditioned by the process of nucleation, from a Gramscian perspective, "[w]hat must next be explained is ... how these currents are born, how they are diffused, and why in the process of diffusion they fracture along certain lines and in certain directions" (Gramsci 1971: 327). A materialist notion of conceptions emphasises that these narratives are not articulated in a social vacuum, but under concrete social conditions that are "given and inherited" (Marx 2010: 146). They are simultaneously the object of hegemonic contestation and tools to make sense of it, they are both shaped by dominant ideologies and at the same time serve as a critique of these.

Two Gramscian arguments can help to shed light on this contradictory character of ideologies. First, Gramsci seeks to assess the relative position of conceptions with regard to the dominant ideologies of the time. He determines a group to be in a state of "intellectual subordination, [if it] adopted a conception which is not its own but is borrowed from another group" (Gramsci 1971: 327). Intellectually subordinate groups thus acquire a sense of the struggle not on their own terms but *on the terms defined by hegemonic groups*. An example studied by Gramsci is the emergence of trade unionism, which seeks to articulate a critique of capitalist social relations but nevertheless operates within the limitations of dominant ideologies, as it ultimately does not threaten the social relations of production (ibid.: 159–161). For the purpose of this study, it is therefore necessary to empirically assess how the hegemonic apparatus "limits the original thought of the popular masses in a negative direction" (ibid.: 420) by "fixing the limits of freedom of discussion" (ibid.: 341). This ideological pressure appears in the form of "a self-limitation which the leaders impose on their own activity" (ibid.: 341). An emphasis of the empirical analysis will therefore lie on establishing whether and in which concrete ways subaltern groups are intellectually subordinate in the Gramscian sense or whether they are capable "to discuss and develop new critical concepts" (ibid.: 341).

A second helpful heuristic is Gramsci's distinction between organic and arbitrary ideologies (see Gramsci 1971: 341 and 376–377). While intellectual subordination approaches subaltern conceptions by studying the *relation between ideologies*, their organicity refers to the degree to which conceptions "respond to the demands of a complex organic period of history" (ibid.: 341), that is, it approaches ideologies from the perspective of *relations of conceptions and structures*. Gramsci's hypothesis is that conceptions with a high degree of organicity are more likely to prevail than those that are arbitrary (ibid.: 341), a hypothesis that will need be assessed empirically in the case of Taiwan. These two criteria will allow for tracking the development of conceptions over the course of successive episodes of hegemonic contestation. Analysing a complete cycle of hegemonic contestation makes it possible to take into account the learning process all groups experience as organic intellectuals discard conceptions, adjust them or articulate new ones as the struggle leaves what Luxemburg (2006: 126) calls a "mental sediment". Thus, we can establish qualitative changes in the groups' "self-consciousness [and] self-knowledge" that can only "be achieved and come to fruition in no way but in the struggle" (both ibid.: 122).

The ways of making sense of one's situation are closely intertwined with the *forms of practice* a movement adopts. These "routine ways of acting collectively" (Barker et al. 2013: 4) "emerge when a subaltern group deploys specific skills and knowledges in open confrontation with a dominant group in a particular place and at a particular conflict over a particular issue" (Nilsen 2009: 126). Hence, a movement's repertoire is a product of a very specific environment, and bears witness to the particular origin of a struggle. Carroll and Ratner (1994: 6 and 13) distinguish between disruptive (or anti-hegemonic, subversive) politics that are aimed at the *dis*organisation of consent and counter-hegemonic politics, which aim to organise consent for an alternative emancipatory project. While disruptive forms of practices, such as sit-ins, can be the result of spontaneous action, the organisation of counter-consent demands the formation of organic intellectuals, which can make the subaltern ideologies coherent and articulate the universality shared by the particularisms. This, in turn, depends on an independent organisational base to disseminate new conceptions and forms of practices.

Eventually, these practices might condensate into a group's *apparatus*, which refers to its organisational capacities, leadership and the extent of its networks of cooperation. It is the result of the "accumulation of successive experience" (Gramsci 1971: 195), which over time coagulates into organisational structures. Again, a group's apparatus does not emerge in a social vacuum, but in a dynamic of struggle. Methodically, the structures of organisation will not be taken for granted as the prerequisite for collective action. Following Luxemburg (2006: 127), collective action will rather be analysed as "the starting point of a feverish work of organization", shifting the empirical attention to "*organizing* rather than organization" (Cox 2014: 49). The establishment of an apparatus "is continually interrupted by the activity of the ruling groups" (Gramsci 1971: 55), and it is therefore necessary to consider these processes of disorganisation that shape the organisational practices of subaltern groups. Examples of this range from attempts to hinder subaltern organisation by posing legal restrictions (such as the Parade and Assembly Act that will be discussed in Chapter 4) or by "the gradual and continuous absorption" (ibid.: 59) of subaltern elites into the hegemonic apparatus to weaken the capacity of a social group to organise, a process Gramsci refers to as transformism.

As shown in Figure 2.1, these three dimensions of hegemonic contestation are methodological distinctions. In the analysis of empirical data, they will be examined

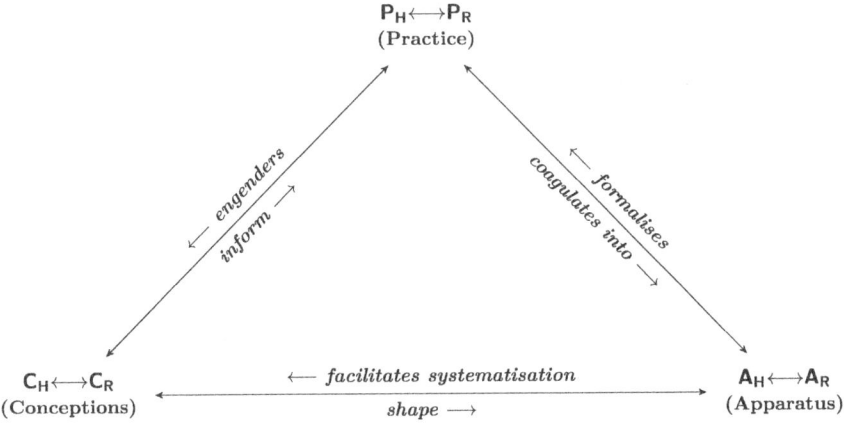

Figure 2.1 Three dimensions of hegemonic contestation

in their continuous dialectical relationships. First of all, each of the dimensions emerges out of the struggle between practices of hegemony (denoted in the figure by the letter H in subscript) and resistance (denoted by the letter R in subscript) as social groups continuously adapt their forms of contestation depending on the other side. Second, the three dimensions are related to each other: Conceptions are engendered by the lived experience, but in turn also inform practice; forms of practice coagulate into the apparatus, but the formalisation of practices through an apparatus also enables certain forms of practice and precludes others, resulting in an effect of path dependency; finally, the apparatus is also shaped by conceptions of struggle, while the emergence of an apparatus in turn provides a group with the capacity to systematically reform the conceptions that arose out of struggle. In the empirical analysis, these dialectical relations will be taken into account.

Process Analysis of Hegemonic Contestation III: Laws of Motion

Both Luxemburg and Lefebvre were concerned with the "law of motion" (Luxemburg 2006: 134) or "mutation" (Lefebvre 1969: 101) of movements. While Luxemburg studied the mass strike in Russia, Lefebvre studied the events of 1968 in France, aiming to understand how the movement emerged over local grievances at the Faculty of Letters and Humanities in Nanterre before it saw a "sudden extension" (ibid.: 120) to the protests in the Latin Quarter and at the Sorbonne that challenged the institutions of France. In each case, the authors identified moments of nucleation, a dialectical relationship of localisation and generalisation, the emergence of internal contradictions and the attempt to forge a unified movement and a constant shifting "from one social arena to another", encompassing the cultural, political and economic fields (Lefebvre 1969: 101–122).

A first aspect of a movement's laws of motion concerns the change in intensity of contestation. Luxemburg observed that movements do not simply comprise one continuous phase of immediate confrontation, but rather consist of a complex cycle of direct confrontation intermitted by phases of retreat, retrenchment and internal organisation. A social movement

> flows now like a broad billow over the whole kingdom, and now divides into a gigantic network of narrow streams; now it bubbles forth from under the ground like a fresh spring and now is completely lost under the earth.
>
> (Luxemburg 2006: 134)

Yet, it "does not cease for a single moment. It merely alters its forms, its dimensions, its effects" (ibid.: 135). Already Marx and Engels conclude in the Communist Manifesto that class struggle has to be understood as a "now hidden, now open fight" (Marx and Engels 2010: 68). This aspect can be theoretically grasped as a dynamic of latent and open phases, highlighting that we have to understand the protest cycle not as separate movements, but as one large movement which is characterised by an "ebb and flow of the wave" (Luxemburg 2006: 126).

What, then, enables us to speak of a protest cycle that undergoes a shift between open and latent phases rather than a simple succession of protests? In empirical terms, we can first detect a continuity of individuals and organisations that appear at various stages of a social movement, allowing us to establish continuities between episodes of a protest cycle. Furthermore, and more crucially, a protest cycle is characterised by the "accumulation of successive experience" (Gramsci 1971: 195). This experience coagulates into new conceptions, new forms of practice and, in particular, a group's apparatus. Activists learn, analyses are revised and new attempts to include or marginalise subaltern are undertaken by the ruling class. Through a careful tracing of these learning processes, it is possible to reconstruct the evolution of hegemonic contestation through open and latent phases. Such a perspective shifts our attention to what happens between the obvious moments of direct contestation.

In addition to the ebb and flow of movements, Luxemburg and Lefebvre paid particular attention to the way movements change their form *during* the phases of open contestation, having observed that movements articulate their appeals at times on the political, economic or cultural terrains. It is not Luxemburg's intention to provide us with a blueprint or a mechanistic model that can predict such "a change of front" (Luxemburg 2006: 121). Rather, she directs our attention to the study of the concrete conditions that shape the form of hegemonic contestation for it is only the analysis of a concrete historical conjuncture that can identify the factors that shape the process. Luxemburg (2019: 286) and Gramsci (1971: 234) agree that the concrete form of struggle is not so much down to the choice of agents on the terrain of struggle, but it is rather delineated by political and social conditions. As such, studying a concrete episode of hegemonic contestation requires constant attention be paid to the ways in which the material but also ideological structures, some of which have grown over decades, shape the terrain of struggle (Myers 2003; Jessop 2003).

In addition to these structural factors, it is the relation among social groups that shapes the form of struggle. As Barker (1996: 10, my emphases) notes, any "movement's development is simultaneously conditioned by its ongoing interaction with *its actual and potential allies* and *its antagonists*". Regarding the confrontation between hegemonic and subaltern groups, a defining characteristic of the latter is that they "are always dominated, even when they rebel and rise up" (Gramsci 1971: 55). Gramsci observes that the subaltern's "tendency toward unification [...] is continually broken up through the initiative of the dominant groups" (Gramsci 2010: 15). These initiatives will be studied relying on the distinctions between force and consent made earlier in this chapter, covering processes of displacement, containment and disorganisation. As discussed with regard to Gramsci's notions of force and consent, this comprises direct forms pressure, including attempts to disorganise disobedient or non-compliant groups. It also includes the "many distinctive features of the state's organization and articulation to the public sphere – electoral, parliamentary, presidential, bureaucratic, administrative, military, state-orchestrated mob violence, etc. – that directly condition *not only* the various struggles on the political stage *but also* struggles to modify the political balance of forces discursively, organizationally, and institutionally" (Jessop 2003: 5).

The authors discussed in this chapter furthermore pay attention to the other aspect mentioned by Barker, namely the movement's *internal* dynamics. Conditioned

Table 2.1 Modi vivendi: managing militant particularisms

Insulation	No significant cooperation among movement currents
Dissociation	Tensions among movement currents are dealt with by taking divergent paths
Subordination	Tensions are dealt with by subordinating competing currents
Integration	Currents are synthesised into one collective political will

by what Harvey calls militant particularisms, "[t]he various undercurrents ... cross one another, check one another, and increase the internal contradictions of the revolution" (Luxemburg 2006: 122). "These [internal] contradictions," Lefebvre (1969: 114) concurs, "give it a powerful impulsion, animate it, and endow it with mobility." While Gramsci was in general appreciative of Luxemburg's work on the mass strike,[7] he emphasised that forging potentially contradictory militant particularisms into a "collective political will" (Gramsci 1971: 228) is not an automatism but requires the ideological and organisational labour of organic intellectuals. It is therefore necessary to clarify, empirically and theoretically, how these spontaneous forms of resistance are forged into a mass movement. Gramsci comments that

> two 'similar' forces can only be welded into a new organism either through a series of compromises or by force of arms, either by binding them to each other as allies or by forcibly subordinating one to the other[.]
> (Gramsci 1971: 168)

With regard to the contradictions of capital, Marx wrote how social contradictions tend not to be resolved but rather "develop a modus vivendi, a form in which they can exist side by side" (Marx 1992a: 103–104). For the purpose of this study, and based on the theoretical arguments outlined here and on the empirical analysis in the following chapter, it is proposed to generalise this observation with regard to the study of social movements that emerge by forming a collective will from a variety of potentially contradictory militant particularisms. Four different modi vivendi (see Table 2.1) were observed over the course of the empirical analysis, each depending on the relation of forces among the involved groups and the particular conditions under which the movement unfolded. Chapters 4 to 6 will discuss the empirical aspect of these forms.

Notes

1 See, for example, Chin and Mittelman (1997), Carroll and Ratner (1994, 1996), Rupert (2003), Worth and Kuhling (2004), Stephen (2011), Nilsen and Cox (2013), Rehmann (2013).

2 See for example: Drainville (1994); Scherrer (1998); Bieling and Steinhilber (2000); Borg (2001); Bieler and Morton (2004); Sekler and Brand (2011); Huke et al. (2015); Shields (2015).

3 Scherrer (1998) therefore rightly notes that his criticism of focusing on domination and neglecting resistance is aimed not at Gramsci himself but rather against neo-Gramscian research practice.

4   See Haug (2000) and Thomas (2009: 102–108) for an overview on the debate about the degree to which Gramsci's terminology was simply a way to avoid censorship by camouflaging sensitive concepts, or whether it actually entails a substantial reformulation of Marxist concepts.
5   In Gramsci's *Prison Notebooks*, the adjective "spontaneous" – particularly in quotation marks, see Thomas (2009: 170–171) – is usually used as a shorthand for the absence of conscious reflection, analysis and criticism.
6   Gramsci refers to the following passage from Marx's (1992b: 426) Preface to *A Contribution to the Critique of Political Economy*: "[I]t is always necessary to distinguish between the material transformation of the economic conditions of production, which can be determined with the precision of natural science, and the legal, political, religious, artistic or philosophic – in short, ideological forms in which men become conscious of this conflict and fight it out."
7   Gramsci (1971: 233) described Luxemburg's *The Mass Strike* as "one of the most significant documents theorizing the war of manœuvre in relation to political science."

Bibliography

Barker, Colin (1996). *'The Mass Strike' and 'The Cycle of Protest'*. Paper presented at the second International Conference on Alternative Futures and Popular Protest, Manchester Metropolitan University, March 1996.
——— (2013). "Class struggle and social movements". In: *Marxism and Social Movements*. Ed. by Colin Barker, Laurence Cox, John Krinsky and Alf Gunvald Nilsen. Leiden: Brill, 41–61.
Barker, Colin, Laurence Cox, John Krinsky and Alf Gunvald Nilsen (2013). "Marxism and social movements: An introduction". In: *Marxism and Social Movements*. Ed. by Colin Barker, Laurence Cox, John Krinsky and Alf Gunvald Nilsen. Leiden: Brill, 1–37.
Bieler, Andreas and Adam David Morton (2004). "A Critical Theory Route to Hegemony, World Order and Historical Change. Neo-Gramscian Perspectives in International Relations". In: *Capital & Class* 28.1, 85–113.
Bieling, Hans-Jürgen, Tobias Haas and Julia Lux (2013). "Die Krise als Auslöser eines neuen europäischen Konfliktzyklus?". In: *Die Internationale Politische Ökonomie nach der Weltfinanzkrise*. Ed. by Hans-Jürgen Bieling, Tobias Haas and Julia Lux. Wiesbaden: Springer, 231–249.
Bieling, Hans-Jürgen and Jochen Steinhilber (2000). "Hegemoniale Projekte im Prozeß der europäischen Integration". In: *Die Konfiguration Europas. Dimensionen einer kritischen Integrationstheorie*. Ed. by Hans-Jürgen Bieling and Jochen Steinhilber. Münster: Westfälisches Dampfboot, 102–130.
Bobbio, Norberto (1979). "Gramsci and the conception of civil society". In: *Gramsci and Marxist Theory*. Ed. by Chantal Mouffe. London: Routledge & Paul Kegan, 21–47.
Borg, Erik (2001). *Projekt Globalisierung. Soziale Kräfte im Konflikt um Hegemonie*. Hannover: Offizin.
Buckel, Sonja (2011). "Staatsprojekt Europa". In: *Politische Vierteljahresschrift* 52.4, 636–662.
Buckel, Sonja, Fabian Georgi, John Kannankulam and Jens Wissel (2014). "Theorie, Methoden und Analysen kritischer Europaforschung". In: *Kämpfe um Migrationspolitik. Theorie, Methode und Analysen kritischer Europaforschung*. Ed. by Forschungsgruppe "Staatsprojekt Europa". Bielefeld: Transcript, 15–84.
Burnham, Peter (1991). "Neo-Gramscian Hegemony and the International Order". In: *Capital & Class* 15.3, 73–92.

Buttigieg, Joseph A. (2005). "The Contemporary Discourse on Civil Society. A Gramscian Critique". In: *Boundary* 32.1, 33–52.

Carroll, William K. and R. S. Ratner (1994). "Between Leninism and Radical Pluralism: Gramscian Reflections on Counter-Hegemony and the New Social Movements". In: *Critical Sociology* 20.2, 3–26.

——— (1996). "Master Frames and Counter-Hegemony. Political Sensibilities in Contemporary Social Movements". In: *Canadian Review of Sociology and Anthropology* 33.4, 407–436.

Chin, Christine B. N. and James H. Mittelman (1997). "Conceptualising Resistance to Globalisation". In: *New Political Economy* 2.1, 25–37.

Cox, Laurence (2014). "'A whole way of struggle?' Western Marxisms, social movements, and culture". In: *Conceptualizing Culture in Social Movement Research*. Ed. by Britta Baumgarten, Priska Daphi and Peter Ullrich. Basingstoke and New York: Palgrave Macmillan, 45–66.

Cox, Robert W. and Michael G. Schechter (2002). *The Political Economy of a Plural World. Critical Reflections on Power, Morals and Civilization*. London and New York: Routledge.

Crehan, Kate (2002). *Gramsci, Culture and Anthropology*. London: Pluto Press.

Demirović, Alex (2011). "Materialist State Theory and the Transnationalization of the Capitalist State". In: *Antipode* 43.1, 38–59.

Drainville, André C. (1994). "International Political Economy in the Age of Open Marxism". In: *Review of International Political Economy* 1.1, 105–132.

——— (2004). *Contesting Globalization. Space and Place in the World Economy*. London and New York: Routledge.

Femia, Joseph (1975). "Hegemony and Consciousness in the Thought of Antonio Gramsci". In: *Political Studies* 23.1, 29–48.

Fontana, Benedetto (2008). "Hegemony and power in Gramsci". In: *Hegemony. Studies in Consensus and Coercion*. Ed. by Richard Howson and Kylie Smith. New York and London: Routledge, 80–106.

Gill, Stephen (2000). "Toward a Postmodern Prince? The Battle in Seattle as a Moment in the New Politics of Globalisation". In: *Millennium* 29.1, 131–140.

Gramsci, Antonio (1971). *Selections from the Prison Notebooks*. Ed. by Quintin Hoare and Geoffrey Nowell-Smith. London: Lawrence and Wishart.

——— (1994). *Letters from Prison*. Vol. 2. Ed. by Frank Rosengarten. New York: Columbia Press.

——— (1995). *Further Selections from the Prison Notebooks*. Ed. by Derek Boothman. London: Lawrence and Wishart.

——— (2007). *Prison Notebooks*. Vol. 3. Ed. by Joseph A. Buttigieg. New York: Columbia University Press.

——— (2010). "The History of the Subaltern Groups: Rome and the Middle Ages in Italy". In: *International Gramsci Journal* 2, 14–20.

——— (2012). *Selections from Cultural Writings*. Ed. by David Forgacs and Geoffrey Nowell-Smith. Chicago: Haymarket Books.

Harvey, David (1996). *Justice, Nature and the Geography of Difference*. Cambridge and Oxford: Blackwell Publishers.

Haug, Wolfgang Fritz (2000). "Gramsci's 'Philosophy of Praxis'". In: *Socialism and Democracy* 14.1, 1–19.

Holloway, John (2012). "Crisis and Critique". In: *Capital & Class* 36.3, 515–519.

Huke, Nikolai, Mònica Clua-Losada and David J. Bailey (2015). "Disrupting the European Crisis. A Critical Political Economy of Contestation, Subversion and Escape". In: *New Political Economy* 20.5, 725–751.

Humphrys, Elizabeth (2013). "Organic intellectuals in the Australian global-justice movement. The weight of 9/11". In: *Marxism and Social Movements*. Ed. by Colin Barker, Laurence Cox, John Krinsky and Alf Gunvald Nilsen. Leiden: Brill, 357–375.

Jessop, Bob (1990). *State Theory. Putting the Capitalist State in its Place*. Cambridge: Polity Press.

———— (2003). *The Political Scene and the Politics of Representation. Periodizing Class Struggle and the State in The Eighteenth Brumaire*. https://www.lancaster.ac.uk/fass/resources/sociology-online-papers/papers/jessop-political-scene.pdf (last accessed on 28/11/2019).

Kannankulam, John and Fabian Georgi (2012). *Die Europäische Integration als materielle Verdichtung von Kräfteverhältnissen. Hegemonieprojekte im Kampf um das 'Staatsprojekt Europa'*. Arbeitspaper Nr. 30, Research Group 'Europäische Integration'. Marburg.

Laclau, Ernesto and Chantal Mouffe (2014). *Hegemony and Socialist Strategy. Towards a Radical Democratic Politics*. 2nd ed. London: Verso Books.

Lefebvre, Henri (1968). *The Sociology of Marx*. London: Allen Lane The Penguin Press.

———— (1969). *The Explosion. Marxism and the French Revolution*. New York and London: Monthly Review Press.

———— (2014). *Critique of Everyday Life*. London: Verso.

Luxemburg, Rosa (2006). "The mass strike, the political party and the trade union". In: *Reform or Revolution and Other Writings*. Mineola, New York: Dover Publications, 101–180.

———— (2019). "The political mass strike". In: *The Complete Works of Rosa Luxemburg. Political Writings*. Vol. 1. Ed. by Peter Hudis, Axel Fair-Schulz and William A. Pelz. London and New York: Verso, 285–289.

Marx, Karl (1992a). *Capital. A Critique of Political Economy*. Vol. 1. New York: Penguin.

———— (1992b). *Early Writings*. London: Penguin Books.

———— (2010). "The eighteenth Brumaire of Louis Bonaparte". In: *Surveys from Exile*. Ed. by David Fernbach. London: Verso, 143–249.

Marx, Karl and Friedrich Engels (2010). "Manifesto of the Communist Party". In: *The Revolutions of 1848*. Ed. by David Fernbach. London: Verso, 62–98.

Morton, Adam David (2006). "The Grimly Comic Riddle of Hegemony in IPE. Where is Class Struggle?". In: *Politics* 26.1, 62–72.

Myers, J. C. (2003). "From Stage-ist Theories to a Theory of the Stage. The Concept of Ideology in Marx's Eighteenth Brumaire". In: *Strategies. Journal of Theory, Culture & Politics* 16.1, 13–21.

Nilsen, Alf Gunvald (2009). "'The Authors and the Actors of Their Own drama'. Towards a Marxist Theory of Social Movements". In: *Capital & Class* 33, 109–139.

Nilsen, Alf Gunvald and Laurence Cox (2013). "What would a Marxist theory of social movements look like?". In: *Marxism and Social Movements*. Ed. by Colin Barker, Laurence Cox, John Krinsky and Alf Gunvald Nilsen. Leiden: Brill, 63–81.

Opratko, Benjamin (2014). *Hegemonie. Politische Theorie nach Antonio Gramsci*. 2nd ed. Münster: Westfälisches Dampfboot.

Overbeek, Henk (2004). "Transnational Class Formation and Concepts of Control: Towards a Genealogy of the Amsterdam Project in International Political Economy". In: *Journal of International Relations and Development* 7.2, 113–141.

Rehmann, Jan (2013). "Occupy Wall Street and the Question of Hegemony. A Gramscian Analysis". In: *Socialism and Democracy* 27.1, 1–18.

Robinson, William I. (2004). *A Theory of Global Capitalism. Production, Class, and State in a Transnational World*. Baltimore: Johns Hopkins University Press.

Rupert, Mark (2003). "Globalising Common Sense. A Marxian-Gramscian (Re-)Vision of the Politics of Governance/Resistance". In: *Review of International Studies* 29, 181–198.

Sassoon, Anne Showstack (1980). *Gramsci's Politics*. New York: St. Martin's Press.

Scherrer, Christoph (1998). "Neo-gramscianische Interpretationen internationaler Beziehungen. Eine Kritik". In: *Gramsci-Perspektiven*. Ed. by Uwe Hirschfeld. Hamburg: Argument, 160–174.

Sekler, Nicola and Ulrich Brand (2011). "Eine 'widerständige' Aneignung Gramscis". In: *Gramsci global. Neogramscianische Perspektiven in der Internationalen Politischen Ökonomie*. Ed. by Benjamin Opratko and Oliver Prausmüller. Hamburg: Argument, 224–240.

Shields, Stuart (2015). "Neoliberalism Redux. Poland's Recombinant Populism and its Alternatives". In: *Critical Sociology* 4.4–5, 659–678.

Stephen, Matthew (2011). "Globalisation and Resistance. Struggles Over Common Sense in the Global Political Economy". In: *Review of International Studies* 37.1, 209–228.

Thomas, Peter D. (2009). *The Gramscian Moment. Philosophy, Hegemony and Marxism*. Leiden and Boston: Brill.

Williams, Raymond (1977). *Marxism and Literature*. Oxford and New York: Oxford University Press.

Winter, Jens (2011). "Dimensionen einer hegemonialen Konstellation. Eckpunkte einer akteursorientierten kritisch-hegemonietheoretischen Forschungsperspektive". In: *Gramsci global. Neogramscianische Perspektiven der Internationalen Politischen Ökonomie*. Ed. by Benjamin Opratko and Oliver Prausmüller. Hamburg: Argument, 145–162.

Worth, Owen and Carmen Kuhling (2004). "Counter-Hegemony, Anti-Globalisation and Culture in International Political Economy". In: *Capital & Class* 28.3, 31–42.

3 The Historical and Structural Origins of the Hegemonic Project

The hegemonic project that aimed to normalise the economic relations between Taiwan and China was the response to an organic crisis of Taiwan's developmental state accumulation strategy that became acute in the 1990s. If we seek to understand its emergence, we have to identify the social forces behind this project and the obstacles they perceived. From a Gramscian perspective, this means first and foremost to analyse the relations of forces among the crucial social groups in Taiwan's society, mechanisms of class inclusion and exclusion, as well as the contradictions arising out of these arrangements. Particular attention has to be paid to the various capital fractions and their relation to politico-ideological dynamics. While others have argued that Taiwan's Small and Medium Enterprises (SMEs) hold the key to understanding the evolution of the developmental state (Dent 2002: 214), this chapter will draw attention to the trajectory of Taiwan's conglomerates. To understand why large enterprises developed from a capital fraction that benefited from Taiwan's neo-mercantilist protectionism to outspoken proponents of liberalisation with China, we have to reconstruct their path within Taiwan's socio-economic development throughout the second half of the twentieth century. Put differently, this chapter examines the dynamics that led to the erosion of the previous developmental historical bloc and the attempted articulation of a common project by Taiwan's business groups.

The first section will argue that the KMT's desire to maintain its autonomy from social forces resulted in the emergence of Taiwan's tripartite economic structure, in which state-owned enterprises (SOEs) controlled the upstream industries, large private enterprises run by capitalists deemed loyal by the KMT controlled the midstream industries as well as the heavily protected domestic market, while the mainly Taiwanese-run – and therefore potentially disloyal – SMEs were forced into the export sector. Section two will analyse the maturation of contradictions of the developmentalist accumulation strategy as well as the state's response to this organic crisis. Faced with the erosion of international recognition, labour shortages, overaccumulation and unsustainable trade deficits with the US, the KMT was forced to abandon the developmentalist accumulation strategy. The emergence of a division within the state apparatus saw the progressive internationalisation of Taiwanese enterprises with the crucial exception of the PRC. The final section will

DOI: 10.4324/9781003395546-3

then analyse the qualitative changes that Taiwan's large business groups underwent from the 1980s onwards. This process will be read against the background of *economic* liberalisation, which changed the parameters of interest formation among the business groups, and *political* liberalisation, providing capital with the terrain to articulate a common project, resulting in the social conditions that made possible the emergence of the hegemonic project.

The Political Origins of Taiwan's Tripartite Economic Structure

When Taiwan was ceded to the R.O.C. after World War II as per the Declaration of Cairo, the island had been a Japanese colony for 50 years. Although the Japanese had invested in infrastructure, industry and agriculture, these investments were tailored to the needs of the Japanese mainland. The key rationale behind the modernisation process in Taiwan was the intention to supply the Japanese Empire with agricultural goods (Gold 1988a: 104–107). In preparation for its war efforts, Japan also expanded heavy industries from the 1930s onwards (ibid.: 107). Consumer goods, on the other hand, were mostly imported from Japan (Gold 1986: 45). While Taiwan saw a steady development of agriculture and industry as a result of colonisation, this era has to be characterised as "a classic dependence or colonial phase, when a foreign power skewed the economic structure, as well as the social and political systems, to the needs of the metropole" (ibid.: 16). Apart from the emergence of a small comprador elite (Gold 1988a: 109–114), the key economic legacy of the colonial era was the absence of a local capitalist class (Ho 1978: 101).

World War II had left Taiwan's infrastructure damaged, and the sudden departure of Japanese elites and bureaucrats further paralysed the island's economy. This vacuum was filled by the KMT, which manned the bureaucracy with R.O.C. officials and took over the monopolistic industries that had previously been controlled by Japan (Wade 1990: 75). For the first few years after 1945, the Nationalist government of the R.O.C. continued the extraction of resources, this time to support the Nationalist army in the Chinese Civil War (Schubert 1994: 198). When the resulting lack of consumer goods and hyperinflation led to public unrest, it was brutally repressed by the R.O.C. governor in 1947 and the following years (Gold 1986: 52–53).

This extractive approach to Taiwan's economy only changed when it became clear that the CCP would win the Chinese Civil War, forcing the Nationalists to retreat to Taiwan (Ho 1978: 102). With the retreat of the R.O.C. party-state to Taiwan in 1949, the island became the object of a modernisation initiative that sought to provide the KMT with the conditions to turn Taiwan into a Chinese model province from which to stage the military operation to retake China. The necessary political condition for this ambition was that the party maintained and consolidated its autonomy from local social forces. While the imposition of martial law (which included the suspension of elections and a ban of associations that were not sanctioned by the state) was the expression of the forceful repression of the local intellectual elite and the working class, the KMT proceeded at the same time to construct a corporatist apparatus that was able to include social forces within the KMT bloc (Ngo 2005: 84).

Land Reform, Original Accumulation and the Re-making
of Class Relations in Taiwan

The cornerstone of this social inclusion was the land reform. During the Chinese Civil War, the US-sponsored Sino-American Joint Commission on Rural Recon- struction had urged the KMT to enact a land reform on the Chinese mainland. But as landlords were a crucial pillar in the Nationalist power bloc, progress was neces- sarily slow and limited. In contrast, on Taiwan, which had been a Japanese colony for five decades, the KMT was not constrained by political allegiances and vested interests (Jacoby 1966: 109–110). Drawing lessons from its failure to maintain power on the Chinese mainland, Chiang Kai-shek swiftly moved towards land re- form measures to de-mobilise the peasants and secure at least their passive consent (Ka and Selden 1986: 1297).

The political economy of the land reform can be deciphered through the lens of the KMT's objective to establish inclusive relations with local social forces. As such, the land reform addressed several key issues: To maintain social stability, the KMT sought to transform tenant-farmers, whose allegiance lay with local land- lords, into owner-cultivators that depended on the KMT (Greenhalgh 1988: 89). Furthermore, the government aimed not only at dismantling the class of landown- ers but also at turning them into capitalists that would contribute resources to the modernisation of Taiwan's economy. This transformation of Taiwan's class struc- ture was accompanied by the establishment of corporatist institutions that aimed to politically bind these classes to the KMT. Finally, the state sought to directly extract a significant share of the agricultural surplus to maintain its military ap- paratus and advance the development of the island's productive forces. The reform measures can therefore best be understood as a process of original accumulation, that is, the attempt to implement class relations that are conducive to the continu- ous accumulation of capital (Marx 1992: 873–940).

The land reform was enacted in three stages. Already in 1949, the KMT car- ried out a rent reduction programme. In the 1940s, about half of Taiwan's farmers were tenants who paid their rent in kind, varying between 40 and 60 per cent of the annual output depending on the quality of the land (Ho 1978: 160). To reduce the burden on farmers and make a larger share of the agricultural surplus available to Taiwan's economic development, the government implemented a rent ceiling of 37.5 per cent of the annual yield. In a second step, the state sold farmland it had appropriated from Japanese owners, transferring about 71,000 hectares of land into the hands of farmers from 1951 onwards (ibid.: 161). The most crucial stage of the land reform, the land-to-the-tiller programme, began in 1953. The government compelled landowners to sell any farmland they owned in excess of 2.9 hectares to the government (ibid.: 162). This land was subsequently resold to the tenants at a price of 2.5 times the annual yield, a process that was completed by the end of 1953 (ibid.: 163). To cement the redistributive effects of the land reform, the maximum farm size of 2.9 hectares is in effect until today, and the transformation farmland into industrial land is highly restricted (Bishai 1991: 55–59).

Over the course of these four years, the landownership structure changed pro- foundly. The sale of public land and the land-to-the-tiller programme affected more than 100,000 landlords and about 330,000 farmer households. Between 1948 and 1953, the percentage of tenant farming was therefore reduced from 44 per cent of the cultivated area to 17 per cent (Ho 1978: 163–164). Ho (ibid.: 168–170) estimates that the land reform nearly doubled the income of the typical farm household. The small size of farms as well as the restrictions on the sale of land, however, limited the land's value as a factor of social mobility, and the need to diversify family income contributed to the proletarianisation of the rural population from the late 1950s onwards (Greenhalgh 1989: 93–97).

While the more equitable income distribution itself already contributed to consolidating the rural population's support for the regime (Greenhalgh 1988: 87), the KMT deepened its social ties to the farmers by combining the land reform with the establishment of corporatist institutions, relying in particular on the Farmers' Associations (FAs) that dated back to the Japanese Empire. At the turn of the century, local landlord-bankers had set up the first FA "which functioned like an all-round service cooperative, providing fertilizer, tools, seeds, and extension services" (Powelson and Stock 1987: 193). Originally set up as cooperatives, the Japanese colonial administration soon assumed control of these associations to exert political authority during the Japanese war effort (ibid.). By then, membership in the FAs had become compulsory, meaning that their total membership exceeded 600,000 farmers (ibid.). In parallel, the Japanese administration had permitted the establishment of rural credit cooperatives that were designed to ease the capital shortage in rural Taiwan (Ho 1978: 63). Their number rose equally fast, from 13 credit cooperatives in 1913 to 443 in 1940 (ibid.).

The KMT recognised the corporatist potential of these organisations and quickly proceeded to reform them into institutions of co-optation and control. FAs and rural credit cooperatives were merged and became the sole source of credit for farmers (Greenhalgh 1988: 93). While membership was not compulsory, the broad range of services provided by the FAs meant that no farmer could avoid a close relation with the local association (Powelson and Stock 1987: 196). The FAs furthermore replaced the landlords as the source of mediation and authority (Jacoby 1966: 110), inverting the associations' character from organisations that represented the farmers' interests into a channel of control for the government (Powelson and Stock 1987: 194).[1]

A crucial ingredient to deepen the farmers' reliance on these associations was the rice-fertiliser barter scheme. Among the Japanese industries taken over by the KMT was the production of chemical fertiliser, a monopoly in production that was complemented by the state's control over fertiliser provided by US aid programmes (Ho 1978: 180–181). While producers of crops other than rice and sugar cane were allowed to purchase fertiliser from state agencies, the only way for farmers producing the former to acquire fertiliser was to exchange it against rice. These institutions meant that with the conclusion of the land reform, the KMT "controlled the peasants politically by the Farmers' Associations and economically by the rice-fertilizer barter" (Gold 1986: 67).

The rice-fertiliser barter scheme, however, was not only driven by the desire to establish corporatist relations with the farmers but also aimed at extracting a large share of the surplus from the agricultural sector. To defend Taiwan from the communist army and eventually take back the Chinese mainland, the KMT sought to maintain its comparatively large military apparatus. The large army was not only unproductive and consumed a large amount of resources – estimated at 12 per cent of the GDP by Ho (1978: 108) – but also absorbed a considerable share of Taiwan's work force, with 14 per cent of Taiwan's male population being in the army in 1952 (ibid.: 107). The government eased this tension in two ways. First, the outbreak of the Korean War put the R.O.C. back on the table as a geopolitical token in the Cold War. In response to the perceived threat of communism in East Asia, the United States aimed to strengthen its anti-communist ally and tripled its economic and military assistance. In total, Taiwan received US\$4.1 billion between 1949 and 1967, US\$2.4 billion of which were military aid (ibid.: 111). The rice-fertiliser barter scheme complemented American aid. As rice farmers had to pay for fertiliser in kind, the government was able to directly appropriate a large part of the agricultural surplus. To this end, the fertiliser was strategically overpriced by approximately 50 per cent (Fei 1987: 74), resulting in what Powelson and Stock (1987: 197) call a "hidden tax" that farmers paid until the abolition of the scheme in 1973 (Francks et al. 1999: 173). The state furthermore siphoned off rice through taxation and as payment for the purchase of farmland, meaning that the government appropriated roughly 50 per cent of all rice that left Taiwan's farms in the 1950s to support its military and bureaucratic apparatus (Ho 1978: 181–182). The rice that was not directly consumed by the state was exported in order to accumulate foreign exchange (Ngo 2005: 97).

Beyond the political inclusion of the farmers and the economic extraction of surplus, the land reform had a third objective, namely the annihilation of Taiwan's landowning class. Prior to the retrocession of Taiwan, this class drew its power from appropriating the agricultural surplus in the form of rent. The largest landlords had furthermore evolved into what Winckler (1988: 165) describes as landlord-bankers who controlled rural credit cooperatives. As a result, they not only secured profits in the form of interest but were also potential rivals of the KMT as patrons to the farmers. Perceived as a threat to state autonomy, the party quickly moved to dismantle the landlords' power base. The above-mentioned reform of rural institutions put rural credit into the hands of the KMT-controlled FAs, further consolidating the patron-client relationship. In addition, the land-to-the-tiller programme directly removed the landlords' control over land and therefore the source of their socio-political power.

The compensation scheme, however, was designed in such a way as to prevent former landowners from becoming discontent (Jacoby 1966: 110). Politically, the KMT aimed to avoid creating unrest among the landlords by integrating them into the KMT bloc, and economically they were indispensable as contributors to the modernisation of Taiwan's economic structure. What the KMT sought to create was a class of politically neutralised capitalists. These aims were met with the particular design of the land-to-the-tiller programme: The former landlords were compensated for two and a half times the amount of the expropriated land's annual yield, 30 per cent of which were paid in stock of former Japanese enterprises and

70 per cent in commodity bonds (Ho 1978: 162). The KMT had taken control of several previously Japanese-owned enterprises in 1945, and the US had since urged the party to privatise these companies (Simon 1988: 141–142). Compensating the landlords in stock of these enterprises was a way to meet this request (Cullather 1996: 17) while simultaneously avoiding the emergence of influential capitalists: By spreading the companies' shares among 40,000 former landlords, it was hoped that no group would be able to gain a controlling majority and emerge as a potential threat to the KMT (Kuo 1998: 88).

Most former landlords, however, sought to sell their shares immediately (Ho 1978: 167), not only because the prospect for Taiwan's private sector to flourish in the 1950s looked dim (Simon 1988: 141, 144), but also because the interest yield of land bonds was four per cent whereas that of bank deposits was at 16 per cent (Ka and Selden 1986: 1298). This set into motion a centralisation of capital, as particularly former landlord-bankers quickly took control of the four companies by buying out the other stockholders. Throughout the 1950s and 1960s, particularly the Taiwan Cement Corporation became the cornerstone of future large business groups, not least because the capitalists were aware of the fact that the KMT was in need of large amounts of cement for its infrastructure projects (Simon 1988: 145).

Import Substitution and the Emergence of Large Enterprises

While the land reform had a profound impact on Taiwan's class structure and freed up resources from the agricultural sector, the 1950s were marked by a struggle within the KMT concerning the question for which purpose to allocate these resources. The state apparatus was divided between a group of bureaucrats that favoured development led by the public sector and those who advocated the establishment of a strong private sector. This struggle over Taiwan's accumulation strategy unfolded against the background of a double crisis of high inflation and a negative balance of payments in Taiwan's external trade relations. The aforementioned lack of consumer goods resulted in rising prices throughout the second half of the 1940s. In 1949, inflation reached 3,500 per cent, mostly driven by the rapid increase of demand when the retreat of the KMT, with its state and military apparatus, brought between 1.5 and two million refugees from the Chinese mainland in addition to the six million people already living in Taiwan (Ho 1978: 104).

Against the background of this crisis, Wade (1990: 387–393), Haggard and Pang (1994: 65–69) as well as Guiheux (2002b: 60–63) identify two competing political projects. The *monetarist* camp formed around important financial agencies in Taiwan, such as the Economic Stabilisation Board (ESB), which was headed by the finance minister (Wade 1990: 389). Marked by the experiences on the Chinese mainland, this group regarded hyperinflation as the biggest threat to KMT rule, as it could not only contribute to social unrest but also put at risk the large military apparatus necessary for retaking the mainland (Guiheux 2002b: 61). To curb inflation, proposed policies included multiple exchange rates to discourage the import of goods that could also be produced in Taiwan, while allowing cheap imports of other goods to control prices (Wade 1990: 390). The monetarists furthermore pursued a balanced budget, while their industrial policy aimed for a large public sector, ensured by a policy that saw the Bank of Taiwan give loans to the public sector only. As these policies envisioned the state as the major agent in Taiwan's economy and would therefore have allocated most of the resources to the public sector and the military, the monetarists secured the support of Taiwan's military apparatus and the managers of SOEs (Guiheux 2002b: 60). The monetarist's vision also appealed to KMT leaders who distrusted the private sector because the majority of businessmen were Taiwanese (Kuo 1998: 90).

These policy propositions were challenged by the *industrialist* camp, which controlled the agencies that were charged with industrial planning, such as the Production Control Board (Wade 1990: 389). The group consisted mainly of American-trained bureaucrats and was supported by mainland capitalists who had come to Taiwan with the KMT (Haggard and Pang 1994: 68). The industrialists concurred with the party's plan to retake the mainland but were sceptical about any short-term success, instead conceiving of it as a long-term project (Wade 1990: 390). Accordingly, they proposed initiatives that were to ensure long-term industrial development in Taiwan, emphasising that private competition was the instrument of choice to achieve the industrial growth that was the necessary condition for national unification. Rather than restricting access to foreign exchange to encourage import substitution, the private sector was to be stimulated by the loosening of foreign trade controls and by exposing it to global competition (Haggard and Pang 1994: 68). The state was to control and allocate raw materials, credit and foreign exchange and thereby encourage private investments in crucial sectors that were not controlled by SOEs (ibid.: 69). Against the monetarists, the industrialists argued that the emphasis on monetary stability, the avoidance of a trade deficit, the implementation of import controls and prudent lending would hinder private investments and therefore run counter to the goal of rapid industrialisation (Wade 1990: 390). Furthermore, they advised against multiple exchange rates, as this could mean that profits could be made through trade rather than production (ibid.). The industrialist current was supported by US-based overseas Chinese economists and US advisers. A major reason for US support was American concern with the monetarists' priority on a military solution of R.O.C.-PRC relations, while the industrialists' plan was compatible with US wishes to see Taiwan compete with the PRC economically rather than militarily, arguing that "Taiwan should be developed as an economic and political showcase for the free enterprise system in Asia" (ibid.: 391).

In the early stages of Taiwan's development, the monetarist camp's policies prevailed. Against the background of hyperinflation, "import substitution industrialisation (ISI) was not so much a choice as a situational imperative" (Cheng 2001b: 26). Similarly, the *fait accompli* of the KMT already having taken control of former Japanese enterprises strengthened the position of those bureaucrats who favoured a large public sector. To reduce hyperinflation, interest rates were raised significantly, at times reaching 125 per cent per annum (Mao and Schive 1995: 36). To promote the substitution of imports, bureaucrats implemented a policy package that combined high tariffs, import controls and multiple exchange rates (Ho 1978: 190–191), effectively formulating what is now referred to as ISI. Until the mid-1950s, nominal tariff rates for imports doubled, while import controls were implemented to stimulate the growth of sectors deemed crucial to supply goods that were demanded in the domestic markets. The government specified several sectors that were to spearhead import substitution and thus reduce the dependence on imports and the resulting trade deficit. In these industries, which included plastics, textiles, synthetic fibres and glass, the import of processed goods was either restricted or prohibited, while imports of machines and raw materials were encouraged through lower rates to promote investment (Cheng 2001b: 26).

To comply with the KMT's desire to prevent the emergence of an influential Taiwanese capitalist class, these industries were mostly left to already-existing large enterprises owned by loyal mainlander entrepreneurs. As state agencies and SOEs not only controlled raw materials as well as the access to credit and foreign exchange, but also the licences to open new factories, the development of the private sector could be strategically steered to ensure the KMT's patronage over these large enterprises (Schubert 1994: 202). A striking example is Taiwan's textile sector. As part of US economic aid, Taiwan received cotton and wheat from the Agency for International Development (AID), which the state channelled to pro-Nationalist capitalists that had fled with the KMT from Shanghai to Taiwan at the end of the civil war, taking their machines with them (Gold 1986: 70). Although any entrepreneur could apply for AID loans, the KMT ensured that most of the assistance was granted to loyal mainlander capitalists to establish large-scale textile and flour milling enterprises (ibid.). Most of the private entrepreneurs who benefited from Taiwan's push towards import substitution were therefore mainlanders: In 1953, 11 textile factories existed in Taiwan, with three being public companies and seven being owned by mainlanders (Mengin 2015: 51). In the late 1950s, the government banned the establishment of new companies in the textile sector altogether, further protecting the existing companies (ibid.). The import substitution policies nurtured a number of large textile enterprises that benefited from protectionist policies to corner the domestic market, allowing them to develop into large business groups during the following decades (Wu 2004: 108–109). Other important sectors were handled in a similar fashion. When a mainlander-owned textile company spun off Yulon Automotive, it too came to benefit from a preferential treatment by the state: The government raised tariffs on the import of vehicles and did not allow the opening of further factories in the sector, after it had forced the only potential Taiwanese competitor into bankruptcy (Mengin 2015: 52–53).

The emergence of large enterprises in Taiwan was, however, kept in check by a corporatist structure based on the three pillars of allocation, limitation and co-optation. As discussed above, the state was in control of the *allocation* of crucial raw materials, such as cotton, wheat and petrochemical products (Chu 1994a; Wu 2004: 112–113). Paired with the ability to withhold licenses for new companies and control credit through state-owned banks, the KMT was not only able to hand-pick loyal capitalists as potential beneficiaries of ISI but also disposed of the instruments that gave it leverage over these companies. Key to this relationship was the control of SOEs, which the state relied on to indirectly control downstream industries (Wade 1990: 179–180). As "private enterprise was profitable only in close alliance with the state" (Wynn 1982: 35), allocation bound large enterprises to the party.

Furthermore, the KMT put *limitations* on the diversification of large enterprises, particularly if they were controlled by Taiwanese. To keep large enterprises from developing into conglomerates, the state restricted the size of enterprises and inter-firm equity flows (Wu 2004: 109). To protect its monopoly of upstream industries and the patron-client relationship that resulted from it, the state prohibited the ex-pansion of midstream industries (such as plastics) into upstream industries (such as petrochemicals) to prevent the vertical integration of business groups (Amsden 1991: 1123). A case in point is Formosa Plastics: After its founder Wang Yung-ching had been hand-picked by leading planning bureaucrats as a Taiwanese suit-able for leading a private company (Cullather 1996: 18), he received a loan of US$670,000 to begin producing PVC in a plant that had been constructed under government supervision and handed to him in 1957, expanding into synthetic fibres a few years later (Gold 1988b: 189; Guiheux 2002b: 67). When Wang sought to expand into upstream industries, proposing to construct a naphtha cracker in 1973, the KMT denied the permit (Amsden 1991: 1125–1126).

The most crucial instrument to influence the emerging capital was the imple-mentation of channels of *co-optation*. Sectors with five or more businesses had to organise a business association with compulsory membership. The three peak associations were of particular importance for the corporatist apparatus (McBeath 1998: 307–308). The Chinese National Federation of Industries (CNFI) groups all the industries in the manufacturing sector, such as steel, textile, chemicals, elec-tronics and the automotive industry. Its top echelons were closely related to the KMT, and the CNFI's leaders have usually been concomitant members of the KMT's central committee (Guiheux 2002b: 87). The General Chamber of Com-merce of the Republic of China (ROCCOC) serves a similar function as the peak association for businesses in the service sector. While these two organisations were dominated by mainlanders, the Chinese National Association of Industry and Com-merce (CNAIC) was established by leaders of large enterprises and was open to Taiwanese (Kuo 1998: 88). It nevertheless exhibited the same character of state-business relations as the two mainlander organisations, and the leading Taiwanese entrepreneurs who had benefited from the land reform were co-opted through these channels. Koo Chen-fu, for instance, first became chairman of the CNAIC and later member of the KMT's Central Executive Committee (Gold 1988a: 115). Although the peak associations were dominated by large enterprises throughout the authori-tarian era, they did not serve to represent the interests of Taiwan's bourgeoisie but rather acted as transmission belts for Taiwan's planning bureaucracy, participating in the implementation of policies (Schubert 1994: 220). To this end, the associa-tions were not only funded by the KMT and the state (ibid.), their leaders were also directly and carefully appointed by the party elite, while the boards of trustees remained largely unchanged until the 1980s as martial law suspended elections even within these organisations (Leng 1996: 83). Local large-scale capitalists were therefore able to continue in the private sector, but they lost any political autonomy (Winckler 1988: 170). From the 1950s to the 1970s, business groups were not a

political force, a situation that would only change when the developmentalist accumulation strategy began to erode during the 1980s (Chu 1994b: 121).

Export Promotion and the Struggle for a Private Sector

Throughout the 1950s, ISI proved to have the desired effects on Taiwan's economic
development. In comparison to 1951, by 1956 Taiwan's GNP had increased by
50 per cent and the industrial sector's relative share of the GNP increased from
27.9 to 36.3 per cent (Jacoby 1966: 273–276). Overall industrial output had nearly
doubled, while the sectors specifically targeted for ISI outperformed the remaining
sectors, with production tripling by 1959 (textile and paper) and 1960 (chemicals),
respectively (ibid.: 281). The increase in domestic output reduced the import dependency in these commodities significantly: While in 1950, imports accounted
for 58.6 per cent of all cotton fabric supply and 82.5 per cent of flour, these numbers had dropped to 2.6, respectively, 5.3 per cent only four years later (Ho 1978:
188). More capital-intensive commodities followed in the years thereafter, with the
import share of synthetic yarn supply, for instance, dropping from 100 per cent in
1954 to 1.4 per cent in 1958 (Ho 1978: 188). The policies had also brought inflation under control, although increased military spending after the PRC attacked the
island of Kinmen in 1954 and 1958, led to temporary spikes.

By the end of the decade, however, several problems resulted in a renewal of the
debates concerning Taiwan's development path. While ISI had successfully stimulated industrial expansion, many of the emerging industries were dependent on
imported raw materials. As the overvalued New Taiwan Dollar (NTD) was an incentive for imports, the overall balance of payments problem persisted (ibid.: 194).
Related to the trade deficit was a shortage of foreign exchange, which resulted in
rising import prices that brought with them a renewed threat of inflation. US aid
was able to mitigate some of these effects, but as the US signalled it would soon
phase out its assistance, Taiwan's bureaucrats began looking for alternative sources
of foreign exchange. Promoting exports was back on the table to address the trade
deficit and the foreign exchange shortage (Cullather 1996: 20). A second problem
concerned the state's fiscal crisis as a result of military expenditure. Due to rising
tensions in the Taiwan Strait, the leadership categorically refused significant spending cuts (Nordhaug 1998: 141). In addition to geopolitical considerations, military
spending represented a crucial element of Taiwan's developmental accumulation
strategy: In the late 1950s, the military apparatus was the largest customer of SOEs,
"buying 65 percent of the island's output of petroleum products and 40 percent of
its cement" (Cullather 1996: 19). But as GDP growth rates began to decline from
the mid-1950s onwards, military spending became a burden. The R.O.C.'s fiscal
deficit rose from NTD 1.3 billion in 1956 to NTD 4.3 billion in 1960, and it was
only US military assistance that covered the difference (Jacoby 1966: 283; Ho
1978: 116). Finally, ISI began to show symptoms of overaccumulation, particularly
in the textile sector where companies were protected from foreign competition but
faced a saturated domestic market (Cullather 1996: 20). ISI policies, such as the
system of multiple exchange rates, had effectively increased industrial output but

at the same time set obstacles to export. The resulting "excess capacity in textiles, paper, rubber goods, and soap" (Ranis 1979: 219) could not be absorbed through domestic demand, and the bureaucracy began pondering ways to ease the pressure.

Against the background of ISI reaching exhaustion, US pressures for an adjustment of Taiwan's accumulation strategy appeared in a new light. US advisers, hoping to showcase capitalist competition as the best way to modernise an emerging economy, urged the Taiwanese government to liberalise exchange and trade regulations, promising additional loans of US$30 million for a prompt implementation of these recommendations (Ho 1987: 245). As the KMT leadership failed to react to these recommendations, the US threatened to withhold aid should Taiwan fail to liberalise and allow a stronger private sector and signalled that economic assistance would be terminated by the mid-1960s (Gold 1986: 73). Contrary to the often-held view that Taiwan's economic bureaucracy embraced the shift towards export promotion only after pressure by the US mounted (e.g. Haggard and Pang 1994: 72, 74; Tsai 1999: 105; Ngo 2005: 97–98, 105), Ho (1987: 243–244) argues that factions within Taiwan's economic bureaucracy contemplated export promotion even *before* US pressure arose. The industrialist camp saw export promotion as a remedy to the economic challenges that Taiwan faced. Already in 1955, K.T. Li, a key bureaucrat educated in Cambridge, proposed to initiate export promotion in the textile sector as a release valve for the sector's excess capacities and a means to provide Taiwan with much-needed foreign exchange to replace US assistance. Furthermore, a growing export sector could absorb the surplus labour and thus meet political ends by co-opting Taiwanese into the economy (Ranis 1979: 219–220).

At the time, his plan was rejected (Ho 1987: 244). Chiang Kai-shek refused to implement steps towards liberalisation on the grounds of Taiwan's "mission" to liberate the mainland (Ngo 2005: 104). To control Taiwan's development path and maintain its relative autonomy from social forces, the KMT wanted to keep the private sector small and close it off from foreign investment (Simon 1988: 141–143). The monetarist camp furthermore insisted that devaluing the NTD would make imports more expensive and therefore lead to inflation. They also held the view that developing countries would not be able to compete with industrialised countries in global markets. More crucially, economic bureaucrats worried about relinquishing control over planning instruments, in particular credit allocation (two-thirds of which went to the government and SOEs at that time). These criticisms found support not only from the military and SOE managers but also from those large enterprises that benefited from protection and were therefore critical of phasing out ISI policies. Even a limited extraversion through the establishment of export processing zones (EPZs) was contested within the state apparatus, with critics arguing that these zones might come at the expense of enterprises outside of the EPZs (Ngo 2005: 99). Instead, the military favoured a secondary phase of import substitution in heavy industries to revive economic growth (Cullather 1996: 21; Ranis 1979: 219).

The struggle was renewed when changing structural conditions induced a shift in the relation of forces within Taiwan's state apparatus. The second Taiwan Strait crisis changed Taiwan's geopolitical position. In August 1958, the PRC began an artillery bombardment of the island of Kinmen, to which Taiwan responded by shelling the Chinese mainland. The United States stifled the crisis by sending the Seventh Fleet into the Taiwan Strait and pledged to guarantee Taiwan's security, if in return Chiang Kai-shek would renounce the KMT's plans to retake the mainland by force (Wade 1990: 392). The realisation that R.O.C. rule would be limited to Taiwan in the foreseeable future strengthened the position of those who favoured a long-term development of productive forces. At the same time, hyperinflation had been successfully contained, leading to the dissolution of the monetarist-controlled ESB. The relation of forces in Taiwan's bureaucracy therefore shifted to the industrialist agencies (Jacoby 1966: 60). When Premier Yu Hung-chun resigned for unrelated reasons in 1958, Chiang Kai-shek replaced him with Chen Cheng, who swiftly installed industrialists in crucial positions in an attempt to overcome divisions within the state apparatus and formulate coherent rather than contradictory policies (Guiheux 2002b: 61; Nordhaug 1998: 141).

This course of events leads Pang (1992: 184–185) to conclude that Taiwan's bureaucracy, faced with the contradictions of ISI, had already decided to shift towards an extraverted accumulation strategy before US pressure was completely articulated. This is supported by K.T. Li's initiative in the mid-1950s, suggesting that the US rather took the role of a midwife to export promotion, acting as a point of reference and further justification for Taiwanese technocrats whose "arguments were reinforced by pressure from the US AID mission" (Ho 1987: 245). More important than the American insistence to transform Taiwan into a free-market economy was the fact that the crisis of ISI provided a window of opportunity for a renewed struggle over Taiwan's industrial path, a struggle that took place under conditions that this time around favoured those bureaucrats that advocated for encouraging private investment. The concrete form of export promotion was not the result of "an overall design or masterplan" (Ranis 1979: 219–220) but rather a compromise among competing groups favouring different rationales of development. The compromise that ultimately shaped the new set of policies was less the expression of competing monetarist and industrialist visions, as by the late 1950s critics of the private sector were mostly side-lined. Rather, a new division had taken its place, namely one between drawing on local capital to further long-term development goals and maintaining the KMT's relative autonomy from these newly emerging social forces.

To this end, several US recommendations were disregarded. To safeguard the party's position, the KMT leadership refused to reduce military spending, privatise its SOEs or the discontinue the rice-fertiliser scheme (Jacoby 1966: 144–147). Furthermore, the state kept control of the banking sector "for fear that the growth of large financial power in the hands of private bankers will eventually challenge economic power of the government" (Fei 1987: 77). The protectionist measures of the domestic market were upheld out of political considerations. To ensure the emerging private sector would focus on exports, the system of multiple exchange rates was abolished in August of 1959, complemented by the liberalisation of the import quota system and the removal of deposit requirements (Balassa 1971: 62–63). Import restrictions on raw materials and intermediate products were relaxed as long as they were destined for export production (Wade 1990: 117). Foreign investment was encouraged, and the establishment of export-oriented enterprises was incentiv-ised through rebates in custom duty, related taxes and access to preferential loans (Ho 1978: 194–196). The NTD underwent a devaluation of about 60 per cent be-tween 1958 and 1961 to ensure the competitiveness of the new enterprises (Wade 1990: 117–118).

From the 1960s onwards, the emerging export sector became a driving force of Taiwan's economic development. The cornerstone of this development was the proliferation of small enterprises: By 1971, 29,278 manufacturing workshops with fewer than ten workers accounted for nearly two-thirds of Taiwan's manufacturing enterprises (Stites 1985: 228), and by the 1980s, these small firms accounted for two-thirds of Taiwan's exports (Lam and Clark 1998: 120). Typically, these small workshops were owned and operated by families, but even medium-sized factories were often partnerships based on kinship or friendship ties (Skoggard 1998: 133).

Yet, the export-oriented sector was not strictly separated from the large enter-prises that focused on the domestic markets. Not only did private large enterprises provide SMEs with intermediate goods, but they also acted as financial interme-diaries and loaned capital to smaller firms that had difficulties in accessing credit due to high collateral demands by state-owned banks (Amsden 1991: 1126–1129; Skoggard 1998: 132). Amsden (1991: 1129) thus concludes, contrary to the often-held view that both sectors functioned separately, that "big and small business need each other." At the other end, SMEs depended on multinational corporations to buy their products. These corporations were not only in a position to dictate prices but also demanded a high degree of flexibility as orders would fluctuate significantly due to factors ranging from the development of the economic situation in the capi-talist centres to changes in fashion trends (Skoggard 1998: 132–133).

Taiwan's small workshops and medium-sized factories responded to these de-mands by developing what Lam and Clark (1998: 120) have termed "guerrilla capitalism", that is, a particular way to organise production to ensure "extreme flexibility in rapidly filling even small orders". Contrary to what the number of enterprises might suggest, the small workshops were often bound to each other in satellite networks of subcontracting agreements, often based on kinship or friend-ship ties (Shieh 1992: 51–77). These arrangements did not so much rely on writ-ten contracts but rather on "traditional morality which includes notions of loyalty, trust, face, and the practice of *guanxi* (personal relations)" (Skoggard 1998: 132). Taiwan's export-oriented SMEs responded to fluctuations in the world market "more as a unified organism than as discrete units" (Lam and Clark 1998: 122). As small-scale manufacturing workshops mostly employed family members and as such did not rely on formal wage relations (Niehoff 1987: 280), global competi-tiveness could be maintained through the particular ways in which family-based satellite production could appropriate unwaged labour rather than through techni-cal innovation (Hsiung 1996: 145). As rural workshops had emerged on the basis of farms without replacing them, households continued farming not only because they would otherwise risk losing the land title, but also because agriculture provided a safety net (Niehoff 1987: 281, 304–306): In times of low global demand, house-hold members could work on the farm to ensure subsistence, while in times of high demand, labour could be shifted from the farm towards the workshop – thereby also absorbing surplus labour that was the result of the introduction of advanced agricultural techniques (Ho 1979: 88–94). Fluctuations in the global market were thus mitigated by the flexibility of kinship-based arrangements, both within the workshop and among the workshops clustered in a subcontracting network.

Despite the high degree of self-exploitation that was the cornerstone of Taiwan's "economic miracle" (Gates 1979: 396–399), Taiwan's rural industrialisation also contributed to maintaining a low level of labour militancy. While large enterprises and especially SOEs used a share of their monopoly profits to pay good wages and provide amenities such as swimming pools, restaurants, schools and cinemas for their employers and their families (Ho 2014b: 61), the profits of small workshops were squeezed between the domestic large enterprises and the multinational corporations. Thus, a set of particular ideological forms emerged from the kinship-based small-scale production. The organisation of the labour process merged characteristics from agricultural work and the manufacturing in the workshop, resulting in social forms that draw on "elements from both capitalist and peasant ideologies of economic production": For instance, unwaged labour by family members and the high degree of self-exploitation in the factory were experienced as a continuation of the work on the fields, which also did not know regulated working hours (Niehoff 1987: 279, 300–302).

The most crucial ideological element that stemmed from Taiwan's shift to export-oriented industrialisation, however, was the prospect of upward mobility. On the one hand, especially the rural industrialisation widened the base of social groups that benefited from Taiwan's economic development, thus reducing "resentment against the capitalist mode of production" (Chu 2001a: 458). On the other hand, workers did have a high degree of awareness regarding economic inequality but accepted these inequalities and other workplace-related grievances (such as long overtime hours and work safety), because the highly flexible system of satellite factories and the low barriers to entering this system fostered their ambition to become their own boss one day, and workers therefore tended to view these grievances from the perspective of a future entrepreneur (Wu 1996: 100; Stites 1985: 229, 242). This proliferation of an "entrepreneurial logic" (Shieh 1992: 214–215) among the workers turned Taiwan into what Shieh (ibid.) calls a "boss island", where hard work and flexibility paved the road to economic prosperity.[2] The result was an ideological configuration which fostered "the social expectation that individuals – not the state, enterprise, or society – were responsible for their own livelihood and that of their family" (Cho and Jessop 2001: 20). The prospect of economic upward mobility compensated, to a certain degree, for the political exclusion and thus contributed to maintaining social stability.

Macro-economically, export-oriented industrialisation did not so much replace but rather complement import substitution. The contradictions of ISI, in particular with regard to the excess capacities of large enterprises, were, however, mitigated as the growing number of export-oriented SMEs turned to Taiwan's large enterprises to buy their intermediary products without intensifying domestic competition (Wu 2004: 98). The particular way of managing the contradictions of ISI resulted in an arrangement that bore within itself the seeds of the next crisis. To support Taiwan as a capitalist country in East Asia, the US did not insist on reciprocity in terms of trade throughout the 1960s and 1970s (Nordhaug 1998: 141). This relationship was formalised in the 1976 Generalized System of Preferences (GSP) that granted Taiwan duty exemption privileges (Werner 1985: 1099). The US policy to grant beneficial access to its domestic market to support the R.O.C. led to what has been labelled a "beneficial dependency" (Tsai 2001: 366) or "US-sponsored export-led growth" (Woo 1991: 462). While this neo-mercantilist accumulation strategy resulted in renewed economic growth and large reserves of foreign exchange, it proved increasingly unsustainable from the early 1980s onwards.

The Organic Crisis of Taiwan's Developmental Accumulation Strategy

Throughout the 1970s, Taiwan began to face multiple crises that converged and became increasingly acute until the mid-1980s. Economically, Taiwan was hit by the oil crisis of 1973. As a result, in 1974 consumer prices rose by 47.5 per cent (Gold 1986: 98), and as Taiwan's exports declined significantly, the economic growth rate fell to one per cent (Trappey 2007: 291). While the immediate effects of the oil crisis were short-lived, this moment revealed the vulnerability of Taiwan's export orientation, which had become a central pillar of its accumulation strategy. The oil shock affected Taiwan in a moment of political uncertainty, as it coincided with the erosion of the Republic of China's claim to represent all of China internationally. In 1971, the R.O.C. lost its seat in the UN Security Council and membership in all UN organisations to the People's Republic of China, after Taiwan and the United States were no longer able to prevent the increasing diplomatic support for China, largely a result of decolonisation, being reflected in the institutions of global politics. Nixon's visit to China the following year heralded the normalisation of US-PRC ties that set in motion a domino effect. Amongst others, Japan, Taiwan's major ally and trading partner in the region, switched diplomatic recognition to the PRC in September 1972. Both the oil crisis and Taiwan's uncertain international status contributed to a decline in foreign investment (Amsden 1991: 1125).

During this political crisis, the internal contradictions of Taiwan's accumulation strategy matured. For one, a shortage of land slowed down industrial growth. Taiwan's population had doubled between 1950 and 1975, and the land shortage contributed to a de-centralised industrialisation in rural Taiwan as land prices in the cities increased from the mid-1960s onwards (Ho 1979). The government was hesitant to allow the conversion of farmland into industrial land for two reasons: First, Taiwan's land reform and the resulting small-scale farming had been a cornerstone of hegemonic inclusion; second, the uncertainties of Taiwan's foreign relations led the government to believe that agricultural land was crucial for Taiwan's food security (Mao and Schive 1995: 58).

Another limiting factor to Taiwan's labour-intensive and export-oriented development strategy was the acute labour shortage. Despite an increase in the labour force of 70 per cent between 1965 and 1979 (Hsu 1982: 846), Taiwan reached a level of full employment by the late 1960s (Gold 1986: 89). Small factories in Taiwan's rural areas alone tripled their work force from 188,000 to 589,000 in the years between 1966 and 1971 (Stites 1985: 228). Women increasingly joined the manufacturing labour force, accounting for one-third of Taiwan's total labour force in the late 1970s (Hsu 1982: 847) and for 85 per cent of the workers in Taiwan's EPZs (Arrigo 1980: 25). Yet, the labour shortage persisted, and by the time male unemployment had fallen to 1.11 per cent in 1980 (Howe 1996: 1180), wages in Taiwan had doubled compared to 1976 (Gold 1986: 98). As rising wages threatened the international competitiveness of Taiwan's export-oriented SMEs, these pursued productivity gains through automation. Between 1987 and 1991, production in manufacturing increased by 14 per cent, while employment in the manufacturing sector decreased by 16 per cent (Schive 1995: 15). Nevertheless, by 1991, unit labour costs had doubled compared to 1982 (ibid.: 66).

A third direct consequence of Taiwan's rapid and intense industrial development was the pollution of air, water and soil (Chi 1994: 26). Environmental concerns were not a priority until the late 1980s, in particular as the KMT considered Taiwan a temporary base until the Chinese mainland had been retaken (Arrigo 1994: 36). A major polluter were the large petrochemical plants that had been rapidly promoted after the oil crisis (ibid.: 34–35). But also Taiwan's export industry, which consisted of a myriad of small factories that were hard to regulate and supervise, contributed to pollution, as especially small electronics manufacturers discharged heavy metals and other pollutants into the environment (Knapp 1996: 789). The three crises of land, labour and the environment were not only objective obstacles to Taiwan's development, they also sparked the emergence of social movements, which contributed to the erosion of the KMT's legitimacy and shaped the process of democratisation (Hsiao 2011).

By far the most acute symptom of the maturing contradictions of Taiwan's neomercantilist accumulation strategy, however, was the trade imbalance with the United States. The export orientation coupled with Taiwan's preferential access to the US market had led to a steady increase of Taiwan's share in US imports (Chen 2001: 343): While in 1962, Taiwan was ranked in 21st position of US imports of manufactured goods, it had risen to number four by 1986 (Wade 1990: 37). Throughout the first half of the 1980s, the American trade deficit rose sharply as Taiwan's exports nearly tripled while Taiwan's protectionist policies meant that imports from the US stagnated, more than quadrupling the trade deficit (Werner 1985: 1098). Between 1976 and 1984, Taiwan's trade surplus with the US grew tenfold (Chou 1990: 201).

From the mid-1980s, the US was no longer able or willing to sustain the trade imbalance, and the US government began to pressure Taiwan into partly opening its domestic markets and allowing the NTD to appreciate. Similar policies were aimed at industrialised countries, including Japan and Germany. In the Plaza Accord of 1985, major industrial countries agreed on letting their currencies appreciate vis-à-vis the US dollar to increase the competitiveness of American goods. As the NTD was pegged to the US dollar, the appreciation of the Japanese Yen contributed to making Taiwan's exports to the US become "supercompetitive" compared to those economies directly affected by the agreement (Wade 1990: 41). This only worsened the trade imbalance between Taiwan and the US, resulting in further attempts by successive American administrations to have Taiwan reduce import tariffs and allow the currency to appreciate to increase imports from the US (Copper 1987: 90). Taiwan was in a weak bargaining position against the United States. Its export economy depended on access to the US markets that were the destination of roughly half of Taiwanese exports (Riedel and Cicognani 1994: 350). The KMT government also sought to compensate for Taiwan's increasing international isolation through the participation in international regimes and organisations, including GATT/WTO, and these plans relied on US support (Tsai 2001: 366–367).

Nevertheless, the Taiwanese government was reluctant to make concessions that would erode its neo-mercantilist accumulation strategy. The trade surplus was the source for foreign reserves, which were seen as an insurance against the increasing international isolation (Chou 1990: 194). In an attempt to avoid a general revision of its trade and economic policies, Taiwan made a series of limited concessions (Chan 1987: 268). Taiwan began sending "Buy American" procurement missions to the US, primarily acquiring agricultural products, but also aircraft and buses, worth US$8 billion between 1978 and 1986 (Wang 1987: 18). Furthermore, early trade liberalisation measures were limited to sectors where the state held a monopoly in an attempt to deflect the pressure from private enterprises (ibid.: 20). Tariff reductions before the mid-1980s also primarily applied to imports of intermediate products or means of production and therefore still did not clash with Taiwan's export promotion policies (Chou 1990: 160).

This organic crisis set the stage for a struggle over Taiwan's future development path. Under Premier Yu Kuo-hwa, the Executive Yuan established the Committee for Economic Reform (CER) to devise proposals for the revitalisation of Taiwan's economy (McBeath 1997: 1150). This committee was remarkable in several ways. First, it included US-trained neoclassical economists, who had become more influential globally since the phenomenon of stagflation undermined Keynesian thinking throughout the 1970s (Chu 2001b: 92). Already in the immediate aftermath of the 1973 oil crisis, these overseas Taiwanese with connections to the Chicago School had proposed far-reaching measures of privatisation to increase the role of the market mechanism (Rubinstein 2013: 39–40). While their recommendations were shelved at that time, their influence within Taiwan's economic bureaucracy increased throughout the 1970s as they joined the Council for Economic Planning and Development (CEPD),[3] which had been downgraded to a vice-ministerial institution in 1973, and the same economists were consulted again a decade later (ibid.). By the time the CEPD was upgraded to ministerial rank again in 1978, it was mostly staffed by economists and began to challenge the Industrial Development Board, which maintained close relations with SOEs, was mostly staffed by engineers and favoured to continue protectionist policies (Wade 1990: 200–204). Against the background of the organic crisis, the neoclassical economists' argument that Taiwan's economic success had been rendered possible by the unleashing of market forces, rather than state intervention, appeared in a new light (ibid.: 221). Second, in an unprecedented move, Premier Yu included representatives of Taiwan's bourgeoisie, including Wang Yung-ching of Formosa Plastics and Koo Chen-fu of the Koos Group, in the CER (Hsia 2019: 92). Hsia (ibid.: 94) suggests that Yu had convened the CER in this form to obtain the backing for a more pragmatic course but that neoclassical economists took advantage of the committee to advance their more radical views.

The CER recommended the liberalisation of foreign trade and investment relations, the deregulation of domestic sectors (including the banking sector), the privatisation of public enterprises and the relaxation of labour laws.[4] Under the formula "liberalise, internationalise, institutionalise", these recommendations became the guiding principle of Taiwan's economic policies (Chu 2001b: 93). In the words of Fredrick Chien, who was CEPD Minister from 1988 to 1990:

> Liberalization allows the economy to be increasingly regulated by the free market. Thus, administrative intervention in private economic activities is being reduced in order to create an equitable and competitive environment for the efficient allocation and utilization of resources. Internationalization expands economic activities by opening up home markets and allowing foreign competition with a view towards encouraging economic, technological, and cultural exchange with foreign countries. Institutionalization streamlines and systematizes economic activities by means of legislation and regulation and is a prerequisite to successful liberalization and internationalization.
>
> (Chien 1989: 187)

While the economic bureaucracy was worried about Taiwan's macro-economic situation, including a lack of domestic demand, excessive saving and a decline in investment (Tsai 2001: 365–366), the political elite was concerned with Taiwan's international status. At this juncture, neoclassical economists successfully presented measures of economic liberalisation as the most adequate remedy for Taiwan's crisis of international recognition. John C.H. Fei (1987: 75–76), himself one of the neoclassical economists consulted on the process, thus argued that "to be a full fledged member of the international economic community of the industrially advanced countries, a country must permit currency appreciation as long as an export surplus persists." The dimension of internationalisation therefore fused the demands by Taiwan's political elite with those of the advocates of liberalisation. Opening up to multinational companies, for instance, came to be seen as an insurance against derecognition, binding the economic interests of Japan and the US to those of Taiwan (Amsden 1991: 1124–1125). Similarly, financial liberalisation became a way to trade "the requisite liberalizing concessions for enhanced recognition as an international player in its own right" (Thurbon 2007: 88). Political elites, however, were able to impose a limit on liberalisation and internationalisation, excluding the People's Republic of China from these initiatives.

After the consensus was reached, trade reforms accelerated after 1986, and Taiwan began to systematically dismantle the two pillars of its neo-mercantilist accumulation strategies (Liu 2002: 980). Export promotion policies, such as preferential loans for export-oriented enterprises, were cancelled (Chou 1990: 82–83).

After the US removed Taiwan from the GSP, Taiwan furthermore adopted policies of diversifying its exports away from the US (Smith 1997: 7). At the same time, protectionist policies were abolished: By the late 1980s, the percentage of items permitted to be imported rose from less than 60 per cent in 1970 to 97 per cent (Smith 1998: 311–312). A tariff reduction affecting 3,500 commodities by 50 per cent on average in 1988 was followed by a further decrease by 23 per cent affecting 4,738 commodities the following year (Chien 1989: 188). Overall, the nominal tariff rate fell from over 26 per cent to less than 11 per cent between 1985 and 1989 (Liu 2002: 977). In addition, Taiwan also removed import bans on a variety of sectors that had previously benefited from protectionist measures, including automobiles, petrochemicals and consumer electronics (Cheng 2001a: 144–145). With regard to financial liberalisation, the government gradually relaxed restrictions on inward and outward remittances to encourage foreign direct investment (Dreyer 1990: 53). Furthermore, the Central Bank of China relaxed foreign exchange controls in 1987 before removing daily fluctuation limits of the exchange rate in early 1989 (Chou 1990: 278).

The effects of these sudden adjustments were significant. Between 1986 and 1989, the NTD appreciated by nearly 50 per cent against the US dollar, prompting a huge loss in competitiveness for Taiwan's export-oriented sector and resulting in a harsh decline of private investment (Chu 1994b: 122). Wedged between the erosion of Taiwan's export model on the one hand and the persistent ban on investments in China on the other, Taiwan's enterprises did not see any potential for profitable investments. Instead, excess capital flowed into the stock and real estate markets (Schubert 1994: 205). Between 1985 and 1986, the annual trading volume on the Taiwan Stock Market grew by 250 per cent while real estate prices in Taipei increased by nearly 450 per cent between 1986 and 1990 (Chou 2001: 65–66). The stock market bubble burst in 1990, when the stock index fell by 78 per cent within eight months (Dreyer 1991: 57).

Faced with these developments, the government decided to reassess the prohibition of China-bound investment. The ban had already proven porous by the mid-1980s, as "adaptable small- and medium-sized enterprises simply rampaged through the official investment ban," often by channelling capital through the Cayman or British Virgin Islands (Chu 1997: 241). These illegal investments were facilitated after the Taiwanese government lifted the travel ban to China in 1987. Rather than clinging to an increasingly ineffective set of restrictions, the government adjusted the regulations to provide a release valve for capital as well as to steer investment flows and thus industrial development in Taiwan. In 1991, the outright ban on China-bound investments was replaced with a highly regulated statute that divided investment projects into three categories: Labour-intensive manufacturing and industries that relied on using raw materials deemed necessary for Taiwan's future industrial development were placed on a permitted list, investments into Chinese infrastructure as well as the service sectors and most crucially the high-technology sector were prohibited, while the remaining projects would be reviewed on a case-by-case basis (Lin 1997: 28–29). Investments furthermore had to be indirect, for example through a subsidiary in a third country or indirect remittance (Leng 1998: 500). These regulations were designed to permit the relocation of SMEs in labour-intensive industries, which had suffered from the appreciation of the NTD, while at the same time encouraging industrial upgrading in Taiwan and thus increasing Taiwan's competitiveness in technology-intensive goods (Weiss 2003: 259–260).

Emerging Social Forces and the Persevering Organic Crisis

The Structural Transformation of Taiwan's Large Enterprises and the Emergence of an Interior Bourgeoisie

Before we turn to the contradictions that would arise from the partial opening of China-bound investment, it is helpful to discuss how the processes of political and economic liberalisation contributed to the transformation of Taiwan's large enterprises. The conglomerates that dominate Taiwan's economy today emerged in three distinct waves and can be categorised into three capital fractions according to their objective position in the global political economy as well as their increasingly congruent political demands and strategies. A first capital fraction can be traced back to the phase of ISI, which Numazaki (1986: 491) further subdivides into three types. A first subgroup consists of business groups owned by former Taiwanese landowners who were compensated in stocks of former state-owned companies and expanded these into business groups. The most prominent example among these is the Koos Group, which was split into the Taiwan Cement and Chinatrust groups in 2003. A second subgroup developed from émigré mainlander industrialists, who brought their textile machinery to Taiwan in 1949, where their enterprises flourished with the help of the KMT. In 1976, nearly one-third of Taiwan's largest business groups had roots in the textile sector, including the Far Eastern Group, the Ruentex Group and the Shin Kong Group, but the founders of the Yulon Group as well as Uni-President had also previously been involved in textile companies (Gold 1988b: 188). A third origin for these earlier business groups were Taiwanese petty capitalists, who were able to expand and diversify their original enterprise. The Evergreen Group, for instance, was founded by Chang Yung-fa, who started his own shipping company with a single used ship after having worked in a shipping enterprise.

These companies made the qualitative step from single enterprises into business groups mostly in the late 1960s. The particular condition that facilitated the formation of business groups has to be seen as an unintended consequence of the government's plan to stimulate investment and export through tax relief for new firms, making it more profitable for entrepreneurs to found new firms rather than expand existing ones (Chung 2001: 725). In addition to these tax incentives, the intent to spread economic risk but also the political consideration to not have single large firms that could be seen as threatening the KMT made the formation of groups of firms the most feasible way to integrate production (Gold 1986: 88). Instead of growing into large enterprises, "a set of legally independent firms [emerged] that link to each other through various economic and social relationships, and operate in a coherent manner" (Chung 2001: 721). In the absence of formal ties that characterise Western large enterprises, companies in Taiwanese business groups are connected by individuals, often family members, holding key positions in enterprises that form a business group (Guiheux 2002a: 207).

Until the 1980s, the core business of more than half of the 100 biggest conglomerates was either in textile, petrochemicals/plastic or food products (Guiheux 1995: 164). With a few notable exceptions, their historical trajectory had placed most of these conglomerates in midstream production (or department I: the production of means of production), acting as suppliers of intermediate products for SMEs that would produce commodities destined for export markets. In contrast to the SMEs established during the export-oriented industrialisation (EOI), the large ISI groups were beneficiaries of protectionist policies and producers for the domestic market and thus tended to be inward looking. As beneficiaries of protectionist measures and certain political and economic concessions by the KMT, these business groups therefore emerged as a typical case of what Poulantzas (2008: 200) calls the *national bourgeoisie*, that is, the "fraction of the bourgeoisie whose interests are linked to the nation's economic development and which comes into relative contradiction with the interests of big foreign capital."

This outlook, however, would change rapidly as a consequence of the economic transformation of the late 1980s. First, business groups involved in the production of intermediate products saw their customers relocate to China after the ban on China-bound investment was lifted. According to Leng (1996: 90), four out of five manufacturers of apparel, toys and footwear had moved to China. Fearing that they would lose their customers to midstream suppliers based in China, Taiwan's business groups began to plan their own investments across the Taiwan Strait to continue the symbiotic relationship with labour-intensive manufacturing companies (Chu 1997: 241). But while SMEs were either allowed to invest in China or were able to circumvent the restrictions, the large-scale projects of Taiwan's conglomerates faced political obstacles: When Formosa Plastics announced it was going to build a petrochemical complex in China (see below), the Taiwanese government pressured Wang into reconsidering the plan, promising preferential treatment if the plant was to be built in Taiwan (Leng 1998: 503). Despite these concessions, Taiwan's conglomerates had changed from beneficiaries of protectionism to critics of cross-Strait restrictions.

The second catalyst for the transformation of interests was the deregulation of service sectors. On the one hand, this had been a central objective of the liberalisation initiative designed to increase economic efficiency by relying on the market mechanism. The Taiwanese government also saw private banks as a prerequisite for the internationalisation of Taiwanese companies, as it deemed state-owned banks unable to provide support for these companies abroad (Thurbon 2007: 94). On the other hand, deregulation was a concession to the business groups that were still barred from investing in China (Ngo 1995: 9–10), as allowing them into "aviation, banking, insurance, public transportation, publishing, securities, shipping, telecommunications, and television" (Chung and Mahmood 2010: 190) would open new spheres of accumulation domestically. However, this only reinforced their shift towards transnational strategies of accumulation, as Taiwan's markets were comparatively small. The liberalisation of the banking sector is a case in point. As the entry barriers into the banking sector were high (Liu 1992: 142), the first 15 private banks established in 1992 were part of large business groups, essentially turning them into financial conglomerates. This situation resulted in a sector characterised by overbanking, making domestic banking persistently un-profitable (Thurbon 2007: 103–104). Banks swiftly began to seek opportunities abroad, and in 1993, a delegation of 15 private Taiwanese banks visited China to probe the possibility of "serv[ing] Taiwanese customers on the mainland" (Baum 1993: 66). But as service sector industries were still prohibited from investing in China, these banks were unable to follow other Taiwanese companies across the Strait. Instead, the government encouraged domestic mergers and acquisitions, and Taiwan saw 15 bank mergers between 1997 and 2001 (Thurbon 2007: 103–104) and the Financial Holding Company Law of 2001 removed barriers between and allowing for the integration of financial services (Brück and Sun 2007: 657). The situation was similar in other newly deregulated sectors. The Evergreen Group, for instance, began to pressure for the normalisation of cross-Strait relations, as its shipping business would benefit from the implementation of direct links between China and Taiwan. This desire only grew stronger after the group established EVA Air, Taiwan's first privately-owned airline (Leng 1996: 91–92).

A second capital fraction developed from electronics companies that were set up as contract manufacturers for overseas customers in the 1970s. Until the mid-1970s, foreign firms dominated Taiwan's electronics industry, with American com-panies tending to produce for exports and Japanese joint-ventures for Taiwan's market (Amsden and Chu 2003: 19–20). Setting up joint-ventures usually required the foreign firm to enter a technical cooperation agreement, which contributed to the transfer of technology and expertise to local Taiwanese firms, thus helping Taiwanese companies to gradually take over the electronics sector (Simon 1992: 105–107). Several of the world's largest original equipment manufacturers (OEMs) and original design manufacturers (ODMs) can be traced back to this era. Hon Hai Precision, known as Foxconn outside of Taiwan, Acer, Kinpo, Inventec, Lite-On and Quanta all evolved from small contract manufacturing companies in the mid-1970s and early 1980s. Throughout the 1980s and 1990s, they upgraded into origi-nal design manufacturing for US companies, spinning off companies that would become the world's leading OEMs and ODMs.[5] In addition to Foxconn, these were Compal (spun off from Kinpo in 1984), Wistron (Acer, 2000) and Pegatron (ASUS, 2008). As labour-intensive ODMs and OEMs produce for the world market, they operate on tight margins and thus began relocating production to China throughout the 1990s to reduce costs and thus maintain their global competitiveness (Fuller 2005: 154–155). Their major interest in cross-Strait relations is thus in the stable flow of capital, needed for the constant expansion and upgrading of their produc-tion facilities, across the Taiwan Strait as well as stable relations between Taiwan, China and the Western countries that were the companies' major markets.

The third capital fraction emerged from Taiwan's state-sponsored initiatives that were devised to induce a process of industrial upgrading after the oil crisis and the labour shortage made the manufacturing of cheap goods for export increasingly precarious (Trappey 2007: 291). Key to this initiative was the establishment of public institutions such as the Industrial Technology and Research Institute (ITRI), which would shoulder the risk involved with entering this technology-intensive sector. The state would also provide the necessary infrastructure by establishing the Hsinchu Science and Industrial Park, often referred to as the "Silicon Valley of the East", which lies in the direct vicinity of two of Taiwan's leading technical universities (Mathews 1997: 30). Enterprises settling in the park would have access to preferential loans, research and development matching funds as well as tax breaks (ibid.). Finally, these initiatives were complemented by a drive, at first informal and then increasingly systematic, to attract Taiwanese who had studied and worked in the US (Saxenian and Hsu 2001: 901–905). The resulting "network of public research laboratories, parastatal organisations, industry parks [and] state- and party-controlled finance institutions" (Nordhaug 1998: 146) led to ITRI spinning off United Microelectronics Corporation (UMC) in 1980 and the Taiwan Semiconductor Manufacturing Company (TSMC) in 1987. Both of these companies are now considered to be among the top four global chip foundries, providing manufacturing capacities for "fabless" (i.e. without fabrication capacities) chip designers, such as Apple, AMD or NVIDIA. Like contract manufacturers, these chip foundries rely on Taiwan's integration into global value chains, and both capital fractions therefore can be considered to belong to what Poulantzas (1974: 166) describes as the *interior bourgeoisie*. Their interest is aligned with those multinational IT firms for whom they produce, which is expressed in a continuous pressure directed at the Taiwanese government to lift restrictions on cross-Strait investment that affect the chip foundries in particular. Unlike the assembly organised by Taiwanese contract manufacturers in China, chip foundries were restricted by the ban on high-tech investment in China to prevent the transfer of technology that is crucial to Taiwan's international competitiveness and national security to China (Fuller 2005: 155–157).

The expansion of conglomerates was reflected in their increasing economic and social significance as indicated in Table 3.1. During the decade between 1977 and

Table 3.1 Economic significance of Taiwan's 100 largest business groups, 1977–2006

Year	Total No. of firms	Ratio sales/GDP	% of employed labour force
1977	651	28.8	5.2
1981	719	28.6	4.8
1986[a]	746	29.4	4.3
1990	815	39.2	4.8
1994	1,021	41.5	5.2
1998	1,362	54.3	7.9
2002	4,825	85.4	9.5
2006	6,038	128.9	24.0

[a] The data for the year 1986 refers to the largest 97 business groups.

Source: Adapted from Chung and Mahmood "Business Groups in Taiwan". In: The Oxford Handbook of Business Groups, 188. © Oxford University Press (2010). Reproduced with permission of the Licensor through PLSclear.

1986, the total sales of these business groups amounted to less than 30 per cent of Taiwan's GDP, while their share of Taiwan's employed work force hovered between 4.3 and 5.2 per cent. This changed markedly during the 1990s, as Taiwan's national bourgeoisie diversified into sectors that had been deregulated and the interior bourgeoisie had consolidated its position in the US-Taiwan-China production chains, leading to both indicators nearly doubling by the late 1990s. The decade also saw a trend towards centralisation: Between 1992 and 1997, Taiwan's Fair Trade Commission rejected only one out of 2,093 applications for mergers (Kuo 2001: 99). Both of these developments were amplified after Taiwan permitted the formation of financial holding companies in 2001, and by 2006, the total sales of Taiwan's 100 largest business groups corresponded to 128.9 per cent of the country's GDP while their share of national employment reached an unprecedented 24 per cent. Although finance is now a central pillar of Taiwan's diversified business groups, they continued their expansion into the transportation, resource, manufacturing and retail sectors, thereby achieving "the integration of the circuits of money capital, commodity capital and productive capital" (Overbeek 2004: 118). Conglomerates had therefore become "the backbone of Taiwan's economy" (Lee and Hsiao 2014: 251), which had long been considered to be dominated by SMEs. Table 3.2 lists Taiwan's ten largest conglomerates in the year 2008. By assets, nine out of ten are financial groups, with Formosa Plastics being the only exception. The picture looks different if groups are ordered by earnings after tax, with Taiwan's IT groups then accounting for six out of the ten largest groups.

Despite the increasing economic significance and the convergence of interests among the various capital fractions in opposition to cross-Strait restrictions, the particular historical trajectories of the conglomerates delayed the formation of a corporate or even political project. One factor that contributed to this delay is the ownership structure of Taiwan's conglomerates. Over the years, the links both within and between groups had been strengthened through intermarriage and

Table 3.2 Taiwan's ten largest business groups by earnings and assets, 2008

	Ten Largest Business Groups	
	By assets	*By earnings*
1.	Linyuan (Cathay)	TSMC
2.	Taiwan Financial	Hon Hai (Foxconn)
3.	Taiwan Cooperative	Chunghwa Telecom
4.	Mega Financial	Far Eastern
5.	Taishin Financial	Fubon
6.	Formosa Plastics	VIA Technologies
7.	Chinatrust	China Steel
8.	Fubon	Quanta Computer
9.	Shin Kong	Mediatek
10.	First Bank	AU Optronics

Source: Adapted from Taiwan Today News (2009).

interinvestment (Leng 1996: 84), and even in 2003 more than half of Taiwan's publicly-listed companies were family-controlled, including nine out of the ten largest groups (Kawakami 2007: 87–88). These links had been further strengthened during the deregulation of the early 1990s, as the sudden opening of new sectors led groups to create joint-ventures to raise the capital necessary for expansion (Chung 2004: 42–44).

Notwithstanding these close relationships among groups, their family-based ownership structure was the decisive element shaping their political strategies: During the authoritarian era, the leaders of Taiwan's large business groups had established close personal connections with the KMT, and several among them (including Koo Chen-fu of the Koos Group and Kao Ching-yuan of the President Group) were members of the party's Central Standing Committee (Leng 1996: 86–87). Continuing to rely on these personal connections to policymakers appeared more promising even during the phase of democratic transition, and thus the conglomerates continued to pursue exclusive benefits rather than organising on a sectoral level or as capital in general (Chu 1994b: 120). The factional struggle that divided the KMT during this time consolidated this symbiosis: Lee Teng-hui, who represented the mainstream faction that advocated the Taiwanisation of the KMT and a more pragmatic foreign policy, courted the large business groups to prevail over the non-mainstream faction, which was strongly entrenched in the party apparatus and saw Lee's course as a threat to the One China principle (ibid.: 127). For the most part, Taiwan's capitalists gladly supported Lee, whom they saw as the most likely candidate to "normalise" economic relations with the PRC (Schubert 1994: 141).

The democratic transition opened up further channels through which business groups sought to expand their direct influence. As democratic reforms progressed, the Legislative Yuan was transformed from a rubber-stamping institution into a body that represented social interests, mostly capital and local factions, that had to be accommodated (Cheng and Chu 2002: 205). Political competition furthermore necessitated the funds for an election campaign, and Taiwan's "diversified business groups became the most sought-after patrons of elective politicians and local factions" (ibid.: 203). Before the 1989 supplementary elections for the Legislative Yuan, eight leading tycoons – including Wang Yung-ching (Formosa Plastics), Stan Shih (Acer) and Kao Ching-yuan (Uni-President) – vented their frustration over the labour and environmental movements in an open letter in the *Economic Daily News*, urging the government to restore social order after the "chaos had not only endangered the lives and property of the public, but also threatened the very survival of enterprises in Taiwan" (Chu 1996: 507–508). Stating that they would support any candidate who could create a reasonable economic environment, they declared an investment strike until the situation was rectified (Ngo 1995: 7–8). At least 65 per cent of the candidates elected into the Legislative Yuan later that year had close connections into Taiwan's private sector, showing the degree to which Taiwan's capital sought to gain a political voice in the process of democratisation (Schubert 1994: 216). On the local level, 18 of the 24 mayors and magistrates elected in the same year were backed by business groups (Chu 1994b: 126).

A first step towards creating an organisational environment that could nourish a common project of Taiwan's bourgeoisie was the political emancipation of Taiwan's business associations. During the process of political liberalisation, business groups were able to transform the corporatist business associations into vehicles of political lobbying while the privatisation of SOEs and the deregulation of previously closed sectors reduced the state's patron power (Schubert 1994: 221). In 1991, the boards of the CNAIC and the ROCCOC were reorganised to reflect these developments, and nearly half of the seats on the board of the CNAIC were occupied by leaders of Taiwan's conglomerates (Leng 1996: 87). Throughout the 1990s, Taiwan's bourgeoisie would increasingly articulate its concerns regarding the normalisation of economic relations with China through these business associations.

The business sector was also able to penetrate various institutions of the state apparatus. In 1990, the Straits Exchange Foundation (SEF) was established as a semi-official organisation to hold low-level talks with China on issues that arose from the increasing economic interactions across the Taiwan Strait. Although the SEF was largely state-funded, the organisation is controlled by a board of trustees that is mainly occupied by representatives of private enterprises (ibid.: 64). While tangible results from this organisation were rather sparse during the 1990s and early 2000s, the establishment of SEF instituted a channel that would allow capital to shape the rapprochement in crucial ways during the Ma Ying-jeou years. In addition to the SEF, Taiwan's business associations were also involved in decision-making processes of the Ministry of Economic Affairs (MoEA), which had become an advocate of cross-Strait normalisation in the early 1990s (Chu 1994b: 117). In order to formulate cross-Strait policies, the MoEA established a Mainland Affairs Committee in 1993 (Mengin 2002: 246). This committee included representatives of peak business associations and was, for instance, involved in adjustments to the lists that distinguish between permitted, prohibited and case-by-case categories for Taiwanese investments in China. Leng (1994: 56) notes that the MoEA tended to follow the recommendations made by the committee for the category of permitted investments.

Finally, the process of democratisation also saw the expansion of capital into what Mengin (2002: 254) calls an "upstream" involvement in the decision-making process by setting up think tanks that provided the necessary channels and expertise. Before the end of martial law in 1987, think tanks were heavily dependent on state funding (McGann 2009: 92), but the political and economic uncertainty resulting from the erosion of the one-party system during the democratic transition led to a proliferation of privately-funded think tanks (Yep and Ngok 2006: 547; McGann 2009: 92). In 1989, Evergreen founder Chang Yung-fa established the Institute for National Policy Research (INPR),[6] the Hualon Group founded the think tank Democracy Foundation and several businesses made the founding of the Taiwan Research Institute and the National Policy Council possible through donations (Kuo 1998: 92; Yep and Ngok 2006: 544–545). A decade later, Chi Mei Corporation founder Hsu Wen-lung would provide funding for the Taiwan Thinktank.

Yet, despite the common interest in the normalisation of cross-Strait relations, no coherent corporate project supported by Taiwan's bourgeoisie emerged throughout the 1990s. While family-owned large business groups benefited from democratisation to enlarge their influence on policymaking (Kuo 1998: 94), these initiatives continued to rely on the close personal relations that leaders of the large groups had forged with KMT leaders over the previous decades. Chu thus ascertains for the early 1990s that Taiwan's bourgeoisie

> shuns the task of building the permanent organisational base and impersonal links necessary for broad-based collective action. As a result, the business community is far from being a cohesive entity in either organisational or ideological terms.
>
> (Chu 1994b: 130–131)

An illustrative example is the 1990 plan by Formosa Plastics to construct a petrochemical complex in the Chinese province of Fujian after the group's project to build a plant in Taiwan had been abandoned due to high land prices and resistance from environmental groups. Formosa Plastics chairman Wang Yung-ching announced that the investment in China would amount to US$5 billion, a sum that was "about equal to Taiwan's total domestic investment between 1980 and 1989" (Leng 1996: 96). Keen on preventing this investment, the Taiwanese government entered into negotiations with Wang. In 1993, Formosa Plastics announced that a plant worth US$9.5 billion would be constructed in Taiwan after the government had agreed on new terms that included preferential loans and land prices (including the use of public land and the permission to reclaim tidal land), a government-funded water supply for the complex, tax breaks and relaxed environmental regulations (Ngo 1995: 11; Leng 1996: 96; Ho 2014a: 8). As long as capital was able to obtain concessions from the government on an individual and exclusive basis, there were few incentives to articulate a common project. This would change in the late 1990s, when the objective urgency for Taiwan's conglomerates to invest in China increased.

The Persevering Contradiction between the Economic and Political Logics

During the authoritarian era, the KMT's neo-mercantilist developmental strategy was driven by the two aspects of national security and economic development. Both were congruent, as economic development was regarded as the prerequisite to prevent Taiwan's incorporation into the PRC and enhance national security (Nordhaug 1998). Privately-owned business groups were not only confined to the domestic market but were also embedded in a tight corset of corporatist institutions, and SMEs exported their goods to the US or other allied countries. But from the late 1980s onwards, capital was increasingly attracted by China's economic potential, first as "work bench" for production and then increasingly as an important market. Liberalisation and internationalisation had induced a transformation of the bourgeoisie's interests, while democratisation and privatisation had reduced the state's capacity to steer private enterprises. The two aims of national security and economic development thus increasingly diverged.

This divergence was reflected in the state apparatus. Although the various institutions did not always pursue a completely coherent policy line during the 1990s, we can generally observe a division between two camps. The MoEA, supported by Taiwan's bourgeoisie, tended to favour the controlled relaxation of cross-Strait regulations (Chu 1994b: 117). A market-induced relocation of labour-intensive manufacturing to China was seen as promoting the upgrading of Taiwan's economy into high-technology and high value-added sectors, securing Taiwan's position in the globalising economy (Leng 1996: 70–71). The CEPD, which had become a base for US-trained neoclassical economists since the mid-1970s, also favoured a market-driven economic development over state intervention (Wade 1990: 220–21). The Mainland Affairs Council (MAC) and the national security apparatus, on the other hand, were concerned about an industrial hollowing out, which would jeopardise Taiwan's security given China's political goals (Leng 1996: 71; Chu 1994b: 117).

Over the years, these camps repeatedly clashed over concrete initiatives that were proposed by the MoEA, such as early attempts to establish direct transportation links across the Taiwan Strait. A turning point was the end of the factional struggle within the KMT, which was sealed when the non-mainstream faction left the party and founded the New Party in 1993 (Cheng and Chu 2002: 207–208). After Lee had consolidated his position within the party, his reliance on Taiwan's bourgeoisie decreased and the balance of forces shifted towards the presidency. The struggle between the business-oriented MoEA and the security-oriented MAC was temporarily resolved by the installation of a third body under the Executive Yuan, the supra-ministerial Mainland Affairs Planning Group, later that year (Mengin 2002: 246). Set up to achieve a better coordination among the ministries that were divided along the lines of political and economic logics, the institutional architecture ensured that ultimately President Lee Teng-hui would have the last say on crucial matters of cross-Strait policymaking (Leng 1996: 62–64).

Nevertheless, Taiwanese investments in China accelerated from 1993 onwards, primarily at the expense of investments in Southeast Asia (Liaw and Wang 2009: 75). Concerned by the increasing capital flows to China, the security-minded presidency conceived the "Go South" policy in summer 1993 intended to redirect investments to Southeast Asia (Liaw 2016: 445). The "Guidelines for Strengthening Economic and Trade Ties with Southeast Asia" were implemented in 1994 (Jing 2016: 15). They provided incentives for Taiwanese businesses to invest in Southeast Asia rather than China, including tax incentives and access to preferential loans (Dent 2003: 268). Furthermore, the government signed investment protection agreements with countries in Southeast Asia, while a similar agreement with China was not yet on the horizon (Deng 2000: 966). SOEs spearheaded the investments, inciting SMEs to follow along. By 1995, Taiwan was the largest foreign investor in Vietnam and Malaysia as well as the third largest in the Philippines (Chen 1996: 454).

The "Go South" initiative was designed to not only provide an economic but also a political counterweight to China: In the absence of formal diplomatic recognition, Lee Teng-hui pursued a "pragmatic diplomacy", an element of which was to increase Taiwan's international visibility and to achieve substantive cooperation through the participation in international organisations (Ngeow 2017: 100–101). Tapping into the potential of the Southeast Asian regionalisation process that was institutionalised in 1992 with the establishment of the ASEAN Free Trade Area was one method to further this goal (Jing 2016: 15). The initiative therefore also involved the intensification of functional cooperation, including "exchanges of visits by political leaders, the upgrading and renaming of Taiwanese representative offices in the region, the signing of bilateral agreements, and the setting up of a ministerial-level dialogue mechanism" (Yang 2018: 9).

Capital, however, continued to push for a normalisation of cross-Strait economic relations. Taiwan's bourgeoisie thus supported an initiative devised by the pro-market CEPD that sought to transform Taiwan into an Asia-Pacific Regional Operations Center (APROC) (Chu 1997: 243). The project was conceived under the aegis of Vincent Siew, who was CEPD chairman in 1993. Vice-chairman Schive Chi, himself a neoclassical economist and former Mont Pèlerin Society fellow, was tasked with the elaboration and implementation. On the one hand, the APROC initiative sought to provide incentives for the companies that relocated their production facilities to China to maintain their headquarters as well as research and development departments in Taiwan (Liaw and Wang 2009: 78). As such, Ngo (2000: 88) suggests that APROC "represents concessions made by the Taiwanese government to the business demand that obstacles to capital regionalization be removed, in exchange for the business community's concession that the government be allowed to guide the course of regionalization". On the other hand, it sought to attract foreign firms to choose Taiwan as the base for their regional headquarters as well as research and development, finance and logistics departments by providing the infrastructure that turned Taiwan into a gateway to Asia for global companies (Liaw and Wang 2009: 78).

At first glance, these aims appear compatible with or even complementary to the "Go South" initiative. However, in order to turn Taiwan into a gateway to Asia, APROC relied on direct links to China. The CEPD went to great lengths to justify the normalisation of cross-Strait transportation (Schive 1995: 49–50). Anticipating criticism, the economic bureaucracy commissioned the US consulting firm McKinsey to prepare a report on the necessity of direct links for the realisation of the APROC initiative (Chu 1997: 243). Schive Chi argued that closer economic relations across the Taiwan Strait would not endanger Taiwan's security, but rather "provide some kind of insurance in our relations with the mainland" (cited in: Taiwan Today 1995).

In a further attempt to defuse the political aspect of direct links, Minister of Economic Affairs Chiang Pin-kung "proposed the idea of opening 'point-to-point' direct air and sea links with mainland China" (Chu 1997: 243). In a similar vein, the Ministry of Transportation and Communications (MOTC) proposed the establishment of "off-shore transshipment zones" or, alternatively, to let Taiwanese and Chinese vessels sail under "flags of convenience" to circumvent the issue of sovereignty (Liu 1996: 220). The thrust towards the normalisation of cross-Strait economic relations, however, reignited the tensions between the CEPD and the MAC, which opposed all of these propositions. When Vincent Siew, one of the architects of the APROC, became chairman of the MAC in December 1994, it appeared as if the contradiction between the political and economic logics had been resolved in favour of the latter (Nordhaug 1998: 151).

The primacy of economic relations, however, was short-lived. As part of his "pragmatic diplomacy", Lee Teng-hui accepted an invitation by his *alma mater*, Cornell University, in 1995. China suspected Lee of advancing an agenda of Taiwan independence and reacted by holding a series of missile tests and military exercises close to Taiwan during the summer of 1995 and prior to the first direct presidential elections in 1996 (Tien 1996: 36). The Taiwan Strait crisis brought the tentative normalisation of cross-Strait relations to an abrupt halt. China postponed the meeting between the SEF and the Association for Relations Across the Taiwan Straits that was supposed to take place in July indefinitely and severed all communication channels with Taiwan (ibid.: 35). In addition to the political fallout, the tensions also had economic effects: At the height of the crisis, the stock market fell 20 per cent and the NTD depreciated by ten per cent, while the capital flight amounted to US$10 billion despite the government injecting more than US$20 billion into the markets to restore investment confidence (Chen 1999: 146), revealing the precarious nature of cross-Strait relations and Taiwan's integration into the global economy.

The missile crisis was grist to the mill of the political forces who had cautioned against closer economic relations with China. Strengthened by winning Taiwan's first direct presidential elections – obtaining 54 per cent of the votes in a four-way race – Lee set out to revise Taiwan's cross-Strait policies. Contradicting earlier statements, Lee announced in August 1996 that APROC was not designed to promote economic interactions across the Taiwan Strait and instructed the Executive Yuan to review the initiative (Leng 1998: 499; Ho and Leng 2004: 734). The CEPD thereupon withdrew its proposal to loosen restrictions on China-bound investments (Deng 2000: 965). The following month, Lee Teng-hui announced what came to be known as the No Haste Be Patient (NHBP) policy. Lee, who only weeks before his US visit had emphasised the complementary and mutually beneficial character of economic relations across the Strait, now urged businesses to keep their roots in Taiwan to secure Taiwan's political survival (Ho and Leng 2004: 734–735). The contradiction between the political and economic logics had now found their expression in the contradiction between the APROC and NHBP initiatives and pervaded the state apparatus at all levels and even within institutions during the same day:

> On one occasion, the Mainland Affairs Council (MAC) and the MoEA jointly stated that Taiwan's economic relations with China should be on the conservative side. On the same day, a task force formed by the same two agencies sent their memo to the Executive *yuan* arguing for more opening toward China so as to enhance Taiwan's competitiveness.
>
> (Ho and Leng 2004: 737)

In early 1997, the MAC specified the new rationale for economic relations with China, announcing that security interests should take priority over economic affairs and that national interest should not be compromised (McBeath 1999: 118). This announcement was followed by a revision of investment guidelines, which stipulated that all investments over US$50 million had to be authorised by the government. Investments into certain services (including real estate and insurance), a variety of infrastructure projects (including transportation and energy) as well as into high-technology sectors were banned altogether, crucially prohibiting Taiwanese computer companies to manufacture complete notebooks in China (McBeath 1999: 118; Tanner 2006: 48). Furthermore, investments in China were limited to 40 per cent of a company's net worth for smaller companies, gradually decreasing to 20 per cent of the company's net worth for enterprises valued US$10 billion or more (Mengin 2015: 159). The regulations forced Formosa Plastics and Uni-President to shelve their planned large-scale investments in China (Cheng 1997: 49). Unsurprisingly, their chairmen, Wang Yung-ching and Kao Ching-yuan, vehemently opposed the new restrictions, and they were joined by Acer's Stan Shih and Evergreen's Chang Yung-fa who were concerned by the ban on high-technology investments and the fading prospect of direct transportation links, respectively (Lin 1997: 40).

NHBP did not prevent cross-Strait investments by Taiwanese companies, as these began to establish shell companies that were registered in tax havens or found other ways to circumvent some of the restrictions (Mengin 2015: 165). As was the case in the late 1980s, the policy therefore mostly affected the large business groups in the high-technology and transportation sectors as well as those that had planned investments into infrastructure projects. More significant than the immediate restrictions were the political uncertainties that cast doubt not only over cross-Strait investments but equally over Taiwan as a stable and reliable investment location. The deadlock in cross-Strait relations effectively brought the APROC project to an end, as it depended on direct links and financial relations with China (Liaw 2016: 454). The military tensions had furthermore called into question Taiwan's ambition to become the gateway to China for foreign companies, and the Asian Financial Crisis dampened the prospects regarding Southeast Asia. After a decade of struggle between pro-market and pro-security forces, the latter had prevailed, motivating Taiwan's bourgeoisie to rethink its strategies regarding the economic dimension of cross-Strait relations.

Conclusion

The analysis of Taiwan's development from a Gramscian perspective brings three aspects to the fore. First, Taiwan's developmental accumulation strategy was conditioned by the particular form of how contradictions were managed against the background of the KMT's attempt to preserve the party's relative autonomy from local social forces after its retreat from the Chinese mainland in 1949. The ideological struggles were shaped by the party's experience of hyperinflation during its time in China on the one hand and development agencies shaped by Western economic thought on the other. The outcome of several major conjunctures was conditioned by this struggle. Both in the mid-1950s and in the mid-1970s, proposals aimed at liberalisation were rejected, only to be reconsidered a few years later when the necessity to find remedies for the objective contradictions of the accumulation strategy had become more urgent. While US pressure played a role in the decision to initiate EOI in the late 1950s and the liberalisation and internationalisation in the mid-1980s, it was by no means the major factor that shaped the outcome, as some observers have argued: Rather, US influence tipped the balance in favour of Taiwanese political forces that had already been pursuing a strategy towards giving market mechanisms a more central role in Taiwan's economic development. The implementation of liberalisation measures was therefore never a direct adoption of US recommendations but instead shaped compromises that reflected the shift in the domestic balance of forces.

Second, the analysis sheds light on the business groups that would become the social driving force behind the rapprochement. The enterprises that emerged during ISI were incorporated into the KMT's hegemonic bloc through a network of corporatist institutions as well as a series of limited economic concessions. As beneficiaries of Taiwan's protectionist policies, these groups were relatively content with the tripartite economic structure that confined them to the domestic market and relinquished Taiwan's dynamic export sector to SMEs. The tacit symbiosis between large business groups and SMEs, however, contributed to the political awakening of these groups as the SMEs, the major customer of midstream intermediate goods, relocated to China while large enterprises were hindered in doing so. At the same time, privatisation and deregulation not only led to the erosion of central developmental planning instruments (such as the monopolies of credit and upstream industries) but also allowed large business groups to diversify into sectors that favoured extraverted accumulation strategies. Together with the erosion of corporatist mechanisms, Taiwan's large business groups, which had hitherto been politically passive, became *the* political force advocating for the "normalisation" of cross-Strait economic relations.

Finally, the contradictions that drove the organic crisis of the 1980s were not *resolved* but rather *displaced*. Before the mid-1980s, the logics of national security and economic development were congruent: Taiwan's national security objective not only benefited from but actually necessitated a rapid industrialisation. The fragmented and incomplete liberalisation of the late 1980s that excluded China, however, brought these logics into contradiction. For Taiwan's bourgeoisie, China was not only an attractive production site but also a future market. The conflict between those elements of the state apparatus that favoured a normalisation of trade and investment relations with China – supported by Taiwan's bourgeoisie – and those that insisted on the primacy of national security – increasingly backed by President Lee Teng-hui – clashed to a greater extent throughout the 1990s. The missile crisis of 1995–96 illustrates the consequences of this contradiction: The already significant immediate economic impact was dwarfed by the political division it nurtured, resulting in inconsistent policy initiatives that cast doubt upon the future economic relations between Taiwan and China and even threatened the conditions of accumulation in Taiwan proper as well as the strategies of transnationalisation pursued by capital. Despite personal access to the president, representation in the Central Standing

Committee of the KMT and the reorganisation of business associations into interest groups, Taiwan's bourgeoisie was unable to overcome the contradictory fusion of politics and economics that was inscribed into the state apparatus and was underlying every aspect of cross-Strait relations. The organic crisis thus persevered.

Nevertheless, the process of political liberalisation in the late 1980s and early 1990s also provided a stage for political competition and thus broadened the terrain for political strategies that Taiwan's bourgeoisie would pursue. Indeed, fractions of Taiwan's bourgeoisie would shift their support to Chen Shui-bian, candidate for the DPP, prior to the elections of 2000. While they were able to obtain limited concessions from the new government, the continued contradiction between the political and economic logics that conditioned cross-Strait relations resulted in the awareness that the normalisation of economic relations across the Taiwan Strait could not be overcome through sporadic and particularistic interventions by Taiwan's bourgeoisie into political society, but had to encompass an intellectual reform and therefore initiatives that unfolded in what Gramsci calls the integral state. The emergence of the hegemonic project as a consequence of this awareness will be discussed in the following chapter.

Notes

1 In addition to Farmers' Associations, Fishermen's Associations, irrigation associations and fruit-marketing cooperatives fulfilled similar or complementary roles in rural Taiwan (Mao and Schive 1995: 34), but will not be discussed here separately due to space limitations.
2 Hsiung (1996: 146) notes, however, that this path was predominantly available for male and not for female workers.
3 At that time, it was called the Council for International Economic Cooperation and Development.
4 For a list of the recommendations formulated by the CER, see Chu (2001b: 94–95).
5 In 2014, five out of the six largest electronics contract manufacturers in the world were Taiwanese (Frederick and Gereffi 2016: 26).
6 The original name was National Policy Research Information Centre.

Bibliography

Amsden, Alice H. (1991). "Big Business and Urban Congestion in Taiwan. The Origins of Small Enterprise and Regionally Decentralized Industry (Respectively)". In: *World Development* 19.9, 1121–1135.

Amsden, Alice H. and Wan-wen Chu (2003). *Beyond Late Development. Taiwan's Upgrading Policies*. Cambridge: The MIT Press.

Arrigo, Linda Gail (1980). "The Industrial Work Force of Young Women in Taiwan". In: *Bulletin of Concerned Asian Scholars* 12.2, 25–30.

——— (1994). "The Environmental Nightmare of the Economic Miracle. Land Abuse and Land Struggles in Taiwan". In: *Bulletin of Concerned Asian Scholars* 26.1–2, 21–44.

Balassa, Bela (1971). "Industrial Policies in Taiwan and Korea". In: *Weltwirtschaftliches Archiv* 106.1, 55–77.

Baum, Julian (1993). "The Unstoppable Tide. Rapid Rise in Taiwan-China Trade Pressures Taipei". In: *Far Eastern Economic Review* 156.20, 66.

Bishai, Martha Fitzpatrick (1991). "The Development of Industrial Land in Taiwan. A Legal Framework for State Control". In: *The Journal of Developing Areas* 26.1, 53–64.

Brück, Sebastian and Laixiang Sun (2007). "Achieving Effective Governance Under Divided Government and Private Interest Group Pressure. Taiwan's 2001 Financial Holding Company Law". In: *Journal of Contemporary China* 16.53, 655–680.

Chan, Steve (1987). "The Mouse that Roared. Taiwan's Management of Trade Relations with the United States". In: *Comparative Political Studies* 20.3, 251–292.

Chen, Qimao (1999). "The Taiwan Strait crisis. Causes, scenarios, and solutions". In: *Across the Taiwan Strait. Mainland China, Taiwan and the 1995–1996 Crisis*. Ed. by Suisheng Zhao. London and New York: Routledge, 127–160.

Chen, Tain-Jy (2001). "Democratization and trade liberalization". In: *Taiwan's Economic Success Since 1980*. Ed. by Chao-Cheng Mai and Chien-Sheng Shih. Cheltenham: Edward Elgar Publishing, 312–346.

Chen, Xiangming (1996). "Taiwan Investments in China and Southeast Asia. 'Go West, but Also Go South'". In: *Asian Survey* 36.5, 447–467.

Cheng, Tun-jen (1997). "Taiwan in 1996. From Euphoria to Melodrama". In: *Asian Survey* 37.1, 43–51.

——— (2001a). "The economic significance of Taiwan's democratization". In: *Taiwan's Economic Success Since 1980*. Ed. by Chao-Cheng Mai and Chien-Sheng Shih. Cheltenham: Edward Elgar Publishing, 120–155.

——— (2001b). "Transforming Taiwan's Economic Structure in the 20th Century". In: *The China Quarterly* 165, 19–36.

Cheng, Tun-Jen and Yun-Han Chu (2002). "State-business relationship in Taiwan. A political economy perspective". In: *Taiwan's Modernization in Global Perspective*. Ed. by Peter C. Y. Chow. Westport: Praeger, 196–214.

Chi, Chun-Chieh (1994). "Growth with Pollution. Unsustainable Development in Taiwan and Its Consequences". In: *Studies in Comparative International Development* 29.2, 23–47.

Chien, Fredrick F. (1989). "Liberalization, Internationalization, and Institutionalization". In: *Journal of Chinese Law* 3.2, 185–192.

Cho, Hee-Yeon and Bob Jessop (2001). *The Listian Warfare State and Authoritarian Developmental Mobilization Regime in the East Asian Anticommunist Regimented Society*. Conference paper prepared for the workshop "In Search of East Asian Modes of Development: Regulationist Approaches," Tunghai University, Taichung, 19-20 April 2001.

Chou, Ji (2001). "Taiwan's macroeconomic performance since 1980". In: *Taiwan's Economic Success Since 1980*. Ed. by Chao-Cheng Mai and Chien-Sheng Shih. Cheltenham: Edward Elgar Publishing, 47–86.

Chou, Yujen (1990). "U.S.-Taiwan trade conflicts (1984–1989). The political economy of accelerated trade liberalization in Taiwan". PhD Thesis. Ohio State University.

Chu, Jou-jou (2001a). "Labour Militancy in Taiwan. Export Integration vs Authoritarian Transition". In: *Journal of Contemporary Asia* 31.4, 441–465.

Chu, Wan-wen (1994a). "Import Substitution and Export-Led Growth. A Study of Taiwan's Petrochemical Industry". In: *World Development* 22.5, 781–794.

Chu, Yin-wah (1996). "Democracy and Organized Labor in Taiwan. The 1986 Transition". In: *Asian Survey* 36.5, 495–510.

Chu, Yun-han (1994b). "The realignment of business-government relations and regime transition in Taiwan". In: *Business and Government in Industrialising Asia*. Ed. by Andrew MacIntyre. Sydney: Allen & Unwin, 113–141.

——— (1997). "The Political Economy of Taiwan's Mainland Policy". In: *Journal of Contemporary China* 6.15, 229–257.

Chu, Yun-Peng (2001b). "Liberalization policies since the 1980s". In: *Taiwan's Economic Success Since 1980*. Ed. by Chao-Cheng Mai and Chien-Sheng Shih. Cheltenham: Edward Elgar Publishing, 89–119.

Chung, Chi-Nien (2001). "Markets, Culture and Institutions. The Emergence of Large Business Groups in Taiwan, 1950s–1970s". In: *Journal of Management Studies* 38.5, 719–745.

——— (2004). "Institutional Transition and Cultural Inheritance. Network Ownership and Corporate Control of Business Groups in Taiwan, 1970s–1990s". In: *International Sociology* 19.1, 25–50.

Chung, Chi-Nien and Ishtiaq P. Mahmood (2010). "Business groups in Taiwan". In: *The Oxford Handbook of Business Groups*. Ed. by Asli M. Colpan, Takashi Hikino and James R. Lincoln. Oxford: Oxford University Press, 180–209.

Copper, John F. (1987). "Taiwan in 1986. Back On Top Again". In: *Asian Survey* 27.1, 81–91.

Cullather, Nick (1996). "'Fuel for the Good Dragon'. The United States and Industrial Policy in Taiwan, 1950–1965". In: *Diplomatic History* 20.1, 1–25.

Deng, Ping (2000). "Taiwan's Restriction of Investment in China in the 1990s. A Relative Gains Approach". In: *Asian Survey* 40.6, 958–980.

Dent, Christopher M. (2002). *The Foreign Economic Policies of Singapore, South Korea and Taiwan*. Cheltenham: Edward Elgar.

——— (2003). "Transnational Capital, the State and Foreign Economic Policy. Singapore, South Korea and Taiwan". In: *Review of International Political Economy* 10.2, 246–277.

Dreyer, June Teufel (1990). "Taiwan in 1989. Democratization and Economic Growth". In: *Asian Survey* 30.1, 52–58.

——— (1991). "Taiwan in 1990. Finetuning the System". In: *Asian Survey* 31.1, 57–63.

Fei, John C. H. (1987). "Economic Developments of Taiwan and the Mainland in 1986". In: *Maryland Series in Contemporary Asian Studies* 79, 73–79.

Francks, Penelope, Johanna Boestel and Choo Hyop Kim (1999). *Agriculture and Economic Development in East Asia. From Growth to Protectionism in Japan, Korea and Taiwan*. London and New York: Routledge.

Frederick, Stacey and Gary Gereffi (2016). *The Philippines in the Electronics & Electrical Global Value Chain*. Report by the Duke University Center on Globalization, Governance and Competitiveness. Duke University.

Fuller, Douglas B. (2005). "Moving along the electronics value chain. Taiwan in the global economy". In: *Global Taiwan. Building Competitive Strengths in a New International Economy*. Ed. by Suzanne Berger and Richard K. Lester. Armonk: M.E. Sharpe, 137–165.

Gates, Hill (1979). "Dependency and the Part-Time Proletariat in Taiwan". In: *Modern China* 5.3, 381–407.

Gold, Thomas B. (1986). *State and Society in the Taiwan Miracle*. Armonk: M.E. Sharpe.

——— (1988a). "Colonial origins of Taiwanese capitalism". In: *Contending Approaches to the Political Economy of Taiwan*. Ed. by Edwin A. Winckler and Susan Greenhalgh. London: M.E. Sharpe, 101–117.

——— (1988b). "Entrepreneurs, multinationals, and the state". In: *Contending Approaches to the Political Economy of Taiwan*. Ed. by Edwin A. Winckler and Susan Greenhalgh. London: M.E. Sharpe, 175–205.

Greenhalgh, Susan (1988). "Supranational processes of income distribution". In: *Contending Approaches to the Political Economy of Taiwan*. Ed. by Edwin A. Winckler and Susan Greenhalgh. London: M.E. Sharpe, 67–100.

——— (1989). "Land Reform and Family Entrepreneurship in East Asia". In: *Population and Development Review* 15, 77–118.

Guiheux, Gilles (1995). "Les conglomérats taiwanais". In: *Économie Internationale* 61.1, 159–172.

——— (2002a). "Enterprises, entrepreneurs, and social networks in Taiwan". In: *Politics in China. Moving Frontiers*. Ed. by Françoise Mengin and Jean-Louis Rocca. New York and Basingstoke: Palgrave Macmillan, 187–211.

——— (2002b). *Les grands entrepreneurs privés à Taiwan. La main visible de la prospérité*. Paris: CNRS Éditions.

Haggard, Stephan and Chien-Kuo Pang (1994). "The transition to export-led growth in Taiwan". In: *The Role of the State in Taiwan's Development*. Ed. by Joel D. Aberbach, David Dollar and Kenneth L. Sokoloff. Armonk: M.E. Sharpe, 47–89.

Ho, Ming-sho (2014a). "Resisting Naphtha Crackers. A Historical Survey of Environmental Politics in Taiwan". In: *China Perspectives* (3/2014), 5–14.

——— (2014b). *Working Class Formation in Taiwan. Fractured Solidarity in State-Owned Enterprises, 1945–2012*. Basingstoke: Palgrave Macmillan.

Ho, Samuel P. S. (1978). *Economic Development of Taiwan, 1860–1970*. New Haven and London: Yale University Press.

——— (1979). "Decentralized Industrialization and Rural Development. Evidence from Taiwan". In: *Economic Development and Cultural Change* 28.1, 77–96.

——— (1987). "Economics, Economic Bureaucracy, and Taiwan's Economic Development". In: *Pacific Affairs* 60.2, 226–247.

Ho, Szu-Yin and Tse-Kang Leng (2004). "Accounting for Taiwan's Economic Policy Toward China". In: *Journal of Contemporary China* 13.41, 733–746.

Howe, Christopher (1996). "The Taiwan Economy. The Transition to Maturity and the Political Economy of its Changing International Status". In: *The China Quarterly* 148, 1171–1195.

Hsia, Chuan-Wei (2019). "Taiwan's Neoliberal Moment. Crisis, Paradigm Competition and the Ascent of Neoclassical Economists". In: *Taiwanese Journal of Sociology* 66, 55–124. (In Chinese).

Hsiao, Hsin-Huang Michael (2011). "Social movements in Taiwan. A typological analysis". In: *East Asian Social Movements. Power, Protest, and Change in a Dynamic Region*. Ed. by Jeffrey Broadbent and Vicky Brockman. New York, Dordrecht, Heidelberg, London: Springer, 237–254.

Hsiung, Ping-Chun (1996). *Living Rooms as Factories. Class, Gender, and the Satellite Factory System in Taiwan*. Philadelphia: Temple University Press.

Hsu, Dave Y. C. (1982). "Measurement of Potential Labor Reserve in Taiwan". In: *Economic Development and Cultural Change* 30.4, 843–861.

Jacoby, Neil H. (1966). *U.S. Aid to Taiwan. A Study of Foreign Aid, Self-Help, and Development*. New York: Frederick A. Praeger.

Jing, Bo-jiun (2016). "Taiwan and Southeast Asia. Opportunities and Constraints of Continued Engagement". In: *Maryland Series in Contemporary Asian Studies* 2016.2, 1–85.

Ka, Chih-ming and Mark Selden (1986). "Original Accumulation, Equity and Late Industrialization. The Cases of Socialist China and Capitalist Taiwan". In: *World Development* 14.10/11, 1293–1310.

Kawakami, Momoko (2007). "The rise of Taiwanese family-owned business groups in the telecommunications industry". In: *Big Business and Economic Development. Conglomerates and Economic Groups in Developing Countries and Transition Economies Under Globalisation*. Ed. by Alex E. Fernández Jilberto and Barbara Hogenboom. London and New York: Routledge, 86–108.

Knapp, Ronald G. (1996). "Rural Housing and Village Transformation in Taiwan and Fujian". In: *The China Quarterly* 147, 779–794.

Kuo, Cheng-tian (1998). "Private governance in Taiwan". In: *Beyond the Developmental State. East Asia's Political Economies Reconsidered*. Ed. by Steve Chan, Cal Clark and Danny Lam. Basingstoke: Macmillan, 84–95.

——— (2001). "Taiwan's Distorted Democracy in Comparative Perspective". In: *Journal of Asian and African Studies* 35.1, 85–111.

Lam, Danny and Cal Clark (1998). "The cultural roots of 'Guerrilla Capitalism' in Taiwan". In: *Beyond the Developmental State. East Asia's Political Economies Reconsidered*. Ed. by Steve Chan, Cal Clark and Danny Lam. Basingstoke: Macmillan Press, 120–130.

Lee, Zong-Rong and Hsin-Huang Michael Hsiao (2014). "Taiwan: SME-oriented capitalism in transition". In: *The Oxford Handbook of Asian Business Systems*. Ed. by Michael A. Witt. Oxford: Oxford University Press, 238–259.

Leng, Tse-Kang (1994). "State-Business Relations and Taiwan's Mainland Economic Policy". In: *American Journal of Chinese Studies* 2.1, 43–64.

——— (1996). *The Taiwan-China Connection. Democracy and Development Across the Taiwan Straits*. Taipei: SMC Publishing.

——— (1998). "Dynamics of Taiwan-Mainland China Economic Relations. The Role of Private Firms". In: *Asian Survey* 38.5, 494–509.

Liaw, Booker C.K. (2016). "State and Business in Taiwan's Economic Diplomacy Under the Lee Teng-hui Administration and the Implications for Current Cross-Strait Relations". In: *Cambridge Review of International Affairs* 29.2, 444–464.

Liaw, Booker C. K. and Yaw-Yih Wang (2009). "Double-Track Decision-Making and the Failure of Taiwan's Asia-Pacific Regional Operations Centre Plan in the 1990s". In: *Tamkang Journal of International Affairs* 13.1, 73–100.

Lin, Teh-chang (1997). "Taiwan's Investment Policy in Mainland China. A Domestic Perspective". In: *Journal of Chinese Political Science* 3.2, 25–45.

Liu, Christina Y. (1992). "Liberalization and globalization of the financial market". In: *Taiwan's Enterprises in Global Perspective*. Ed. by N. T. Wang. Armonk: M.E. Sharpe, 123–149.

Liu, Lawrence S. (1996). "Aspiring to Excel. The Uneasy Case of Implementing Taiwan's Asia-Pacific Regional Operations Center Plan". In: *Columbia Journal of Asian Law* 10.1, 199–244.

Liu, Meng-Chun (2002). "Determinants of Taiwan's Trade Liberalization. The Case of a Newly Industrialized Country". In: *World Development* 30.6, 975–898.

Mao, Yu-kang and Chi Schive (1995). "Agricultural and industrial development in Taiwan". In: *Agriculture on the Road to Industrialization*. Ed. by John Williams Mellor. Baltimore: Johns Hopkins University Press, 23–66.

Marx, Karl (1992). *Capital. A Critique of Political Economy*. Vol. 1. New York: Penguin.

Mathews, John A. (1997). "A Silicon Valley of the East. Creating Taiwan's Semiconductor Industry". In: *California Management Review* 39.4, 26–54.

McBeath, Gerald A. (1997). "Taiwan Privatizes by Fits and Starts". In: *Asian Survey* 37.12, 1145–1162.

——— (1998). "The Changing Role of Business Associations in Democratizing Taiwan". In: *Journal of Contemporary China* 7.18, 303–320.

——— (1999). "Foreign Direct Investment (FDI) Management and Economic Crisis in Asia. Taiwan's Changing Strategy". In: *MIR: Management International Review* 39.4, 105–135.

McGann, James (2009). *Think Tanks and Civil Society in Mainland China, Hong Kong, and Taiwan*. Philadelphia: Foreign Policy Research Institute.

Mengin, Françoise (2002). "Taiwanese politics and the Chinese market. Business's part in the formation of a state, or the border as a stake of negotiations". In: *Politics in China. Moving Frontiers*. Ed. by Françoise Mengin and Jean-Louis Rocca. New York and Basingstoke: Palgrave Macmillan, 232–257.

——— (2015). *Fragments of an Unfinished War. Taiwanese Entrepreneurs and the Partition of China*. Oxford: Oxford University Press.

Ngeow, Chow Bing (2017). "Taiwan's Go South Policy. Déjà vu All Over Again?". In: *Contemporary Southeast Asia* 39.1, 96–126.

Ngo, Tak-Wing (1995). "Business Encirclement of Politics. Government-Business Relations Across the Taiwan Strait". In: *China Information* 10.2, 1–18.

——— (2000). "Business strategy, state intervention, and regionalization in East Asia". In: *The Dialectics of Globalization. Regional Responses to World Economic Processes: Asia, Europe, and Latin America in Comparative Perspective*. Ed. by Menno Vellinga. Boulder: Westview Press, 83–99.

——— (2005). "The political bases of episodic agency in the Taiwan state". In: *Asian States. Beyond the Developmental Perspective*. Ed. by Richard Boyd and Tak-Wing Ngo. Oxon: RoutledgeCurzon, 83–109.

Niehoff, Justin D. (1987). "The Villager as Industrialist. Ideologies of Household Manufacturing in Rural Taiwan". In: *Modern China* 13.3, 278–309.

Nordhaug, Kristen (1998). "Development Through Want of Security. The Case of Taiwan". In: *Forum for Development Studies* 25.1, 129–161.

Numazaki, Ichiro (1986). "Networks of Taiwanese Big Business. A Preliminary Analysis". In: *Modern China* 12.4, 487–534.

Overbeek, Henk (2004). "Transnational Class Formation and Concepts of Control: Towards a Genealogy of the Amsterdam Project in International Political Economy". In: *Journal of International Relations and Development* 7.2, 113–141.

Pang, Chien-Kuo (1992). *The State and Economic Transformation. The Taiwan Case*. New York: Garland.

Poulantzas, Nicos (1974). "Internationalisation of Capitalist Relations and the Nation-State". In: *Economy and Society* 3.2, 145–179.

——— (2008). "On social classes". In: *The Poulantzas Reader. Marxism, Law and the State*. Ed. by James Martin. London and New York: Verso, 186–219.

Powelson, John P. and Richard Stock (1987). *The Peasant Betrayed. Agriculture and Land Reform in the Third World*. Boston: Oelgeschlager, Gunn & Hain.

Ranis, Gustav (1979). "Industrial development". In: *Economic Growth and Structural Change in Taiwan. The Postwar Experience of the Republic of China*. Ed. by Walter Galenson. Ithaca and London: Cornell University Press, 206–262.

Riedel, James and Maria Luisa Cicognani (1994). "Economic Relations between Taiwan and the United States". In: *Journal of Asian Economics* 5.3, 349–366.

Rubinstein, Murray A. (2013). "The evolution of Taiwan's economic miracle 1945-2000. Personal accounts and political narratives". In: *Technology Transfer Between the US, China and Taiwan. Moving Knowledge*. Ed. by Douglas B. Fuller and Murray A. Rubinstein. London and New York: Routledge, 25–46.

Saxenian, AnnaLee and Jinn-Yu Hsu (2001). "The Silicon Valley-Hsinchu Connection. Technical Communities and Industrial Upgrading". In: *Industrial and Corporate Change* 10.4, 893–920.

Schive, Chi (1995). *Taiwan's Economic Role in East Asia*. Washington, DC: Center for Strategic and International Studies.

Schubert, Gunter (1994). *Taiwan. Die chinesische Alternative*. Hamburg: Institut für Asienkunde.

Shieh, Gwo-shyong (1992). *'Boss' Island. The Subcontracting Network and Micro-Entrepreneurship in Taiwan's Development*. New York: Peter Lang.

Simon, Denis Fred (1988). "External incorporation and internal reform". In: *Contending Approaches to the Political Economy of Taiwan*. Ed. by Edwin A. Winckler and Susan Greenhalgh. London: M.E. Sharpe, 138–150.

––––––– (1992). "Taiwan's strategy for creating competitive advantage. The role of the state in managing foreign technology". In: *Taiwan's Enterprises in Global Perspective*. Ed. by N. T. Wang. Armonk: M.E. Sharpe, 97–122.

Skoggard, Ian (1998). "The structure and spirit of development in rural Taiwan". In: *Beyond the Developmental State. East Asia's Political Economies Reconsidered*. Ed. by Steve Chan, Cal Clark and Danny Lam. Basingstoke: Macmillan Press, 131–141.

Smith, Heather (1997). "Taiwan's Industrial Policy in the 1980s. An Appraisal". In: *Asian Economic Journal* 11.1, 1–33.

––––––– (1998). "The Determinants of Manufacturing Protection in Taiwan". In: *The Developing Economies* 36.3, 305–331.

Stites, Richard W. (1985). "Industrial Work as Entrepreneurial Strategy". In: *Modern China* 11.2, 227–246.

Taiwan Today (1995). *The Deregulator*. 1st November 1995. https://taiwantoday.tw/print. php?unit=8&post=12578&unitname=Economics-Taiwan-Review&postname=The-Deregulator (last accessed on 03/09/2020).

Taiwan Today News (2009). *Linyuan Group the no. 1 Taiwan conglomerate in total assets*. 24th October 2009. http://www.taiwantodaynews.com/index.php/linyuan-group-the-no-1-taiwan-conglomerate-in-total-assets (last accessed on 29/11/2015).

Tanner, Murray Scot (2006). *Chinese Economic Coercion against Taiwan. A Tricky Weapon to Use*. Santa Monica: RAND Corporation.

Thurbon, Elizabeth (2007). "The developmental logic of financial liberalization in Taiwan". In: *Institutions and Market Economies. The Political Economy of Growth and Development*. Ed. by W. R. Garside. London: Palgrave Macmillan, 87–111.

Tien, Hung-mao (1996). "Taiwan in 1995. Electoral Politics and Cross-Strait Relations". In: *Asian Survey* 36.1, 33–40.

Trappey, Charles (2007). "The impact of the WTO on Taiwan's and China's electronics industry". In: *Economic Reform and Cross-Strait Relations. Taiwan and China in the WTO*. Ed. by Julian Chang and Steven M. Goldstein. Singapore: World Scientific Publishing, 285–318.

Tsai, Ming-Chang (1999). "Geopolitics, the State, and Political Economy of Growth in Taiwan". In: *Review of Radical Political Economics* 31.3, 101–109.

––––––– (2001). "Dependency, the State and Class in the Neoliberal Transition of Taiwan". In: *Third World Quarterly* 22.3, 359–379.

Wade, Robert (1990). *Governing the Market. Economic Theory and the Role of Government in East Asian Industrialization*. Princeton: Princeton University Press.

Wang, Philip T.Y. (1987). "Trade Relations between Taiwan and the U.S.". In: *Journal of Third World Studies* 4.2, 14–21.

Weiss, Linda (2003). "Guiding globalisation in East Asia. New roles for old developmental states". In: *States in the Global Economy. Bringing Domestic Institutions Back In*. Ed. by Linda Weiss. Cambridge: Cambridge University Press, 245–270.

Werner, Roy A. (1985). "Taiwan's Trade Flows. The Underpinning of Political Legitimacy?". In: *Asian Survey* 25.11, 1096–1114.

Winckler, Edwin A. (1988). "Elite political struggle 1945–1985". In: *Contending Approaches to the Political Economy of Taiwan.* Ed. by Edwin A. Winckler and Susan Greenhalgh. London: M.E. Sharpe, 151–171.

Woo, Jung-En (1991). "East Asia's America Problem". In: *World Policy Journal* 8.3, 451–474.

Wu, Nai-teh (1996). "Class identity without class consciousness? Working-class orientations in Taiwan". In: *Putting Class in Its Place. Worker Identities in East Asia.* Ed. by Elizabeth J. Perry. Berkeley: Institute of East Asian Studies, University of California.

Wu, Yongping (2004). "Rethinking the Taiwanese Developmental State". In: *The China Quarterly* 177, 91–114.

Wynn, Sam (1982). "The Taiwanese 'Economic Miracle'". In: *Monthly Review* 33.11, 30–40.

Yang, Alan H. (2018). "Unpacking Taiwan's Presence in Southeast Asia. The International Socialization of the New Southbound Policy". In: *Issues & Studies* 54.1, 1–30.

Yep, Ray and Ma Ngok (2006). "Money, Power and Ideas. Think Tank Development and State-Business Relations in Taiwan and Hong Kong". In: *Policy & Politics* 34.3, 535–555.

4 Reformist Resistance against the Black Box

Technocratic Management and the Structured Spontaneity of the Wild Strawberry Movement

The election of Chen Shui-bian in 2000 appeared to open up the possibility to at least partly meet the demands of Taiwan's bourgeoisie. Prior to the elections, the DPP had promised to lift the policy of No Haste Be Patient and thus attenuate the politicisation of economic relations between Taiwan and China. For reasons that will be discussed in this chapter, however, few of Chen's initiatives brought tangible results. Instead, Chen embarked on a course that resembled that of his predecessor Lee Teng-hui. The year 2008 then marks a turning point in Taiwan's recent political history. After eight years under President Chen Shui-bian and the DPP, the double elections of 2008 represented not simply a victory by Ma Ying-jeou and the KMT, but rather a watershed: In the legislative elections of January 2008, the party increased its voting share from less than 35 per cent in the previous election to gain an absolute majority of more than 51 per cent, leaving the pan-blue coalition with a three-quarters majority in the Legislative Yuan. Two months later, Ma Ying-jeou won the presidential elections with a majority of 58.45 per cent. These results suggest a broad public support for the party's platform that had emphasised the necessity of normalising economic exchanges with the PRC to reinvigorate Taiwan's economy.

Yet, only a few months after Ma took office, the first ever visit of Chen Yunlin, then chairman of the Chinese quasi-governmental Association for Relations Across the Taiwan Straits (ARATS), to Taiwan in November 2008 sparked protests that evolved into a social movement. What would soon come to be known as the WSM provided a first challenge to the KMT's attempt to portray the negotiations across the Taiwan Strait as a mere technocratic project, the aim of which was to normalise trade relations without jeopardising Taiwan's political status as a *de facto* independent country. For several weeks, students occupied a central square in Taipei and other public spaces throughout the island. Ultimately, the WSM failed to sustain its challenge and faded away throughout the months of December and January without any of its demands being met.

At first glance, several aspects of these developments appear puzzling. Why did this movement emerge only months after Ma Ying-jeou and the KMT were overwhelmingly elected on a platform that emphasised the benefits of a pragmatic approach towards cross-Strait negotiations? Why did the movement, which was directly prompted by the developments in cross-Strait relations, forego any direct

DOI: 10.4324/9781003395546-4

references to China, instead relying on a narrative framework that put issues of human rights to the fore? And why was it Taiwan's young "Strawberry Generation", thought to be uninterested in politics and unwilling to bear the hardship of taking responsibility, that became the cause's mouthpiece?

These elements provide us with a direction for this chapter's line of investigation. The following sections will question the dominant interpretation of the WSM as simply a spontaneous movement that failed due to a lack of preparation. It is exactly this apparent unpreparedness and spontaneity that deserves our attention. Analysing it in depth will unveil that we have to speak of a *structured* spontaneity that reflects the material and ideological conditions at the time. A first indication is the movement's label itself, which consists of two building blocks, the previously mentioned pejorative label "Strawberry Generation" on the one hand and a reference to the "Wild Lily" student movement that took place in 1990 during Taiwan's democratisation on the other. This particular historical articulation will provide a seam at which we can tear apart the dynamics of hegemonic contestation in late 2008. To adequately understand the form of the WSM, we have to unravel the ideological and material limitations, brought about in large part by hegemonic interventions since the turn of the century.

To this end, the following section will reconstruct how Taiwan's bourgeoisie organised itself as a leading social group, and section two will analyse how these social and political forces rearticulated the ideology of cross-Strait relations. Section three provides a process analysis of hegemonic activities, namely the inclusion of subaltern social forces and the marginalisation of potentially counter-hegemonic forces. The final section then shows how these hegemonic activities can account for the particular form of the WSM as the response to both a narrowing ideological terrain and the hegemonic disorganisation of subaltern apparatuses.

Emergence and Condensation of a Hegemonic Apparatus

During the last years under Lee Teng-hui, the conditions of accumulation had worsened from the perspective of Taiwan's capital in two ways. On the one hand, the NHBP policy had severely restricted capital's ability to freely make investment decisions with regard to China. On the other hand, Lee Teng-hui's political stance was hanging over the Taiwan Strait like the sword of Damocles. As the crisis of 1995–96 had shown, the Chinese side was inclined to interpret Lee's discourse as affronts that could spiral into a political crisis, endangering Taiwan's investment environment. At the centre of this constant threat was the particular politicisation of economic relations with China, as the government sought to control the flow of capital on the grounds of a political logic, a practice that stemmed from the authoritarian era, when the developmental state intervened in the market in ways it thought to be beneficial to Taiwan's development.

But in the course of liberalisation during the 1980s, Taiwan's bourgeoisie had emancipated itself from the KMT and the state apparatus economically, and now, under the conditions of democratisation, it sought to emancipate itself politically as well. Throughout the late 1990s, Taiwan's bourgeoisie repeatedly urged the government to stop intervening in investment decisions. Its major demand was to liberate economic interactions across the Taiwan Strait from extra-economic interventions and give free reign to the logic of capital. In part, these demands were articulated through the large business associations. The CNFI had urged the government to establish the three links, demanding that "politics should not interfere with economy", a position shared by Taiwan's other large business associations (Chen 2018: 95, 105). Several influential individual capitalists – including Wang Yung-ching (Formosa Plastics), Chang Yung-fa (Evergreen) and Kao Ching-yuan (Uni-President) – became particularly vocal after they were forced to abandon plans for large-scale investments in China due to political pressure (Lin 1998: 190).

Changes in the political landscape provided a window of opportunity to rearticulate state-business relations. In view of a chance at winning the 2000 presidential elections, the DPP adopted a more moderate stance on cross-Strait relations. Although the New Tide faction within the party adhered to the NHBP policies and advocated strengthening Taiwan's industrial base, the moderate Formosa faction, in line with capital's demand for the de-politicisation of economic relations across the Strait, favoured an approach labelled "go west boldly" (Chao 2004: 697). Promoting the economic integration with China, they argued, would turn Taiwan into a link between China and the world and therefore also reduce the likelihood of military aggression by China (Rigger 2001a: 130).

Ultimately, the debate resulted in the compromise "strengthen the base and go west" (Fell 2016: 58). For Wu (1999: 570–571), the retention of the "go west" element demonstrates the influence of the business community on the DPP's cross-Strait policy, and after the new course had been agreed, the party began consulting with leaders of large conglomerates, including Formosa Plastics and the Evergreen Group (Rigger 2001a: 139). Although the DPP's compromise did not embrace the outright de-politicisation of economic relations across the Strait, it sought to soften the dichotomy of security and economy that had so far characterised Taiwan's China policy. As the party's 1999 "White Paper on China Policy for the 21st Century" states:

> In Taiwan's interest, cross-strait trade has been an important part of the economic development in Taiwan. However, national security risks should be considered as well. The traditional perception puts economic and security interests in opposition to each other. The current governmental restrictions on navigation, trade and investment are formulated from this assumption. But such measures are outdated.
>
> (Democratic Progressive Party 1999)

Chen Shui-bian confirmed that, should he be elected, his presidency would be marked by the normalisation of cross-Strait relations. In another white paper, he outlined a roadmap that offered crucial concessions to Taiwan's bourgeoisie. He promised to "promote comprehensive normalization of the relations between Taiwan and China" and "to conduct negotiations and consultations with the Beijing government on all kinds of matters through all channels soon" (Chen 2002: 65, 69). Crucially, topics to be covered during these negotiations included direct transportation links, agreements on investment protection, the establishment of trade agencies as well as the lifting of the NHBP policy (ibid.: 70–79).

The DPP furthermore moved towards reconciling the increasingly moderate stance on cross-Strait relations with its ideological cornerstone, Taiwan independence. Aware that a declaration of independence stood in contradiction to the prospect of normalising cross-Strait relations, the party adopted the position that a formal declaration of independence was unnecessary as Taiwan was already a sovereign and independent country. In a reversal of its long-held commitment, the party reassured its electorate, Taiwan's bourgeoisie as well as the Chinese Communist Party that a DPP government would not upset the status quo by holding a referendum on Taiwan independence (Rigger 2001a: 131–132).

Although KMT candidate Lien Chan had also criticised the NHBP policy, he was still Lee Teng-hui's Vice President, protégé and chosen successor (Wu 2001: 41). Hence, a few days before the elections, major tycoons who had been critical of the KMT's course under Lee Teng-hui came forward to endorse Chen Shui-bian, including Evergreen Group founder Chang Yung-fa, Acer's Stan Shih and Hsu Wen-lung of Chi Mei Corporation (Rigger 2001a: 193). Ultimately, Chen benefited from a split in the pan-blue camp, as former Governor of Taiwan Province James Soong chose to run on an independent ticket after the KMT had picked Lien Chan as its candidate. On 18 March 2000, Chen Shui-bian won the presidential elections with 39.3 per cent of the vote, narrowly beating Soong (36.8 per cent), while KMT candidate Lien Chan only received 23.1 per cent of the votes.

After assuming office, Chen demonstrated his willingness to reach out to China, not only suggesting that cross-Strait negotiations should take place in the pragmatic "1992 spirit" that had characterised the first meeting between the SEF and ARATS, but even stating that unification would not be excluded as a potential outcome of these negotiations if the Taiwanese people supported it (Wu 2001: 43). What complicated his early years was the fact that his inauguration coincided with the bursting of the "dot-com" bubble (Rigger 2004: 183). As Taiwanese companies were (and still are) among the world's largest contract manufacturers for the IT sector, Taiwan's stock market fell by 50 per cent until the end of the year, exports declined by 20 per cent and the unemployment rate reached a historical high of 5.3 per cent (Wu 2001: 44; 2002: 32). Normalising economic relations across the Taiwan Strait therefore also became a central element of Chen Shui-bian's efforts to mitigate the economic difficulties Taiwan was facing (Wu 2001: 45).

Early progress, however, was limited. Not only were China's reactions to Chen's overtures cold, scepticism towards lifting the restrictive policies regarding investments in and trade with China was also voiced from within Chen's own government. Among others, Vice President Annette Lu opposed the liberalisation of cross-Strait restrictions, as did labour representatives, pro-independence groups and a number of economists (Tanner 2006: 51).

The conglomerates that had pinned their hopes on the DPP's commitment to lift the NHBP policy increased their pressure. In November 2000, Wang Yung-ching hosted a dinner with 12 other leading tycoons to discuss the issue of cross-Strait liberalisation before meeting with Premier Chang Chun-hsiung the next morning (Taipei Times [TT] 2000). At the occasion, Wang emphasised that "[t]he economy should be the top priority, not politics", underlining that opening the three links was necessary to maintain the competitiveness of Taiwan's industries (TT 2000). When the government failed to act on the demands of the business sector, Wang called on Chen Shui-bian to accept the One China principle to "turn this crisis into an opportunity" (TT 2001d), a position the President could not adopt without antagonising the DPP's supporters.

Chen, now under considerable pressure from Taiwan's bourgeoisie, convened the Economic Development Advisory Conference (EDAC) (Kastner 2004: 23). This body was established to formulate a national consensus on Taiwan's economic development, with a particular emphasis on the issue of cross-Strait relations. The composition of EDAC suggests that it was not so much an open debate, but rather a vehicle to universalise the interests of Taiwan's bourgeoisie by giving it the appearance of general consensus. While the member list included representatives from the government, political parties, think tanks and other social groups, Taiwan's bourgeoisie provided a significant share of EDAC members: Among others, Wang Yung-ching (Formosa Plastics), Morris Chang (TSMC), Robert Tsao (UMC), Rock Hsu (Kinpo), Jeffrey Koo (Chinatrust), Barry Lam (Quanta), Stan Shih (Acer), Douglas Hsu (Far Eastern), Henry Kao (Dah An Commercial Bank), Frank C. Huang (Powerchip Semiconductor Corporation), Tsai Wan-tsai (Fubon Group) as well as Koo Chen-fu (Koos Group and SEF chairman) participated in the conference (Office of the President, Republic of China (Taiwan) 2001). In addition, Taiwan's business associations CNAIC, CNFI, ROCCOC and the National Association of Small and Medium Enterprises (NASME) sent representatives, while Taiwan Electrical and Electronic Manufacturers' Association (TEEMA) was present through its chairman Rock Hsu. Finally, several organic intellectuals of organisations that will be discussed in more detail below took part, with the National Policy Foundation (NPF) being represented by three members, the Cross-Strait Common Market Foundation (CSCMF) through its chairman Vincent Siew (as "financial expert"), while Jeffrey Koo, head of the Third Wednesday Club (TWC), participated in his capacity as CNAIC chairman. EDAC thus encouraged Taiwan's bourgeoisie to coordinate their demands, moving towards a corporate project.

The final report of the panel on cross-Strait relations bears striking similarities with the demands articulated by business over the past decade and the DPP's "strengthen the base and go west" compromise: Departing from the principle that "[t]he ROC government should spare no effort to improve the local investment climate and initiate positive trade and economic interactions with the Chinese mainland" in order to "increase Taiwan's competitive edge", the normalisation of economic relations across the Taiwan Strait was portrayed as a "win-win" situation (Government Information Office 2001). The panel recommended establishing the three links and replacing NHBP by a policy that would strengthen the competitiveness of Taiwan's leading industries while letting sunset industries move to China (ibid.).

On the final day, the conference unanimously passed the recommendation to replace NHBP with a policy of "active opening, effective management". After the conference, Wang Yung-ching published a 13,000-word essay entitled "Face Taiwan's economic situation and take necessary countermeasures" (Wang 2001). He praised Chen Shui-bian's initiative, but also expressed the growing impatience of the business sector. Unless the recommendations were swiftly implemented, Taiwan's "industry [would be] helpless and [could] only wait to die" (ibid.). Failing to act upon the "irreversible natural trend" of cross-Strait integration would jeopardise the competitiveness of Taiwanese companies and thus lead to a hollowing out of Taiwan's industry, while "adopt[ing] a pragmatic attitude" would "create a bright development prospect" for all of Taiwan and thus bring about a "win-win situation" (ibid.).

The same month, however, Chen Shui-bian's situation was complicated when former President Lee Teng-hui re-entered the political stage. Alarmed by the KMT's departure from the political course he had pursued, he founded the Taiwan Solidarity Union (TSU) in August (Wu 2002: 44). Before the parliamentary elections in 2001, the TSU shifted the electoral discourse towards the issue of identity, and as the Chen government was facing a dire economic situation and – unlike before the 2000 elections – had little to gain from continuing an economy-centred campaign, it chose to follow the TSU in criticising the KMT for moving closer towards the CCP (ibid.: 36–38). With the TSU, now part of the pan-green camp, strictly opposing any measures that might accelerate the industrial "hollowing out" of Taiwan, Chen faced further obstacles in his pursuit of opening the three links (Rigger 2003: 42–43).

Although his government lifted various restrictions on cross-Strait investment after EDAC – allowing Taiwanese high-technology companies to relocate the production of older generations of semiconductors to China – it appeared that Chen's initiative of normalising economic relations across the Taiwan Strait was exhausted. While the government unilaterally opened the "three mini-links" between the islands of Kinmen and Matsu and China in 2001, their economic relevance was negligible and "amounted to no more than Taiwan's decriminalization of the hitherto illegal small trade between fishermen from the two sides" (Wu 2002: 33). In addition to the TSU, Chen was also criticised by the MAC and Vice President Annette Lu (Brown 2001: 74; Rigger 2004: 183). In the summer of 2002, he moved towards a more confrontational stance with China, stating that the Taiwan Strait had "one country on each side" and that Taiwan might "go its own way" if China failed to respond to his overtures (Rigger 2003: 47). In the run-up to the 2004 elections, Chen entertained the possibility of holding a referendum on a new constitution, after which the Taiwan Affairs Office (TAO) stated that China would not tolerate "referendums to conduct separatist activities" (ibid.). Not only had Chen failed to depoliticise economic relations across the Taiwan Strait, from the perspective of Taiwan's bourgeoisie, his volatile positions on cross-Strait relations had the potential to jeopardise the small gains that the government had made during the term.

As the 2004 elections approached, Taiwan's conglomerates were frustrated by Chen's failure to accomplish substantial steps towards liberalisation and feared that his increasingly confrontational stance on cross-Strait relations would preclude any progress in the future (Dean 2004a: 22). Formosa Plastics chairman Wang Yung-ching published a one-page advertisement in Taiwan's major newspapers, urging candidates to refrain from "radical moves" (ibid.: 23). The chairmen of Acer, Evergreen and Uni-President also publicly voiced their frustration with the failure to normalise economic relations across the Strait (Chen 2018: 123, 137–138). The KMT, on the other hand, had by now not only distanced itself from Lee Teng-hui but had also adopted a more carefully formulated position on the issue of unification, with Lien Chan stating that reunification was no longer the only option (Dean 2004b: 26). Furthermore, the pan-blue camp had now united Lien and Soong on a single KMT ticket for the presidential elections, avoiding the split that arguably cost the pan-blue camp the previous elections. On the eve of the elections, Evergreen founder Chang Yung-fa indirectly but unmistakably voiced his support for Lien Chan (TT 2004), signalling that influential representatives of Taiwan's bourgeoisie had now thrown their support behind the KMT.

Yet, as the ballots closed on 20 March 2004 and the 12 million votes were counted, Chen Shui-bian came out ahead by a margin of less than 30,000 votes or 0.22 per cent. While his election in 2000 appeared to be a "historical accident" made possible by the split in the pan-blue camp, his re-election confronted the forces supporting the normalisation of economic relations across the Strait with a new situation. KMT leaders considered new options, and Lien Chan in particular was keen on finding ways of cooperating with the Chinese Communist Party to prevent steps towards Taiwan's independence. From the perspective of Taiwan's capital, such a cooperation was the most likely path towards the normalisation of cross-Strait relations they so eagerly awaited.

This moment therefore represents catharsis in the Gramscian sense. Over the past decade, Taiwan's capital fractions had gradually united in their opposition against the politicised nature of economic relations across the Taiwan Strait to pursue what Gramsci calls an "economic-corporate" project: They coordinated and articulated their common interests, approached various political parties and governments with their appeals no longer only individually but also through business associations and intervened in public discourse to argue that Taiwan's economic development was "obstructed ... by traditional ideological elements" (Gramsci 1971: 168). The year 2004 marks the passage from this economic-corporate phase, characterised by lobbying efforts of Taiwan's capitalist class, to the hegemonic phase that is characterised by the awareness

> that one's own corporate interests, in their present and future development, transcend the corporate limits of the purely economic class, and can and must become the interests of other subordinate groups too. This is the most purely political phase, and marks the decisive passage from the structure to the sphere of the complex superstructures ... bringing about not only a unison of economic and political aims, but also intellectual and moral unity, posing all the questions around which the struggle rages not on a corporate but on a 'universal' plane.
>
> (Gramsci 1971: 181–182)

The particular form of fusing political and economic interests will be discussed in the following section, but at its core was the prevention of Taiwan independence to allow for the normalisation of cross-Strait economic relations. To this end, three organisational centres that already existed in an embryonic form – the National Policy Foundation (NPF), the Third Wednesday Club (TWC) and the Cross-Strait

Common Market Foundation (CSCMF) – were transformed into the pillars of the hegemonic apparatus.

To adequately understand the role of these organisations in the rapprochement, it is necessary "to measure the 'organic quality' of the various intellectual strata and their degree of connection with a fundamental social group, and to establish a gradation of their functions and of the superstructures from the bottom to the top" (ibid.: 12). Already those think tanks that emerged during the period of democratisation depended on the fusion of economic and political interests (McGann 2009: 93). During the period of political and ideological uncertainty, Taiwanese capitalists funded think tanks, the influence of which ultimately relied on the personal relationships between the founders and policymakers (Yep and Ngok 2006: 543–544). Based on the integration of these interests, think tanks then served as vehicles for establishing quasi-diplomatic relations with countries to which Taiwan did not maintain official relations. The three organisations that will be discussed below are no exception to this. The particular political, historical and ideological circumstances under which the rapprochement was about to unfold made these think tanks the adequate vehicle to initiate a systematic dialogue both among Taiwanese political and capitalist forces as well as with the political elites in China. On the one hand, their cross-Strait activities can be seen as what Gill describes as "consciousness-raising forums where individuals representing elements of the state and civil society in affiliated countries can come to know and influence each other" (Gill 1991: 122).

The first of these centres attempting to fuse the concrete needs of Taiwan's bourgeoisie with those of political forces on either side of the Taiwan Strait is the TWC, named after its regular lunch meeting on the third Wednesday of each month. Its central figure was Chiang Pin-kung, a key technocrat under Lee Teng-hui who led the Ministry of Economic Affairs from 1993 to 1996 and the CEPD from 1996 until 2000. In 1999, he initiated the TWC as a business organisation for Taiwan's largest conglomerates with the aim of improving their conditions for international economic cooperation (Third Wednesday Club [TWC] 2020). The TWC only accepts financially healthy conglomerates that are among Taiwan's 100 largest business groups. The combined annual revenues of its 78 members amount to US$700 billion, roughly US$100 billion higher than Taiwan's GDP (TWC 2020). According to the TWC, these meetings can be understood as small-scale consciousness-raising forums providing a platform for

> senior government leaders from various ministries to elaborate on government policies, assess current economic condition and global situation [sic], and provide guidance for the private sector's business development. On the other hand, member enterprises of the Club may also take the opportunity to make propositions and policy recommendations directly to the government.
>
> (TWC 2020)

In 2002, the TWC furthermore began to organise delegations to China, resulting in various memoranda of understanding with business associations across the Taiwan Strait (TWC 2020). Chiang had advocated for a relaxation of cross-Strait restrictions since the early 1990s to improve the competitiveness of Taiwan's industries and mitigate the country's international isolation (Leng 1996: 70–71). The focus of the TWC therefore was neither the establishment of elite networks (like the NPF, see below) nor conceptual innovation (like the CSCMF, see below). Rather, it served as a channel to ensure that the political forces organising the rapprochement attended to providing "hands-on" functional benefits that would improve the immediate conditions of accumulation for Taiwan's conglomerates. This technocratic character is reflected in the "Twelve-Point Consensus" that was the outcome of Chiang's China trip in 2005, covering issues such as direct transportation, investment protection as well as negotiations about common IT standards (National Policy Foundation [NPF] 2005). On his return from China, Chiang established the SINOCON Industrial Standards Foundation, which organises one to two meetings of the Cross-Strait Information Industry and Technology Standards Forum per year to negotiate common industrial standards for high-tech industries (Poong 2008). SINOCON's board consists of IT company chairpersons, including representatives of Quanta, Hon Hai, HTC, MediaTek and TSMC.

The TWC is embedded in the wider hegemonic apparatus through its chairmen and board members. Chiang himself was Vice Chairman of the KMT from 2000 to 2012, and it was in this capacity that he visited China in 2005. From 2000 until 2018, he was also Vice Chairman of the NPF. The first TWC chairman was Koo Chen-fu, who, in addition to heading the Koos Group, was also a member of the KMT's Central Standing Committee and had been chairman of the CNAIC between 1961 and 1994. Due to his political connections and his corporate contacts, Koo also chaired the SEF, the organisation that is the institutional expression of Taiwan's "tycoon diplomacy" in the particular case of cross-Strait relations. Chiang's career in the technocratic state apparatus, his relation to the large conglomerates as well as the KMT and NPF, and his experience in the negotiations of functional agreements with the Chinese side made him the obvious candidate to head the SEF after the KMT came into power.

Even though the SEF receives the majority of its funding from the government, it is controlled by the Board of Trustees that largely consists of corporate representatives (Leng 1996: 64). And while the SEF has no formal ties with the TWC, the personal overlap between the two organisations is striking: All four chairmen of the TWC since its establishment in 1999 – namely Koo Chen-fu, Chiang Pin-kung, Jeffrey Koo and Rock Hsu – were at some point either heading the SEF or, in the case of Jeffrey Koo, members of its board. Of the SEF's 35 board members in summer 2008, seven were also board members at the TWC, while another four SEF board members represented conglomerates that were also corporate members of TWC. Despite the lack of formal ties, both organisations were therefore shaped by similar interests, and through the SEF and SINOCON, the conglomerates could project their interests into negotiations with China (Table 4.1).

A second crucial pillar of the hegemonic apparatus is the CSCMF, headed by Vincent Siew. Similarly to Chiang Pin-kung, Siew had been part of the KMT's economic bureaucracy throughout the 1990s. He preceded Chiang as Minister of Economic Affairs, overseeing the first wave of privatisation and deregulation. He then took charge of the CEPD, where he devised the APROC initiative. Following his stint at the CEPD, he headed the MAC until Lee Teng-hui appointed him as

Table 4.1 The involvement of Taiwanese conglomerates in cross-Strait channels (selection)

	Representation in organisational centres		Participation in cross-Strait channels		
	CSCMF	TWC	SEF Board	KMT-CCP Forum	Cross-Strait-CEO Summit
Cathay	•	○	•	•	•
Chinatrust		•	•	•	•
Core Pacific		○		•	•
Evergreen		○	•	•	•
Far Eastern		•	•	•	•
Farglory	•	○		•	
Formosa Plastics		•		•	
Fubon		○	•	•	•
Hon Hai (Foxconn)		•		•	•
Hua Nan	•	○	•	•	•
Inventec	•	○	•	•	
Kinpo (Compal)	•	•	•		
Lite-On		○		•	
Powerchip		○		•	•
Quanta				•	
Ruentex		○	•	•	
Shin Kong		•	•		•
Taiwan Cement	•	•	•	•	•
Taiwan Glass		•	•	•	•
TSMC	•	○	•	•	•
Uni-President	•	○	•	•	•
Walsin Lihwa	•	○	•	•	•
Want Want		•	•	•	•
Yulon	•	○	•	•	•

Notes: With regard to the TWC column, a group that is a corporate member is represented by a (○). If it is furthermore represented on the TWC's board, it is represented by a (•). SEF board membership refers to the period between 2008 and 2016. Source: Author's compilation.

premier in 1997. After failing to win the elections running for Vice President on the KMT ticket in the year 2000, he became one of the KMT's vice chairmen, but he also sought to condense his expertise as well as his political and business contacts into his own organisation.

His key ideological contribution was the idea of a common market across the Taiwan Strait, conceived of as a modus vivendi for the organic crisis that would operate on a "functional" and apolitical level, thereby circumventing the intricate political issues that had been the obstacle to a normalisation of economic exchanges between Taiwan and China. In January 2001, he presented his ideas at the American Enterprise Institute in Washington, D.C. He diagnosed a necessity "to replace orthodox and conservative views with new concepts" and called for "new thinking and new approaches to old problems" (Siew 2001). His own proposition was to set aside political differences and focus on economic issues. Once the principle of "win-win" had taken "the place of past tensions", the resulting "normal relations between two important economies" would then pave the way for political integration (ibid.).

In March 2001, Siew established the CSCMF with the support of 20 tycoons, who each invested NTD five million into the organisation (Sutter 2002: 53). Among these were TSMC chairman Morris Chang, Uni-President chairman Kao Ching-yuan, Leslie Koo of Taiwan Cement, Kenneth Yen of Yulon, Chiao Yu-lon of Walsin Lihwa and Wu Tung-liang, Chairman of the Taishin Bank (China Post 2001).[1] Supporting the foundation financially gave these businessmen preferential access to Chinese leaders. The seemingly apolitical framework allowed Siew, accompanied by a dozen of business leaders, to be among the first former KMT government members to travel to China and meet Vice-Premier Qian Qichen and TAO chairman Chen Yunlin in May 2001.

One of the major activities of the CSCMF is to organise the Taiwanese delegation to the Boao Forum for Asia, conceived as the Asian counterpart to the World Economic Forum. At the Boao Forum, Siew and his delegation, consisting mainly of CSCMF board members who are chairmen of large business groups, met with political and economic leaders, culminating in a meeting with Hu Jintao in 2008. At that point in time, the Ma–Siew ticket had already won the 2008 presidential elections, meaning that Siew met Hu as Vice President-elect. The CSCMF has also acted as a co-organiser for the Straits Forum (see Chapter 5), the Cross-Strait CEO Summit (co-organised with the TWC, see Chapter 6) as well as the Cross-Strait Competitiveness Forum (organised by the Taiwan Competitiveness Forum).

The organisation seeks to "obtain the consensus of the domestic industry, government, academia, and elites from all walks of life" to then "use this consensus as the basis for our counterparts in mainland China" (Cross-Strait Common Market Foundation [CSCMF] 2001c). To this end, the foundation established two departments. The Research Department is tasked with "collect[ing] opinions from industry, government, academic circles and social elites" (CSCMF 2001a). The Integrated Planning Department organises the various activities of the foundation, compiles and publishes its research results, and establishes exchange networks with scholars, business leaders and other social elites (CSCMF 2001a). The CSCMF therefore assumes the functions of a corporate organic intellectual by aggregating the needs of various social forces, articulating coherent and systematic conceptions and disseminating these by reaching out to Taiwan's civil society. The dissemination of the common market idea will be discussed below.

The third, and arguably most crucial, pillar of the emerging hegemonic project was the NPF. Like the two organisations discussed above, it emerged during the organic crisis that reached its political expression in the election defeat of the KMT in the year 2000. Immediately after Lien Chan had lost the presidential election, he became chairman of the KMT, and the party injected US$30 million into the Lien Chen-tung Cultural and Education Foundation, a small foundation with an annual budget of US$20,000 that Lien had established in 1993, upgrading it into the KMT's party think tank. Lien grouped a number of influential former KMT government officials with backgrounds in economic or cross-Strait policy, including Chiang Pin-kung, Su Chi (former MAC chairman) and Kao Koong-lian (former MAC vice chairman) around him, "with the main objective of preparing the KMT's prospective return to power" in 2004 (Yep and Ngok 2006: 544). The foundation expanded significantly over the years, and by 2009, the NPF's staff consisted of 41 senior fellows, 37 full-time researchers, 350 part-time researchers, 223 advisers and 22 administrative personnel (NPF 2009: 6). The think tank also benefited from Lien's personal network: Under Lee Teng-hui, Lien had been Minister of Foreign Affairs, Prime Minister and Vice President, and his family was connected to Taiwan's large bourgeoisie through close friendship and marriage (Ngo 1995: 9). As of 2009, the NPF was funded by donations from the business sector (NPF 2009: 1).

After the Lien Chan and James Soong ticket failed to win the 2004 presidential elections, both the KMT and the CCP considered new options. After the legislative elections of December 2004, the KMT initiated cross-Strait contacts (Huang 2015: 107). The NPF was the proper vehicle for this initiative, as it had assembled the necessary expertise on cross-Strait relations, had developed the necessary organisational capacities and – as a think tank – was less likely to give the visits the semblance of political negotiations. These contacts resulted in Chiang Pin-kung's "Icebreaking Journey" to China of March 2005. After meeting Jia Qinglin, chairman of the Chinese People's Political Consultative Conference, and Chen Yunlin, chairman of the TAO, the "Twelve-Point Consensus" was announced. More importantly, Jia asked Chiang to extend the CCP's invitation to Lien Chan. Four weeks later, Lien made the so-called "Journey of Peace" to China, which culminated in the Lien–Hu meeting, the first direct talks between KMT and CCP leaders in 60 years (R3). Their common declaration, the "Five-Point Vision" (Taiwan Affairs Office of the State Council, PRC [TAO] 2005), became the roadmap for the rapprochement. Reaffirming their common opposition to Taiwan independence, Lien and Hu committed to (1) the resumption of cross-Strait negotiations on the basis of the 1992 consensus as soon as possible; (2) negotiations for a peace agreement; (3) the institutionalisation of cross-Strait economic exchanges, including the "Three Links", agricultural trade and a common market; (4) consultations on Taiwan's participation in international activities, in particular the World Health Organization (WHO) and (5) the establishment of a party-to-party platform to hold "consultations on issues related to the vital interests of compatriots on both sides of the strait, inviting people from all walks of life to participate, and organising discussions on measures to intensify cross-strait exchanges" (TAO 2005).

The party-to-party platform was realised the following year in the form of the Cross-Strait Economic, Trade and Culture Forum (or KMT-CCP Forum). Originally, this forum was supposed to be complemented by a Cross-Strait Peace Forum held in Taiwan. The Taiwanese government, however, rejected the NPF's application to invite a Chinese delegation, and the plans were abandoned (R17). Thus, all ten meetings of the KMT-CCP Forum between 2006 and 2015 have been held in various cities throughout China. During this time, one meeting took place per year with the exception of 2006, which saw two meetings, and 2014, when the channel was suspended due to the Sunflower Movement.

The agenda was outlined by the KMT and the CCP, with the NPF being the organisational centre of the forum on the Taiwanese and the TAO on the Chinese side (R17). The final agenda for each meeting was decided after preliminary meetings between the NPF and the TAO (R17). The issues discussed at the forum (see Table 4.2) show that the forum combined pro-active and re-active elements. Among

Table 4.2 Meetings of the KMT-CCP Forum (2006–2015)

No.	Date	Location	Major Issues	Recommendations
1st	Apr. 2006	Beijing	Economic, financial and agricultural cooperation; direct transportation and tourism	7 joint recommendations 15 unilateral policies
2nd	Oct. 2006	Boao	Agricultural cooperation	7 joint recommendations 20 unilateral policies
3rd	Apr. 2007	Beijing	Direct transportation and tourism	6 joint recommendations 13 unilateral policies
4th	Dec. 2008	Shanghai	Financial cooperation and investment; service industry	9 joint recommendations 10 unilateral policies
5th	Jul. 2009	Changsha	Cultural exchanges and educational cooperation	6 joint recommendations
6th	Jul. 2010	Guangzhou	ECFA follow-up negotiations; industrial cooperation; service industries and media	22 joint recommendations
7th	May 2011	Chengdu	Nuclear safety; ECFA follow-up negotiations (goods and services); cultural cooperation and youth exchanges; youth employment and entrepreneurship	19 joint recommendations
8th	Jul. 2012	Harbin	Peaceful Development; service trade agreement; finance and investment; cultural and educational exchanges; media cooperation	17 joint recommendations
9th	Oct. 2013	Nanning	Service trade and trade in goods agreements; financial cooperation; research and development; media cooperation; youth entrepreneurship	19 joint recommendations
10th	May 2015	Shanghai	Grassroots and youth participation in cross-Strait exchanges; Belt and Road initiative	9 joint recommendations

Source: Author's compilation.

the pro-active issues promoted by the forum were direct links, tourism, agricultural cooperation as well as common market initiatives. On the re-active side, the forum addressed issues of finance (in response to the global financial crisis), cultural cooperation (in response to the WSM, see Chapter 5), nuclear safety (after the Fukushima nuclear accident) as well as grassroots and youth participation (after the SFM). As such, the forum has to be considered not only a crucial site for shaping the dynamics of cross-Strait relations but also as an indicator for how hegemonic groups interpreted various phases of hegemonic contestation.

Due to the broad range of issues being addressed, uncritical accounts of the KMT-CCP Forum hailed it as a mechanism that ensured the "participation of Taiwan's civil society" (Hu 2010: 8) in cross-Strait negotiations. The discussion above, however, has documented the organic quality of the organisational centres of the rapprochement, and the forum is no exception. The Taiwanese delegation, usually consisting of 150 to 300 members (R17), comprised leaders of the KMT as well as other pan-blue parties (i.e. the People First Party (PFP), the New Party and the Non-Partisan Solidarity Union), KMT legislators, staff of the NPF and individual experts or consultants invited by the think tank depending on the issues to be discussed. In addition, a significant number of Taiwan's conglomerates, business associations as well as China-based Taiwan Business Associations (TBAs) participated in the forum. Table 4.1 shows that there was a considerable overlap between the business groups that were represented at the KMT-CCP Forum and those that were members of the TWC, the SEF board or the Cross-Strait CEO Summit.

The forum had two instruments, "joint recommendations" and "unilateral policies", at its disposal. *Joint recommendations* refer to the announcement of a list of agreements that were reached during the forum, outlining more concrete forms of cooperation or the steps necessary to implement initiatives. Many of the agreements later signed between SEF and ARATS were first outlined at the forum in joint recommendations. Unlike joint recommendations, *unilateral measures*, also announced at the Forum's closing ceremony, usually entail concrete preferential policies, which are implemented by China and bring tangible benefits to Taiwanese who travel to or live, work or study in China. Especially while the KMT was still in the opposition, this was a way to directly shape the relation between Taiwan and China. Their announcement during the closing ceremony of the forum – and thus in the presence of politicians, think tank representatives, academics and business leaders – bestows upon the recommendations and measures an appearance of a broad social consensus. From 2009 onwards, unilateral policies were announced at the Straits Forum to further amplify this effect.

These means were employed to serve two ends. First, joint recommendations and unilateral measures launched concrete initiatives that responded to demands that Taiwan's capitalist class had articulated for over a decade, in particular with regard to the "normalisation" of economic relations and the consolidation of a stable accumulation environment. The forum, for instance, laid the groundwork for SEF-ARATS agreements on the Three Links (prepared at the 1st and 3rd forum), investment protection (4th forum) as well as ECFA and the CSSTA (from the 1st forum onwards). In addition, the agreements and unilateral measures opened whole sectors for Taiwanese businesses, including Chinese tourism to Taiwan and access to China's media market. One of the unilateral measures announced at the first forum concerned Chinese procurement missions to Taiwan. During the onset of the global economic crisis, these missions served to buy commodities from Taiwanese conglomerates, with early procurement missions each signing deals worth several billion US$ (Chien and Hsieh 2010: 18). The second aspect of these instruments was to organise consent for the cross-Strait rapprochement. In particular, the unilateral measures created opportunities for Taiwanese who were not part of the capitalist class. This and the following chapters will illustrate this process with recourse to specific examples below.

The class character of the rapprochement lies in the organisational centres that provided the infrastructure for the rapprochement (see Table 4.3). For more than a decade, Taiwan's bourgeoisie had demanded the normalisation of economic exchanges across the Taiwan Strait, and the political constellation of the early twenty-first century provided the window of opportunity to realign their interests with those of the pan-blue camp and raise the corporate-economic project to the level of a political project. Relying on organic intellectuals who had experience as members of the government and were well connected to Taiwan's bourgeoisie, three "collective" organic intellectuals emerged during the organic crisis and provided the terrain for a fusion of political and capitalist interests. In turn, Taiwan's bourgeoisie funded these organisations and was substantially involved in their

Table 4.3 Centres of the Hegemonic Apparatus, 2005–2008

	National Policy Foundation	*Cross-Strait Common Market Foundation*	*Third Wednesday Club*
Associated channels	KMT-CCP Forum	Boao Forum; Straits Forum; Cross-Strait CEO Summit; Cross-Strait Competitiveness Forum	SEF-ARATS meetings; Cross-Strait Information Industry and Technology Standards Forum; Cross-Strait CEO Summit
Key figures	Lien Chan, Chiang Pin-kung	Vincent Siew	Chiang Pin-kung
Social base	KMT party apparatus and selected representatives from business and academia	Large conglomerates, predominantly from the high-technology and finance sectors	Large conglomerates
Functions	Organisation of an intra-elite consensus among capitalist and political forces; providing structures of material inclusion	Articulation of a narrative that aligns political and economic aspects; providing structures of ideological inclusion	Improve the conditions of cross-Strait accumulation; negotiate technical aspects

Source: author's compilation.

cross-Strait activities, ranging from technical negotiations to high-level meetings between the KMT and the CCP. The central role of these three organisations underlines the qualitative change of the strategies pursued by Taiwan's bourgeoisie: While they still relied on personal connections to organic intellectuals, such as Chiang Pin-kung and Vincent Siew, these relations now coagulated into a particular institutional form that allowed for the accommodation of interests of the national and interior bourgeoisies and enabled them to speak with one voice.

The Hegemonic Rearticulation of Cross-Strait Ideology

The organisational centres of the rapprochement both rested on and promoted a particular set of conceptions. The major aim of what Gramsci calls the "intellectual and moral reform" that necessarily complements the structural reforms that are the main objective of a hegemonic project was to reconcile two particular interests that had hitherto stood in contradiction to each other, namely those of a political and an economic kind. The ideological initiative furthermore sought to do so in such a way that the rapprochement was not seen as a threat, nor as driven by particular interest, but as being in the general interest of all Taiwanese. This ideological framework aims to depoliticise cross-Strait relations by relying on three strategies. The first consists of *naturalising* the rapprochement, that is, of draining all social interest from it by portraying it as part of the inevitable and quasi-natural process of globalisation. The second was to *normalise* it by arguing that the restrictions on cross-Strait trade and the absence of negotiations with China were the exception that had to be rectified. The third strategy was to depict the rapprochement as *necessary*, i.e. there being no alternative if Taiwan wanted to effectively respond to the pressures of globalisation, avoid isolation and maintain its economic prosperity.

The conceptions that constitute the ideological framework were not freely conceived "out of thin air". Rather, the rearticulation of this reformed ideological narrative is best understood as a "change in the relative weight that the elements of the old ideologies used to possess" (Gramsci 1971: 195). The organisational centres introduced above aggregated the diverse particular interests and continuously offered conceptual elements that would ultimately form a rather coherent framework in which the elements mutually reinforced each other. The resulting ideological complex *appeared* to not rely on revolutionary conceptual innovations, but rather as a slight adjustment of extant discourses that were already rooted in common sense. The hegemonic centres furthermore contributed to the dissemination of these conceptions, either through direct interventions in public discourse, for instance, by writing opinion pieces for newspapers or holding public speeches, or by emphasising that these conceptions were the prerequisite for the exchanges, consultations and negotiations across the Strait that were organised by these groups.

The whole structure of the ideological framework is shown in Figure 4.1. It illustrates the fusion of particular interests on the left and the increasing universalisation towards the right. It furthermore grasps the separation of political and economic dimensions. Crucially, the elements of this narrative cannot be adequately understood if discussed separately. The following interpretation therefore also

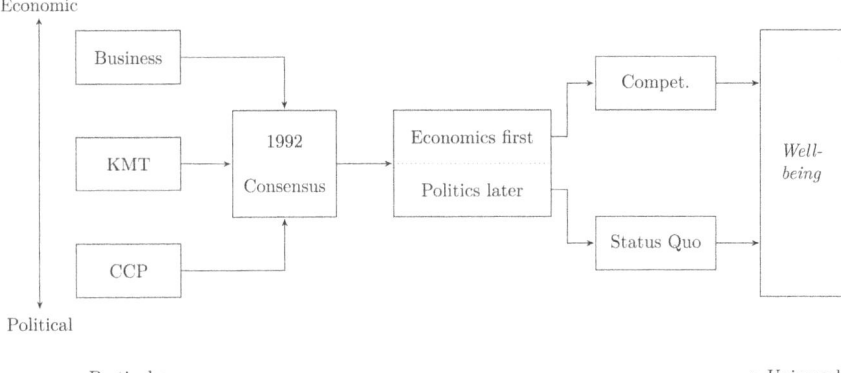

Figure 4.1 The ideological structure of the cross-Strait rapprochement

Source: Adapted from Beckershoff (2014b: 8). Reprinted with permission by *Spectrum: Journal of Global Studies*

takes into account the relation among the various elements, unveiling not only the underlying particular interests of the rapprochement, but also the ways in which the ideological reform contributed to their obscuration.

The *1992 consensus* is both the most crucial and most misunderstood ideological element of the cross-Strait rapprochement. It refers to an alleged consensus reached after the 1992 SEF-ARATS meeting in Hong Kong, stating that both sides of the Taiwan Strait subscribed to "One China" but had their respective interpretations, Taiwan understanding it as the R.O.C. and China as the PRC. Proponents of the formula have since pointed to this factual basis as well as the improvements its adoption by the KMT brought to cross-Strait relations. Critics like Lee Teng-hui and Tsai Ing-wen, on the other hand, have disputed that there ever was an agreement, attributing it to Su Chi who in 2006 stated that he had coined the notion in the year 2000 to mean "One China, respective interpretations" (Hickey 2013: 4–6; Wei 2016: 78–89). For most academic observers, the 1992 consensus is just the old wine of the One China Principle – that is that both the PRC and the R.O.C. belong to One China – in new bottles (Hickey 2013: 6), either to serve as a "flexible expression" (National Institute for Defense Studies 2002: 218) of One China and thereby introduce an element of "creative ambiguity" (Bush 2013: 12) for policymakers or to provide a "sugarcoated" (Tseng 2016: 1223) version of it to make it more palatable to the Taiwanese public.

Rather than trying to unearth the factual basis of the 1992 consensus, Wei (2016: 78) argues that the key to appreciating the new quality that the 1992 consensus exhibits over the orthodox One China principle lies in analysing it within the context from which it emerged: Su Chi coined the term in the immediate aftermath of Taiwan's 2000 presidential elections, weeks after the defeat of the KMT but before Chen Shui-bian's inauguration. This transitional phase was marked by a heightened political, ideological and economic uncertainty, and as this chapter has shown, it was this uncertainty that worried both political and capitalist social forces. At this point in time, Su was still chairman of the MAC, and the 1992 consensus was likely addressed not primarily at China but at the future Taiwanese government. As will be argued below, Taiwan's bourgeoisie welcomed this proposition immediately.

Extant analyses, however, have the tendency to assess the notion of the 1992 consensus through its *political form*, neglecting its *social content*. To understand why the 1992 consensus became the cornerstone of the rapprochement and had such a lasting effect on the dynamics of cross-Strait relations, it is indispensable to decipher why it was ultimately endorsed by Taiwan's large conglomerates. From a materialist perspective, the 1992 consensus differs from One China not only in the label but in the underlying social and political logics. The One China principle was the conceptual expression of the Chinese Civil War and the period of geopolitical competition that followed it. Cross-Strait relations during that period were characterised by mutual denial, confrontation, the ultimate aim of unification, and thus framed as a zero-sum game. The underlying logic entailed a politicisation of cross-Strait economic exchanges that justified the restrictions of trade, investment and direct transportation. This logic continued to be effective even after the end of the authoritarian era in Taiwan and fundamentally contradicted the interests of Taiwan's bourgeoisie.

The 1992 consensus, on the other hand, was the expression of a struggle over the relation of politics and the economy *within* Taiwan as the country's accumulation strategy shifted from the US and Japan towards China. The 1992 consensus reflected these struggles, and the emphasis shifted from unification to the prevention of Taiwan independence. Mutual dependency replaced mutual denial, cooperation took the place of confrontation and cross-Strait relations were no longer presented in zero-sum but positive-sum terms. Vincent Siew emphasises this distinction between the One China principle and the 1992 consensus: He sees the former as the origin for "One China dispute" over sovereignty issues (Siew 2001) and proposes "the 1992 consensus – one China with both sides having different interpretations – [as a way] to remove the political barriers toward future cross-strait economic cooperation" (cited in: TT 2001f). The 1992 consensus thus became the cornerstone of overcoming the division between economic and political logics. Adopting this approach made it possible for the KMT to find common ground with the CCP in the opposition to Taiwan independence. In contrast to the One China principle, the logic underlying the 1992 consensus was compatible with the demands by Taiwan's capitalist class, which opposed both strict isolation as well as Taiwan independence, as the second half of the 1990s had proven the disruptive effect political crises could have on accumulation. In addition, the conceptual reform promised the resumption of cross-Strait talks, thus providing a channel for Taiwan's bourgeoisie to realise its demands. The crucial quality of the 1992 consensus therefore is that it reconciled the particular interests of pan-blue political and capitalist forces in Taiwan, which was the necessary prerequisite for the hegemonic project.

It is therefore inaccurate when Wei (2015: 72) argues "that an economic logic was attached in a sociolinguistic way to the 1992 consensus" only after 2008. Taiwan's bourgeoisie had repeatedly called for a return to the One China principle or the 1992 consensus during the phase of economic uncertainty of the early 2000s. Wang Yung-ching of Formosa Plastics, for instance, appealed to the Taiwanese people to accept "one China, separate interpretations" (cited in: Cheng 2001) to allow for economic cross-Strait cooperation in July 2001. EDAC, through which Taiwan's bourgeoisie hoped to realise its economic-corporate project, was another occasion for similar calls. Prior to the conference, 14 presidential advisers, including Acer chairman Stan Shih, petitioned President Chen Shui-bian to accept some form of "One China", which they regarded as necessary to break the cross-Strait stalemate that was hurting Taiwan's economic development (Yang 2001). Several DPP members proposed that the normalisation of cross-Strait economic relations might be achieved if the party agreed to "uphold the so-called 1992 consensus, existing or not" (cited in: TT 2001c), an appeal that was echoed by several business associations that "urged a return to the 1992 consensus" (TT 2001e). It was therefore not the 2008 election that made it possible to charge the 1992 consensus with an economic logic but the opposite: Because the 1992 consensus expressed the interests of Taiwan's capitalist class, it had their support and could become a cornerstone of Ma Ying-jeou's election platform that made his and the KMT's election victory possible.

The 1992 consensus was sporadically mentioned throughout the early 2000s but only became the hegemonic principle of the rapprochement when the party-to-party platform began to emerge from 2005 onwards (Wei 2016: 82–84). Having coined the term during his last weeks as MAC chairman, Su Chi brought the notion to the NPF where he would serve as the convenor of the National Security Division. There it became the conceptual framework for the Lien–Hu meeting in 2005 and the subsequent meetings of the KMT-CCP Forum. Subsequently, the 1992 consensus was integrated into the KMT's policy guidelines in August 2005 (Kuomintang 2005), before Ma Ying-jeou adopted it as one of the crucial pillars for his election platform the following year (Office of the President, Republic of China (Taiwan) 2014). In his inaugural address, Ma Ying-jeou stated that "based on the '1992 Consensus,' negotiations should resume at the earliest time possible" (Ma 2008), and the formula that is attributed to the 1992 meeting of SEF and ARATS came full circle when talks between these two organisations resumed three weeks later in Beijing.

Where the 1992 consensus allowed for the fusion of political and capitalist interests, the notion of *"economics first, politics later"* contributed to the *"apparent separation of politics and economics"* (Bieler and Morton 2004: 100). The developmental state of the authoritarian era "governed the market" as a matter of course (Wade 1990), and trade with China was outright prohibited until the late 1980s. Issues such as direct transportation remained highly politicised afterwards on the grounds of national security and concerns that the outflow of capital to China would "hollow out" Taiwan's industrial base: "San tong [i.e., the Three Links] is a political, not an economic issue" (cited in: Baum 1992: 21), a KMT legislator remarked during the first debates about liberalising contacts in the early 1990s. After protests of Taiwan's bourgeoisie against the NHBP policy went unheard (Chen 2018: 94–96), the government change coinciding with the economic crisis in the year

2000 provided a fresh opportunity for Taiwan's bourgeoisie to mobilise against the extra-economic interventions into investment decisions. Wang Yung-ching stated that economics should have the priority over politics, adding: "If businesses want to invest anywhere around the world, including China, the government shouldn't stop them" (TT 2000). His position was echoed by others, and Morris Chang of TSMC, for instance, called the restrictions a "blatant interference" in his business (Dolven and Kruger 2002: 34).

Again, the interests of pan-blue political as well as capitalist forces coincided. For Taiwan's bourgeoisie, the de-politicisation of economic relations with China would open up new paths towards accumulation, while the KMT, which sought to reach out to the CCP, would benefit from negotiations with China being perceived as disinterested, technocratic and thus apolitical. The organic intellectuals at the NPF and the CSCMF translated capital's criticisms into a coherent framework and concrete propositions. After returning from his trip to China in January 2001, Kao Koong-lian, writing in his capacity as NPF fellow, argued in an opinion piece "that 'economics first, politics second' is the only option left to break the cross-strait stalemate" (Kao 2001). He thus proposed not simply a separation of economics and politics, but rather a reversal of the hitherto predominant logic: The normalisation of economic relations, Kao argues, would have a positive effect on the political relations between the two sides of the Taiwan Strait. The dynamism of cross-Strait relations also demanded new ways of thinking, as "stubbornly clinging to the same old framework will only delay opportunities for the two sides to benefit each other" (ibid.), a phrase reminiscent of Vincent Siew's call for abandoning orthodoxies made in the same month.

Siew himself presented his conceptual suggestions regarding the relation of the political and economic realms a few weeks later. Like Kao, he departs from the demands of Taiwan's bourgeoisie, postulating that "economics, not politics, should be the top priority" (TT 2001f). Against the "inevitable international trends" of globalisation, the practice of political intervention, he argued, was thus not only harmful but also futile (Siew 2001). Instead, he contrasts it with the mutually ben-eficial results of market-driven integration: "Economic integration on both sides of the Taiwan Strait should occur naturally, in areas of economic activity where entrepreneurs seek mutual opportunities" (ibid.). As market forces were to condi-tion this process, Siew argued that his "proposal involves no political implications at all" and thus allows for "both sides [to] put aside their political differences and ideologies" (TT 2001f). On the basis of the 1992 consensus and by prioritising the economy, cross-Strait relations would enter "into a new era" (Siew 2001).

Siew developed the abstract formula "economics first, politics later" into a set of concrete initiatives. These consisted of measures amounting to negative integra-tion, that is, the gradual removal of barriers to the direct flow of capital, goods and services. Beginning with the lifting of the NHBP policy and the opening of the Three Links, integration would gradually deepen – e.g. through the introduction of a common currency or the harmonisation of labour regulations – and ultimately result in a common market (ibid.). The mutual trust engendered by this process would also entail the potential for positive integration, a "step by step integration of politics", and thus pave the way for a "sharing of sovereignty" in the long term (Siew 2001). The formula of "economics first, politics later" is thus a crucial ideological element that contributes to the portrayal of the rapprochement, including the consultations and negotiations through the KMT-CCP and SEF-ARATS channels, as the disinterested, apolitical and therefore technocratic management of technical issues that arise from the allegedly inevitable and natural trend of globalisation. Like the 1992 consensus, these conceptions were disseminated successfully. During his "Journey of Peace", Lien Chan presented a vision of the rapprochement that is akin to Siew's:

> For both sides to truly achieve a win-win situation in all aspects of economy and trade, we have to step up and accelerate. However, there are various mechanisms in place today, such as so-called 'tariffs' and other issues. … We wish to avoid these concerns and refer to the common market, and for our common market, we will follow the path that everyone has taken under the system of free trade and open economies. What does this path consist of? As you all know, it begins with the reduction or removal of trade barriers, followed by the free circulation of production factors, including personnel, capital and goods; then comes the transfer of technology and information; afterwards, it is the currency union and even the harmonisation of policies; and after that the coordination of the entire economy and trade.
>
> (Sina.com 2005a)

The hegemonic initiative of the common market therefore became "the concrete form in which every intellectual and moral reform presents itself" (Gramsci 1971: 133). Reconciling the demands of capitalist and political forces, Siew's notion was declared a priority objective in the "Five-Point Vision" at the Lien–Hu meeting (TAO 2005) as well as several meetings of the KMT-CCP Forum. Subsequently, the common market was endorsed by the KMT's 17th National Congress, adopted into the KMT policy guidelines in 2005 and then became a central element of the Ma–Siew election platform (Fell 2016: 60–62). At the SEF, Chiang Pin-kung ensured that the talks regarding the first concrete steps towards a common market were "being conducted according to the principle of 'economics first, politics later'" (Lai 2008). The SEF-ARATS channel signed the ECFA in 2010, which is considered the first building block of Siew's vision.

Based on this dissociation, the allegedly separate economic and political realms were then infused with two distinct social logics. The political, and implicitly the social, dimension of cross-Strait relations was subjected to the narrative of *Status Quo*, signifying that the *de facto* independent political status of Taiwan would be maintained and the alternatives of *de jure* independence or unification would not be considered immediately. In the early 2000s, public support for the Status Quo was as high as 90 per cent, either as a short-term temporary arrangement before Taiwan's political status was to be decided or as a long-term solution (Rigger 2001b: 103, 111). The formula, as Dreyer (2006a,b) explains, first emerged as a diplomatic framework, resulting from the historical failure to resolve the One China question.

As a notion filled with several meanings over time and by various agents, Dreyer (2006a) dismisses it as "a largely meaningless phrase and a dangerous ambiguity".

Here, however, we are not so much interested in its geopolitical dimension but rather its significance for attempts to legitimate Taiwan's cross-Strait policies domestically. Given the high support for the Status Quo, Taiwan's leaders sought to portray their cross-Strait approaches as safeguarding it, implying that their policies respected not only the preferences of the electorate but also did not significantly revise Taiwan's political status. After his "special state-to-state relationship" remarks, Lee Teng-hui suggested that the Status Quo had been in place since the amendments to the R.O.C. constitution in 1991, as a result of which Taiwan abandoned its ambition to govern the Chinese mainland. For him, the intensification of economic interactions across the Strait posed a threat to that Status Quo. His understanding thus sanctioned the attempts by his government to restrict cross-Strait economic interactions through the Go South and NHBP policies. His successor, Chen Shui-bian, pledged in his 2000 inaugural address to "not promote a referendum to change the status quo with regard to the question of independence or unification" (Chen 2000). When, due to the circumstances discussed below, the Chen government did organise a referendum on the future of cross-Strait relations in 2004, the United States accused Chen of seeking to change the Status Quo. The DPP government, in turn, justified the referendum as protecting the Status Quo: Joseph Wu, at that time Deputy Secretary-General of the Presidential Office, wrote in an opinion piece that "independence is the real status quo" (Wu 2004).

The KMT, however, sought to actively encourage economic relations across the Taiwan Strait, and therefore had to reassure Taiwan's electorate that their policies would not challenge the Status Quo by promoting unification. As both the 1992 consensus and the common market idea received criticisms to this effect,[2] Ma Ying-jeou embedded the rapprochement project within a Status Quo narrative by adopting the "Three Noes" – no negotiations with the CCP on unification, no declaration of independence and no use of force – during the election campaign (Dumbaugh 2008: 3). By describing the 1992 consensus as the basis for maintaining the Status Quo, Ma furthermore reinforced the interlock among these elements of the conceptual framework. The Status Quo as defined by Ma's Three Noes corresponds to capital's demand for a stable investment environment, which neither the governments of Lee Teng-hui nor Chen Shui-bian were able to provide. At the same time, it absolves capital from its involvement in the transformation of cross-Strait relations. Informed by a very narrow and formalistic understanding of the political, the notion of Status Quo purports that the dynamism of cross-Strait relations is confined to the sphere of economic relations, where private interest can be legitimately exercised without affecting public interest. The capillary and molecular changes that affect the material basis from which the political superstructure arises are obscured by the overemphasis on the question of independence vs. unification.

The economic realm, on the other hand, was embedded in a narrative of *competitiveness*, designed to legitimate the unleashing of the particular interests of Taiwan's bourgeoisie as the driving force of the rapprochement. The element of competitiveness had been introduced by Taiwan's bourgeoisie as a way to naturalise the intensification of economic relations across the Taiwan Strait and to delegitimate restrictions on cross-Strait investments. Taiwan's bourgeoisie could rely on support from foreign capital, as both the American and the European Chambers of Commerce in Taipei repeatedly urged the government to lift restrictions on cross-Strait exchanges (TT 2005b; China Daily 2006).

The organic intellectuals of the rapprochement integrated the element of competitiveness into their ideological framework, shifting the emphasis from a negative and particularistic framing to a positive and universalistic one. For this purpose, they could draw on the contribution by Wang Yung-ching, who had already argued in a similar direction. To mitigate the declining competitiveness of Taiwan's companies, Wang called for lower taxes and the privatisation of state-owned enterprises, but also for the liberalisation of cross-Strait relations. This would not *weaken* Taiwan's economy, Wang argued, but *strengthen* it (Wang 2001). The ideological conception of competitiveness thus contributed to legitimating the economic dimension of the rapprochement in two ways. First, it obscured the particular interest of Taiwan's bourgeoisie by portraying the issue of normalising cross-Strait economic exchanges as a necessary response to the quasi-natural and inevitable trends of globalisation. As such, liberalisation was not a political question but one imposed by the laws of competition under globalisation. This was the angle pursued by Vincent Siew (CSCMF 2001b; Siew 2001). It was in this way that Ma Ying-jeou justified the normalisation of economic cross-Strait exchanges as an economic necessity rather than a political project (Hu 2010: 7).

In addition to naturalisation, the notion also lent itself to universalising the market-driven rapprochement. By emphasising that catering to the competitiveness of Taiwan's businesses was in the general interest of Taiwan as a whole – by safeguarding Taiwan's economic strength and therefore its economic and political survival – it obscured the political and capitalist interests the rapprochement served. As such, the conceptual element of competitiveness drew on a history of debates on trade liberalisation, beginning with the "liberalisation and internationalisation" initiative of the 1980s (see Chapter 3), which it sought to fulfil by extending it to China, the final piece of the puzzle. It also reflects the struggles of the 1990s: Already Chiang Pin-kung had argued that allowing non-competitive industries to relocate to China would ultimately promote a process of industrial upgrading in Taiwan and thereby benefit the country (Leng 1996: 70–71). But these earlier initiatives failed to deliver full liberalisation due to the politicisation of economic relations with China, internal opposition and the DPP's isolation in cross-Strait relations. Only the emerging hegemonic apparatus was able to provide the ideological and material foundations for the liberalisation project that had been initiated two decades earlier, as the alignment of political and capitalist forces provided the project with the capacity to universalise the underlying interests which were now being presented as "the motor force of a universal expansion" (Gramsci 1971: 182).

The NPF contributed to the dissemination of this particular framing of competitiveness. Su Chi stated that the competitiveness of Taiwan's semiconductor industry depended on the lifting of cross-Strait restrictions (TT 2001b), and Lien Chan had already promised to boost Taiwan's competitiveness during the campaign for the 2004 elections (TT 2003). Only after the establishment of the KMT-CCP plat-form, competitiveness became central to the project. Having reached a consensus on the common market with Hu Jintao during the "Journey of Peace" in 2005, Lien Chan spoke in front of representatives from TBAs in Shanghai to portray the com-mon market as a response to Taiwan's declining competitiveness:

> Today, Taiwan is facing another crucial moment due to cross-Strait relations: where shall we go? Almost all the world's major countries have already set their sights on or entered the mainland to enhance their competitiveness and expand their markets. In such an environment, we are likely to suffer serious negative effects, if we were to keep a closed mind.
>
> (Sina.com 2005a)

In his inaugural address of May 2008, Ma Ying-jeou then fused all these aspects together, emphasising that Taiwan's future depended on embracing the trend of globalisation, which in turn necessitated the normalisation of economic exchanges across the Taiwan Strait:

> The new administration's most urgent task is to lead Taiwan through the daunting challenges from globalization. … Islands like Taiwan flourish in an open economy and wither in a closed one. This has been true throughout history. Therefore, we must open up and deregulate the economy to unleash the vitality of the private sector. This will strengthen Taiwan's comparative advantages.
>
> (Ma 2008)

Finally, the rapprochement promised to improve the life of Taiwanese in general. In speeches and debates, this element was often vaguely referred to as a state of general *well-being* or *win-win*. The hegemonic framework emphasised how the rapprochement would contribute to the avoidance of negative outcomes, ranging from economic issues (such as the decline of competitiveness) to political ones (such as tensions or war as the result of a formal declaration of independence), either of which would affect Taiwan's survival as a *de facto* independent polity. In addition, proponents of the rapprochement argued that improving relations with the PRC would entail positive outcomes, which Ma Ying-jeou summarised as a "peace dividend" (Taiwan News 2010). These included Taiwan's participation in international organisations, in particular the World Health Assembly, and the Asian process of regionalisation, as well as the prospect of a peace agreement with China.

Hegemonic Inclusion and Marginalisation Between 2005 and 2008

Hegemonic Inclusion of the Subaltern: The Case of Taiwan's Farmers

As discussed in Chapter 3, Taiwan's agricultural sector had been crucial in main-taining social stability since the years of the land reform. Despite earlier moves towards liberalising Taiwan's agricultural sector, first due to US pressure in the 1980s and later during World Trade Organization (WTO) negotiations, agricultural produce was still relatively protected as of the early 2000s. The rapprochement, however, sought a "normalisation" of trade relations with the PRC that would potentially change this. Taiwan's farmers were customarily regarded as the group that had the most to lose from trade liberalisation across the Taiwan Strait due to the potential influx of a large quantity of inexpensive agricultural produce from China. Taiwan's small average farm size, which was a crucial pillar of the farmers' integration into the hegemonic bloc forged by the KMT, now acted as a barrier limiting the international competitiveness of Taiwan's agricultural sector. Even though the importance of the agricultural sector had declined over the decades, the potential impact of trade normalisation would affect the lives of hundreds of thousand rural Taiwanese, and discontent farmers were seen as a potential force of resistance against the rapprochement.

This sentiment was based on a history of farmer mobilisation since the late 1980s. Despite the exploitative character of the KMT's hegemonic architecture, the inclusion of peasants had contributed to social stability since the land reform. Whenever this equilibrium was threatened, Taiwan's farmers proved a serious force to be reckoned with. The first notable mobilisation against the government emerged during the wave of liberalisation that was the result of US pressure in the 1980s. Given the decadelong hegemonic inclusion of Taiwanese farmers, the KMT entered negotiations with the confidence it could minimise concessions affecting Taiwan's industrial export sector by offering Taiwan's agricultural sector as a "sacrificial lamb", expecting only limited domestic resistance (Li 1998: 591–592).

But when Taiwan's agricultural imports doubled within the decade as a result of these concessions, farmers felt betrayed (ibid.: 586). Not only did they organise several large-scale demonstrations, they also sought to emancipate themselves politically from the corporatist FAs by establishing independent organisations with the help of the emerging political opposition (ibid.: 594). On 20 May 1988, the police violently dispersed a large-scale farmer protest in Taipei, resulting in over 100 arrests (ibid.: 592–593). In an attempt to retain hegemonic inclusion, the government reacted to the increased farmer militancy by laying out a series of social reforms that included a pension system for farmers, crop insurance, improved service provision by FAs and pollution control in rural areas (Mao and Tu 1993: 99). Taiwan's negotiations to join the WTO saw another rise in farmer activism. In February 1998, five thousand pig farmers came to Taipei from all over the country to protest the liberalisation of pork meat. They took their protest to the MoEA and the Council of Agriculture (COA), but also the American Institute in Taiwan, the *de facto* embassy of the US, throwing pig dung and eggs at the latter (Pan 2005: 90–91).

The mobilisation potential of farmers was proven on another occasion when in 2001, the DPP moved towards eradicating "black gold" political corruption, a central element of the party's election platform (Rigger 2001c: 959). Among the first targets selected by the government were the credit departments of farmers' and fishermen's associations (CDFFA), which provided crucial financial services to their one million members. In the years prior to this initiative, the non-performing loan ratio of Taiwan's 288 local CDFFAs had accelerated at an alarming rate, rising from five per cent in December 1995 to over 21 per cent in March 2002 (Leou 2006: 116). While a share of this increase could be attributed to farmers being unable to service their debt (due to the impact of a recent earthquake, an epidemic among pigs as well as financial difficulties caused by the liberalisation measures to meet the WTO conditions), it was the lending practices of CDFFAs, based on political considerations and disregarding economic risk assessments, that were the major contributing factor, causing local credit cooperatives to be at the centre of several scandals of corruption and embezzlement (Sato 2004: 233, 241–243).

However, FAs were also a major pillar of the KMT's hegemonic apparatus that had been forged during the authoritarian era, and the FAs' role in mobilising voters during local elections persisted into the democratic era (Hsu 2009: 299–300; Leou 2011: 225–228). Early in the legislative period, the DPP had already attempted to curtail the mobilising potential of FAs by passing amendments to the Farmers' Associations Act with the objective of preventing individuals who had been sentenced on corruption charges to run for positions in FAs (TT 2001a). The reorganisation of the FAs' credit departments was therefore not simply an issue of financial reform, but also an expression of the DPP's "vital interest in fundamentally changing the political rules of the game" (Göbel 2004: 15) by dismantling a crucial part of the KMT's rural power base.

Between September 2001 and July 2002, the government assumed control of 36 CDFFAs with the aim of restructuring them before transferring them to commercial banks (Leou 2006: 116–117). In August, the government announced severe restrictions on CDFFAs with a high non-performing loan ratio. In response, the FAs demanded the abolishment of the new policies, the return of the 36 CDFFAs that had already been taken over, as well as the establishment of a national bank for agriculture as an alternative to tackle the problems of CDFFAs (ibid.: 120). The FAs were able to mobilise 120,000 farmers to participate in a large-scale protest in Taipei, forcing the government to withdraw its plans to reform the CDFFAs (Hsu 2009: 300). In the aftermath, the Minister of Finance as well as the chairman of the COA resigned, while the American credit rating agency Standard and Poor's downgraded Taiwan's credit rating as the failure to reform the CDFFAs was taken as a sign that the government would abandon its financial reform plans altogether (Leou 2006: 113–114). Although the DPP had the support of the general public to eradicate "black gold" politics, its frontal assault on the rural power base of local factions and the KMT failed due to the mobilisation capacities of FAs and local factions in both the streets and the political realm. Not only was the DPP defeated in this particular power struggle, the failed attempt to weaken the local factions and thereby the KMT even raised the latter's awareness of mutual dependence and contributed to reinvigorating their alliance (Huang and Wang 2010: 20).

These episodes demonstrate the farmers' (and the FAs') willingness and ability to mobilise when faced with measures that threatened their material interests. It is therefore not surprising that agricultural cooperation, together with the implementation of the "three direct links", was the most prominent issue in the early stage of the hegemonic project: Not only was it an element in the "Twelve-Point

Consensus" announced during Chiang Pin-kung visit in March 2005, the "Five-Point Vision" of the Lien–Hu meeting in April and the communiqué released after the meeting between Hu Jintao and James Soong, but also Hu Jintao, Wen Jiabao, the TAO and China's Ministry of Agriculture all repeatedly emphasised that facilitating Taiwanese agricultural exports was a priority in cross-Strait exchanges (Mainland Affairs Council [MAC] 2005a).

The subsequent steps towards promoting the export of Taiwanese agricultural produce to China can therefore be interpreted as the attempt to ensure that the hegemonic project's aim of cross-Strait liberalisation was "coordinated concretely with the general interests of the subordinate groups" (Gramsci 1971: 182). The major aim was to convince Taiwanese farmers that not only were they not threatened by the rapprochement as they were by the trade liberalisation with the US and after Taiwan's WTO accession, but to ensure their active consent as beneficiaries of the process. The particular interests of Taiwan's bourgeoisie were universalised by direct economic concessions aimed at creating Taiwan's largest export market for agricultural produce, and thus adjusting the hegemonic inclusion of Taiwan's farmers from the increasingly precarious domestic arrangement towards a new cross-Strait equilibrium.

Immediately after the visits of Chiang Pin-kung and Lien Chan, China announced a set of preferential policies which removed tariffs for 15 kinds of Taiwanese fruit (Wong and Wu 2016: 356). The Chinese side invited the Taiwan Provincial Farmers' Association to negotiate further steps, but their role as the key negotiator in cross-Strait agricultural issues was blocked by the DPP government, which threatened to withhold government subsidies that constitute 85 per cent of the association's budget (Wei 2013: 652). Nevertheless, the Taiwan Provincial Farmers' Association participated in events that sought to promote Taiwanese agricultural produce in China to take advantage of the reduced tariffs. In October 2005, together with several Chinese organisations, it co-organised a Cross-Strait Agricultural Cooperation Forum that was held to envisage the concrete implementation of the agreements reached between Hu Jintao and Lien Chan during their meeting (Sina.com 2005b). One month later, the Xiamen Association of Cross-Strait Agricultural Exchanges and Cooperation was established to speed up the processing and distribution of Taiwanese imports (China.com.cn 2005).

The cooperation was significantly expanded after the agricultural issue became the main focus of the second KMT-CCP Forum, themed "Strengthening Cross-Strait Cooperation and Realising Mutual Benefit and Win-Win Agriculture on Both Sides of the Strait", in Boao in October 2006. The first KMT-CCP Forum in April that year (as well as most of the subsequent forums) consisted mostly of business representatives, including several of Taiwan's most prominent tycoons, and dealt with questions of production and accumulation. The emphasis on agriculture at the second forum, by contrast, was less motivated by immediate economic benefits for Taiwan's bourgeoisie, but rather aimed at creating the conditions most favourable for Taiwan's farmers, a subaltern class.

At the closing ceremony, both parties announced seven joint recommendations (Taiwan.cn 2006a) before TAO chairman Chen Yunlin outlined 20 unilateral policies regarding the implementation of the agreements (TAO 2006). To make the export of perishable Taiwanese fruit to China a viable option, the joint recommendations called for measures to ensure the smooth and rapid transport of farm produce from Taiwan to China (Taiwan.cn 2006a). The unilateral measures announced by TAO chairman Chen Yunlin addressed the provision of preferential treatment in quarantine approval, inspection and release, as well as a further facilitation of customs clearance (Taiwan.cn 2006c). The relevant Chinese agencies subsequently implemented measures to facilitate inspection and quarantine procedures by giving Taiwanese imports priority treatment around the clock at the port declaration site, reducing the time for clearance from one or two days to 30 minutes (TAO 2006; Tsai 2005). The establishment of a "green corridor" for Taiwan's fresh agricultural products meant that vehicles transporting agricultural produce from Taiwan across a road network spanning 27,000 km across all of China's provinces benefit from reduced toll charges, special toll gate lanes and other preferential treatment (China. org.cn 2006; Taiwan.cn 2006c).

A second dimension emphasised in the joint recommendations was assistance in the sale of Taiwanese farm produce in China (Taiwan.cn 2006a). The TAO directed the relevant agencies to support farmers and farmer organisations in participating in product exhibitions and sales activities (Taiwan.cn 2006c). Various local governments subsequently included agricultural produce in extant cross-Strait trade fairs or established new platforms. The PRC's Ministry of Agriculture, the Ministry of Commerce and the TAO had already organised a Cross-Strait Agricultural Cooperation Exhibition and Taiwan Agricultural Products Fair at the Shanghai Exhibition Center in 2005 to showcase Taiwanese fruit and establish contacts to wholesale customers and distributors. Similar expos later proliferated across China, often co-organised by the Taiwan Province Farmers' Association. On the side of distribution, a Taiwan Fruit Trade Centre offering preferential treatment was opened in Xiamen in 2006. Distributors who settled in the centre were exempted from cold storage fees and one year of rent. Four similar centres in Fujian Province and one in Shanghai soon followed, as did cross-Strait agricultural e-commerce trading platform in Nantong, Jiangsu province (People's Daily 2010).

Another joint recommendation addressed the issue of counterfeit fruit (Taiwan. cn 2006a). Chinese agricultural producers had introduced Taiwanese seeds to China, cultivating fruit that was later sold as Taiwanese (Central People's Government of the PRC 2006). To "safeguard the legitimate rights and interests of farmers from Taiwan", the TAO specified that the relevant agencies in China had to "protect the brand and image of Taiwanese fruits" by improving the supervision of the fruit market and the enforcement of the Anti-Unfair Competition Law as well as the Advertising Law (Taiwan.cn 2006c). One month later, the State Administration for Industry and Commerce of the PRC instructed local authorities to crack down on counterfeit Taiwanese fruit and false advertising, enforcing regulations that distinguish between "fruit of Taiwanese origin" and "fruit of Taiwanese variety" by clearly stating the place of origin on the packaging (Central People's Government of the PRC 2006; Taiwan.cn 2006b). The TAO furthermore encouraged Taiwanese producers and distributors to register their own trademarks (Taiwan.cn 2006c).

Organisations such as the All China Federation of Supply and Marketing Cooperatives held conferences to inform those trading in Taiwanese fruit about intellectual property rights, brand management as well as marketing. The above-mentioned trade fairs, exhibitions and conventions furthermore contributed to promoting Taiwanese fruit as exotic luxury commodities, and the Chinese government also mobilised state-run media to raise awareness of Taiwanese brands and promote the consumption of Taiwanese fruit (Tsai 2005).

While these measures were designed to "unleash" the market forces to stimulate the cross-Strait fruit trade, in exceptional cases Chinese authorities resorted to more direct means. Direct procurement had already been announced as one of the unilateral measures during the first KMT-CCP Forum. When a huge surplus led to a decline in prices in bananas in 2006 and oranges in 2007, China signed deals with the Taiwan Provincial Fruit Marketing Cooperative and local FAs to buy 2,000 tons of bananas and 1,200 tons of oranges (China Post 2007). After the election of Ma Ying-jeou, this practice continued. For the year 2010, for instance, Chinese and Taiwanese agencies agreed that 3,000 tons of fruit, including bananas, pineapples and oranges, would be acquired through these channels (Global Times 2010).

In June of the same year, the Economic Cooperation Framework Agreement was signed between the SEF and ARATS. As part of the agreement, China further opened its agricultural sector to Taiwan without insisting on reciprocity as part of the "five concessions" announced by TAO director Wang Yi during the negotiations (Romberg 2010: 2–3). This led to a final agricultural initiative worth being discussed. In March 2011, the state-owned Shanghai Fisheries Group agreed with the Tainan-based Shinejia Foods Co. to buy milkfish at a guaranteed price. 100 farming households of the Syuejia District of Greater Tainan in southern Taiwan were contracted to each provide 18,000 kg of milkfish for a total volume of US$4.5 million (Keng et al. 2017: 962). Unlike the direct procurement of sporadic surpluses, contract farming not only meant that farmers had a reliable purchaser for their fish, but it also led to a more permanent direct hegemonic intervention in that district. Similarly to Taiwanese fruit, milkfish was promoted during fairs and exhibitions in China (TT 2012).

Several factors may have contributed for Syuejia to be chosen for this showpiece initiative. The district was one of the DPP's rural strongholds in southern Taiwan. After the textile industry had relocated to China in the 1980s and 1990s, Syuejia was left with a relatively large farming population specialised in milkfish, which under the provisions of the ECFA early harvest list could now be traded across the Taiwan Strait tariff-free. Many of the fish farms, however, had been devastated by the typhoon Morakot in 2009, adding to the economic hardships of the local population (Keng et al. 2017: 961–962). This particular constellation meant that this district was suited as a "test laboratory" for a pilot initiative aimed at assessing the ideological effects of cross-Strait agricultural cooperation.

Extant research on the impact of these agricultural initiatives pursues one of two approaches. Wei (2013) looks at it from a state-centric perspective of inducing an "economic dependency", concluding that the promotion of agricultural trade across the Taiwan Strait "did not make Taiwan's fruit exports dependent on the Chinese market" (ibid.: 646). While recent data casts doubt on this conclusion (see below), this chapter also argues that economic dependency was not the aim of the initiative. Rather, it was designed to shape how Taiwanese farmers perceived the cross-Strait rapprochement. The second strand of literature aims to assess whether these initiatives changed voting behaviour. Looking at the earlier phase of the hegemonic project, Wong and Wu (2016: 359) conclude "that Beijing's agricultural concessions ended up failing to undermine the DPP's electoral support in the 2008 presidential election". With regard to the 2012 elections, the district of Syuejia attracted particular attention. Again, these studies mostly agree in their conclusion that the agricultural dimension of the rapprochement did not entail any significant change in voting behaviour in Syuejia (Batto 2014: 26–29; Cabestan 2016: 292; Wei et al. 2016: 6).

Keng et al. (2017: 962–964), however, rightly question whether voting patterns are necessarily the best indicator to assess the effects of agricultural cooperation. Their approach based on fieldwork in Syuejia reveals that local farmers have indeed changed their perception of agricultural exchanges across the Taiwan Strait and, by extension, the rapprochement as a whole. Responding to a survey conducted among the district's farmer households, "91.9 per cent felt that the programme had greatly boosted their income and that terminating the programme would significantly impact their livelihood" (ibid.: 966). In addition, 98.4 per cent were very satisfied or satisfied with the programme, and 96.8 per cent had applied for the programme the following year (ibid.: 967). 83.9 per cent said their impression of China had significantly improved due to the programme, and 72.6 per cent supported cross-Strait cooperation not only on economic but also on political issues (ibid.: 969). Furthermore, a more rigorous analysis of statistical data does indeed show that "Syuejia's voting patterns have considerably and persistently changed since the introduction of contract farming" (Keng et al. 2017: 975).

Agricultural cooperation across the Taiwan Strait restructured Taiwan's fruit trade significantly. Figure 4.2 shows Taiwan's exports to China in comparison to the exports to the US, documenting a considerable increase in exports to China in the year 2005, the first year of cross-Strait agricultural cooperation. In the years prior to the election of Ma Ying-jeou, the trade volume increases slowly but constantly before rising sharply from 2008 onwards. Table 4.4 shows the structural shift that was initiated in 2005: Taiwan's export volume to China increased from a mere US$260,000 in the year 2003, accounting for 0.6 per cent of Taiwan's fruit exports, to US$150 million by 2019, accounting for just under 80 per cent of the country's exports. The data suggests a significant increase after the early unilateral measures of 2005, the election victory of the KMT in 2008 and the signing of ECFA in 2010, before the election of Tsai Ing-wen in January 2016 coincides with a plateauing of trade volume throughout the years 2016 and 2017. Whatever the impact on voting behaviour may have been, the structural shift is undeniable. During the decade of systematic promotion of cross-Strait fruit trade between 2005 and 2015, the absolute export volume to China grew by the factor 50. Whether or not Taiwanese fruit farmers have adjusted their views on the rapprochement

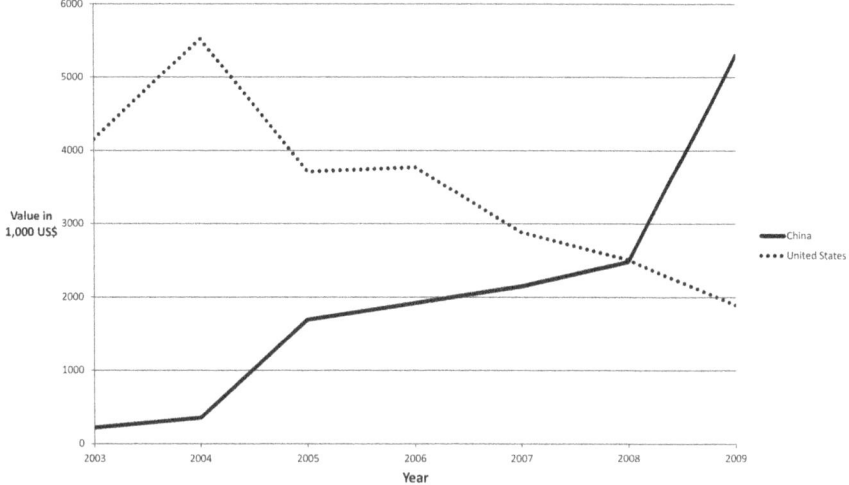

Figure 4.2 Taiwanese fruit exports to China and the United States, 2003–2009

Source: Customs Administration, Ministry of Finance (Taiwan, R.O.C.).

in similar ways in which Syuejia's milkfish farmers have cannot be answered at this point. What can be said with certainty is that the rapprochement has brought about a structural reversal in agricultural trade and therefore in the *objective* base for their interest.

Table 4.4 Taiwanese fruit exports, 2003–2019

Year	Total fruit exports Value (in US$ 1,000)	Fruit exports to China Value (in US$ 1,000)	Share of exports to China
2003	41,491	261	0.6%
2004	36,178	370	1.0%
2005	32,071	1,694	5.3%
2006	38,389	1,930	5.0%
2007	44,289	2,155	4.9%
2008	44,676	2,482	5.6%
2009	44,991	5,317	11.8%
2010	55,683	10,807	19.4%
2011	65,803	11,433	17.4%
2012	64,888	16,482	25.4%
2013	87,473	37,225	42.6%
2014	92,255	46,684	50.6%
2015	130,613	85,272	65.3%
2016	112,816	85,553	75.8%
2017	110,209	83,043	75.4%
2018	141,341	105,442	74.6%
2019	191,769	150,671	78.6%

Export category: Chapter 8 (edible fruit and nuts; peel of citrus fruit or melons).

Source: Customs Administration, Ministry of Finance (Taiwan, R.O.C.).

Hegemonic Marginalisation: The Case of Pro-independence Forces

A crucial factor that allowed the KMT to boast its own success in cross-Strait negotiations was the fact that the party was able to contrast its own accomplishments with the limited results achieved by DPP government. The DPP's limited success, however, was not for lack of initiative: After first overtures beginning with Chen's election in 2000, the government proposed negotiations on a variety of technical issues from 2004 onwards, but as the party-to-party platform between the KMT and CCP emerged in the same time frame, the Chinese government could afford to stall, decline or even ignore the overtures of the Taiwanese government. The hegemonic apparatus provided the means to not only negotiate benefits for Taiwan's bourgeoisie and the subaltern group of farmers, but it also lent itself to amplifying the impression that the DPP's alleged "ideological" approach to cross-Strait relations contributed to Taiwan's international political and economic isolation while the KMT's pragmatic approach was able to achieve tangible benefits for the Taiwanese.

This dimension was already apparent during the fruit negotiations that were discussed above. In July 2005 – a few weeks after the Lien–Hu meeting – the PRC suggested negotiations on the issue of fruit trade to the Taiwanese government. The DPP government proposed the Taiwan External Trade Development Council (TAITRA) as the official organisation authorised to conduct the negotiations for Taiwan, a proposal that was shunned by China as TAITRA was set up to promote Taiwan's *international* trade relations, while the CCP sought to treat it as a domestic matter (Wei 2013: 651). China instead preferred to negotiate with a Taiwanese delegation that was composed of a broader alliance of groups, including the provincial and local FAs as well as the Taiwan Provincial Fruit Marketing Cooperative (TT 2005a). The fruit negotiations were conducted through the above-mentioned channels, precluding the involvement of organisations authorised by the DPP government. Relying on informal negotiations and the implementation through unilateral measures, the CCP was able to bypass the government, thus not only isolating the DPP but also driving a wedge between the party and the southern Taiwanese agricultural regions (R9), where the party had secured the majority of its votes in the 2004 elections (Hsu 2009: 299).

The government was comparatively successful regarding the issue of direct cross-Strait flights. In the absence of scheduled flights between China and Taiwan since the Civil War, people flying across the Taiwan Strait had to take connecting flights, usually in Hong Kong or Macao. Even a limited number of cross-Strait charter flights in 2003 had to include a stopover in these places, increasing both the duration and the cost of flights. A first step towards mitigating this situation was a series of negotiations on direct cross-Strait flights for the holiday period of the Lunar New Year 2005. As the CCP made the resumption of the SEF-ARATS channel conditional on the DPP's acceptance of "One China", a concession the DPP was reluctant to make, an alternative framework was considered. Ultimately, two private entities, the Taipei Airlines Association and the China Civil Airlines Association, accompanied by government officials in the capacity of consultants, met for negotiations in Macao and reached an agreement within two hours (Bellows

2005: 115; Tung 2005: 201). Between 29 January and 20 February, and for the first time since the retreat of the KMT to Taiwan, 48 direct charter flights took place across the Taiwan Strait (Jacob 2005: 331). While planes still had to pass through Hong Kong's air space, a stopover was not necessary.

Over the following years, the cooperation on direct flights gradually expanded to further holidays and even cargo charter flights. The so-called "Macao model", that is, negotiations on technical issues through private organisations, became the DPP's preferred option for similar negotiations (R7). Encouraged by the limited yet tangible results of these negotiations, the MAC suggested that discussions on cross-Strait tourism should be held "as soon as possible based on the model of the 'Macao talks'" (MAC 2005b). By this time, however, the party-to-party platform between the KMT and the CCP was being established, and during a visit by Chiang Pin-kung, the KMT delegation and the TAO stated that follow-up negotiations should adopt the party-to-party model (MAC 2005b). Nevertheless, the DPP government remained hopeful that progress could be made during the final two years of Chen Shui-bian's term. Following the Macao model, the MAC authorised the establishment of the Taiwan Strait Tourism Association (TSTA) in August 2006 as the designated agency to negotiate a tourism agreement with its Chinese counterpart, the Cross-Strait Tourism Exchange Association (CTEA) (MAC 2006). Early signs were encouraging as both organisations initiated talks immediately. Joseph Wu described these negotiations as "smooth" and, given that both sides had reached a consensus on technical aspects, expected Taiwan to open up to Chinese tourists before the end of the year (MAC 2006). Even after the Tourism Bureau of Taiwan's MOTC stated in December that this goal would not be met, negotiations still appeared to make progress (MAC 2006). The TSTA and the CTEA held a third and fourth round of tourism talks in January 2007, and a fifth round in March (MAC 2007). With both organisations having "reached consensus in many aspects", Wu was adamant that negotiations were "entering the final stages", a statement reaffirmed by his successor Chen Ming-tong on 27 April (MAC 2007).

The next day, however, the 3rd KMT-CCP Forum opened in Beijing to discuss the topics of direct flights and cross-Strait tourism. The composition of the delegation reflected the issues on the agenda: In addition to the usual party and business representatives, it comprised delegates from four Taiwanese airlines, several hotel groups as well as a number of associations from the tourism and travel sectors (Taiwan.cn 2007). Three of the forum's six recommendations dealt with issues of cross-Strait links. The first called for the promotion of direct cross-Strait flights as well as cooperation between the aviation industries on both sides of the Strait, the second one urged both sides to let non-governmental organisations negotiate agreements on maritime transportation, while the fifth recommendation endorsed the swift realisation of a cross-Strait tourism agreement (Ministry of Commerce of the PRC 2007). The unilateral measures announced at the forum facilitated travel for Taiwanese citizens by allowing further cities to issue landing visas, and Taiwanese airlines were permitted to set up offices in China while also benefiting from measures designed to promote cooperation with Chinese airlines on issues such as aircraft maintenance, ground service and strategic partnerships.

At the forum's closing ceremony, Shao Qiwei, director of China's National Tourism Administration, contrasted the pragmatic and productive negotiations with the Taiwanese opposition parties through the KMT-CCP channel with the disruptive attitude of the Taiwanese government. He stated that the five rounds of negotiations between the TSTA and the CTEA had reached a consensus on a large number of tourism-related issues (MAC 2007) and blamed the stalling of negotiations on the Taiwanese government's unwillingness to recognise cross-Strait tourism as *domestic* travel (Central People's Government of the PRC 2007). Arguably, this was a clear signal that the CCP preferred to negotiate with the opposition parties rather than giving the DPP any credit during the remainder of Chen Shui-bian's term (R7). By contrast, negotiations would later move very quickly after Ma Ying-jeou was elected. Within a month, both sides signed agreements on cross-Strait weekend charter flights and tourism during the first SEF-ARATS meeting, and a mere six weeks would pass between Ma Ying-jeou's inauguration on 20 May and the arrival of the first Chinese tourists on 4 July 2008. The SEF-ARATS agreement, extensively prepared in the KMT-CCP Forum (R18), gave the KMT government an early success, consolidating its image as a pragmatic party after years of negotiations under the previous government had brought few results.

During the final years of Chen Shui-bian's term, the DPP government was faced with a dilemma: Without accepting the 1992 consensus, it was excluded from substantial negotiations in cross-Strait relations, with only limited instruments to prevent the opposition parties from interacting with the Chinese side. Subscribing to the 1992 consensus, however, was not conceivable without jeopardising the party's conceptual principles. The ideological framework of the hegemonic project therefore acted as a gatekeeper to the terrain of the cross-Strait rapprochement, exerting what Jessop (1990: 260) describes as "a system of strategic selectivity, i.e. as a system whose structure and *modus operandi* are more open to some types of political strategy than others." In the case of the rapprochement, this system favoured "pragmatic" political strategies. These were compatible with capital's need for a stable accumulation environment, opened negotiations that resulted in improved accumulation conditions in China and, by extension, also furthered the political goal of the rapprochement, namely the prevention of Taiwan independence. By contrast, the rapprochement isolated social forces that pursued strategies – often labelled as "ideologically" motivated – that might contribute to a disruption of accumulation across the Taiwan Strait. Although the conceptual expression of this strategic selectivity was the 1992 consensus, this process is by no means reducible to its ideological dimension. Without the institutional apparatus of the hegemonic project, China might have very well succeeded in isolating Chen Shui-bian in similar ways as it had tried to coerce Lee Teng-hui during the second half of the 1990s. But the case of Lee had already revealed the limitations of coercive measures. The new quality that surfaced after 2005 was the element of consent, which became not only complementary to coercion but predominant over it.[3] Only the hegemonic apparatus was able to organise consent to the rapprochement, whether in the form of concessions to Taiwan's farmers or by improving the conditions of accumulation for Taiwan's bourgeoisie. As a result, the strategic selectivity contributed not only to the isolation of the DPP but simultaneously provided the Taiwanese voter with a concrete alternative: the "pragmatic" KMT.

Faced with the domestic and international isolation, partly brought about by the establishment of the KMT-CCP platform, Chen Shui-bian's policies became increasingly desperate (Fell 2011: 91). Constrained strategically by the hegemonic project, the president pursued options that were largely limited to symbolic value, as a former MAC senior official concedes:

> Therefore he [Chen Shui-bian] considered that radicalisation is probably one way to go, and he decided to announce the 'ceasing to function' of the National Unification Council and the name-rectification. He changed the name of the Chiang Kai-shek Airport, the Chiang Kai-shek Memorial, he changed Chunghwa Post Office into Taiwan Post Office, all these kinds of things, and then it led to seeking of membership in the WHO and seeking membership in the UN by having a referendum. All these kinds of things were President Chen's instinct as a politician, to secure his position in Taiwan. But, of course, all these kinds of things led to more difficulties between Taiwan and China and to more difficulties between Taiwan and the United States.
>
> (R5)

Constraining the DPP government's strategic options therefore further amplified the contrast between the "ideological" and "pragmatic" approaches to cross-Strait interactions. At times, the DPP even internalised the hegemonic pressure by sanctioning its own members: After individual party members accepted the KMT's invitation to the KMT-CCP Forum and participated in its 2009 edition, the DPP chose to expel both of them from the party (Beckershoff 2014a: 233).

The Structured Spontaneity of Taiwan's Wild Strawberry Movement

A Brief Account of the Protests Surrounding the SEF-ARATS Talks

The Wild Strawberry Movement erupted around the second round of talks between the SEF and the ARATS. The first round of these meetings since 1998 had been held in Beijing in June 2008, only a little more than three weeks after the inauguration of Ma Ying-jeou, resulting in two agreements. The second round of talks can be considered historical as it was the first time ever that these organisations met for substantial negotiations on Taiwanese soil. The agenda listed the signing of four agreements on direct flights, shipping and postal services (the Three Links) as well as food safety (a reaction to the recent contaminated milk scandal in China that affected several children in Taiwan). Security measures were increased significantly after ARATS Vice Chairman Zhang Mingqing – travelling to Taiwan in a private capacity as a scholar – had been shoved to the ground during a protest a few days earlier (Romberg 2009: 6–8).

Headed by ARATS chairman Chen Yunlin, the 60-member delegation arrived at Taoyuan Airport on 3 November. The Taiwanese police had dispatched 2,000 officers to escort the delegation from the airport to the Grand Hotel in Taipei, where Chen Yunlin was set to stay for the five days of the trip. While several groups, among them the DPP, held organised protests, many individual protesters spontaneously went to the streets along the route from the airport to the hotel, waving the official R.O.C. flag and chanting that "Taiwan was not part of China". Suggesting the statehood of Taiwan, and therefore being potentially offensive to the Chinese delegation, the police intervened and confiscated the flags, at times forcibly removing protesters from the scenes.

On 6 November, two separate protests were held. Several ten thousand people – the highest estimate being 200,000 (Formosan Association for Public Affairs [FAPA] 2008: 9) – followed the DPP's call to join the "Yellow Ribbon Siege", named after the coloured ribbons reading "Taiwan is my country" in Chinese and English. The DPP had originally planned to blockade the guest house near Taipei's Presidential Palace, where Chen Yunlin was set to meet with Ma Ying-jeou in the late afternoon. When it became clear that the authorities had moved the meeting forward by several hours to avoid the siege, crowds became angered. Protesters attempted to break through the police cordon, throwing bottles and stones at the security forces. In the ensuing scuffle, several people were injured. Over the five days of the visit, 149 police officers and about 100 protesters were injured according to the police.

Not far away, a separate and smaller group came together at the Executive Yuan, the seat of Taiwan's government. Shocked by the police action during the previous days, National Taiwan University (NTU) professors and students formulated three demands: an apology by Ma Ying-jeou for the "state sponsored violence" over the previous days; the resignation of police officers who "abused their authority" and an amendment of the Assembly and Parade Act that served as the legal foundation of the "suppression of human rights" (Wild Strawberry Movement [WSM] 2008a). During the night from 6 to 7 November, the police dispersed participants of the sit-in. The activists quickly regrouped on Liberty Square, an open space in front of the Chiang Kai-shek Memorial Hall, where they reconstituted themselves as the WSM. Over the coming days, the movement attracted further participants and quickly spread throughout Taiwan, with sit-ins emerging in Tainan (8 November), Taichung (9 November), Kaohsiung and Hsinchu (10 November) as well as Chiayi (12 November) (WSM 2008e). Under the *leitmotif* of human rights, these sit-ins would soon adopt a wide-ranging portfolio of practices, including art projects, public debates, seminars and concerts. The efforts to mobilise broader strata of Taiwan's society culminated in a demonstration on 7 December with 4,000 participants.

Despite these efforts, the movement is remembered for its inability to mount an effective challenge against the government, with none of its demands being met. As students became increasingly exhausted as the sit-in drew on with no substantial concessions by the government in sight, the number of participants dwindled over the weeks. Having already declined to fewer than 100 protesters, the remaining students were forcibly removed from Liberty Square by the police in the early hours of 11 December. Although this coercive action marks the end of the movement's mobilisation in the public spaces of Taipei, it should not be taken as the decisive turning point. Rather, the following sections will argue that the movement ultimately succumbed to its internal limitations. While most accounts of the movement highlight its spontaneous character and the lack of organisation as the most important elements that prevented a sustained challenge (R21; R29), this view neglects that the activists responded to structural conditions that were the product of developments outside of the students' control. Rather than overemphasising the spontaneity, which undoubtedly was a defining feature of the WSM, we have to consider the fact that this spontaneity was structured not simply by individual decisions or the outcome of intra-group struggles, but more importantly by molecular forms of hegemonic intervention that posed ideological and material constraints on the movement.

Ideological Determinants of the Wild Strawberry Movement

The WSM's own conceptions focused on the issue of human rights. On an immediate level, the human rights narrative appears as a direct response to the police interventions that characterised the government's reaction to spontaneous protests. Yet, the specific articulation of this narrative, in particular its historic reference to the martial law era and a social movement that took place during Taiwan's democratisation, was not a foregone conclusion. Other possible frames of reference were also discussed among the students (R21). These included the fact that in the first place the protests were originally directed against and explicitly referred to the visit of a Chinese delegation, representatives of a state that until today claims sovereignty over Taiwan. And indeed, the very first press release by the movement put to the fore that free speech and free assembly as basic democratic rights had been impeded to please China (WSM 2008c).

At this juncture, these elements could have provided potential cornerstones to articulate a counter-narrative that would have explicitly focused on *current* developments. Yet, as the movement consolidated, they were relegated to an implicit and secondary status, while the historical reference to the martial law era took the spotlight. This development was by no means accidental but a conscious choice by activists. To comprehend how this choice was conditioned by the ideological and material conditions that were produced through molecular activities in the years prior to the KMT's election victory, it is necessary to evaluate the movement's conceptions in relation to the dominant ideology and its effects on the common sense.

The first ideological factor concerns the lack of an established and reliable counter-narrative on which the movement could have drawn. The obvious candidate was the China-sceptic narrative, politically represented by the DPP and other pro-independence organisations. This route was chosen by a group that constituted itself on 2 November, one day before the Chinese delegation arrived. Tsay Tingkuei, then chairman of the independence-leaning Taiwan Association of University Professors (TAUP), had initiated a hunger strike on 25 October to demand changes to the referendum law. According to Tsay, the "United Front tactics" pursued by the KMT undermined Ma Ying-jeou's promise that Taiwan's future would be decided by 23 million Taiwanese. Tsay regarded a referendum as the most feasible path to put the power back into the hands of the people. The legal obstacles inscribed in the referendum law, however, made this impossible and ultimately protected the government from the people's will. During his hunger strike, Tsay therefore formed the Alliance of Referendum for Taiwan (ART), a pro-independence group that explicitly related their demands for legal reform to the current KMT-CCP cooperation, and therefore to the hegemonic project (R36).

The activists of the WSM consciously decided not to follow this path. In their view, an articulation of the movement's conception around the principles of Taiwan independence or China was more likely to harm the movement than to resonate with Taiwan's society, as the recent election suggested DPP had failed to convince the general public that their China-sceptic approach was the most promising response to Taiwan's pressing problems. Molecular interventions by the hegemonic apparatus had contributed to a view that contrasted the KMT's "pragmatism" with the DPP's "ideological" approach: While the talks between proxies of the DPP government and China in Macao had come to nothing, the KMT, despite being an opposition party, negotiated unilateral concessions from the PRC. When President Chen and Taiwan faced the Severe Acute Respiratory Syndrome epidemic in international isolation, Lien Chan and Hu Jintao agreed to discuss Taiwan's "meaningful participation" in international organisations.[4] And after eight years of standstill across the Taiwan Strait, SEF and ARATS were about to sign agreements on direct transportation, a central demand from Taiwanese business groups, thought to benefit Taiwan's economy.

China's double-pronged approach between 2005 and 2008 to isolate the Chen government and negotiate concessions with the KMT had contributed to Chen's increasingly confrontational stance and the above-mentioned symbolic politics during the last 18 months of his presidency. This not only reinforced the "pragmatic vs. ideological" contrast but also cast doubt on whether the China-sceptic political project was a convincing way to overcome pressing problems of the Taiwanese economy and international isolation. If the activists needed any further justification for their hesitation, this was delivered when the DPP was caught up in a political scandal just three weeks before the WSM: Seven of its party members (including several former ministers, magistrates and councillors) were detained on the suspicion of corruption, and Chen Shui-bian himself was arrested on corruption charges on 11 November (FAPA 2008: 12–13).

These developments made activists refrain from articulating the movement with explicit references to the only established narrative that was critical of the rapprochement (R21). None of the three major demands mentioned China or the government's pro-China policies. Instead of emphasising the immediate circumstances of the police action (i.e. the visit by the Chinese delegation), protesters framed these as violations of the Assembly and Parade Act, which in turn was seen as a relic from the authoritarian era. This entailed a de-politicisation of the movement's narrative to reduce the risk of being associated with the pan-green camp.

The attempt to appear as non-partisan or even apolitical was also reflected in the movement's practice. As one observer remembers: Activists at the protest site in Chiayi drew a line on the square that all people affiliated with political parties were not allowed to cross, unless they removed any banner, badge or sign that would identify them as supporting the pan-green camp (Ho 2011).[5]

This attempt to insulate the movement from the China-sceptic narrative therefore should be considered a *negative ideological effect* of the hegemonic project, as it narrowed the ideological terrain on which a potential critical project could be articulated. The China-sceptic project had been marginalised not only in terms of substantial political outcomes, but also in terms of affective attractiveness to those seeking an alternative vision to the KMT's pragmatism.

A second ideological factor can be considered a *positive ideological effect* of the hegemonic project, as it offered a persuasive interpretation of Taiwan's current crisis and possible solutions to it. For nearly a decade, organic intellectuals had disseminated the narrative that Taiwan's prosperity depended on its integration into the global economy and that – in the light of recent shifts in global production networks – this integration in turn was now dependent on a normalisation of economic exchanges with China. By association, the plausibility of this argument reinforced the ideological elements that were seen to be the necessary condition of the rapprochement that epitomised the KMT's pragmatic approach, in particular the 1992 consensus and the principle of "Economics first, politics later". After the election of Ma Ying-jeou, the hegemonic narrative therefore aligned with people's experience, adding to its persuasive power in economic terms. Given that China had already made unilateral concessions since 2005 and ARATS and SEF had signed several agreements thought to be beneficial for Taiwan, there was no immediate reason to believe that a further deepening of economic ties with China would not fulfil the promise of safeguarding Taiwan's prosperity.

The narrative's appeal was, crucially, amplified by the onset of the global economic crisis in 2007–2008, which had severe repercussions in Taiwan. As shown in Figure 4.3, the economy contracted in the third quarter of 2008 and slumped by more than 7.5 per cent in the fourth quarter, the time of the WSM. Given that Taiwan's extraverted economy either directly or indirectly depended on consumption (mainly of electronic consumer goods) in those areas of the world hit most severely by the crisis, such as the United States and the European Union, access to the growing markets in China was said to become even more crucial for Taiwan's enterprises and, by extension, to their workers. Indeed, many of the hegemonic initiatives at the time can be seen as an attempt to convince Taiwan's population that China was Taiwan's "ticket out of the crisis": With the agreement on cross-Strait tourism, Chinese authorities channelled millions of tourists to Taiwan, and after the 16 November announcement of the TAO, Chinese provinces began sending procurement missions to Taiwan. Between May 2009 and September 2010, the largest 11 of these alone placed orders worth US$20 billion (Chien and Hsieh 2010: 18).

Against this background, the promise of a "rapprochement dividend" (in terms of employment and educational opportunities, demand for Taiwanese goods,

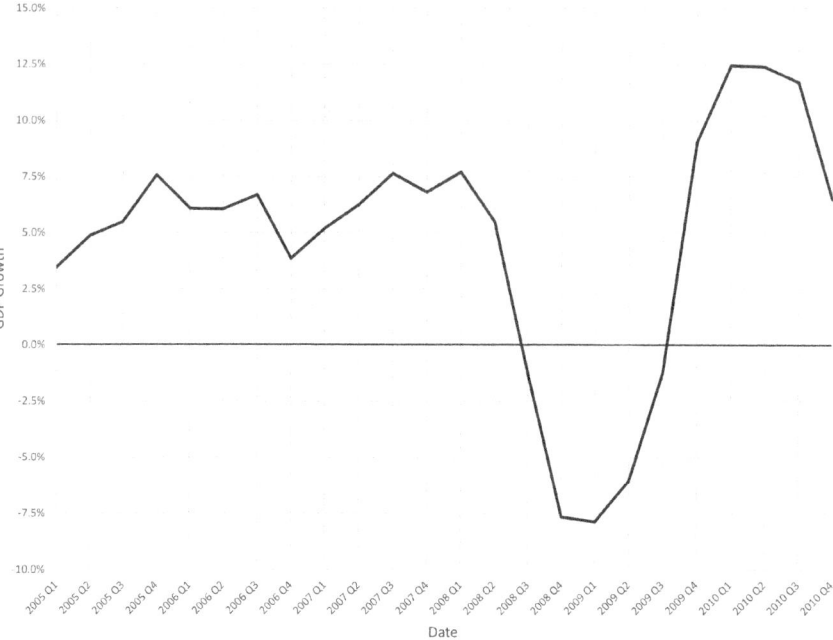

Figure 4.3 Quarterly GDP growth in Taiwan, 2005–2010

Source: Directorate General of Budget, Accounting and Statistics, R.O.C.

acquisition of agricultural produce, participation in international organisations, etc.) appeared particularly compelling. This should by no means be taken to suggest that Taiwan's citizens suddenly favoured unification. In fact, poll data shows that from this point onwards, Taiwanese identity rose to unprecedented levels. It rather suggests that the pragmatism of the 1992 consensus radiated into the China-sceptic narrative and thereby reconciled some of its elements with the pragmatic approach. In other words, identifying oneself as Taiwanese and pursuing pragmatic opportunities arising from the rapprochement came to be seen as compatible. Especially among the young generation, employment opportunities in China no longer stood in conflict with their identity as Taiwanese (Chen 2009: 11). By absorbing and neutralising ideological elements previously thought to be in opposition to the normalisation of cross-Strait relations, the pragmatic narrative had become the new common sense, plausibly portraying the rapprochement as the solution to Taiwan's urgent problems without threatening the affective elements of Taiwaneseness. In late 2008, there was an actual support for the KMT's course, which even the movement did not dare to question. As one activist put it:

China was not seen as a threat at that time. The big majority [of Taiwan's population] shared the opinion that opening up to China was good for everybody.
(R21)

This statement is supported by opinion polls from that time. According to a survey commissioned by the MAC in August 2008, 73 per cent of respondents approved the government's stance to handle economic issues first and discussing political questions at a later point in time (MAC 2008a: 3–4). Even a poll from December 2008, during the time frame of the WSM, suggests that respondents were in favour of tangible benefits provided by the rapprochement: 80.1 per cent considered using the newly opened direct flight routes to China, 67.9 per cent thought the opening of direct transportation links to be beneficial to Taiwan's international competitiveness and 61.7 per cent regarded these links to have a positive impact on Taiwan's economic development (MAC 2008b: 2–3). Similarly, the early success of the Ma government was perceived as having a positive impact on the political relations across the Taiwan Strait, with 64.2 per cent of the respondents describing cross-Strait relations as "more relaxed" than under the previous government (MAC 2008b: 3). The approval extended to the ideological and organisational dimensions of the rapprochement: About 70 per cent of the public approved the 1992 consensus as the basis of cross-Strait negotiations, a similar number of respondents expressing that they were in favour of continuing negotiations through the SEF-ARATS channel (MAC 2009: 3–7). Interestingly, it was in particular the young generation in Taiwan that expected economic exchanges across the Taiwan Strait to be beneficial for Taiwan: 51.66 per cent of those aged 40 or younger at the time of the WSM expected the opening to be beneficial for Taiwan (compared to 41.72 per cent of the general population), while a further 22.51 per cent at least did not expect them to worsen (compared to 17.48 per cent of the general population) (Rigger 2011: 76).

These surveys suggest that the technocratic narrative was firmly rooted within the common sense of Taiwan's society at that time. In Gramsci's (1971: 120) words, the hegemonic project was "capable of creating … a period of expectation and hope". The only established alternative, the China-sceptic narrative, had been exhausted due to its inability to provide a positive vision for Taiwan's future before collapsing due to a series of political scandals. The negative and positive ideological effects of the hegemonic project put severe limitations on the movement's attempt to critically scrutinise and challenge the ideological foundations of the rapprochement. Considering themselves unable to criticise the common sense, the activists chose to circumvent the dominant ideology by framing the protest in universalistic principles seemingly unrelated to the actual political and socio-economic developments. While this articulation was a conscious choice on behalf of the movement, it was by no means a voluntary or merely spontaneous consideration: It rather reflects the structural effectiveness of the hegemonic project at this point in time. In a sense, the hegemonic separation of the rapprochement's socio-economic content from its political form appears mirrored in the form of resistance: As the movement attempted to generalise its criticism on the grounds of universalistic principles of democracy and human rights, the political form itself was moved to the centre of attention, albeit drained from any socio-economic content. And while the hegemonic ideology took its appeal by promising future benefits, the WSM drew on the past.

Material Determinants of the Wild Strawberry Movement

In addition to these ideological constraints, we have to consider material determinants that resulted in a weakened and highly fragmented movement apparatus in late 2008. A crucial factor in the pre-2008 erosion of practice, conceptions and apparatus relates to the organisational relationship of social movements and the DPP. When the DPP had been formed by political activists in 1986, it found itself at the centre of an emerging wave of social movements against the authoritarian KMT. To counter corporatist mass organisations that had been set up and were controlled by the Kuomintang, the DPP participated in the establishment of movement-oriented civil society organisations, such as the Taiwan Labor Front (TLF) and the Taiwan Association for Human Rights (TAHR) (Lee 2014: 440). To facilitate the coordination with these and other movements, the party set up a Department of Social Movements in May 1987 (Ho 2005: 406).

Over the following two decades, the close relationship between the party and social movements would prove to be a double-edged sword. Several developments support Lee's (2014: 437) characterisation of these groups as "dependent movements" that benefited of the DPP having taken power in some ways but suffered in others due to the close relationship. First, to appear as a reliable party ready to take government responsibilities, the DPP moved towards pragmatism in the years prior to the 2000 elections. As part of this process, it closed down its Department of Social Movements (Ho 2010: 11). Furthermore, once in power, the DPP backtracked on several of its progressive election promises (such as the improvement of labour standards and halting the construction of a nuclear power plant) after these plans were met with resistance (Ho 2005: 412), consolidating its profile as a pragmatic party at the expense of its relation to social movements that had long pressed for these reforms. Second, the party's relation towards social movements assumed a form that is best described with the Gramscian notion of transformism: Experienced activists were absorbed into the DPP hierarchy and became ministers in Chen's cabinet, while the younger ones worked as their assistants (ibid.: 408–409). The government furthermore found ways to increase the state-funding of these groups (ibid.: 410) and established committees through which "movement activists enjoyed a more routinized access to influence upon the process of formulating and implementing policies" (Ho 2014: 110–111).

These developments contributed to an overall decline in activism during the DPP years. The Labour Day parade on 1 May was held only twice during the eight years after 2000, and despite the WSM and other protests against the ARATS visit, 2008 was the year that saw the fewest protests between 2006 and 2013 (Ho 2014: 101, 106; 2018: 110–111). Crucially, most activism-oriented student groups at Taiwanese universities that had previously been central hubs for organising protests and recruiting activists lay dormant by the time of the WSM, a process that had begun already in the 1990s (Chen 1998: 238; see also Chapter 5).

While the "dependent movements" were included in the new arrangements, "independent movements" faced new obstacles. Many activists saw the DPP's election victory in the year 2000 as a unique historical juncture and felt that they should refrain from criticising a party that was perceived as vulnerable to political and social pressures from the pan-blue camp. Criticising the DPP while it was in office, they feared, might contribute to weakening a party that had long supported social movements. As movements had partly been integrated into institutionalised channels, street protests outside of these channels came to be seen as illegitimate. From 2005 onwards, that is when the government's inability to deal with the hegemonic project became apparent and weakened the China-sceptic narrative, independent movements "realised that they ha[d] to fight even under a DPP government" (R24). The movements that emerged during that time, such as those against the construction of a chemical plant in Kuokuang or against the destruction of a historical site from the Japanese colonial era in favour of an infrastructure project in Losheng, were met with criticism from other activists. The following observations from respondents capture how the split between "dependent" and "independent" movements was consolidated and reproduced through forms of mutual scepticism:

> [The Losheng] movement was against the DPP, which was in charge at that time. [Veteran activists] from the Wild Lily Movement do not understand the real movement. These scholars think we are too radical and too aggressive. … The Wild Strawberry Movement put a tag on us: '*left unificationists, pro-China.*' But actually, a lot of people are pro-independence, just not in the sense of the DPP. A lot of the democracy movements depended on the DPP. [The rationale was:] 'First unite with the DPP, then solve the other problems.' But Losheng was directed against the DPP, so we were branded pro-unification. … The Losheng movement was therefore not directly involved in the Wild Strawberry Movement. We also did not like the Ma government, but we did not want to be close to the DPP.
>
> (R33)

Conversely, a participant of the WSM frames the Losheng activists in terms of a "leftist anti-neoliberalism" thought to be incompatible with the political goals of pan-green Taiwan independence:

> Anti-neoliberals do not see that China has a special quality. [Emphasising the element of] anti-free trade means: 'China is not different to all other countries'. This neutralises China into just another country – but it is special to Taiwan! They don't see the elephant in the room, or they strategically tone it down. … Leftists are antinationalist, we do not have a very good relation with them.
>
> (R21)

The government's transformism had therefore not only resulted in a low overall intensity of social movements, it had also contributed to a sense of alienation among groups. As movements split into a "dependent", reformist, pro-independence camp supported by Wild Lily Movement (WLM) veterans on the one side and an "independent", radical, anti-neoliberal camp sceptical of the DPP on the other, the apparatus was fragmented, conceptions increasingly diverged and obstacles to common forms of practice arose. This rift, which emerged around the principal question of the relation of social movements to the DPP and the role of its China-sceptic narrative, carried over into the WSM.

A final material factor regards the hegemonic inclusion of Taiwan's farmers. As discussed above, farmers had previously organised large-scale protests when political initiatives of trade liberalisation threatened their interests. Crucially, during the late 1980s, the Democratic Student Union supported the farmers' protest against trade liberalisation (Wright 1999: 1003). This group was critical not only of the authoritarian KMT government but also of the bourgeois leadership of the opposition movement and attempted to forge connections to independent labour and farmer groups (Chen 1998: 217). Importantly, the year 2008 did not see any form of a farmer-student alliance (or at least mutual support), suggesting that the hegemonic inclusion of Taiwan's farmers was successful in maintaining the farmers' subaltern passivity. As such, the hegemonic activities towards the inclusion of potential critics narrowed the field of potential alliances.

Limits of Hegemony, Limits of Resistance: The Reformist Path to Hegemonic Contestation

The WSM therefore emerged under conditions that had negative effects on the formation of unified and systematic forms of resistance. Yet, against the background of these constraints, it is misleading to depict the WSM's forms of resistance as spontaneous if this is meant to be understood as accidental or contingent. We rather have to reconstruct the process of how forms of hegemonic intervention and forms of resistance ultimately structured the process of contestation. This analysis will rely on the three analytical dimensions of hegemonic contestation as discussed in Chapter 2, beginning with the apparatus before discussing the movement's conceptions and practice.

It was the weak and fragmented apparatus that characterised the mobilisation phase of the movement. After years of muted student activism, the lack of independent organisations made it impossible to mobilise experienced activists at short notice. Instead, the initiators of the movement were in contact over PTT, a popular social media platform in Taiwan. This board consists of two sections, with PTT1 being organised along topics while users have individual boards on PTT2. The original call to assemble at the Executive Yuan was published by NTU sociology Professor Lee Ming-Tsung on his *personal* site on PTT2, from where it was forwarded to other personal boards (Hsiao 2017: 43). This meant that in the constitutive hours of the protest, mobilisation relied on activating pre-existing social networks (ibid.). Thus, it is not surprising that many of the early participants who followed the call to the Executive Yuan were NTU students closely connected to university professors, some of whom were members of the Dalawasao student group (He 2009: 120). This allowed the initial group to assemble the movement literally overnight. However, the fact that it was initiated mostly through social networks from the NTU alienated other social movement groups, especially those connected to Losheng (Ho 2011). Furthermore, the lack of organisational links to political or social forces resulted in the inability to forge alliances with workers, farmers or other subaltern groups. The movement therefore formed around NTU professors, several of whom had experienced the WLM, and a significant number of inexperienced students.

This highly fragmented and underdeveloped apparatus limited the articulation of convincing conceptions that could not only mobilise and unite but also provide a systematic analysis. Both the ideological and material factors discussed above played a role. The lack of exchange with other movements, such as Losheng, contributed to the disconnection of the WSM's conceptions from everyday life struggles, and the movement instead drew on the past (ibid.). The first indication of this is the name of the movement. While the movement was first referred to as "*TWAction 1106*" or "*Action 1106*" (the numbers referring to the first day of the movement, 6 November), it was renamed Wild Strawberry Movement on 9 November after a meeting of protesters from various movement locations (WSM 2008e). This designation is made up of two components: the label "strawberry generation" – a common description of the young generation being soft and therefore easily bruised under pressure, such as hard work – and the WLM of 1990 (Rigger 2011: 65–66). But the references to the WLM do not end here. Instead of putting the current issue of the cross-Strait rapprochement in the spotlight, the WSM presented itself as a direct continuation of the WLM that emerged during Taiwan's democratic transition. In order to evoke this historical continuity, activists articulated what they felt was the common denominator with the WLM: the struggle against a (neo)authoritarian Kuomintang. The movement's first protest statement thus begins by framing the police actions observed during the previous days in exactly this light:

> These acts have included arbitrary searches and prohibitions, seizure and destruction of property, physical assault, dispersion, and even arrest and detention. … This is a proliferation of state sponsored violence that is provoking and attacking civil society. All these oppressive acts, which ignore human rights and democratic values are reminiscent of martial law. … In only a few short days, the liberal democracy that the people of Taiwan have fought so hard for has nearly collapsed amid massive police presence in the city, and the atmosphere of fear and repression that it brings. Behind its police state-like barricades, our government remains blinded by its delusions of a 'meeting of historic proportions', and indulges itself in its receptions and banquets. Through this all, the peoples' constitutionally guaranteed rights to freedom of speech and movement have been cast aside, and even forgotten.
>
> (WSM 2008c)

It is in the light of these explicit references to the authoritarian era that the activists wanted the public to interpret the police actions of the previous days: not as a one-time misconduct by individual police officers, but rather as an indication of a structural development that was undermining Taiwan's democratic system. The statement furthermore articulates both a synchronic and a diachronic relationship.

Both are constitutively interwoven, as is best captured by a statement made by Professor Lee, the initiator of the movement, on the first night of the sit-in: "The state has stretched its evil hand into civil society where democracy has struggled for 30 years" (quoted in Beck 2010). In synchronic terms, the juncture is framed in a dichotomous "state versus civil society" opposition. It suggests that a liberal conception of the relation between state and society is at work, which ultimately made it difficult for the movement to recognise that civil society itself was the terrain on which the struggle was fought. In its diachronic dimension, the WSM is then framed as a continuation of the WLM's anti-authoritarian and pro-democratic mission. From here, a prognostic framing emerges, setting the movement on a course towards continuing the fight for democracy and human rights by way of what could be called a form of "defensive reformism".

As far as the counter-narrative is concerned, it reflected the ideological constellation at that time. Evading any contentious topics, activists proposed criticising technocratic management as autocratic management. Against the systematic de-politicisation of cross-Strait relations, as pursued by the hegemonic project, the movement attempted a conscious re-politicisation by demanding that even the technocratic management of the rapprochement had to adhere to the democratic principles of Taiwan's legal and political systems. The students were well aware of the negative and positive ideological factors discussed previously:

> The argument was framed as a human rights issue instead of a China-Taiwan issue, because of the fear that it would be too controversial – and also because President Chen was arrested in November.
>
> (R21)

These conceptions were then condensed into the movement's central demands, of which the revision of the Assembly and Parade Act merits a closer look as it provides several insights into the constitutive moments of the movement. As the authorities had justified their actions as a response to violations of the Assembly and Parade Act by protesters during the Chen Yunlin visit, it appears to be a self-evident demand. Activists argued that the functioning of Taiwanese democracy depends on a vibrant civil society, and that civil society can only function under conditions of free speech (WSM 2008a). The Assembly and Parade Act, however, curtailed this freedom by prohibiting any protest that was not permitted in advance. In the eyes of the activists, this procedure was "left over from the authoritarian days of martial law, gravely damag[ing] the right to free speech" (WSM 2008a). It is this third demand that creates a conceptual link to the authoritarian era around which the narrative of neo-authoritarianism was constructed.

It is, however, telling that the students initially had only agreed on the first two demands, an apology by Ma Ying-jeou and the resignation of police officers. The demand to revise the Assembly and Parade Act was added at the suggestion of the professors (Ho 2011). Again, the material constraints provide some context. In the absence of conscious leadership among the students, professors tipped the balance towards consolidating the "defensive reformism" that was in-spired by the WLM. It indicates the central role held by the professors in provid-ing direction in the early phase of the movement. When the movement was then "handed over" to students (Ho 2011; WSM 2008e), the movement's ideological parameters had already been defined. Over the following days, a new hierarchy of demands emerged, and by 10 November the students had made legal reform the central demand: "Emphasis is placed on demanding the revision of the Assembly and Parade Act, with the slogan 'Parade and Assembly Law is unconstitutional, human rights are disappearing'" (WSM 2008e). The framing of the WSM as a struggle for basic human rights and against the return of martial law in Taiwan had therefore been consolidated at the cost of disregarding potential alternatives, especially those that were more likely to resonate with the everyday experience of the students themselves.

The WSM echoed its assumed predecessor not only in name and conceptions, it also adopted its defining forms of practice. The characteristic feature of the WSM's practice was the return to Liberty Square in front of Taipei's Chiang Kai-shek Me-morial Hall in the form of a sit-in. It was the same location where the WLM had taken place in 1990, constituting the tradition that in order to be perceived as a so-cial movement, a protest has to assemble at that square (Lee 2017: 210–211). It also repeated the attempt to be distinctly non-partisan. Although the DPP held a protest on the same day, 6 November, activists not only refrained from coordinating these protests but also resorted to the aforementioned ban on partisan badges, banners and other signs (WSM 2008e).

The sit-in furthermore adopted direct democracy as the central decision-making process. Any decision was first debated in a thorough discussion, before being voted on in a general assembly (usually taking place each night at 7 pm). On the one hand, the practice of direct democracy was a critique *in actu* of what was perceived as autocratic management by the KMT and the opaque mode of negotia-tion across the cross-Strait channels. On the other hand, it grew out of necessity: While social media, in this case PTT, allowed for mobilising people at short no-tice, these channels were more likely to recruit movement *participants* rather than movement *organisers*, and in the absence of leaders or proven structures, direct democracy was the only possible way to set the direction of the movement (Hsiao 2017: 48). It is therefore an expression of the material constraints, in particular the weak apparatus, of the time.

This procedure contributed to discontent within the movement (R21). One par-ticipant noted that a lot of time was lost on discussing issues (Hsiao 2017: 48). The lack of representative mechanisms also favoured participants with more time at their disposal: As the composition of the group, and therefore the voting constella-tions, fluctuated throughout the day, participants who could afford to spend more time at the protest site to convince people or force votes to be held at certain times had more weight (R34). The same participant described this feature of the move-ment as "the tyranny of structurelessness" in reference to the book of the same title by Jo Freeman (R34). Furthermore, the commitment to relying on the sit-in as the central form of practice tested the endurance of the participants, contributing to a slow decline in numbers. As one participant succinctly describes:

> For the masses, the square is an open place where they come and go just as they like. If you have finished class, or are hungry or can't sleep, you go there; if you have to go to work, the weather is cold or you are tired, you leave. On an ordinary day, the scene in front of the Memorial Hall is bleak during daytime, with very few people, only the cadres remain at the scene to keep it all up; only after nightfall, you can see the crowd gradually emerge. But due to the erratic habits of the masses, no one can tell whether those who came today will vote the same as yesterday, and no one knows if those who are there at this moment will come tomorrow. The responsible ones have no power and those who have power have no responsibility. And so, the direct democracy of Wild Strawberry is destined to be a tragedy and a farce.
>
> (cited in Lee 2017: 219–220)

Other forms of practice reinforced the narrative focus on human rights. A "human rights statue" was erected at Liberty Square (Beck 2010), and regular seminars were held on the issues of democracy and human rights (WSM 2008e). Several art projects were conceived in a similar vein: Besides holding candlelight vigils to "mourn human rights in Taiwan", three students volunteered to be locked in a cage for 24 hours (WSM 2008e), and in late November participants staged a funeral service for human rights (WSM 2008b).

This emphasis did allow the establishment of links with human rights associations. It triggered messages of solidarity by the non-governmental organisations (NGOs) Amnesty International, Freedom House, Reporters without Borders and the US-based Formosan Association of Human Rights. On a more practical level, the movement was able to obtain organisational support by the TAUP and the Taiwan Bar Association for the preparation of a demonstration on 7 December (under the motto "warming up for Human Rights Day"), which was attended by 3,000 to 4,000 people. To underline their criticism of the Assembly and Parade Act, the organisers did not file for a permit before the demonstration. A concert that was held in support of the WSM took place under the slogan "Music Trumps Nationality. Human Rights Know No Borders." The movement then culminated on 10 December, the International Human Rights Day, which in the year 2008 marked the 60th anniversary of the Universal Declaration of Human Rights.

The subaltern conditions of disorganisation and intellectual subordination thus mutually reinforced each other, resulting in the movement's main contradiction, namely between the demands of the movement (necessitating a long-term perspective) and the chosen forms of practice (which were difficult to sustain in the long term). The lack of an independent apparatus necessitated the practice of direct democracy and the form of a sit-in. This proved to be difficult to sustain. By 20 November, the number of protesters in Taipei had declined to about 70 per day, while attendance at other sites reached only single digit numbers (WSM 2008f). At that time, the movement was aware that it was "at risk of losing popular support and momentum", with part of the blame being attributed to media coverage shifting to the unfolding Chen Shui-bian scandal and the resulting unfavourable politicisation of the movement (WSM 2008f).

The movement's forms of practice made the WSM susceptible to displacement and stalling. The government gladly picked up the movement's central demand of revising the Assembly and Parade Act, thus deflecting the focus away from cross-Strait negotiations in general and the Chinese delegation in particular. The government could also resort to delaying tactics: The KMT and the DPP began discussions on the amendment, and both the government and the opposition drafted bills. By the time it became clear that none of these would be submitted to a vote in parliament, the movement had already disbanded.

The limitations of the movement's conceptions can be described as a twofold subordination. First, the human rights narrative was subordinate to the current dominant ideology insofar as it focused on the political *form* of the rapprochement. As argued above, this resulted in draining the struggle of its socio-economic content, a condition that was reinforced by stating the grievances in legal terms. From an organisational perspective, this legal narrative proved too narrow: It reproduced the WSM's inability to provide points of contact that might have enabled it to include other movements and social groups, and thus consolidated the fragmentation of activist groups. Second, the subordination to the historical narrative of martial law made it too abstract, as the emphasis on historical links with the WLM came at the expense of a fresh analysis that could have made it more relatable to the broader public. Although there is ample evidence to document the particular experience of excessive police action, the attempt to universalise it and ultimately warn of the return of the martial law period did not resonate with broad strata of Taiwan's society. The Wild Lily generation had still experienced the whole weight of authoritarianism in their everyday life on campus: The Nationalist ideology was part of entry exams and undergraduate classes, students were assigned KMT-affiliated counsellors who lived among the students in the dormitories, the state controlled all campus associations and every publication had to pass a review by a committee before it could be distributed (Wright 2012: 107). Their movement was derived from experience, and it grew out of everyday practice and political activism that was anchored in these experiences. Nearly 30 years later, the claim that authoritarianism was returning hardly resonated with the everyday experience of the majority of Taiwanese.

The twofold subordination of the movement's conceptions precluded any attempt to politicise current sources of discontent, such as the economic crisis, stagnating real wages, urban renewal or land grabbing in Taiwan's rural areas. The analysis shows that this was due to the fact that neither the WSM's conceptions nor its practices were organically derived from or suited to the struggle at hand. Gramsci's distinction between organic and arbitrary ideologies can be applied to both the WSM's conceptions and practice. As the human rights narrative and the forms of practice that went along with it had been borrowed from WLM, they were the product of different social, economic and political circumstances. They had been organic to the social structure and the concrete struggles at that time. Two decades later, the same conceptions failed to resonate with the current social structure and struggles and were therefore unsuited to any attempt at effective universalisation. They had become arbitrary.

As Gramsci suggested, however, the failure of a movement may initiate a process of systematic reflection. Already at the height of the movement, the WSM's activists became aware of its shortcomings. The first group to not only articulate but also put into practice a new approach was the Wild Strawberries in Taichung. In a release dated 28 November, they addressed the limitations of both the human rights narrative and the practice relying on sit-ins:

> Through the medium of literature, music, public forum and etc., we explored the issue of human rights as the start and expanded our analysis and examination to the issues such as environmental protection and farmers' rights. … We believe that it is more effective to go into the campus and reach out to more people rather than staying in the Citizens Square and talking to the same people to mutually strengthening [sic] our belief. We will create a broader dialogue space through networking, assembly and discussions to generate resonant echoes. With the precious memory of the warmth and peace at the Citizens Square, we have also come to realize the questions and challenges ahead when we resolved to this action of outreach to the campuses and communities. Still, we are not afraid or even withdrawn because we are ready. Only by taking this action can we review, improve, break through and revitalize the movement. We want to emphasize that the switch from the sit-in at the Citizens Square to the outreach action does not mean the end of the Taichung Wild Strawberries movement. We seek for the transformation of campaign to carry on our mission.
>
> (WSM 2008d)

This statement is a strikingly accurate road map for the transformation of student activism that would unfold over the following months. Once the need to construct an independent apparatus became evident, the Taipei branch of the movement followed suit. The last sporadic sit-ins were ceased on 4 January 2009 to redirect resources to a new base in Taipei, called the WildBerry House. Conceived to serve as "the root for strawberries spreading our beliefs and ideas at the campuses and through the country" (WSM 2009), it was opened on 11 January but closed down only a few months later.

This new direction, however, continued beyond the short-lived experiment of the WildBerry House. As the students vacated the squares in Taiwan's largest cities, they set into motion a process of reflection and discussion. The list of lessons drawn from the failure of the movement consists of many items: Students vowed to maintain and consolidate contacts established during the movement (R21), expand the networks among various groups (R22), maintain common activities (R23) and train leaders or movement organisers (R24).[6] As students returned to their campus, old dormant student clubs were reactivated and new clubs were established, a process that will be discussed in the following chapter. This process was facilitated by the emergence of central hubs beyond the university campus. A case in point are spaces such as the *Go Straight Café* (2009–2012) and the *Café Philo* (2010–2016) in Taipei. By organising talks and podium discussions on a wide range of social issues, concerning both the national and the local levels, these locations served as spaces of discussion and exchange among a variety of social movements that had previously existed in their respective local contexts. These forums contributed to broadening the general interest in these issues, bringing together activists, NGOs, academia and the general public.

Finally, political and civil society organisations came to pursue a similar aim. In the light of the election defeat and the resurgence of social movements, the DPP reconsidered its relation to social movements. In February 2009, the party reopened its Department of Social Movements (R37), and chairwoman Tsai Ing-wen declared that year to be the "year of social movement" (Ho 2014: 112). A year later, the DPP-affiliated Youth Synergy Foundation was founded (ibid.: 113). By organising training workshops and common "activism field trips" with a mix of experienced and inexperienced activists, it helped to establish contact among activists, teach them techniques of social activism and bring them into contact with local grievances (R35). These activities would prove to be crucial in the articulation of organic ideological forms.

From this process of reflection emerged an ideological element that would become central to the counter-hegemonic narrative over the coming years, as activists began to refer to the rapprochement's form as a *Black Box*.[7] This was nothing other than the attempt to analytically connect the various molecular hegemonic interventions to a larger project, and this narrative would gradually replace the WSM's claim that martial law was returning to Taiwan. The notion of the *Black Box* represents a confession of the inadequacy of the dichotomous "neo-authoritarian state against civil society" narrative and at the same time expresses the realisation as well as a criticism of the opaqueness that characterises the rapprochement. It, finally, defines the task of systematically analysing the relationship of these seemingly disparate changes. Going beyond the focus on the political form of the rapprochement, the Anti-Media Monopoly Movement would move towards understanding civil society as a terrain of struggle, developing a sensitivity towards the socio-economic content and the cultural form of the hegemonic project.

Conclusion

Having failed to advance their corporate interests during both the KMT government of Lee Teng-hui and the DPP government of Chen Shui-bian, Taiwan's bourgeoisie seized the opportunity of the KMT's second consecutive electoral defeat in 2004 to initiate a common project, relying on a set of organisational and conceptual centres that can be subsumed under the notion of a hegemonic apparatus. Building on the organisational capacities of these groups, the hegemonic forces conducted an intellectual reform and reached out to the CCP. Through the KMT-CCP Forum, these political and capitalist forces were not only able to obtain material concessions from the Chinese side but also contributed to marginalising the DPP and maintaining the subaltern passivity of Taiwan's farmers. Crucially, the hegemonic activities were also instrumental in shifting the focus of the 2008 election debates from the issue of identity to that of the economy, where the KMT prevailed – not least due to its track record in negotiating with the CCP. The overwhelming election victory by Ma Ying-jeou and the KMT appeared to suggest that the rapprochement had secured broad public support. Yet, the ARATS visit in November 2008, the first tangible actualisation of the hegemonic cross-Strait channels on Taiwanese soil, became the catalyst for the social contestation of the rapprochement.

While it is certainly justified to characterise the WSM as spontaneous, it was by no means incidental or without underlying structure. It rather confirms the claim that "'pure' spontaneity does not exist in history" (Gramsci 1971: 196). In this case, the ways the leading groups had reorganised the common sense along the lines of the dominant ideology and reshaped – or more precisely: *severed* – social relations resulted in the erosion of movement apparatuses and conceptions. Consequently, the specific form of the WSM is only decipherable in the light of the hegemonic project. By tracing the effectiveness of molecular hegemonic interventions and shedding light on the contradictions that structured the resistance against it, we arrive at a richer understanding of spontaneity.

Despite its reliance on arbitrary ideologies, the WSM marks the emergence of the reformist current of social mobilisation against the cross-Strait rapprochement. With scholars and NGOs at its core, including the Taiwan Democracy Watch founded by scholars during the WSM, it proceeded to systematise the Black Box narrative from a perspective that maintained its core demands of democratic accountability and adherence to constitutional standards, but at the same time increased its organicity. The WSM's significance lies therefore not so much in its immediate success (or failure), but rather in its role as a catalyst that set into motion a process of systematic analysis in Taiwan's activist groups. It has to be concluded that the WSM did not so much end in January 2009 as it transitioned from an open to a *latent phase*. Here, the question has to be raised which factors contributed to the WSM entering a latent phase rather than fading away. This issue will be studied in more detail in the following chapters. Suffice it to outline two factors here. First, past experience had shown that the DPP was not a reliable political force to represent the concerns of social movements, especially since in 2009 another step towards "pragmatisation" was on the cards. While activists welcomed the DPP's renewed attention to movements, they were now aware that a liberal, centrist and bourgeois party would never be able to represent their various concerns. Activists vowed to maintain pressure whichever party was in power. Second, in contrast to the WLM, the WSM had not ended in success. Activists felt that their mission had not been accomplished, but at the same time were convinced that a more organised and better prepared resistance could indeed make a difference.

This analysis furthermore shows that social activism at the time was not as monolithic as some accounts suggest. The WSM in fact only represented a certain current within Taiwan's activist groups. This is not without consequences for our understanding of hegemonic contestation in Taiwan. On the one hand, it leads to a more adequate understanding of the WSM itself. It shifts our attention to the movement's inability to connect to contemporaneous activist groups, which not only explains the relative weight of WLM veterans in the movement at decisive junctures but in turn also accounts for the reliance on historical references and the human rights focus. On the other hand, the discovery of these early splits is crucial to understanding the trajectory of Taiwan's social movements over the subsequent years. In particular, it makes the tensions between the reformist and radical currents in the Sunflower Movement appear in a different light. The analysis of the movements that would unfold over the following years will therefore need to pay special attention to the respective trajectories of the currents and the relation of forces between them.

Finally, the social resistance of 2008 also marked a turning point for the hegemonic project. Despite its failure, the WSM suggested that a potential for resistance, however diffuse, existed in Taiwan's society. While the direct material inclusion of farmers had secured their passive consent, the indirect forms of material and ideological inclusion offered to the younger generations had failed to do so. The leading social and political forces therefore significantly expanded their attempts to secure consent to the cross-Strait rapprochement. The focus shifted towards the creation of a wide network of social and cultural activities, altering the character of molecular interventions to such a degree that we can speak of a qualitatively new phase of hegemonic contestation. This "Cultural Turn" raised the process of struggle to a new level and brought about new contradictions, which will be at the centre of the following chapter.

Notes

1 The foundation's board mostly consists of chairmen of Taiwanese conglomerates (see Table 4.1).
2 See for example: Wu (2002: 36), Jacobs (2012: 235) and Fell (2016: 60–62).
3 Coercive measures did, however, continue to play a role. One example is the PRC's Anti-Secession Law, which was passed in 2005 and stipulates that the PRC shall resort to non-peaceful means if Taiwan chose to declare independence, if a "major event" occurred that would result in the separation of Taiwan from China or if all possibility of peaceful unification was lost (Bellows 2005). China also applied coercive measures to individual representatives of Taiwan's bourgeoisie who had supported the DPP (see Chapter 5 and Mengin 2015: 197–199; Tanner 2006: 127–129).
4 Taiwan was eventually invited to participate in WHA meetings under the label of "Chinese Taipei" in April 2009.
5 A similar practice had been in place at the Wild Lily Movement, where it had been inspired by the 1989 Tiananmen Square protests (Chen 1998: 237; Wright 2012: 119–120).
6 Incidentally, this mirrors the aftermath of the WLM (Wright 2012: 116).
7 An early mention of this was by Tsai Ing-wen in November 2008 (see Tsai 2008).

Bibliography

Batto, Nathan F. (2014). "Continuity in the 2012 presidential and legislative elections". In: *Political Changes in Taiwan under Ma Ying-jeou. Partisan Conflict, Policy Choices, External Constraints and Security Challenges*. Ed. by Jean-Pierre Cabestan and Jacques deLisle. London and New York: Routledge, 15–36.

Baum, Julian (1992). "Flags follow trade". September 17. In: *Far Eastern Economic Review*, 155.37, 20–21.

Beck, Scott (2010). *Taiwan's Quest for Self-Determination and the Language of Resistance. An Analysis of Social Unrest in Taiwan*. http://www.kon.org/urc/v9/beck.html (last accessed on 24/03/2019).

Beckershoff, André (2014a). "The KMT-CCP Forum: Securing Consent for Cross-Strait Rapprochement". In: *Journal of Current Chinese Affairs* 43.1, 213–241.

——— (2014b). "Seizing the Transnational: Ideology, Hegemony, and the Doubling of China-Taiwan Relations". In: *Spectrum: Journal of Global Studies* 6.1, 1–21.

Bellows, Thomas J. (2005). "The Anti-Secession Law, Framing, and Political Change in Taiwan". In: *Asian Journal of Political Science* 13.2, 103–123.

Bieler, Andreas and Adam David Morton (2004). "A Critical Theory Route to Hegemony, World Order and Historical Change. Neo-Gramscian Perspectives in International Relations". In: *Capital & Class* 28.1, 85–113.

Brown, David G. (2001). "Of Economics and Elections". In: *Comparative Connections* 3.3, 73–80.

Bush, Richard C. (2013). *Uncharted Strait. The Future of China-Taiwan Relations*. Washington, DC: Brookings Institution Press.

Cabestan, Jean-Pierre (2016). "Cross-Strait integration and Taiwan's new security challenges". In: *Taiwan and the 'China Impact'. Challenges and Opportunities*. Ed. by Gunter Schubert. London and New York: Routledge, 282–300.

Central People's Government of the PRC (2006). *The State Administration for Industry and Commerce requires all localities to stop and investigate counterfeit Taiwanese fruits*. (In Chinese). 19th October 2006. http://www.gov.cn/jrzg/2006-10/19/content_418673.htm (last accessed on 06/08/2020).

——— (2007). *The Director of the Tourism Administration Shao Qiwei delivered a speech on mainland residents traveling to Taiwan*. (In Chinese). 29th April 2007. http://www.gov.cn/jrzg/2007-04/29/content_602293.htm (last accessed on 16/08/2020).

Chao, Chien-min (2004). "National Security vs. Economic Interests. Reassessing Taiwan's Mainland Policy Under Chen Shui-bian". In: *Journal of Contemporary China* 13.41, 687–704.

Chen, Chien-Kai (2018). *Political Economy of China-Taiwan Relations. Origins and Development*. Lanham, Boulder, New York, London: Lexington Books.

Chen, Hsin-Hsing (1998). "New Democracy and Old Society. A Personal Journey Through Student and Grassroots Activism in Taiwan". In: *Science as Culture* 7.2, 217–241.

Chen, Shiuan-Ju (2009). "Searching for Consensus in Cross-Strait Relations". In: *Issues & Insights* 9.4, 1–38.

Chen, Shui-bian (2000). *Taiwan Stands Up. Presidential Inauguration address*. USC US-China Institute. 20th May 2000. https://china.usc.edu/chen-shui-bian-%E2%80%9Ctaiwan-stands-presidential-inauguration-address%E2%80%9Dmay-20-2000 (last accessed on 21/08/2020).

——— (2002). "China Policy White Paper Across the Century". In: *Chinese Law & Government* 35.5, 64–88.

Cheng, Allen T. (2001). *The United States of China. How business is moving Taipei and Beijing together*. Asia Week. 6th July 2001. http://web.archive.org/web/20010709185810/http://www.asiaweek.com/asiaweek/magazine/business/0,8782,165847,00.html (last accessed on 19/08/2020).

Chien, Shiuh-Shen and Chenglin Hsieh (2010). *Political Economy of Taiwan-China Transnational Interactions. A Perspective of Provincial Exchange and Procurement*

Delegations. http://web.bp.ntu.edu.tw/DevelopmentStudies/Data/ACDS_2nd_B11.pdf (last accessed on 01/06/2012).

China Daily (2006). *US askes Taiwan to end trade limits*. 27th May 2006. http://www.chinadaily.com.cn/china/2006-05/27/content_601790.htm (last accessed on 22/07/2020).

China Post (2001). *KMT's Siew launches 'common market'*. 27th March 2001. https://chinapost.nownews.com/20010327-138825 (last accessed on 20/08/2020).

———— (2007). *China to buy 1,200 tons of surplus oranges from Taiwan*. 13th January 2007. https://chinapost.nownews.com/20070113-133684 (last accessed on 03/08/2020).

China.com.cn (2005). *The Xiamen Cross-Strait Agricultural Exchange and Cooperation Association was established on the 7th*. (In Chinese). 8th November 2005. http://www.china.com.cn/overseas/zhuanti/ln/txt/2005-11/08/content_6022710.htm (last accessed on 05/08/2020).

China.org.cn (2006). *Chinese Mainland Opens 'Green Channel' for Taiwan Farm Produce*. 31st May 2006. http://www.china.org.cn/english/features/poverty/169983.htm (last accessed on 04/08/2020).

Cross-Strait Common Market Foundation (2001a). *Introduction to the Foundation*. (In Chinese). https://web.archive.org/web/20031123190851fw_/http://www.crossstrait.org:80/version1/subpage1/sp1-5/sp1-5-2b.htm (last accessed on 12/08/2020).

———— (2001b). *The Relationship between the Cross-Strait Common Market Foundation and Enterprises*. (In Chinese). https://web.archive.org/web/20040111205436fw_/http://www.crossstrait.org:80/version1/subpage1/sp1-3d.htm (last accessed on 12/08/2020).

———— (2001c). *Understanding the Foundation*. (In Chinese). https://web.archive.org/web/20040111205029fw_/http://www.crossstrait.org:80/version1/subpage1/sp1-3c.htm (last accessed on 12/08/2020).

Dean, Jason (2004a). "Losing Business". February 19. In: *Far Eastern Economic Review*, 22–23.

———— (2004b). "The Strait Grows Wider". March 4. In: *Far Eastern Economic Review*, 24–27.

Democratic Progressive Party (1999). *White Paper on China Policy for the 21st Century*. 28th November 1999. http://www.taiwandocuments.org/dpp01.htm (last accessed on 09/08/2020).

Dolven, Ben and David Kruger (2002). "Silicon Rush". February 14. In: *Far Eastern Economic Review*, 30–34.

Dreyer, June Teufel (2006a). *The fictional 'status quo,' Part 1*. Taipei Times. 20th December 2006. https://taipeitimes.com/News/editorials/archives/2006/12/20/2003341215 (last accessed on 21/08/2020).

———— (2006b). *The fictional 'status quo,' Part 2*. Taipei Times. 21st December 2006. https://taipeitimes.com/News/editorials/archives/2006/12/21/2003341352 (last accessed on 21/08/2020).

Dumbaugh, Kerry (2008). *Taiwan's 2008 Presidential Election*. Washington, DC: Congressional Research Service.

Fell, Dafydd (2011). "The polarization of Taiwan's party competition in the DPP era". In: *Taiwan's Democracy. Economic and Political Challenges*. Ed. by Robert Ash, John W. Garver and Penelope B. Prime. London and New York: Routledge, 75–98.

———— (2016). "The China impact on Taiwan's elections. Cross-Strait economic integration through the lens of election advertising". In: *Taiwan and the 'China Impact'. Challenges and Opportunities*. Ed. by Gunter Schubert. London and New York: Routledge, 53–69.

Formosan Association for Public Affairs, ed. (2008). *Taiwan Communiqué 121*.

Gill, Stephen (1991). *American Hegemony and the Trilateral Commission*. Cambridge: Cambridge University Press.

Global Times (2010). *Mainland buys surplus fruits*. 13th June 2010. http://www.globaltimes.cn/content/541775.shtml (last accessed on 06/08/2020).

Göbel, Christian (2004). "Beheading the Hydra. Combating Political Corruption and Organised Crime". In: *China Perspectives* 56 (November/December), 14–25.

Government Information Office (2001). *Final Summary Report, Mainland Affairs Division*. Economic Development Advisory Conference. 26th August 2001. http://web.archive.org/web/20011024041557/http://www.taipei.org/press/mac0828.htm (last accessed on 10/08/2020).

Gramsci, Antonio (1971). *Selections from the Prison Notebooks*. Ed. by Quintin Hoare and Geoffrey Nowell-Smith. London: Lawrence and Wishart.

He, Donghong (2009). "My Taipei 'Wild Strawberry' Notes". (In Chinese). In: *Reflexion* 11 (February), 118–132.

Hickey, Dennis V. (2013). "Wake Up to Reality. Taiwan, the Chinese Mainland and Peace Across the Taiwan Strait". In: *Journal of Chinese Political Science* 18.1, 1–20.

Ho, Ming-sho (2005). "Taiwan's State and Social Movements under the DPP Government, 2000–2004". In: *Journal of East Asian Studies* 5.3, 401–425.

——— (2010). "Understanding the Trajectory of Social Movements in Taiwan (1980–2010)". In: *Journal of Current Chinese Affairs* 39.3, 3–22.

——— (2014). "The resurgence of social movements under the Ma Ying-jeou government. A political opportunity structure perspective". In: *Political Changes in Taiwan under Ma Ying-jeou. Partisan Conflict, Policy Choices, External Constraints and Security Challenges*. Ed. by Jean-Pierre Cabestan and Jacques deLisle. London and New York: Routledge, 100–119.

——— (2018). "The rise of civil society activism in the Ma Ying-jiu era. The genesis and outcome of the Sunflower Movement". In: *Assessing the Presidency of Ma Ying-jiu. Hopeful Beginning, Hopeless End?* Ed. by André Beckershoff and Gunter Schubert. London and New York: Routledge, 109–131.

Ho, Tung-hung (2011). *My Notes on the 'Wild Strawberries'*. http://www.erenlai.com/en/focus/2011-focus/new-energy-in-taiwans-social-movements/item/4546-my-notes-on-the-wild-strawberries.html (last accessed on 24/03/2019).

Hsiao, Yuan (2017). "Virtual ecologies, mobilization and democratic groups without leaders. Impacts of Internet media on the Wild Strawberry Movement". In: *Taiwan's Social Movements under Ma Ying-jeou. From the Wild Strawberries to the Sunflowers*. Ed. by Dafydd Fell. London and New York: Routledge, 34–53.

Hsu, Jinn-yuh (2009). "The Spatial Encounter between Neoliberalism and Populism in Taiwan. Regional Restructuring Under the DPP Regime in the New Millennium". In: *Political Geography* 28.5, 296–308.

Hu, Lingwei (2010). "The Basic Features and Challenges of Cross-Strait Relations in the New Era". In: *American Foreign Policy Interests* 32.1, 5–12.

Huang, Hsin-ta and Yeh-lih Wang (2010). *Local Factions after Twin Transitions of Government in Taiwan. Decaying or Transforming?* Paper presented at the 2010 Annual Meeting of the American Political Science Association, 2–5 September, Washington, DC. https://papers.ssrn.com/sol3/papers.cfm?abstract_id=1642470.

Huang, Wei-Hsiu (2015). "The Role of the KMT in the Ma Ying-Jeou Administration's Mainland Policy Making. A Case Study of the KMT-CPC Platform". In: *Journal of Contemporary East Asia Studies* 4.2, 93–118.

Jacob, Jabin T. (2005). "Direct Flights Take Off. Cross-Straits Relations Remain Grounded". In: *China Report* 41.3, 331–339.

Jacobs, J. Bruce (2012). *Democratizing Taiwan*. Leiden: Brill.

Jessop, Bob (1990). *State Theory. Putting the Capitalist State in its Place*. Cambridge: Polity Press.

Kao, Koong-lian (2001). *Economic links must come first*. Taipei Times. 24th January 2001. https://taipeitimes.com/News/editorials/archives/2001/01/24/0000071021 (last accessed on 17/08/2020).

Kastner, Scott L. (2004). *If trade follows the flag, why does commerce flourish across the Taiwan Strait?* Unpublished Manuscript.

Keng, Shu, Jean Yu-Chen Tseng and Qiang Yu (2017). "The Strengths of China's Charm Offensive. Changes in the Political Landscape of a Southern Taiwan Town under Attack from Chinese Economic Power". In: *The China Quarterly* 232, 956–981.

Kuomintang (2005). *Kuomintang Policy Guidelines. Democracy, Peace, New Hope*. (In Chinese). http://www1.kmt.org.tw/article.aspx?mid=33&aid=1756 (last accessed on 12/08/2020).

Lai, Shin-Yuan (2008). *Outcome and Explanation of the 2nd 'Chiang-Chen Talks'*. Mainland Affairs Council. 7th November 2008. http://www.mac.gov.tw/public/data/962917463671.pdf (last accessed on 29/07/2020).

Lee, Stanley (2017). "The Invisible Student Movement. Reflections on the History of Taiwan Student Movement and Related Issues". In: *Taiwan: A Radical Quarterly in Social Studies* 106.4, 207–224. (In Chinese).

Lee, Yoonkyung (2014). "Diverging Patterns of Democratic Representation in Korea and Taiwan. Political Parties and Social Movements". In: *Asian Survey* 54.3, 419–444.

Leng, Tse-Kang (1996). *The Taiwan-China Connection. Democracy and Development Across the Taiwan Straits*. Taipei: SMC Publishing.

Leou, Chia-feng (2006). "Financial reform under the KMT and the DPP (1996–2004). Has the DPP government done a better job?". In: *What Has Changed? Taiwan Before and After the Change in Ruling Parties*. Ed. by Dafydd Fell, Henning Klöter and Bi-yu Chang. Wiesbaden: Harrassowitz Verlag, 107–127.

——— (2011). "Democratisation and Financial Governance. The Politics of Financial Reform in Taiwan (1988–2008)". PhD Thesis. School of Oriental and African Studies, London.

Li, Chien-pin, (1998). "Domestic Bargaining in Taiwan's International Agricultural Negotiations". In: *Asian Survey* 38.6, 585–602.

Lin, Gang (1998). "China's relation with Taiwan in retrospect". In: *China Review 1998*. Ed. by Joseph Y. S. Cheng. Hong Kong: The Chinese University Press, 187–208.

Ma, Ying-jeou (2008). *Inaugural address*. USC US-China Institute. 20th May 2008. https://china.usc.edu/ma-ying-jeou-%E2%80%9Cinaugural-address%E2%80%9D-may-20-2008 (last accessed on 19/08/2020).

Mainland Affairs Council (2005a). *Mainland's Taiwan Policy and Work, 2005*. https://www.mac.gov.tw/en/News_Content.aspx?n=EE8E4A0BF2004468&sms=3591176AC6FB66EF&s=20C3FE7745F8B850 (last accessed on 05/08/2020).

——— (2005b). *Major Events across the Taiwan Strait*. 2005 July–2005 December. https://www.mac.gov.tw/en/News_Content.aspx?n=1C6028CA080A27B3&sms=6F070A2443531120&s=6B0F6BAEC6193B30 (last accessed on 16/08/2020).

——— (2006). *Major Events across the Taiwan Strait*. 2006 July–2006 December. https://www.mac.gov.tw/EN/News_Content.aspx?n=1C6028CA080A27B3&sms=6F070A2443531120&s=4773608F226124D4 (last accessed on 16/08/2020).

——— (2007). *Major Events across the Taiwan Strait.* 2007 January–2007 June. https://www.mac.gov.tw/EN/News_Content.aspx?n=1C6028CA080A27B3&sms= 6F070A2443531120&s=BE8A73D3A0435784 (last accessed on 16/08/2020).

——— (2008a). *Percentage Distribution of the Questionnaire on 'The Public's View on Current Cross-Strait Relations'.* August 2008. http://ws.mac.gov.tw/001/Upload/OldFile/ public/Attachment/96315264474.pdf (last accessed on 09/04/2019).

——— (2008b). *Percentage Distribution of the Questionnaire on 'The Public's View on Current Cross-Strait Relations'.* December 2008. http://ws.mac.gov.tw/001/Upload/ OldFile/public/Attachment/96314575479.pdf (last accessed on 09/04/2019).

——— (2009). *Combined Analysis Report on Public Opinion Surveys on Cross-Strait Relations in 2008.* January 19, 2009. https://ws.mac.gov.tw/001/Upload/OldFile/public/ Attachment/96314283469.pdf (last accessed on 09/04/2019).

Mao, Yu-kang and Chaw-hsia Tu (1993). "Current agricultural problems and policies of Taiwan". In: *Agricultural Policy and U.S.-Taiwan Trade.* Ed. by D. Gale Johnson and Chi-ming Hou. Washington, DC: The AEI Press, 79–105.

McGann, James (2009). *Think Tanks and Civil Society in Mainland China, Hong Kong, and Taiwan.* Philadelphia: Foreign Policy Research Institute.

Mengin, Françoise (2015). *Fragments of an Unfinished War. Taiwanese Entrepreneurs and the Partition of China.* Oxford: Oxford University Press.

Ministry of Commerce of the PRC (2007). *Joint Proposals of the Third Cross-Strait Economic, Trade and Cultural Forum.* (In Chinese). Department of Taiwan, Hong Kong and Macao Affairs. 30th April 2007. http://tga.mofcom.gov.cn/article/zt_jmwhlt/subjectkk/ 200704/20070404629127.shtml (last accessed on 16/08/2020).

National Institute for Defense Studies (2002). *East Asian Strategic Review 2002.* Tokyo: Ministry of Defense.

National Policy Foundation (2005). *The Twelve-Point Consensus between Vice Chairman Chiang Pin-kung's delegation and Director Chen Yunlin.* (In Chinese). https://www.npf. org.tw/5/21 (last accessed on 13/08/2020).

——— (2009). *The National Policy Foundation.* Taipei: National Policy Foundation.

Ngo, Tak-Wing (1995). "Business Encirclement of Politics. Government-Business Relations across the Taiwan Strait". In: *China Information* 10.2, 1–18.

Office of the President, Republic of China (Taiwan) (2001). *The Office of the President Makes Public the List of 125 EDAC Members.* 19th July 2001. https://english.president. gov.tw/NEWS/784 (last accessed on 10/08/2020).

——— (2014). *President Ma meets Professor Kishore Mahbubani, Dean of Lee Kuan Yew School of Public Policy at National University of Singapore.* 27th November 2014. https://english.president.gov.tw/NEWS/4541 (last accessed on 29/07/2020).

Pan, Chun-Ying (2005). "The Preliminary Study of Taiwan Peasants-Movement". (In Chinese). Unpublished Thesis. National Taiwan Normal University.

People's Daily (2010). *Economist: ECFA to boost cross-Strait agricultural cooperation.* 15th July 2010. http://en.people.cn/90001/90776/90882/7067549.html (last accessed on 04/08/2020).

Poong, Hwei-luan (2008). "State and business in the high-tech industry. A case study of technical standard setting". In: *Cross-Strait at the Turning Point. Institution, Identity and Democracy.* Ed. by I Yuan. Taipei: Institute of International Relations, National Chengchi University, 294–315.

Rigger, Shelley (2001a). *From Opposition to Power. Taiwan's Democratic Progressive Party.* Boulder: Lynne Rienner Publishers.

———— (2001b). "Regional Perspectives and Domestic Imperatives. Maintaining the Status Quo: What It Means, and Why the Taiwanese Prefer It". In: *Cambridge Review of International Affairs* 14.2, 103–114.

———— (2001c). "The Democratic Progressive Party in 2000. Obstacles and Opportunities". In: *The China Quarterly* 168, 944–959.

———— (2003). "Taiwan in 2002. Another Year of Political Droughts and Typhoons". In: *Asian Survey* 43.1, 41–48.

———— (2004). "Taiwan in 2003. Plenty of Clouds, Few Silver Linings". In: *Asian Survey* 44.1, 182–187.

———— (2011). "Looking Toward the Future in the Taiwan Strait. Generational Politics in Taiwan". In: *SAIS Review of International Affairs* 31.2, 65–77.

Romberg, Alan D. (2009). "Cross-Strait Relations. 'Ascend the Heights and Take a Long-Term Perspective'". In: *China Leadership Monitor* 27.

———— (2010). "All Economics is Political. ECFA Front and Center". In: *China Leadership Monitor* 32.

Sato, Yukihito (2004). "Democratization and Financial Reform in Taiwan. The Political Economy of Bad-Loan Creation". In: *The Developing Economies* 40.3, 226–251.

Siew, Vincent (2001). *Toward the Creation of a 'Cross-Strait Common Market'*. Cross-Strait Common Market Foundation. https://web.archive.org/web/20130901031240/http://crossstrait.org/version3/index.html (last accessed on 05/12/2019).

Sina.com (2005a). *Lien Chan's speech to representatives of Taiwanese Business Associations*. (In Chinese). 3rd May 2005. http://news.sina.com.cn/c/2005-05-03/10065806299s.shtml (last accessed on 21/08/2020).

———— (2005b). *The 2005 Cross-Strait Agricultural Cooperation Forum will open in Chengdu today*. (In Chinese). 19th October 2005. http://news.sina.com.cn/c/2005-10-19/07257204798s.shtml (last accessed on 05/08/2020).

Sutter, Karen M. (2002). "Business Dynamism Across the Taiwan Strait. The Implications for Cross-Strait Relations". In: *Asian Survey* 42.3, 522–540.

Taipei Times (2000). *Wang Yung-ching slams politicians over economy*. 24th November 2000. http://www.taipeitimes.com/News/biz/archives/2000/11/24/0000062822 (last accessed on 29/11/2015).

———— (2001a). *Amendment aims to clean up farmers' associations*. 5th January 2001. http://www.taipeitimes.com/News/front/archives/2001/01/05/0000068471 (last accessed on 04/08/2020).

———— (2001b). *Chang's change of heart sign of China's chip boom*. 2nd October 2001. https://taipeitimes.com/News/twbiz/archives/2001/10/02/0000105453 (last accessed on 22/08/2020).

———— (2001c). *DPP's advisors call for change to China trade*. 28th July 2001. https://taipeitimes.com/News/local/archives/2001/07/28/0000096045 (last accessed on 19/08/2020).

———— (2001d). *Formosa's Wang says 'one China' must be accepted*. 20th June 2001. http://www.taipeitimes.com/News/front/archives/2001/06/20/0000090748 (last accessed on 29/11/2015).

———— (2001e). *Panel clashes on China*. 1st August 2001. https://taipeitimes.com/News/biz/archives/2001/08/01/0000096699 (last accessed on 19/08/2020).

———— (2001f). *Siew sees economics as key to China ties*. 31st March 2001. https://taipeitimes.com/News/local/archives/2001/03/31/0000079786 (last accessed on 20/08/2020).

——— (2003). *Lien promises loyalty to Republic of China.* 24th October 2003. https://taipeitimes.com/News/taiwan/archives/2003/10/24/2003073117 (last accessed on 22/08/2020).

——— (2004). *Evergreen tycoon switches support from Chen to Lien.* 20th March 2004. https://www.taipeitimes.com/News/taiwan/archives/2004/03/20/2003107050 (last accessed on 10/08/2020).

——— (2005a). *MAC says it won't send envoys to Beijing fruit talks.* 25th July 2005. https://taipeitimes.com/News/taiwan/archives/2005/07/25/2003264964 (last accessed on 15/08/2020).

——— (2005b). *Taiwan's economy needs change, urgently: ECCT.* 27th October 2005. http://www.taipeitimes.com/News/biz/archives/2005/10/27/2003277614 (last accessed on 22/08/2020).

——— (2012). *TAITRA to use traditional dishes to promote milkfish.* 25th March 2012. http://www.taipeitimes.com/News/taiwan/archives/2012/03/25/2003528667 (last accessed on 08/08/2020).

Taiwan Affairs Office of the State Council, PRC (2005). *Press Communiqué on Hu Jintao's Talks with Lien Chan.* (In Chinese). 29th April 2005. http://www.gwytb.gov.cn/speech/speech/201101/t20110123_1723800.htm (last accessed on 17/08/2020).

——— (2006). *Press Conference (2006-5-17).* (In Chinese). 17th May 2006. http://www.gwytb.gov.cn/xwfbh/201101/t20110106_1679257.htm (last accessed on 04/08/2020).

Taiwan News (2010). *No 'peace dividend' for Taiwan people.* 8th January 2010. https://www.taiwannews.com.tw/en/news/1150087 (last accessed on 23/08/2020).

Taiwan.cn (2006a). *Common proposal passed at cross-Straits agricultural co-op forum.* 18th October 2006. http://big5.taiwan.cn/english/key/sr/af/Focus/200905/t20090507_889421.htm (last accessed on 06/08/2020).

——— (2006b). *Taiwan Affairs Office of the State Council: The mainland is actively implementing the results of the Cross-Strait Agricultural Cooperation Forum.* (In Chinese). 15th November 2006. http://www.taiwan.cn/jm/ny/xgpl/200611/t20061115_319877.htm (last accessed on 06/08/2020).

——— (2006c). *The mainland launched 20 new policies and measures to expand and deepen and cross-strait agricultural cooperation.* (In Chinese). 17th October 2006. http://agri.taiwan.cn/zcfg/201311/t20131119_5226673.htm (last accessed on 06/08/2020).

——— (2007). *List of Representatives of the Third Cross-Strait Economic, Trade and Cultural Forum.* (In Chinese). 28th April 2007. http://big5.taiwan.cn/zt/jmkj/3lajmwhlt/jmltdbmd/200807/t20080725_708050.htm (last accessed on 16/08/2020).

Tanner, Murray Scot (2006). *Chinese Economic Coercion against Taiwan. A Tricky Weapon to Use.* Santa Monica: RAND Corporation.

Third Wednesday Club (2020). *Introduction of San-San-Fe.* http://www.sansanfe.org.tw/english/ (last accessed on 13/08/2020).

Tsai, Ing-wen (2008). *Chairperson Tsai Ing-wen's summary of the Yellow Ribbon Siege.* (In Chinese). 8th November 2008. https://www.facebook.com/notes/1023538741392685/ (last accessed on 04/04/2019).

Tsai, Ting-I (2005). *The Beijing-Taipei fruit fracas.* Asia Times. 26th August 2005. http://web.archive.org/web/20161112142402/http://www.atimes.com/atimes/China/GH26Ad02.html (last accessed on 05/08/2020).

Tseng, Chien-yuan (2016). "Exposing the 'One China' Principle". In: *Contemporary Chinese Political Economy and Strategic Relations. An International Journal* 2.3, 1217–1224.

Tung, Chen-yuan (2005). *Cross-Strait Charter Flights Arrangement. A viable Model for Taiwan-China Negotiation?* UNISCI Discussion Papers No. 9.

Wade, Robert (1990). *Governing the Market. Economic Theory and the Role of Government in East Asian Industrialization*. Princeton: Princeton University Press.

Wang, Yung-chin (2001). *Face Taiwan's economic situation and take necessary counter-measures*. (In Chinese). http://www2.fpg.com.tw/html/mgz/abu/abu_pdw_dtl11.htm (last accessed on 08/08/2020).

Wei, Chi-hung (2013). "China's Economic Offensive and Taiwan's Defensive Measures. Cross-Strait Fruit Trade, 2005-2008". In: *The China Quarterly* 215, 641–662.

——— (2015). "Producing and Reproducing the 1992 Consensus. The Sociolinguistic Construction of the Political Economy of China-Taiwan Relations". In: *Asian Security* 11.1, 72–88.

——— (2016). "China-Taiwan Relations and the 1992 Consensus, 2000–2008". In: *International Relations of the Asia-Pacific* 16.1, 67–95.

Wei, Mei-Chuan, Yao-Nan Hung and Chen-Yuan Tung (2016). "The Economicization of the Cross-Strait Relationship. The Impact of the Cross-Strait Economic Relationship on the 2012 Presidential Election in Taiwan". In: *Issues & Studies* 52.2, 1–29.

Wild Strawberry Movement (2008a). *Action Statement 1108*. 10th November 2008. http://taiwanstudentmovement2008.blogspot.com/2008/11/action-statement-1108.html (last accessed on 12/12/2017).

——— (2008b). *Lament for Civil Rights*. 21st November 2008. http://taiwanstudentmovement2008.blogspot.com/2008/11/ode-to-death-of-civil-rights.html (last accessed on 12/12/2017).

——— (2008c). *Protest Statement*. 10th November 2008. http://taiwanstudentmovement2008.blogspot.com/2008/11/protest-statement.html (last accessed on 12/12/2017).

——— (2008d). *The Transformation of the Taichung Wild Strawberries*. 30th November 2008. http://taiwanstudentmovement2008.blogspot.com/2008/11/rationale-transformation-of-taichung.html (last accessed on 12/12/2017).

——— (2008e). *Wild Strawberries Major Events*. 3rd December 2008. http://taiwanstudentmovement2008.blogspot.com/2008/12/wild-strawberries-major-events-113-121.html (last accessed on 12/12/2017).

——— (2008f). *Wild Strawberries Movement Situation Report*. 21st November 2008. http://taiwanstudentmovement2008.blogspot.com/2008/11/nov-20-taipei-wild-strawberries.html (last accessed on 12/12/2017).

——— (2009). *Opening Ceremony of WildBerry House*. 11th January 2009. http://taiwanstudentmovement2008.blogspot.com/2009/01/opening-ceremony-of-wildberry-house.html (last accessed on 24/03/2019).

Wong, Stan Hok-wui and Nicole Wu (2016). "Can Beijing Buy Taiwan? An Empirical Assessment of Beijing's Agricultural Trade Concessions to Taiwan". In: *Journal of Contemporary China* 25.99, 353–371.

Wright, Teresa (1999). "Student Mobilization in Taiwan. Civil Society and Its Discontents". In: *Asian Survey* 39.6, 986–1008.

——— (2012). "Taiwan: Resisting control of campus and polity. Between protest and powerlessness". In: *Student Activism in Asia*. Ed. by Meredith L. Weiss and Edward Aspinall. Minneapolis: University of Minnesota Press, 101–124.

Wu, Joseph (2004). *Independence is the real status quo*. Taipei Times. 6th January 2004. https://taipeitimes.com/News/editorials/archives/2004/01/06/2003086572 (last accessed on 21/08/2020).

Wu, Yu-Shan (1999). "Taiwanese Elections and Cross-Strait Relations. Mainland Policy in Flux". In: *Asian Survey* 39.4, 565–587.

——— (2001). "Taiwan in 2000. Managing the Aftershocks from Power Transfer". In: *Asian Survey* 41.1, 40–48.

——— (2002). "Taiwan in 2001. Stalemated on All Fronts". In: *Asian Survey* 42.1, 29–88.

Yang, Mengyu (2001). *Taiwan National Policy Adviser urges recognition of One China Principle*. (In Chinese). BBC. 21st July 2001. http://news.bbc.co.uk/hi/chinese/news/newsid_1450000/14500831.stm (last accessed on 19/08/2020).

Yep, Ray and Ma Ngok (2006). "Money, Power and Ideas. Think Tank Development and State-Business Relations in Taiwan and Hong Kong". In: *Policy & Politics* 34.3, 535–555.

5 The Contested Emergence of the China Factor

Resisting the Cultural Dimension of the Rapprochement

The years following the Wild Strawberry Movement did not see an immediate renewal of large-scale direct contestation. The absence of open struggle, however, should not be mistaken for the inactivity or decline of either the hegemonic or the subaltern groups. Rather, as this chapter will demonstrate, the Anti-Media Monopoly Movement of 2012 was preceded by a latent phase that was marked, on the one hand, by a significant transformation of hegemonic activities and, on the other, by the establishment of local dissident groups, the formation of networks among them, the training of cadres and attempts to systematically articulate conceptions that were able to express the experiences of the previous years

During this latent phase, the site of struggle shifted towards the realm of culture. A first pebble that would signal the oncoming avalanche was loosened in September 2010 when the acting governor of Shaanxi province led a business delegation consisting of 500 members to Taiwan. Over the course of a week, the Chinese delegation met with KMT and business leaders, visited science and industrial parks and signed procurement deals worth US$800 million. On the surface, this appears to be another of the procurement missions discussed in Chapter 4. This particular visit, however, exhibited a number of characteristics that went beyond the previous cases. First, we can observe a new emphasis on the cultural dimension of cross-Strait relations. In addition to meeting with Taiwan's political and capitalist elites, the delegation also visited universities and schools and attended cultural events that addressed the historical links between Shaanxi and Taiwan (Chien and Hsieh 2010: 9). Second, the visit was accompanied by extensive and favourable coverage in several of Taiwan's major daily newspapers, including a three-page special report in the China Times (Engbarth 2011). As it would later turn out, official Chinese agencies had paid for these reports, which were disguised as news coverage rather than being marked as advertisements. This practice of embedded marketing, or advertorials, would become the first point of nucleation for the AMM that would erupt two years after these events.

This episode exemplifies two aspects that will be more closely studied in this chapter. First, it marks the expansion of hegemonic activities into Taiwan's civil society proper. While the rapprochement was driven by social forces organising within Taiwan's civil society even before 2009, the hegemonic project had

DOI: 10.4324/9781003395546-5

attempted to maintain the narrative of a "Status Quo." According to this narrative, the transformation of cross-Strait relations necessitated the management of technical aspects by a state bureaucracy drained of all particular social interests while shielding Taiwan's political and civil society. After the challenge of the WSM, however, the rapprochement increasingly relied on molecular interventions that were directly aimed at transforming Taiwan's civil society. These dynamics, amounting to what will be referred to as the "Cultural Turn" of the hegemonic project, represent a qualitatively new stage of hegemony, the workings of which require being studied in more detail. Second, unlike the sudden eruption of the WSM, the AMM was the culmination of a series of low-intensity mobilisations in response to these refined instruments of molecular intervention. Although these separate moments of resistance would ultimately be forged into a broader alliance, the movement was in no way as homogeneous as some studies suggest. Rather, the various points of nucleation engendered a number of movement currents that evolved along distinct trajectories, developing different and at times competing conceptions and forms of practice. The integration of these currents not only proved to be a challenge for the social movement but also shaped the open phase of hegemonic contestation in substantial ways.

The analysis of these aspects will lead us to the question regarding the social and political character of the AMM, best illustrated by its relation to the issue of China. While the WSM was characterised by its attempt to avoid raising the China question, the extant literature unequivocally agrees that it was the AMM that introduced the "China Factor" as a counter-hegemonic principle into Taiwan's social movement environment (e.g., Rawnsley and Feng 2014: 108; Yuen 2014: 74; Kaeding 2015: 211; Rawnsley et al. 2016; Ebsworth 2017: 74; Wu 2017: 437; Ho 2018: 115–116; Wong and Wright 2018: 89). This characterisation, however, comes with a caveat: Just as the movement was not as homogeneous as often portrayed in this body of literature, the China Factor was arguably not a conceptual fixture of the AMM. It only emerged *after* the high point of mobilisation, and even then, it was fiercely contested within the movement. This assumption of fixed ideological conceptions and homogeneity obscures the internal tensions within the movement and with it a decisive source of dynamics of this phase of contestation. To avoid reifying the China Factor as the central organising principle of the AMM, this chapter will instead seek to analyse it as a *product* of contestation not only between hegemonic and resisting groups but also among the latter. Only if we carefully reconstruct the tensions within the movement rather than obscuring them, can we shed light on its puzzling aspects: Why did the movement abandon the strategy of continuously occupying a public space in favour of more selective and momentary actions? And why did the issue of China now dominate the movement's conceptions, after activists had actively avoided it during the WSM?

To answer these questions, it is inadequate to take the China Factor as a point of departure, nor is it sufficient to simply attribute its emergence to the inventiveness of the dissident groups. Following Luxemburg's (2019: 286) argument that the form of contestation reflects its material conditions rather than simply the creativity of activists, this chapter seeks to understand how the apparatus, conceptions and forms of practice mutually evolved under the condition of molecular interventions by the hegemonic project. It will argue that, first, the hegemonic shift towards the realm of culture was both a reaction to the WSM and a catalyst to the emergence of the AMM. Second, despite various alternatives student groups ultimately relied on Taiwanese nationalism in the form of the China Factor, because it was able to politicise both the Chinese nationalism promoted by the hegemonic project and the supposedly "apolitical" pragmatism that had spread among Taiwan's subaltern classes. And, third, that it was the long phase of accumulation of grievances that gave rise to several points of nucleation and thereby structured the terrain of struggle even before the student dissident groups entered the scene. It was therefore only after the high point of the broad movement that the students could assert their ideological perspective which had emerged from their organisational proximity to a select few organic intellectuals.

To this end, the following section aims to understand why and how hegemony changed after 2008. This includes an analysis of the adjustments of the hegemonic apparatus, hegemonic activities as well as the rationale behind the renewed emphasis on culture. Section two will trace how the adjustments to the hegemonic apparatus made in reaction to the challenge of social contestation enabled new forms of hegemonic activities. Studying new forms of molecular interventions, such as the intensification of people-to-people exchanges, but especially the increasing cross-Strait cooperation in the media sector, will help us account for the shift of the site of hegemonic contestation and the resulting effects on ideology and politics. Section three provides a reconstruction of the latent phase of the social movement in Taiwan, with an emphasis on the establishment of structures of cooperation. The fourth and final section will then integrate these insights into a process analysis of the AMM. This chapter will pay particular attention to potential alternatives, contradictions and tensions that arose within the movement and therefore propelled it forward.

The Cultural Turn of the Hegemonic Project

In the aftermath of the Wild Strawberry Movement, the forms of hegemonic intervention changed profoundly. The first KMT-CCP Forum after the WSM, held in July 2009 in Changsha, initiated a shift towards the cultural dimension of the rapprochement. Instead of the previous focus on agriculture and economic cooperation, issues of education, people-to-people exchanges and media cooperation dominated the agenda. The following year, the second edition of the Straits Forum took place in Fujian province with a distinct focus on culture, bringing together Taiwanese and Chinese organisations from the realms of religion, art, literature as well as print and broadcasting media. These developments signalled a remarkable shift from economic competitiveness to common cultural heritage and a renewed emphasis on Chinese nationalism.

The simple reference to a common cultural heritage shared by Taiwan and China was not a new element in cross-Strait interactions. Already the PRC's 'Message to compatriots in Taiwan' of 1979 focused on kinship (Hughes 2014: 125–126), before it became a leitmotif of the rapprochement as cross-Strait interactions began to intensify in the late 1980s and 1990s. When Vincent Siew (2001) outlined his vision of a common market across the Taiwan Strait in 2001, he suggested that "collective cultural heritage and traditions" were a crucial dimension of the project. Arguing that "[c]ooperative economic and trade relations will develop naturally where there is complementarity in economic conditions and similar cultural and social backgrounds among producers" and that, conversely, "economic unity would encourage the development of social and cultural coalitions, and pave the way for political integration" (ibid.), he established the view that the economic and cultural dimensions of the rapprochement not only were mutually reinforcing but that the latter also contributed to the naturalisation of the former.

Subsequently, the ice-breaking meeting between Lien Chan and Hu Jintao in 2005 adopted Chinese nationalism as the foundation of party-to-party negotiations (Wu 2011: 64): Both sides of the Taiwan Strait were seen as "descendants of the Yellow Emperor" (Hughes 2014: 125) and therefore shared the historical mission to achieve "the great rejuvenation of the Chinese Nation." The KMT-CCP Forum that emerged from these exchanges inherited this ambition, as is reflected in its formal title "Cross-Strait Economic, Trade and Culture Forum."

And yet, despite these continuities the year 2009 marks a significant break. Previously, the cultural element was largely limited to the purely discursive level, and it was the economic element that dominated the material dimension of cross-Strait interactions. The qualitatively new element of what effectively amounts to the "Cultural Turn" of the hegemonic project consists of the attempt to provide a material structure specifically designed to promote a resonance between the conceptions of the hegemonic project (articulated ideology) and the everyday conduct of people affected by it (lived ideology).

This transformation can be attributed to two developments that coincided in the years after 2008. On the one hand, the most urgent demands of Taiwanese capital had been met: Crucial agreements on direct transportation links had been implemented within the first year of the Ma Ying-jeou government, agreements on investment protection and financial cooperation had recently been signed, and the negotiations on the ECFA were well underway. At the same time, the direct provision of benefits had contributed to keeping crucial potentially counter-hegemonic groups, such as Taiwan's farmers, in a state of subaltern passivity. With these initial goals having been realised and the KMT in power, the hegemonic project could move towards expanding its aims – from a focus on conditions of accumulation to conditions of reproduction – and refining its means accordingly. On the other hand, not only the timing but also the form and content of the Cultural Turn suggest that it was a systematic reaction to the challenge of the Wild Strawberry Movement. The very fact of social resistance itself had suggested the incompleteness and precariousness of hegemonic inclusion. The movement implicitly challenged not only the social form of the rapprochement, namely elite negotiations behind closed doors without any meaningful participation of subaltern groups, it also presented a critique of the rapprochement's content, namely the focus on elite interest that served Taiwan's interior and national bourgeoisie. As will become apparent in this chapter, the Cultural Turn sought to address precisely these critiques.

From a Gramscian perspective, this turn towards cultural issues can be interpreted as a shift in the strategies of universalisation from inclusion to naturalisation. Naturalisation refers to the attempt to obscure the particular character of the interests that drive social dynamics by depicting them not as the outcome of social struggle but as natural or at least "apolitical" developments that are independent of relations of domination and exploitation. Until the WSM, the universalisation of the rapprochement depended on portraying it as the disinterested management of technocratic issues that was agnostic to political and class interests and arose as the by-product of a quasi-natural increase of economic exchanges. In its material dimension, this narrative relied on the attempt to include potentially sceptical social forces through the direct provision of benefits. The WSM, however, showed that the "22k generation," named after the monthly wage a university graduate could expect, had not been successfully included and went on to challenge – albeit in incomplete and contradictory ways – the elitist and exclusive form of the rapprochement, which operated not only under the exclusion but also to the detriment of subaltern classes and Taiwan's democracy.

In response, the narrative of quasi-natural economic integration was amended by a narrative of a shared culture, which can be summarised as follows: It is not the particular interests of capitalist and political elites that drive the rapprochement, but a common historical destiny of the Chinese people, which had been separated by historical tragedy. Despite temporary political differences, both sides share a language, a history as well as relations of kinship, and both sides would be better off once this wound had been healed. In contrast to the rather bland narrative of technocratic management, the Cultural Turn sought to mobilise the affective dimension of these cultural resources to enthuse the Taiwanese people even where immediate economic and material opportunities failed to materialise.

Crucially, the Cultural Turn was more than a revision or expansion of the rapprochement's discursive elements. It was, rather, a refinement of the instruments of molecular intervention – to be discussed in detail below – that were designed to introduce new ways of acting, thinking and feeling. In Gramsci's (1971: 348) words, these have to be understood as elements of a "cultural battle to transform the popular 'mentality'". Gramsci emphasises that introducing elements of the "official ideologies" (i.e., as articulated by the organic intellectuals of hegemonic groups) into the common sense is facilitated if forms of practice that resonate with these ideologies are already in place. The key to understanding the Cultural Turn of the hegemonic project, therefore, does not lie in the analysis of its *discursive* but rather its *material* dimension, i.e., the introduction of new forms of practice. The following sections will examine the efficacy of molecular interventions to mould routines and practically organise the ways people relate to each other.

To this end, it is helpful to trace the molecular operation from the hegemonic centres to their effect on concrete social relations and forms of practice. As it is the revised apparatus that enables new forms of hegemonic interventions, the account of such a process has to begin with the adjustments made to it. While the KMT-CCP Forum was retained as the organisational centre of the rapprochement, the new phase was characterised by a proliferation of subordinate channels across the

Taiwan Strait, most of which focused on social groups that had previously been ignored, including Taiwan's youth, workers and women. In contrast to the direct provision of benefits designed to secure the consent of Taiwan's farmers, the hegemonic project increasingly relied on indirect forms of inclusion through market forces and the dissemination of forms of social practice.

Although the KMT-CCP Forum had achieved its primary goal – the marginalisation of the Taiwan independence movement and the KMT's return to power – the channel was not suspended after the 2008 Taiwanese elections. In an attempt to avoid the party-to-party platform becoming a separate power centre, however, the Ma government moved towards enclosing it in a tight corset (R5). To reduce the impact of his prestige and close relations to Chinese leaders, KMT Honorary Chairman Lien Chan was now accompanied by KMT chairman Wu Poh-hsiung (Romberg 2008: 8). Furthermore, the government asserted its presence in the forum. The agenda, previously set by the NPF, was now partly defined by the government to include issues raised by the MAC, the SEF and the National Security Council (NSC) (R18). Furthermore, the delegation now included representatives of Taiwan's executive branch, such as high-level representatives of the CEPD, the Financial Supervisory Commission and other cabinet-level agencies with interests in cross-Strait affairs (Beckershoff 2014: 224). The inclusion of KMT legislators also ensured a tight interlock with the legislative branch. Finally, the resumption of SEF-ARATS talks enabled the organisers of the forum to delegate some of the more technical negotiations, thus releasing resources for a re-orientation of party-to-party talks. As a result, the government strengthened its role in the forum at the expense of the KMT party apparatus (R17). Conversely, major architects of the hegemonic apparatus assumed positions in Taiwan's state apparatus: Chiang Pin-kung (TWC and NPF) and Kao Koong-lian (NPF) led the Straits Exchange Foundation, Su Chi moved to the NSC and Vincent Siew became Vice President. Lien Chan, who had initiated the reorganisation of the NPF and the party-to-party platform, represented Taiwan at Asia-Pacific Economic Cooperation between 2008 and 2012, meeting Hu Jintao five times.

The 2009 edition of the forum in Changsha is characterised by a shift from agricultural and economic issues, which had dominated the agendas over the previous years, to the topics of culture, media, education and society. The announced purpose of the forum was to deepen educational and cultural cooperation, thought to be of "far-reaching significance for the continued peaceful development of cross-Strait relations" (NPF 2009), and the common legacy of Chinese culture was chosen to serve as the ideological "cement" (Gramsci 1971: 328) that could unify the various elements of the rapprochement into one coherent project:

> An enduring and brilliant Chinese culture is our common legacy. It is an important link joining people on both sides. Given these new circumstances, we should promote and deepen cross-Strait cultural and educational exchanges and cooperation, encourage identification with Chinese culture, and create a new era for the Chinese nation.
>
> (NPF 2009)

This re-orientation is reflected in the composition of the delegations. At the fourth forum, held the previous year in Shanghai, only 27 (or 7.2 per cent) of the 377 participants were affiliated with the educational or cultural sectors.[1] The majority of these were representatives of universities of either side of the Strait. In Changsha, 247 (or 46.3 per cent) of the 534 participants were now representing the educational, cultural and media sectors. Furthermore, the diversity within the sectors was increased. Whereas in the previous meeting, participants from these sectors mainly came from a few select key institutions, the educational sector was now represented by delegation members from primary and middle schools, vocational colleges and language institutes. In addition to professors, teachers and administrative staff, 60 students from Chinese and Taiwanese universities participated. Beyond the educational sector, the delegations covered cultural foundations, museums, art galleries, operas, theatres, as well as dance and ballet groups. Furthermore, nine religious groups were present, covering Christian, Buddhist and Daoist denominations. Finally, the delegations included members of the press, publishing, film production, television drama and animation industries.

While the minutes of the negotiations are not publicly available, the closing declaration confirms that cultural issues were at the centre of the Changsha forum. The first five of the six joint recommendations, the central instrument through which the forum expresses consensus and aligns parties and governments on both sides, deal with cultural exchanges and cooperation. The first four recommendations call for both sides to encourage the organisation of festivals and fairs, create a common cultural industry to increase the cooperation in television and film production, promote educational exchanges and facilitate the mutual recognition of academic credits and degrees. The shortest of the five recommendations, finally, addresses the issue that would prove to be the most contentious over the following years and result in the AMM: Both governments were advised to "encourage the media to strengthen exchanges and cooperation across the Strait" (NPF 2009). This set of tasks represents the founding document and roadmap of the hegemonic project's Cultural Turn. It aims to advance the fusion of cultural, economic and political aspects of the hegemonic narrative by establishing the material infrastructure capable of promoting media and educational cooperation as well as the intensification of people-to-people exchanges.

A crucial element of the hegemonic apparatus that would be tasked with the implementation of this roadmap is the Straits Forum. The Straits Forum was first held in 2009 and quickly became a central pillar of the cross-Strait rapprochement. At first glance, it stands in stark contrast to the two other organisational centres of the rapprochement, the KMT-CCP and the SEF-ARATS channels, in almost every respect. While the party-to-party channel has a monolithic structure, the Straits Forum is de-centralised. It is conceived as a platform for about three dozen events (see Table 5.1) that are spread over several cities in Fujian province. In contrast to the exclusive character of the KMT-CCP and the SEF-ARATS channels, the new forum is open to people from all walks of life, operating as a mass event that is co-hosted by 60 organisations from both China and Taiwan and, according to official statements, brings roughly 10,000 Taiwanese to China each year. The

Table 5.1 Selection of sub-fora at the Straits Forum, 2009–2019

Title	'09	'10	'11	'12	'13	'14	'15	'16	'17	'18	'19
Economic sub-fora											
Cross-Strait Maritime Transportation	•										
Cross-Strait Tourism Forum	•	•									
(Pingtan Tourism Development Seminar)		•									
Cross-Strait Air Transport Development Roundtable		•									
Straits Financial Forum		•	•		•	•	•	•	•	•	•
Cross-Strait Accounting Forum			•								
Straits Real Estate Forum			•								
Cross-Strait Logistics Forum				•	•						
Straits Science and Technology Expert Forum				•	•	•	•	•	•	•	•
Cross-Strait Common Home Forum						•	•	•	•	•	•
Cross-Strait Entrepreneurship and Venture Capital Development Forum							•	•			
Cross-Strait Economic and Trade Industry Association Meeting (Cross-Strait Chamber of Commerce Economic Forum)	•			•							
Media, culture and education sub-fora											
Cross-Strait Film and Television Exhibition (Film and TV Production Summit)	•	•	•	•	•	•	•	•	•	•	•
Strait Press and Publication Industry Development Forum		•	•	•							
Chinese Medicine Development and Cooperation Seminar	•	•	•	•							
Cross-Strait University Symposium						•	•	•			
Cross-Strait Vocational Education Forum					•	•					
Koxinga Cultural Festival	•		•	•							
Martial Arts Competition	•		•	•						•	•
Cross-Strait Hakka Summit		•	•						•	•	•
Mazu Cultural Activity Week	•	•	•					•			•

(Continued)

Table 5.1 (Continued)

Title	'09	'10	'11	'12	'13	'14	'15	'16	'17	'18	'19
Cross-Strait Temple Fair			•	•	•	•	•	•	•	•	•
Fujian–Taiwan Buddhist Culture Exchange Week			•	•	•						
Minnan Culture Festival			•								
Folk Belief Exchange					•	•					
Chinese Culture Development Forum										•	
Fujian and Taiwan Art and Literature Forum										•	
Cross-Strait Choir Festival		•		•							
People-to-people exchanges											
Cross-Strait Youth Forum	•		•	•	•	•	•	•	•	•	•
Cross-Strait Youth New Media Cultural Innovation Forum								•	•	•	•
Cross-Strait Youth Cultural and Creative Products Fair								•	•	•	•
Fujian–Taiwan Youth Employment and Entrepreneurship Meeting				•	•	•					•
Cross-Strait Workers Forum	•	•	•	•	•	•	•	•	•	•	•
Cross-Strait Women's Forum		•	•	•	•	•	•	•	•	•	•
Cross-Strait Marriage and Family Forum				•							•
Cross-Strait Village and Township Exchange Meeting	•		•	•							
Taiwan County Promotion Conference											
"Same Name Village" Networking Activities											
Cross-Strait Welfare Forum					•	•	•		•	•	•
Cross-Strait Think Tank Forum						•	•		•	•	•

Source: author's compilation, adapted from the Straits Forum website (http://www.taiwan.cn/hxlt/)

formal negotiation setting of the closed elite channels is contrasted with the nearly folkloristic events that are taking place in Fujian: Due to the various martial arts competitions, calligraphy events, mass weddings, art exhibitions as well as dance and choir performances, their appearance resembles that of a carnival. Beneath this appearance, however, operates a carefully designed mechanism of hegemonic intervention.

Fujian, the province directly opposite to Taiwan across the Strait, was not chosen by accident. For one, this location makes it possible to avoid places with an immediate political connotation, such as Beijing or Nanjing. More importantly, the location of Fujian itself is a rather crucial ingredient of the event: It is a crystallisation point of Chinese-Taiwanese history as an article about the Straits Forum published in China's official English-language magazine *Beijing Review* acknowledges:

> Fujian and Taiwan share the same cultural origin. People from both sides have many things in common. They speak the same language, *minnan hua*, listen to the same opera, drink the same tea, and worship the same Mazu Goddess. They were separated in 1895 when China's Qing Dynasty (1644-1911) lost a war to Japanese aggressors and was forced to cede Taiwan. The Cross-Straits Forum aims to bridge the two sides.
>
> (Zhang 2010)

It is these cultural resources that the Straits Forum seeks to mobilise, and they are therefore featured in all forms of practice and discourse at the Straits Forum. In addition to the emphasis on the shared cultural heritage of Fujian and Taiwan, this narrative achieves another feat: By dating the separation of Taiwan and China to the Sino-Japanese war of 1895 instead of the KMT's retreat to Taiwan in 1949, it obscures the source of cross-Strait tensions (namely the Chinese Civil War) and instead aims to construct a shared history of suffering from Japanese imperialism.

This narrative is regularly invoked in official statements, both at the Straits Forum and at other cultural cross-Strait events. A representative example is the following statement by KMT Honorary Chairman Wu Poh-hsiung. At the occasion of the visit by a cultural exchange delegation from Fujian province, he pointed out that

> there is an economic bridge between the two sides, and there is also a cultural bridge. The economy allows the two sides to join hands, and the culture connects the hearts of the people. Most people of Taiwan have their ancestral homes in Fujian ... Fujian is more likely than any other province to build a bridge for cross-Strait economic, trade and cultural exchanges.
>
> (China News Service 2011)

Tang Guozhong, leader of the Chinese delegation, added that

> culture is the root, culture is the soul, culture is the foundation, and culture is power. The Fujian-Taiwan culture is an integral part of the long-standing and

splendid Chinese culture. It is an important link connecting the national feelings of compatriots on both sides of the Taiwan Strait and a powerful driving force for the cooperation and exchange between Fujian and Taiwan. … Deepening cooperation means using culture as a source of mutual trust, seeking common ground while reserving differences, [seeking] mutual benefit and win-win.

(ibid.)

A central *leitmotif* of the rapprochement narrative, "mutual benefit and win–win," therefore persists. Crucially, though, it is no longer seen in purely economic but also in affective terms. Echoing Vincent Siew's remarks from a decade earlier, culture is now framed as a *prerequisite* for economic interactions, said to provide a foundation of mutual trust on which the "economic bridge" can be constructed. While the economic aspect of the cross-Strait rapprochement had been designed to appeal to a sense of rationality of "self-interested" and "benefit-maximising" Taiwanese subjects, the cultural linkage is supposed to speak to the heart in order to overcome the lack of trust of which the WSM was a concrete manifestation.

One ingredient to create this trust is the inclusion of previously marginalised groups. In an attempt to refute the claims that the rapprochement is an elite project, the Straits Forum aims to be perceived as a peer-to-peer grassroots event. The organisational architecture emphasises that the various events are organised by a large number of civic associations. From the Taiwanese side, Farmers' Associations, youth and women's associations, labour organisations, religious groups and many other sports and cultural associations are present. In contrast to the hand-picked guests of the KMT-CCP Forum and the bureaucratic elite of the SEF-ARATS channel, it appears as if the Straits Forum not only involves a significantly larger number of people but also invites participants from a variety of social backgrounds. The forum therefore aims both at re-orienting the hegemonic project towards its cultural dimension and, in doing so, broadening its social basis.

Despite these efforts to convey a grassroots image of disinterested civic associations, the process is actually shaped by groups closely related to the organisational centres of the hegemonic project. Four features cast doubt on its supposed grassroots nature. First, the Chinese side is represented by government agencies or the CCP and its mass organisations. Co-organisers include the TAO, the Fujian Provincial People's Government and several relevant ministries, as well as the All-China Federation of Trade Unions, the All-China Youth Federation, the All-China Women's Federation and the All-China Taiwan Compatriots Association. This ensures that the CCP's political aims are represented in all sub-fora.

A second factor is the presence of Taiwan's conglomerates. All six major business associations – the ROCCOC, the CNAIC, the CNFI, the Taiwan Federation of Industries (TFI), the TEEMA, and the NASME – are actively involved as co-organisers of the Straits Forum. Together with the Association of Taiwan Investment Enterprises on the Mainland (ATIEM), the umbrella business association of Taiwanese companies operating in China, these represent the interests of all Taiwanese capital fractions. In addition to the umbrella associations, specific branch associations from media industries (e.g., the Taiwan China Radio and Television Program Production Commercial Association and the Taipei Film and Television Program Production Commercial Association) are also present, as are individual media enterprises from Taiwan (Want Want Media Group, United Daily News Group, TVBS, Eastern Broadcasting). The list of organisers also comprises associations that in fact have to be considered the civic arm of capital due to the composition of their boards, their leadership and mission, as well as their funding sources. Beyond the CSCMF and the TWC (see Chapter 4), these groups include the China Cross-Strait Cultural Trade Development Association and the Small and Medium Enterprise Foundation Taiwan, which was founded by long-time NASME chairman Roscher Lin.

Third, a closer look at the remaining Taiwanese co-organisers of the various sub-fora reveals that many of these are deeply connected to the KMT and its former mass or state-corporatist organisations of the martial law era. A few examples suffice: One of the Taiwanese co-organisers of the Cross-Strait Workers Forum is the *Cross-Strait Labor Development Exchange Association*. Its chairwoman, Ho Tsai-feng, is both a legislator for the KMT as well as a member of its Central Standing Committee. Prior to her involvement in the cross-Strait labour association, she was a leading official at the KMT-affiliated Chinese Federation of Labor (CFL), before heading the Chinese General Labor League that split from the CFL in 2000 (Kamimura 2010: 157). The other Taiwanese co-sponsor of the Cross-Strait Workers Forum is the *Chung-Hua Cross-Strait Labor Relations Development Association*, headed by Yao Chiang-lin. Yao, who is also a KMT Central Standing Committee member, established the organisation in 2010 as a potential counterpart to the All-China Federation of Trade Unions after leaders of the latter had encouraged him to do so.

The Taiwanese associations that co-host the Strait Forum's various youth events provide a similar picture: *Chinese Youth International* was founded by Jeanne Tchongkoei Li, who had previously headed the KMT Central Committee's Department on Youth Affairs before chairing the KMT-affiliated China Youth Corps. Former board members of Chinese Youth International include Su Chi as well as former or current representatives or advisors of the MAC, the SEF, the CSCMF as well as presidents and CEOs of Taiwanese banks and high-technology companies. The board of directors of the *Ten Outstanding Young Persons Foundation,* chaired by then-President of the Legislative Yuan and KMT member Wang Jin-pyng, includes members who have central positions at the CNAIC, TFI or CNFI.

The *R.O.C. Women's Association Headquarters* is led by Huang Ciao-yun, a former representative in Taiwan's now-abolished National Assembly for the pan-blue PFP. The chairman of the *Chinese Culture Promotion Association*, Chao Yi, is also a member of the KMT party apparatus as well as the KMT-affiliated think tank NPF, where he compiled reports on television cooperation across the Taiwan Strait, and former vice president of and current consultant to the Eastern Media Group. The association's board members include CEOs from newspapers and real estate companies. These examples illustrate that the "civic organisations" allegedly representing Taiwan's youth, women and workers are tightly woven into the hegemonic apparatus, reflecting its particular configuration by fusing political and capitalist interests and projecting these onto the cultural terrain.

The fourth feature that casts doubt on the alleged grassroots nature of these exchanges is therefore the ideological leadership of hegemonic groups across the Straits Forum and its related exchanges. Unlike the KMT-CCP Forum, it is not the individual delegation members that are hand-picked but the participating organisations, and as we have seen, these subscribe to the ideological framework of the rapprochement. This is confirmed by the speeches held at the various sub-fora, which all emphasise the various elements of the adjusted hegemonic narrative: First, they praise the unprecedented achievements of the previous meetings and provide a bright outlook on the mutually beneficial future of cross-Strait relations; second, these benefits are conditional on upholding the 1992 consensus and a further deepening of exchanges; and third, the peaceful development across the Strait is conditional on the common effort to rejuvenate the Chinese nation.

The overview of the Straits Forum's sub-fora over the years as shown in Table 5.1 provides helpful insights into its role within the hegemonic apparatus. First, it appears as if the character of the Straits Forum was adjusted early on. The first edition of the Straits Forum suggests that it was initially conceptualised as an implementation platform for the agreements that were conceived in the KMT-CCP Forum and signed through the SEF-ARATS channel. The economic sub-fora of the 2009 and 2010 editions of the Straits Forum therefore mainly dealt with the recently signed agreements regarding tourism, maritime and air transportation as well as finance. The focus, however, then quickly shifted to activities that emphasised the grassroots character of the event. From the second edition onwards, the Cross-Strait Workers Forum and the Cross-Strait Women's Forum as well as the Hakka event were added, followed by the Temple Fair and a Buddhist activity a year later as the attempt to draw on cultural resources that suggest a common history linking the two sides of the Taiwan Strait became a defining feature. This indicates that the Straits Forum's character was slightly refined after the WSM, shifting its focus from the implementation of agreements towards the inclusion of subaltern groups. The flexible organisational architecture of the forum allowed it to be continuously adapted to react to the dynamics of hegemonic contestation, albeit with a temporal lag. In the aftermath of the AMM and the SFM, for instance, the youth focus was refined by complementing the general Cross-Strait Youth Forum with more specialised events on vocational training, youth employment and youth media.

Two central instruments – preferential policies and means of molecular inclusion – are at the forum's disposal to project its ideological forms in a molecular way. Preferential policies have been assumed from the KMT-CCP Forum and work in the same fashion: They are merely the announcement of unilateral measures taken by the PRC designed to benefit Taiwanese citizens travelling to or living in China as well as enterprises operating there. Delegating the announcement of preferential policies from the party-to-party channel to the Straits Forum entails an effect of obscuration: While in fact, these unilateral decisions are a double-edged generosity of the CCP that is conditional on upholding the 1992 consensus, their announcement at the KMT-CCP Forum made them appear as the outcome of negotiations between these two parties; their announcement at the Straits Forum, however, bestows on them an aura of inclusive grassroots cooperation, designed to contribute to the universalisation of these measures. The unilateral implementation of legal frameworks by the PRC opens up new strategies to groups that are part of the hegemonic bloc, but it also allows for new forms of hegemonic intervention. Early examples of preferential policies aimed at the estimated one million Taiwanese citizens who live in China include measures to facilitate travel, the recognition of diplomas, access to degree programs and vocational examinations as well as to previously restricted professions (such as in the health care or education sectors), and access to services regarding work, marriage and social security that are comparable to those of Chinese citizens. Other policies provide Taiwanese companies with access to infrastructure (such as industrial parks) as well as markets by loosening restrictions in highly regulated sectors, such as the media. Preferential policies are an instrument that enables the Chinese side to react to developments in cross-Strait relations. A few examples with regard to the media sector will be discussed below.

The second instrument consists of the Straits Forum's means of molecular inclusion, including the indirect intervention by satellite networks that disseminate ideological forms and permeate Taiwan's civil society. While the Straits Forum meets only once per year, the dozens of youth, women, labour, business and religious associations that participate in it continuously organise their own activities and are therefore able to project forms of practice all year round. These activities serve as multipliers of the hegemonic apparatus within Taiwan's civil society and continuously mould social forms of everyday life. Due to the atomised character of these activities, a systematic analysis of their extent is beyond the scope of this study. A look at the two major Taiwanese co-organisers of the youth-focused events at the Straits Forum, however, shall suffice to illustrate this capillary mode of including Taiwanese citizens in these satellite events. *Chinese Youth International* organises a dozen events per year, including annual cross-Strait debate and singing competitions as well as science and technology camps. Each of these involves upwards of 25 Taiwanese participants. The *Ten Outstanding Young Persons Foundation*, according to its own website, had organised 68 cross-Strait training exchange camps by 2014, involving more than 3,000 students from over 120 colleges and universities. It had also received nearly 40 delegations from China. Many other associations arrange similar activities. The official Taiwan.cn website reported on cross-Strait youth exchanges taking place every single week. The wide range of activities covers summer camps, vocational training events, internship and employment programmes, science and art competitions, literature camps, baseball and rugby tournaments, e-sport and short film contests, martial arts exchanges and joint visits to historical sites that commemorate the "martyrs of the Anti-Japanese War." Catering to all conceivable personal preferences, these associations are a crucial interface that translates the hegemonic project into a large variety of entry points through which individuals become involved in cross-Strait exchanges.

From a Gramscian perspective, the Straits Forum represents a qualitatively new phase of the rapprochement. First, it contributed significantly to the extension of the hegemonic narrative. Until the challenge of the WSM, the legitimation of the hegemonic project relied primarily on the promise of economic benefits. The Cultural Turn introduced an affective dimension, namely the common destiny to fulfil the historical mission of reuniting a "family" that was divided through foreign imperialism in 1895. This common destiny is no longer conceived as a bureaucratic project to be negotiated by elites behind closed doors, but as an enterprise that is realised through the active participation of people from all walks of life. This active participation in the rapprochement, furthermore, was no longer dependent on economic or political interests but on individuals pursuing their personal interests in the seemingly apolitical spheres of sports, literature, religion, etc.

Second, the Straits Forum created the impression that previously neglected groups were now included through grassroots associations. As the analysis has shown, however, this inclusion was not the result of subaltern groups actively and successfully struggling for representation. Rather, the Straits Forum promotes a passive form of inclusion under the leadership of hegemonic groups, as the participation of these associations is highly conditional on subscribing to the hegemonic narrative. While proponents of the Straits Forum claim that it "can faithfully reflect the people's true views on cross-strait relations"[2], it is rather the case that the associations serve to transmit hegemonic principles into the broader strata of Taiwan's society. Ultimately, they do not represent subaltern interests but neutralise them.

Third, the presence of these groups provided the hegemonic project with new mechanisms to extend the material basis for its ideology. The inclusion of pseudo-grassroots organisations is important not simply because of their ability to mobilise delegations to the forum and in doing so lend it the semblance of expressing the interests of subaltern groups; more crucially, by continuously arranging their own events throughout the year they affect the lives of tens if not hundreds of thousand Taiwanese, projecting hegemonic forms of social practice into Taiwan's social fabric. These activities are also aimed at fostering more substantial and *lasting* relationships across the Taiwan Strait, which research has shown to contribute to the Taiwanese developing more favourable views of China than incidental contacts (Wang and Cheng 2017: 238).

To assess the significance of these developments, it is here helpful to recall Gramsci's thoughts on the materiality of ideology. A praxeological account of hegemony examines not only how narratives are articulated and disseminated but also how molecular interventions "change practical activity as a whole" (Gramsci 1971: 344) to align lived ideology with articulated ideology. In other words, the narrative of the rapprochement appears as more appealing and less arbitrary to those who are an active part of it. The Cultural Turn of the hegemonic project, therefore, is the true Gramscian moment of the rapprochement: Instead of political parties or quasi-governmental organisations, hegemonic functions are delegated to "'private' enterprise" (Gramsci 1971: 60) in the form of a network of associations, foundations and similar seemingly apolitical groups. While the early phase of the hegemonic project was characterised by its monolithic form and the reliance

Table 5.2 Character of the Hegemonic Project, 2005–2012

	Monolithic Mode	Capillary Mode
Apparatus	Centralised E.g.: *KMT-CCP Forum*	Diffuse E.g.: *Straits Forum and its satellite network*
Hegemonic Activities	Continual E.g.: *Regular meeting of the KMT-CCP Forum*	Continuous E.g.: *Activities by sports or cultural associations*
Object of hegemonic inclusion	Social groups E.g.: *Farmers*	Individuals E.g.: *Individuals seeking employment, educational or recreational opportunities*
Form of hegemonic inclusion	Direct E.g.: *Direct procurement missions targeting Taiwan's agricultural surplus produce*	Indirect E.g.: *Implementing structures that provide opportunities for individuals*

Source: author's compilation.

on the direct provision of benefits to social groups as a whole, as was the case with Taiwan's farmers, this network exerts a "'diffused' and capillary form of indirect pressure" (ibid.: 110) that interpellates individuals as atomised subjects of the hegemonic process. These adjustments contribute to the increasingly heterogeneous experiences of hegemony, hindering attempts to discern a hegemonic centre. Table 5.2 summarises the features of the earlier monolithic and the post-WSM capillary modes of hegemony. These categories are not to be understood as dichotomous but rather as a continuum with more and more aspects of the hegemonic process moving from the left towards the right column.

The Hegemonic Character of Cross-Strait Media Cooperation

Gramsci (2012: 389) set out to study "how the ideological structure of a dominant class is actually organized: namely the material organisation aimed at maintaining, defending and developing the theoretical or ideological 'front'". The wide range of activities promoted by the hegemonic apparatus suggests several potential case studies for a more detailed examination of how the cultural dimension of hegemony was organised. The extant literature on people-to-people exchanges across the Taiwan Strait tends to focus on the increasing cooperation in tourism. These studies ask how practices of cross-Strait tourism affect imaginations of territory, sovereignty and identity (Zhang 2013). They show that the outcomes are rather contradictory: While the promotion of cross-Strait tourism is found to contribute to a more nuanced understanding of Taiwanese history and culture by Chinese tourists (Qiu et al. 2015: 83; Chung et al. 2016; Pan et al. 2020), inbound cross-Strait tourism does not appear to foster a common understanding for Taiwanese locals (Wang and Cheng 2017: 238); it does, rather, seem to contribute to a growing sense of alienation (Rowen 2014: 68). This suggests tourism has little potential as a cultural hegemonic strategy and should instead be more adequately understood as a conditional economic measure made possible by the SEF-ARATS agreements and designed to benefit Taiwan's tourism and retail sectors (Chiang 2012: 251): Between 2008 and 2016, tourism from China was a US$19 billion industry (Pan et al. 2020: 6), a stream of revenue that was carefully directed to benefit Taiwan's large enterprises (Rowen 2016: 143).

This section will study cooperation in the media sector for two reasons: Given the vast range of activities promoted by the Straits Forum (youth, sports, religion, agriculture, etc.), a detailed analysis of the multitude of "atomised" exchanges is beyond the scope of this study. This is exacerbated by a lack of literature on the majority of these forms of cooperation, as little has been published on exchanges involving women, workers and youth associations. More importantly, it was ultimately the media sector that would prove to be the most contentious issue in Taiwan. Cross-Strait media cooperation was the catalyst for the AMM, and its analysis therefore allows us to relate the process of hegemonic intervention to the emergence of grievances and social mobilisation.

Taiwan's Media Sector and the Lure of the Chinese Market

The AMM emerged from grievances regarding the state of Taiwan's media sector in general and the attempt by the Want Want Group to expand into the cable operating business in particular. When the movement emerged in late 2011 and 2012, this was mainly in response to Want Want chairman Tsai Eng-meng's publicly expressed pro-China stance. Critics argued that Want Want represented "a *different* kind of media capital" (Lin and Lee 2017: 37, my emphasis), and at first glance, Tsai Eng-meng's pro-China stance is indeed striking. This section, however, will provide the structural context to these dynamics: Seen against the background of the developments discussed in this section, a more nuanced picture emerges, showing that the mergers and acquisitions in Taiwan's media sector were first and foremost reactions to structural change, such as barriers to and opportunities for accumulation. Reducing the monopolisation of Taiwan's media sector to the political stance of business leaders or the CCP's attempt to influence Taiwan's public opinion obscures how structural imperatives compel capital to diversify within Taiwan and expand to the Chinese market, as Marx and Engels put it, "on pain of extinction" (Marx and Engels 2010: 71).

The dynamics that shaped Taiwan's media sector in the late 2000s and early 2010s have their origin in the period of media liberalisation during the 1990s. During the authoritarian era, media outlets were either directly controlled by the party-state or had KMT representatives on the editorial boards (Rawnsley et al. 2016: 67). As restrictions were lifted, new newspapers and television channels were established. The presence of conglomerates in the cable operating business can be traced back to this time: After the legalisation of cable television in 1993, "Taiwan's business conglomerates paid more attention to the "new" profitable service and became interested in cable television operation" (Chen 2002: 41). As such, the media sector reflects general developments that could also be observed in banking, telecommunication and transportation at the same time (see Chapter 3). For the large enterprises in Taiwan, the de-regulation of these sectors was simply another opportunity to expand.

Although the cable market was characterised by a highly competitive structure early on, Taiwan's large conglomerates ultimately prevailed. Those cable operators that were part of a large business group had the capacity to raise capital, relinquish short-term profits for long-term accumulation and operate at temporary losses in order to succeed under these competitive conditions (ibid.: 42, 44). A wave of mergers and acquisitions initiated a process of capital concentration until only the most powerful operators remained. Among them were the United Communications Group, a subsidiary of the Koos Group (active in finance, real estate, manufacturing, tourism), and the Eastern Multimedia Group, part of the now dismantled Rebar Group (textiles, banking and insurance, food, real estate and construction) (Chen 1999: 209–213).

By the early 2000s, within less than ten years, the five major operators accounted for 82 per cent of cable subscribers (Rawnsley and Rawnsley 2006: 238). The centralisation through acquisitions and mergers was accompanied by a process of diversification as media enterprises began to integrate their various activities resulting in business groups combining, among others, television broadcast, cable and satellite operation, advertising as well as newspapers and magazines (Chen 2002: 53). At the same time, they reached a regulatory barrier to growth, as competition laws capped the maximum number of subscribers served by one operator at one third of all subscribers and limited subscription fees to a fixed maximum monthly rate (Curtin 2007: 154–155). The conglomerates unsuccessfully lobbied the government to ease these restrictions. Several cable operators set eyes on the Chinese market, but the political climate did not allow for substantial cooperation across the Taiwan Strait. When some of the media groups were affected by the fallout from the *dot-com* bubble, a wave of divestment began that would characterise the coming years (ibid.: 155).

The government's decision to allow foreign investors to hold up to 80 per cent of cable operators heralded an interlude of foreign capital domination in Taiwan's cable sector (Thomas 2005: 177). Around the turn of the century, Taiwan Broadband Communications was acquired by Carlyle while the Koos Group entered a joint-venture Star TV, then owned by Rupert Murdoch, transforming the United Communications Group into China Network Systems (CNS) (Curtin 2007: 154). Faced with the limited possibilities for growth, the Koos Group sold CNS to the South Korean private equity firm MBK in 2006 (Tucker and Mitchell 2006). In the same year, Carlyle took control of Eastern after having sold Taiwan Broadband Communication to the Australian investment bank Macquarie.

Newspapers and television stations also faced pressure to diversify through mergers and acquisitions. China Times, operating at a deficit like most newspapers, acquired CTi TV in 2002 and China TV in 2005 (Hsu 2014b:: 135), while the Eastern Media Company took control of the Commons Daily newspaper in 2000 (Chen 2010b: 20). These groups suffered from a general decline in advertisement revenue that was exacerbated by the global financial crisis. In the decade after 2005, newspaper advertising revenue fell by 65 per cent, and while television advertising revenue remained stable (except for a contraction during the financial crisis), the overcrowded market meant that in effect the average revenue per channel decreased as ever more channels competed over the same amount (Rawnsley and Gong 2011: 334–335; Hu 2017: 218; Huang 2017: 31–32).

As much as the onset of the global financial crisis sharpened the contradictions within Taiwan's media sector, it also presented an opportunity for Taiwan's conglomerates: In the aftermath of the financial crash, the private equity firms that controlled Taiwan's cable operators sought to sell their assets to raise capital. Conversely, Taiwan's conglomerates found a renewed interest in the cable sector as several developments aligned. First, the general trend towards digital convergence, that is, the integration of diverse activities in mobile communication, cable, internet and television into one seamless digital communication platform, had reached Taiwan. Despite the earlier restrictions on business models in the cable television sector, cable operators now became attractive again as broadband internet breathed new life into the sector (Kwong 2010). Conglomerates that owned telecommunications companies (such as Fubon through Taiwan Mobile, Far Eastern through Far-EasTone and later Hon Hai Precision through Asia-Pacific Telecom) or television channels (such as Want Want China Times and Eastern Media, who together would form Want Want China Broadband) began to set eyes on the cable operators owned by foreign capital. Second, the long-awaited access to the Chinese market appeared more likely than ever before. Since the Lien-Hu meeting in 2005, the rapprochement had progressively deepened, and after Ma Ying-jeou and the KMT won the 2008 elections, conglomerates were optimistic that they could finally unleash the "go west" spirit and overcome the obstacles that had posed limits to accumulation over the previous decade. Finally, the late 2000s were a period of heightened ideological uncertainty. Similar to what Gramsci (2012: 387) observed after the First World War in Italy, when trusts and banks scrambled to buy Italian newspapers in times of organic crisis, the Taiwanese conglomerates that depended on the normalisation of cross-Strait relations increased their involvement in the media sector. Taiwan's seven 24/7 news channels, in particular, are part of everyday life in Taiwan, and their broadcasts frame political debates and transmit ideological narratives. But as the case of Jimmy Lai's difficulties to find cable operators that would carry his Next TV channel had revealed, owning a television channel was insufficient to reach audiences unless cable operators were willing to broadcast it (Hsu 2014a: 533–534). Under these circumstances, assuming direct ownership of the cable operators appeared imperative.

What emerges from this contextualisation is a picture of broader structural transformations at work. The acquisitions and diversifications of Taiwanese conglomerates appear to be compelled by larger economic trends beyond the control of a single company let alone business owner. Given the regulatory barriers to growth, the decline in advertisement revenues and market saturation in general, media groups of all political orientations pro-actively attempted to set foot in the Chinese market. These efforts also show that the cross-Strait orientation of media groups pre-dates the KMT-CCP cooperation, and that the media conglomeration in Taiwan is therefore not a consequence of the rapprochement. If anything, media conglomeration is one of its underlying catalysts, given that Taiwanese business groups not only lobbied for access to the Chinese market but were in many cases also willing to support political forces which could take substantial steps towards realising this ambition. It is therefore necessary to not overemphasise the political motivations of Taiwanese conglomerates.

Despite the media sector's efforts to enter the Chinese market, two kinds of obstacles – regulatory and political – remained (Chen 2006: 63–64). Given the nature of means of ideological production, China's media sphere is already tightly regulated, and the CCP systematically utilised these restrictions to coerce individual Taiwanese companies deemed to support China-critical views: Authorities could block market access, deny visa applications to journalists (Wu and Lambert 2016: 46) or withhold permits for branch offices in China (Huang 2017: 32). For Taiwanese companies aiming to expand into China, they needed Chinese authorities to not only refrain from this coercive use of regulations but also lift those restrictions that applied to all foreign enterprises in China.

Political obstacles were therefore at the top of the agenda. In a broader sense, this necessitated the reduction of general uncertainty in cross-Strait relations, as developments such as they could be observed during the government of Chen Shui-bian endangered cross-Strait accumulation in general. In a narrow sense, business groups had to find ways to dispel doubts about their stance on the rapprochement. Being perceived as leaning towards pro-independence positions had become a burden for their plans to expand into the Chinese market. Taiwanese media companies adapted to this situation in two ways. One path was that of *passive submission* to the hegemonic project: Media outlets began to avoid reporting on issues deemed sensitive to the CCP, such as the 1989 protests in Tiananmen Square, Falun Gong, Xinjiang and Taiwan independence. This is the route several pro-DPP media outlets took, *de facto* internalising the CCP's censorship demands (ibid.). The alternative was a form of *active integration* into the hegemonic apparatus through participation in the Straits Forum or its satellite networks. This was not only a way to demonstrate commitment to the ideological lines of the hegemonic project, but also granted access to actively participating in the negotiation and institutional shaping of the rapprochement. In return for a direct involvement in the Straits Forum, China would not only refrain from coercive measures, but would also reward this active commitment by providing domestic investment partners for joint ventures, paying for advertorials or even allocating direct subsidies (Hsu 2014a: 522). To different degrees, Want Want China Times, the United Daily News Group, TVBS and Eastern Broadcasting as well as many publishers actively participated in the Straits Forum. The next section will examine how this process contributed to the cooperation in the media sector.

Media Cooperation and the Hegemonic Apparatus

Both the regulatory and political aspects were addressed by the hegemonic apparatus, which facilitated the media cooperation across the Taiwan Strait in three complementary ways: through measures of selective de-regulation, the provision of infrastructure and by establishing and coordinating channels that ensured the integration of social forces into the project. Already during Chiang Pin-kung's visit to China in 2005, both sides agreed to promote media cooperation between the two sides. The Changsha Forum then laid out the agenda for a process left to market forces, which were steered through the selective removal of regulatory barriers. The early stages were characterised by sporadic exchanges and measures. In January 2008, for example, the State Administration of Press, Publication, Radio, Film and Television of the People's Republic of China (2008) announced that television dramas co-produced by Taiwanese and Chinese companies would be treated as domestic productions, facilitating the otherwise lengthy review process for foreign content. In 2009, the SEF organised the visit of a delegation of Taiwanese media representatives to meet the TAO and the ARATS in China to establish channels of contact between the two sides (Huang 2017: 30–31). One of the outcomes was the inclusion of films in the ECFA. Annex IV of the ECFA's Early Harvest List, which lists the liberalisation measures to take effect until the implementation of a Service Trade Agreement, stipulates that "Chinese language motion pictures produced by production companies in Taiwan … may be imported for distribution in the Mainland on a quota-free basis" (World Trade Organization [WTO] 2010: 54–55). The fact that the media sector, together with banking, insurance and transportation, was selected for this list demonstrates its importance.

It was only once the Straits Forum had been established that these aspects were addressed in a more systematic fashion. At that time, the event in Fujian comprised one specialised sub-forum for television and film and another for press and publishing. The Taiwanese co-organisers include the Want Want and United Daily groups as well as Eastern Broadcasting and TVBS. Regarding the civil society organisations that participated in these fora, the general observations discussed above apply: Participating groups from the Taiwanese side are either characterised by a high degree of cross-representation between these associations and Taiwan's conglomerates (e.g., in the case of the Taipei Newspapers Association) or, as in the case of the Cross-Strait Chinese Publishing and Logistics association, they have been purposefully set up to promote the cross-Strait interests of Taiwan's media businesses.

With regard to de-regulation, these sub-fora served as platforms where Taiwanese conglomerates as well as Taiwanese and Chinese authorities negotiated piecemeal steps toward market access for Taiwanese companies. This process consisted of two stages. First, selective markets in China were opened to Taiwanese firms as a relief measure aimed at compensating the decline in advertisement revenues, embedded in the narrative that the growing Chinese market presented the only opportunity for the crisis-ridden Taiwanese publishing companies. Second, the long-term target of these measures was the integration of cross-Strait media under the banner of a unified Chinese culture, the ultimate goal being the increase of global competitiveness of the cross-Strait media industries and the expansion into overseas markets.

It was the third Straits Forum that tackled the (de-)regulatory measures that the fifth KMT-CCP Forum had called for. Five preferential policies were announced for a pilot phase, mostly benefiting Taiwanese companies active in media-related services. With regard to minimum capital requirements for printing and packaging companies, Taiwan-owned firms were now treated equal to Chinese enterprises. Taiwanese companies were further allowed to set up wholly-owned firms or joint ventures in book pre-production as well as audio-visual services and production, and Fujian province would recognise copyright certificates issued by Taiwanese authorities (Straits Forum 2011). Although these initiatives were limited to Fujian province, they marked a first step towards meeting the demands of Taiwanese firms. Other policies were aimed at Taiwanese workers. For instance, the provincial government opened up vocational qualification examinations to Taiwanese employed in press and publication units in Fujian (Straits Forum 2013). These policies have consolidated the general trend that Taiwanese creative workers increasingly see China as their future (Zhao 2016: 57).

The fifth Straits Forum marked the shift towards infrastructural initiatives, establishing a set of complementary institutions in Fujian. A Straits National Digital Publishing Industry Base was set up to integrate resources related to digital books and newspapers, digital printing as well as online and mobile games. It is complemented by a Cross-Strait Copyright Center, the Fujian and Taiwan Newspaper Research Exchange Center and an Education and Training Center in Fujian, which provides the infrastructure for the preferential policies designed to attract talent from Taiwan (Straits Forum 2013). A plan regarding digital media seeks to promote the formation of industrial clusters by establishing "standards, platforms, industrial chains, capital markets, project cooperation, talent training and exchanges, and jointly promote the development of the digital publishing industry" to not only "build a relatively complete digital publishing industry chain", but also provide means that are "conducive to the spread of Chinese culture" (Zhang 2012). Together with the preferential policies, these initiatives mould the way the emerging digital industry develops: as an *already-integrated cross-Strait industry*, guided by and reinforcing the hegemonic principle of a common Chinese culture.

These initiatives were increasingly embedded in capillary satellite networks that extended the reach of the hegemonic apparatus beyond the main channels. As with all other activities of the Straits Forum, seemingly disinterested associations were a central pillar of these networks. By participating in the KMT-CCP Forum, the Straits Forum as well as academic media forums, and by receiving and organising cultural delegations on a provincial level and between associations as well as meetings with TAO and potential media partners in Fujian, the above-mentioned Chinese Culture Promotion Association, for instance, serves as a liaison not only between the various cross-Strait channels but also among political and capitalist interests. As such, it is in a position to receive the various interests of political and capitalist social forces, to reconcile and accommodate them, and to reintroduce them into the hegemonic apparatus via policy papers and recommendations.

Provincial delegations were another element of the satellite networks, beginning from early 2009. Within 20 months, 24 of China's province-level administrative divisions had sent delegations, at times consisting of up to 2,000 members (Chien and Hsieh 2010: 5). They increasingly participated in cultural events, such as artefact exhibitions, performances, but also religious events or signing ceremonies for partnerships among universities from both sides of the Taiwan Strait (ibid.: 8-11, 19). One of these culture-oriented delegations was mentioned above. In April 2011, the delegation from Fujian, headed by Tang Guozhong, who as director of the party's provincial Publicity Department was charged with ideological work, arrived for a ten-day visit in Taiwan. The interlock with the hegemonic apparatus is expressed in his meeting with Tseng Yung-chuan, then Deputy Speaker of the Legislative Yuan, who in turn would lead the Taiwanese delegation to the third Straits Forum a few weeks later. During the visit, Chinese and Taiwanese firms signed agreements to co-produce a TV series as well as an animated film (China News Service 2011), showcasing the recently relaxed regulations.

Another outcome of this delegation therefore regards the establishment of cross-Strait partnerships. At an event that was part of the trip, the Want Want Group and the Fujian Daily Newspaper Group announced that they had agreed to co-produce the *Cross-Strait Media* magazine. The magazine was launched in October later that year and is published in both traditional and simplified Chinese characters. Similarly, the previously pro-independence newspaper *Commons Daily*, now owned by Eastern Multimedia, began to share news content with the *Straits Herald*, which also belongs to the Fujian Daily Group (Hsu 2014b:: 174), while Eastern Broadcasting reached a deal to screen a documentary series produced in Fujian. Another form of partnership was the establishment of joint ventures such as the Straits Book Co., set up by Chinese and Taiwanese publishers to provide services to the emerging cross-Strait publishing industry, including "logistics and distribution, import and export business, copyright agency, copyright trade, exhibition activities, special lectures, and marketing promotion" (Straits Forum 2010).

The Want Want China Times Group and Fujian Daily cooperated not only on producing content but also held various Cross-Strait Media Forums since 2009 (Huang 2020: 94–95, 98). In 2015, these forums were moved to Beijing by establishing the annual Cross-Strait Media Summit, now co-organised by the Want Want and Beijing Daily groups. The move to Beijing suggests that media cooperation was at the time considered crucial enough to be shifted from the provincial level in Fujian towards the central government. More than 100 media outlets from both sides of the Taiwan Strait participate in this forum, including subsidiaries of the Want Want Group, United Daily, TVBS, Eastern Broadcasting as well as business associations and cultural foundations (Cole 2019).

It is one of the many seminars, forums and fairs that are closely intertwined with the hegemonic apparatus and therefore have to be considered as satellite events of the Straits Forum. The integrated and networked character of these channels is partly acknowledged through the formula "One Forum, Three Exhibitions" (一论坛、三展会), referring to the Straits Forum and three cross-Strait exhibitions: the Cross-Strait Book Fair, the Straits Printing Technology Exhibition and the Straits Copyright Expo. While the Straits Forum's major task is the coordination of social groups that are actively integrated into the hegemonic project, the related exhibitions focus on sales and marketing, also integrating those publishers that are not actively part the hegemonic apparatus. This process is complemented by an academic exchange platform for cross-Strait publishing. The "Cross-Strait Chinese Publishing Forum" holds an annual seminar, inviting scholars from both sides to assess the state of the industry and propose policies, covering issues such as soft power, digitalisation and textbooks.

The de-regulation of the cross-Strait media sector reawakened the interest of Taiwanese conglomerates. As Table 5.3 shows, the decade since the KMT's return to power has seen a series of major media acquisitions by business groups. With Tsai Eng-meng (Want Want Group), the Tsai brothers (Fubon Group), the Wei brothers (Ting Hsin Group), Terry Gou (Hon Hai Precision) and Lin Yu-lin (Hong Tao Group), five of the six wealthiest Taiwanese (as of 2015) were involved in failed or successful attempts to take over media outlets or cable operators, and foreign private equity firms have largely withdrawn. The most prominent of these

Table 5.3 Major media mergers and acquisitions in Taiwan by conglomerates, 2008–2018

Year	Target	Outcome
2008	China Times Group	Acquired by Want Want Group, outbidding Jimmy Lai's Next Media
2009	kbro	Fubon subsidiary Taiwan Mobile agrees to acquire kbro but fails to get regulatory approval
2010	kbro	Acquired by Tsai brothers of Fubon through Dafu Media
2011	TVBS	Cher Wang (HTC) acquires stakes in TVBS Media Group before taking full control of the group in 2015
2011	CNS	Want Want Group set to acquire CNS, but fails to get regulatory approval
2012	Next Media	A consortium led by Jeffrey Koo Jr. (Chinatrust), William Wong (Formosa Plastics) and Tsai Eng-meng (Want Want) reaches a deal with Jimmy Lai to acquire the print outlets under Next Media but withdraws the offer during the regulatory review
2013	Next TV	Jimmy Lai sells Next TV to ERA Communications chairman and land developer Lien Tai-sheng
2014	Gala TV	Acquired by Formosa Plastics Group from private equity firm EQT Partners AB
2014	CNS	Ting Hsin Group agrees to acquire CNS from MBK Partners, outbidding the Far Eastern Group, but the deal falls through after Ting Hsin is involved in a food scandal
2014	Asia-Pacific Telecom	A subsidiary of Hon Hai Precision merges with Asia-Pacific Telecom
2016	CNS	FarEasTone and Morgan Stanley Private Equity set to acquire CNS before withdrawing after the regulatory process is deemed unlikely to succeed
2017	Taiwan Broadband	Acquired from Macquarie by Hon Hai Precision-related Dynami Vision
2018	CNS	Acquired by property-developer Hong Tai Group through a charity foundation
2018	Eastern Broadcasting	Acquired by property-developer Mao Te International Investment

Source: author's compilation.

acquisition attempts, involving Tsai Eng-meng's Want Want China Times Group, would prompt the AMM and the emergence of the counter-hegemonic principle of the "China Factor." Before we discuss the emergence of these protests, it is helpful to address how the aforementioned molecular transformations contributed to the rise of pragmatism in Taiwan.

Pragmatisation as the Outcome of Hegemonic Pressure

As the discussion above has shown, a significant share of hegemonic activities was embedded in a narrative of Chinese nationalism. The motifs that were regularly invoked include those of a community of destiny of the two sides of the Taiwan Strait, relations of kinship, as well as the shared trauma of Japanese imperialism. Those initiatives related to Fujian province furthermore emphasised the more specific cultural affinities between Fujian and Taiwan, including the shared dialect as well as common folk beliefs, both of which provided points of reference for concrete people-to-people exchanges. On the basis of this ideological framework, the Cultural Turn promoted people-to-people exchanges and other forms of cultural cooperation through a capillary network.

Yet, despite this orchestrated effort, there is no indication that Taiwanese relinquished their local identity. On the contrary, the self-identification as Taiwanese reached a historic high after the KMT came into power. However, it would be imprudent to assume that the hegemonic project had no effect on the ideological terrain on which Taiwanese become aware of their everyday desires and political convictions. As discussed in Chapter 4, the aim of the hegemonic project and its concrete initiatives was not to promote Chinese unification, but rather to defuse those elements of Taiwanese identity that had the potential for political explosiveness, such as providing the basis for the political project of Taiwan independence.

What we can observe is that, against the background of the rapprochement, the issue of identity was somewhat transformed. As Shelley Rigger (2016: 72) notes, the rising self-identification as Taiwanese did *not* result in a similar increase in the desire for independence, with the latter remaining at a stable level. In other words, self-identifying as Taiwanese no longer inevitably entailed what had long been seen as its organic and logical political expression. This decrease of importance in political discourse can be attributed to two major developments. First, Ma Ying-jeou and the KMT had refrained from making identity a central issue during the campaign for the 2008 elections, instead building a platform around the issue of Taiwan's economic development and the economic benefits of cross-Strait interactions (Fell 2011: 103). Ma's pledge to the status quo in cross-Strait affairs – condensed into the formula of "Three Noes" – furthermore mitigated fears about a swift move towards unification, thereby defusing the polarisation of the issue of identity that had characterised the two terms under his predecessor Chen Shui-bian.

Identity became less important not only in shaping the political discourse but also in informing everyday activities. The hegemonic project had weaved a tightly-knit fabric of concrete opportunities for individuals. In contrast to the fierce political battles of the late 1990s and early 2000s, the rapprochement did not interpellate

Taiwanese as a collective political subject but based on private interests, personal considerations and individual preferences: as tourists, worshippers of Mazu on a pilgrimage, students seeking a promising education, young graduates escaping Taiwan's job market in the hope to obtain an internship in a company that develops online games or to even found a start-up company in China, participants in Kung Fu, baseball or esports tournaments, or as appreciators of literature and film. Despite the political dimension that the hegemonic project attributed to cross-Strait exchanges, embracing the opportunities offered by these exchanges was not only based on apolitical choices but also contributed to divorcing political persuasions from individual decisions. More than the mantra of a unified Chinese nation, it was this atomisation of choice that was driving the pragmatisation of cross-Strait interactions.

An example of particular relevance for this chapter is that of Taiwan's students. As early as 2009, the two major concerns of the younger generation were Taiwan's economic situation and stability in cross-Strait relations, resulting in their "support [for] a strong and stable relationship with China" and accounting for the fact that 61 per cent of young voters had supported Ma Ying-jeou the previous year (Chen 2009: 10). Young voters were attracted by the tangible benefits that the Cultural Turn of the rapprochement provided based on the agreements of the KMT-CCP Forum at Changsha: After Taiwanese students in China received the same status as local students (i.e., same tuition fees as well as access to scholarship programmes and basic medical insurance), the number of Taiwanese enrolled at Chinese universities increased by 48 per cent from 7,364 to 10,870 within four years after 2011 (Lin 2019: 192). An increasing number of these students were considering a long-term future in China rather than returning to Taiwan after graduation (Wang 2015: 12).

The crucial point is that identity does not appear to be a prohibitive element in considering opportunities in China. Although three-quarters of the young Taiwanese surveyed by LePesant (2012: 75) identified as either "Taiwanese" or both "Taiwanese and Chinese (Huaren)" and generally supported Taiwan independence, they acknowledged that Taiwan's economy depended on closer economic ties with China, and a majority of about 62 per cent saw China as an opportunity compared to 25 per cent who saw it as a danger. Taiwanese identity is therefore divorced from a pragmatic pursuit of opportunities in China (Chen 2009: 11–13). Furthermore, Taiwanese and Chinese identities were not conceived as mutually exclusive: A majority of young Taiwanese agreed with Ma Ying-jeou's statement that "the peoples on both sides of the strait are the descendants of the Emperors Yan and Huang" (LePesant 2012: 75). To a certain degree, this suggests that a Taiwanese self-identification and pursuit of opportunities in China as well as the dichotomy between Taiwanese and Chinese elements of identity were reconciled. In this sense, pragmatism is not so much "the willingness to *compromise* on the issue of a nationalist identity", as Liao et al. (2018: 65, my emphasis) define it, but rather the fact that it was possible to participate in and benefit from increased cross-Strait interactions *without* having to compromise one's own identity.

The negative complement to this active pragmatism is a form of resignation or political paralysis, which I encountered in many conversations with students during my fieldwork in Taiwan in 2011 and 2012. Although these young people raised doubts, however vague, whether the rapprochement was beneficial to Taiwan, they perceived it as inevitable. With regard to the increasing economic interaction across the Taiwan Strait, the lure of China due to educational and employment opportunities, and the rise of China in global politics in general, they simply wondered: "what could we possibly do?" The systematic survey conducted by LePesant (2012: 76), diagnosing a "fatalistic attitude" among students, supports this impression.

What is striking are the parallels to the views held by Taiwanese businesspeople operating in China. These had long pursued opportunities independent of their personal political convictions, adopting what can be described as a "don't ask, don't tell" approach: Politics is seen a private matter best kept out of business decisions and interactions with Chinese officials (Schubert 2010: 81). As the example of the media industry shows, even Taiwanese companies that have a pro-independence position sought to expand into the Chinese market (Huang 2017: 35). This separation of political and personal identity from economic activities is at the core of cross-Strait pragmatism. This form of pragmatism, originally a prerequisite for cross-Strait investment, was universalised to 'non-economic' activities as well as more social groups within Taiwan, and the systematic provision of opportunities for Taiwanese citizens through the hegemonic apparatus played an important part in that process.

Despite these developments, even in the early January of 2012, the election victory by the KMT was far from certain. In the weeks before the elections, Taiwan's capitalist social forces chose to openly voice their support for the 1992 consensus (and, by extension, Ma Ying-jeou and the KMT), again pleading with voters to be pragmatic in their decision and "do the rational thing": Foxconn founder Terry Gou labelled Ma an "experienced, outstanding helmsman" (Standing 2012). HTC chairwoman Cher Wang said that the 1992 consensus "ensures peace and stability" while describing the alternative, implying the election of Tsai Ing-wen, as "unpredictable," and Evergreen founder Chang Yung-fa warned that abandoning the 1992 consensus might jeopardise Taiwan's economy (Ger 2012: 83). Other tycoons to voice their support for the 1992 consensus included Douglas Hsu (Far Eastern Group), Wang Wen-yuan (Formosa Plastics) and Frank Liao (Chi Mei Corporation), while representatives of Taiwan's small and medium enterprises warned that abandoning the 1992 consensus could "spoil the future opportunities of Taiwan" (China.org.cn 2012). Led by UMC's honorary vice-chairman Jason Hsuan, 128 owners of high-tech enterprises based in the Hsinchu Science and Technology Park came forward, stating that while everybody had a personal preference for a colour (i.e., a party), it was important to consider the future of Taiwan's economy in the upcoming elections (China News Service 2012). The day before the ballot, this group sponsored an advertisement in the *Apple Daily*, emphasising that "[i]n the present economic conditions, whoever supports the 1992 Consensus maintains stable relations between the two sides of the strait, which allows us in turn to govern without fear and to continue to take care of our employees and their families" (cited in: LePesant 2012: 78). In all of these interventions, the basic message was clear:

electing an "unpredictable" Tsai Ing-wen would "rock the boat," while the 'experienced' Ma Ying-jeou was the pragmatic choice.

Although these purposeful interventions might have benefited Ma Ying-jeou, the key to understanding his re-election does not lie in a momentary episode. Rather, the pragmatism that had been advocated by Taiwanese capital since the 1990s and had since become the cornerstone of the hegemonic project had been successfully universalised to a degree that it had taken root in Taiwan's society. Even young pro-independence voters who identified as Taiwanese ultimately saw China as an opportunity rather than a threat, and a majority of Taiwanese were in favour of a "more proactive interaction with regard to cross-Strait economic and trade exchanges" (Liao et al. 2018: 78).

More than its eventual electoral defeat, this fundamental development called into question the relevance of the DPP. Given the gradual yet constant move toward cross-Strait pragmatism, these circumstances were bound to be reflected in the party's political imaginations and strategies. Against the background of the DPP's defeat, "[a] number of party leaders and public figures ... reiterated that the DPP's major weakness was its approach to China, and that a 'no change' attitude would compromise the party's future opportunities to regain power" (Schubert 2018: 44–46). The DPP considered adopting a pragmatic position towards China that would allow it to participate in cross-Strait interactions (Ger 2012: 83). A major advocate of finding common ground with the Chinese government was Frank Hsieh, a former prime minister under Chen Shui-bian and the DPP's presidential candidate for the 2008 elections. In the immediate aftermath of the elections, he urged the party to adopt a cross-Strait policy that was closer to the approach of the KMT (Romberg 2012a: 17–18). Even Tsai Ing-wen acknowledged the need for adjusting the party's approach to cross-Strait relations, stating that "you cannot understand China by sitting at home" (Taipei Times [TT] 2012a). Over the course of the summer, several DPP members travelled to China, albeit in private capacity, to explore potential openings for a more proactive approach to the CCP, culminating in Frank Hsieh's trip to China. While the official reason for the visit was a bartender competition, Hsieh also probed high-level officials of China's cross-Strait institutions, meeting both Wang Yi, director of the TAO, as well as Chen Yunlin, chairman of ARATS (Romberg 2012b: 11–12). This process led to adjustments of the party apparatus, with the China Affairs Department being reinstated in July before a China Affairs Committee was established in November to study potential paths to engage China. These arguments about the direction of the DPP meant that the party embarked on a path towards pragmatism just as social contestation moved to an open phase.

Organising Resistance in the Shadow of Hegemony

To understand the particular form of student participation in the AMM, it is necessary to reconstruct the specific trajectory of student group involvement. This trajectory was largely conditioned by the lessons activists had drawn from the failure of the WSM, resulting in new forms of organisation that were characterised by the formation of networks both among student groups as well as between these groups and Taipei-based NGOs. Two distinct phases will be discussed in this section. The first phase consists of the WSM activists' return to campus, where they established new or revitalised dormant campus groups that tended to focus on local issues of everyday life. The second phase is characterised by the establishment of cross-campus networks.

The Proliferation of Local Student Groups after the Wild Strawberry Movement

The WSM had introduced students from all over Taiwan to social struggle. Although most participants regarded the movement as a failure, it had a profound impact on student consciousness. Many students thought it imperative to conserve the momentum of activism, prompting them to conduct a systematic analysis of the movement's defining characteristics and discuss possible ways to transform the kinetic energy of the post-WSM environment into durable structures. In their analysis, student activists attributed the failure of the WSM to two of its major features. First, the movement was characterised by a lack of organisational structures (R25). Thus, students were ill-equipped and ill-prepared when the initial protests suddenly erupted into a full-blown movement (R21). Second, and closely related to the first feature, the movement then committed to a form of organisation without leaders (R21). It was therefore a movement of few organisers and many participants (R20), and activists felt this had contributed to a lot of time being taken up by discussions that not always yielded substantial results. They concluded that it was necessary to establish lasting structures that were able to train cadres who would ensure a more efficient decision-making process in the future (R24). This was the most important "mental sediment", to use the words of Luxemburg (2006: 126), of the WSM.

The crucial question that remained was that of the adequate organisational form to achieve the desired results. After the WildBerry House in Taipei closed as it posed a significant financial burden to the initiators (He 2009: 131) and contradicted the de-centralised character of the movement, the activists ultimately decided to return to the campus and organise students there (R22; R25; R29). In doing so, they drew on Taiwan's history of the so-called dissident societies (異議性社團, *yìyì xìng shètuán*), a term used to refer to movement-oriented campus groups that originated after the Wild Lily Movement in the early 1990s (Lee 2015). Student groups understood themselves as rooted in the everyday student experience, making them, according to Wei Yang, the adequate vehicle to cultivate student consciousness through grassroots practice (Lin 2011). Adopting the form of student papers, campus magazines or reading clubs meant that the groups were not limited to one kind of activity or one issue. In what follows, the terms student group, dissident society and campus group will be used interchangeably to refer to all of these forms of organisation. The discussion will largely be limited to those groups shown in Table 5.4 that would later be among the most active in the Youth Alliance against Media Monsters (YAMM). These can be distinguished into three generations based on the time of their establishment. The groups that were formed during the era of

Table 5.4 Selection of YAMM-related student groups

Name	Campus	Est.	Name (Chinese)	05/2011 THU	12/2011 Festival	01/2012 Vote	03/2012 NTU	03/2012 Tuition	05/2012 1 May	07/2012 YAMM
NTU Continent	NTU	04/1972	台大大陸社		•		•		•	•
Dalawasao	NTU	1987	台大濁水溪社		•		•		•	•
Ideology Study Club	SCU	1987	東吳大研社	•	•	•	•	•	•	•
People Workshop	THU	09/1989	東海人間工作坊	•	•	•	•	•		•
Black Ditch Club	FJU	1991	輔大黑水溝	•	•	•	•		•	•
Club of Seeds	NCCU	2000	政大種子社			•	•			•
Consciousness Paper	NTU	01/2008	台大意識報		•		•		•	•
CollectThinking	NUK	06/2008	高大軻仔糶社							○
Crowtopia	Middle Schools	08/2008	烏鴉邦中學生校園民主促進會		•	•	•		•	•
02 Society	NCKU	12/2008	成大零貳社	•	•	•	•		•	•
Taiwan Humanities Society	NTNU	2009	師大人文學社	•	•	•	•		•	•
Radical Notes	NTHU	03/2010	清大基進筆記	•	•	•	•		•	•
Outexpert	AU	2010	亞洲不學無術丈量室			•	•			○
Anti-Corporatization Front	NCKU	08/2011	反大學法人化陣線			•	•			•
Praxis in South	Cross-campus	07/2011	行南文化協會	•	•	•	•		•	•
Movement Club	CCU	09/2011	中正大學牧夫們社		•		•			•
Interesting Society	NYMU	09/2011	陽明大學有意思社							•
CGU Talk	CGU	09/2011	長庚庚云			•	•			•
FreeTakao	NSYSU	09/2011	中山放狗社			•			•	
NTPUCross	NTPU	02/2012	台北大學翻牆社			•	•		•	○

Source: author's compilation.

Note: • group was a constitutive member; ○ group participated in or co-organised events democratisation as well as in the aftermath of the WSM will be discussed in this section, while those that were established in 2011 will be part of the following one.

The first wave of dissident societies was established before or during Taiwan's democratisation in the late 1980s and the early 1990s, and most of these were active during the WLM in the early 1990s. With the notable exception of the *People Workshop* based at Taichung's Tunghai University (THU), these were founded at universities in the Taipei area. Although a few of the major groups of that time reach back to the 1970s, they underwent a process of reorganisation in the second half of the 1980s, and traditional groups such as the influential *NTU Continent*, *Dalawasao* (also NTU) or the *Ideology Study Club* at Soochow University (SCU) were adapted to intervene in the struggle for political change. However, many of these traditional student groups had become defunct by the time of the WSM, largely as a consequence of the general decline in social activism over the previous decade (see Chapter 4 and Lee 2017). In the Taipei area, these dormant clubs were revitalised by the influx of students who had experienced the WSM.

More than half of the groups that would later form the YAMM were established during a second wave after the WSM. What is striking is the geographic distribution: While the majority of first-wave dissident groups was established in the Taipei-area, only three out of the 11 newly-established groups of the second wave were located at universities in the north. Eight were founded in central or southern Taiwan, which had until then lacked campus-based movement groups. This wave of establishing new dissident clubs began with *02 Society* in Tainan, which was formed by WSM activists already during December 2008. It was followed by the *Taiwan Humanities Society* (Taipei), *Radical Notes* (Hsinchu) and *Outexpert* (Taichung) within a year and a half after that. This process can be understood as the condensation of local WSM branches, harnessing the WSM's de-centralised mode of resistance that consisted of loosely connected protest sites at various campuses throughout Taiwan. While this decentralisation was at first seen as a major shortcoming of the movement, it facilitated the local rooting of student activism after 2008. The major task of these reactivated and newly established dissident societies was to put into practice the lessons drawn from the analysis of the WSM by systematically developing conceptions and forms of practice. In their self-conception, some clubs prioritised theoretical analysis (e.g., Hsieh 2010), while others, according to *Radical Notes* member Wei Yang, sought to cultivate consciousness through grassroots activities (Lin 2011). In practice, most groups adopted a combination of various forms of practice including reading groups, workshops, discussions and talks, film screenings, print and online publications as well as local protest initiatives.

To better grasp the character of the student movement, it is necessary to take a look at the issues that preoccupied the campus groups during that time and the conceptions that emerged from these. Although the fluctuation of members and the variety of issues addressed by student clubs preclude the reduction of any of the groups to one current, several tendencies are worth discussing, as these would later contribute to competing visions of the student movement as a whole. In this early phase, the outlook of the various student groups was largely conditioned by two factors: their trajectory and the local issues they had to confront. Remarkably, the groups that had emerged during the struggle against authoritarianism in Taiwan were less influenced by the Wild Strawberry Movement and its themes of authoritarianism and human rights. Instead, they had developed radical conceptions in response to local consequences of the economic and social dynamics that emerged after Taiwan's democratisation. Especially the Taipei-based groups – including *NTU Continent*, the *Consciousness Paper* and the *Club of Seeds* – had been involved in struggles over nearby urban development projects, such as Losheng or Treasure Hill, an informal settlement in Taipei designated for demolition. The *Club of Seeds*, based at the National Chengchi University (NCCU), furthermore played a crucial role in the labour struggle by the university's cleaning staff. The *People Workshop*, based in central Taiwan, was similarly deeply conditioned by its local environment. The group was strongly influenced by Taiwan's Central Science and Industrial Park, which neighbours the campus of THU. Being directly affected by Taiwan's developmentalism shaped the group's conceptions of issues regarding land, labour and the environment (Chen 2010a). Another factor for the relative dominance of radical groups in the north, according to Lee (2017: 213–214), was that they had been more resilient during the decline of activism in the early 2000s. Pro-independence groups had been content with the election success of the DPP and thought it was not opportune to criticise Chen Shui-bian and his government. Radical groups, by contrast, were carried by the international wave of the anti-globalisation and anti-war movements of that time, which contributed to their survival.

The involvement in local movements further consolidated the development of radical conceptions: To better understand the concrete struggles the groups were involved in, they organised reading groups on Marxist theory (e.g., *NTU Continent*, *People Workshop*) and workshops that approached both the issues of developmentalism (urban renewal, land grabbing, etc.) as well as issues of everyday student life from the perspective of capital and labour (People Workshop 2011) or the crisis of capitalism (People Workshop 2012). A few of the post-WSM groups also adopted a radical perspective. The most notable example is *Radical Notes*, co-founded by Chen Wei-ting and Wei Yang. Chen had grown up in Miaoli, where he was involved in fierce land struggles. After his experience of the WSM, he enrolled at National Tsing Hua University (NTHU), setting up the *Rural Reading Club* in 2009, where students studied the land issue in Taiwan's countryside. At this time, the group also formed a relationship with the Taiwan Rural Front (TRF). After the establishment of *Radical Notes*, the activists broadened their perspective to all issues of social life, always maintaining a focus on questions of land and labour. Similar to the *People Workshop*, the conceptions developed by *Radical Notes* were therefore also profoundly shaped by the land struggles that occurred nearby due to the planned expansion of the Central Science and Industrial Park.

The alternative trajectory is best exemplified by the *02 Society*[3] formed by Lin Fei-fan in December 2008. Conceptually, the group retained its lineage to the WSM and its central themes of human rights, martial law and authoritarianism. However, it expanded the narrative to include nationalist conceptions, as displayed by a statement published on the occasion of the Lunar New Year 2009. In what can be considered its founding document, the *02 Society* warned of a threat greater than the global economic crisis, which had reached its peak during that time: "This threat comes from our government; this threat comes from China on the opposite side [of the Taiwan Strait]; this threat comes from the shadow of past authoritarianism" (02 Society 2009). The authors declared that during the past year, Taiwan's people had experienced "the violation of universal values such as freedom and human rights, or even the loss of national dignity and sovereignty", and lamented the fact that "the spirit of 'defending one's homeland' is forgotten" (ibid.). This situation could only be improved if the citizens of Taiwan were to reaffirm their identity:

> From now on, all citizens of Taiwan must understand their own rights and defend them to the death. From now on, every Taiwanese must know where they came from, how to take root, and to continue taking root. From now on, whether you are a child, a young, middle-aged or elderly person, you must know that you are Taiwanese.
>
> (ibid.)

To emphasise its lineage to the WSM, the group held vigils on the movement's anniversary, showed documentaries, and organised lectures and discussions on the WSM. More than the other groups, the *02 Society* not only conserved the momentum but also the conceptions of the movement from which it emerged. The nationalist element was reinforced by additional events, including a weekly "China Salon" that was moderated by Chinese dissident Wang Dan. While the *02 Society* also addressed the consequences of Taiwan's developmentalism, including environmental degradation and land grabbing, human rights and democracy remained the conceptual principle of the group, although the erosion of Taiwan's democratic system was increasingly attributed to the Chinese Communist Party in addition to the KMT.

The implications of these different conceptual approaches are best exemplified by the currents' positions on the issue of student rights. Being rooted in campus life, most dissident societies were involved in matters that affected the everyday life of students. The concrete issues ranged from strict dormitory regulations, rising tuition fees and transportation on campus to restrictions on establishing new campus groups. Their interpretations, however, differed considerably. Groups like the *02 Society* mainly saw these regulations as remnants of the authoritarian era. Lin Fei-fan framed the restriction of student autonomy as an issue of human rights, while Huang Kuo-chang, himself a veteran student activist of the Wild Lily era, described democratisation as an "unfinished battle" of the student movement of the 1990s (Lin 2011). From this perspective, university regulations "left over from the *old era* still restrict the autonomy of students in the current era of the universal values of human rights and freedom" (02 Society 2010, my emphasis).

The radical view on student rights emphasised the role of universities in a capitalist society (e.g., People Workshop 2008): "in a capitalist society, the form and content of education will inevitably have to meet the needs of capital" (Hsu 2011).

If elements of authoritarian regulations survived into the 2010s, it was because they resonated with the needs of capitalist reproduction. Similarly, Chen Wei-ting, in a contribution to the campus magazine *Radical Notes*, attributes the rising living costs, stagnating wages and their consequences on the everyday life of students to the dynamics of capital accumulation and the need to continuously adjust the system of higher education to meet the needs of accumulation (Chen 2010c). The *People Workshop* developed a perspective from which tuition fees could only be understood against the background of neoliberalisation and commodification of higher education and where the question of dormitories was necessarily related to urban renewal. These conceptions had significant implications for the practice of dissident societies: If student life on campus was mainly conditioned by legacies of the martial law era, as some groups argued, the situation could be remedied through reforms. By contrast, the radical perspective emphasised that the conditions of student life are continuously reproduced under capitalism, meaning that only systematic change could result in student autonomy.

Horizontal Organisation: Establishing Networks of Cooperation

After consolidating their foundation on campus, the groups slowly moved towards a second phase that was characterised by the establishment of networks of cooperation. This phase followed a distinct pattern, and it is helpful to first discuss the factors that contributed to this pattern. The dominant factor at this stage was the analysis of the structural differences between the north of Taiwan on the one hand and the central and southern regions on the other. A comprehensive critique of this phenomenon that students called "Taipei-centrism" appeared in a special issue on this question in the campus magazine *Praxis in South*. Although these articles date from the later stages of this phase and are therefore in all likelihood more mature and systematic than earlier arguments, a look at the various contributions of this publication sheds light on the self-conception that shaped the activism of the newly-established groups in the south.

Lee (2012) argues that Taiwan's particular mode of integration into the global economy induced a constant migration to the north, first due to industrial employment opportunities, then increasingly affecting education, media and other sectors. According to Lin (2012c), Taipei's structural advantage also exerted a gravitational pull on the cultural sector, with funding structures cementing "Taipei's long-term monopoly of art and cultural resources" and reproducing the peripheral position of the south. A similar picture emerges in tertiary education. Nearly two-thirds of all Taiwanese students are enrolled in the north of the country, where 70 per cent of educational resources are pooled in the pursuit of creating global universities (Hsu 2012a). These processes favoured the formation of distinct identities: While the economic and cultural development brought about a certain internationalisation of northern identity, the south tends to be locally rooted, not only due to a sense of relative deprivation but also because southern Taiwanese were more dissatisfied with the authoritarian era and thus tended to support the DPP (Hsieh 2012).

This Taipei-centrism, the contributing authors argue, necessarily had an effect on student activism. According to Pan (2012), Taipei has historically been the centre of social movements not because residents in the south had fewer reasons to collectively mobilise, but rather because the concentration of intellectual resources in Taipei prevented southern cities from developing a vibrant civil society of their own. Building on the various aspects discussed in the other contributions, Lin Fei-fan draws two major conclusions for the practice of southern dissident societies (Lin 2012b): The first is the need to overcome the historical marginalisation of southern activism. He points out that dissident societies at northern universities can trace back their legacy to the 1980s. Although they had been less active during the years prior to the re-emergence of student activism in Taiwan, these groups had preserved the experience of previous social movements and also remained in contact with Wild Lily veteran activists-turned-intellectuals. By contrast, the dissident groups in the south "start from scratch and create history" (ibid.). The second difference related to the historical circumstances is one of issues: Northern groups, Lin (ibid.) observes, are preoccupied with contesting exploitation, commodification and similar consequences of neoliberal developmentalism, as Taiwan's north is the region where these contradictions are more pronounced. Southern activism, on the other hand, is primarily motivated by the distinct southern identity, the region's relative structural deprivation, as well as Taiwan's history of authoritarianism and the process of transitional justice.

The conscious engagement with the political and socio-economic structures that resulted in activist subjectivities that are quite distinct from those in the north conditioned their practice over the following years. Most crucially, it accounts for two strategies: It led to the increasingly systematic cooperation among southern groups in order to compensate for their lack of experience. This found its expression not only in inter-campus exchanges and mutual support for protests but also in a continuous support for the establishment of new groups. It furthermore provides the context for the southern groups reaching out to NGOs in order to compensate for the lack of historically grown relations on which the northern groups could rely. Dissident societies in the south particularly sought to cooperate with like-minded NGOs that were concerned with authoritarianism, transitional justice and democracy – and increasingly China's impact on these issues – to develop the capacity to project the southern voice into the northern centres of power.

Throughout the year 2009, the exchanges between dissident societies took the form of a series of bilateral meetings, involving, among others, the *People Workshop*, *Outexpert* and the *Black Ditch Club* (Su and Shadow 2016). A first example of cooperation that not only involved multiple groups from the south but also instituted the first instances of cooperation with Taipei-based NGOs was the ECFA Watcher Student Alliance. In April 2010, Lin Fei-fan initiated this group to monitor the negotiation and implementation of the Economic Cooperation Framework Agreement, a preferential trade agreement between China and Taiwan. The alliance – consisting of Tainan's *02 Society* (NCKU) and student activists from National Sun Yat-sen University (NSYSU), National University of Kaohsiung (NUK) as well as National Kaohsiung Normal University (NKNU) – argued that the agreement was harmful to Taiwan's democracy and called for a referendum and the addition of a human rights clause (ECFA Watcher Student Alliance 2010). In June, the Alliance joined the Cross-Strait Agreement Watch (CSAW), a coalition initiated by Taiwan Democracy Watch (TDW) and joined by about two dozen NGOs, including the TAUP, the TAHR, Taipei Society and the TLF. While a detailed look at this coalition is beyond the scope of this study, it constituted a remarkable step towards overcoming the marginalisation of southern dissident societies. Participating in CSAW not only established personal connections with Lai Chung-chiang, Wu Jieh-min (both TDW) and Huang Kuo-chang (Taipei Society) – which will be discussed at a later point – but would provide a model for the later instances of student-NGO cooperation during the Anti-Media Monopoly and Sunflower Movements.

The increasing cooperation of dissident societies resulted in the THU exchange of May 2011. Student activists proposed the idea for this event at a vigil during the Kuokuang chemical plant protests. Originally planned as a bilateral event involving the *People Workshop* and *02 Society*, further groups expressed interest in joining, and plans to hold a larger meeting were agreed (Wei 2016: 88). In addition to the host *People Workshop*, eight other groups participated: *Radical Notes*, *Ideology Study Club*, *Club of Seeds*, *Black Ditch Club*, *Crowtopia*, *Outexpert*, *02 Society* and *CollectThinking* (see Table 5.4). With six groups from central and southern Taiwan being joined by three established clubs from the Taipei-area, this was the first significant event that systematically compared the conceptions and forms of practice of both older and newer as well as radical and nationalist-leaning groups (Su and Shadow 2016). It was at the THU exchange that several of the later YAMM and Black Island Nation Youth Front (BIY) leaders met for the first time (Chen 2012c; Su and Shadow 2016).

This exchange and the conscious effort to establish cooperation networks served as the inspiration for further dissident groups. The momentum was further reinforced by a two-day 'Consensus Camp' organised by *02 Society* in August 2011 (02 Society 2011). This camp sought to address the needs of both extant societies by proposing concrete steps to deepen forms of cooperation and of students who sought advice on how to establish new groups. Both of these aims were realised: During the month of September alone, four dissident societies were established, marking the third wave of student club formation.[4] Furthermore, the cross-campus group *Praxis in South* was set up as a campus magazine for seven universities in the southern cities of Tainan, Chiayi and Kaohsiung. This group is not only the product of cooperation between southern student groups but also a major instrument to deepen it: Based on the experience that "the themes and content selected by the media are mostly about Taipei", the magazine not only wanted to simply report on issues concerning the south, but also vowed to "abandon the perspective of looking at the world from Taipei" by disseminating the views developed by southern activists (Praxis in South 2012).

The second outcome of the Consensus Camp was the Southern Wave Music Festival in December 2011. While about 20 dissident societies participated in the event organised by the *02 Society*, the festival went beyond earlier internal exchanges as these groups addressed themselves to the general public. Not only did the concert showcase the capacity of the groups to organise a large event, but it also drew on and consolidated the relations with NGOs, as the TAUP and the *Lee Teng-hui Association for Democracy* acted as sponsors of the event while the TRF set up a farmers' market at the venue. The dissident groups and other NGOs set up exhibitions and booths at the concert venue to inform visitors. The southern groups, which largely organised the event, also used it as a vehicle to publicise what they called the "taking a stance" theory (Lee 2017: 215–216), that is, to pursue an open re-politicisation of the student movement based on national identity with the aim of defeating the KMT during the 2012 elections:

> We dare not state our political position, we are scared of being labelled … we cannot talk about our love for the land … No! On this day we want to be young, take a stance, talk about our dreams, choose our future!
> (Southern Wave Music Festival 2012)

Another example that displays the elements of south-south cooperation as well as student-NGO cooperation was the "I want to go home to vote!" campaign of early January 2012. This initiative grew out of the activists' concern that many young Taiwanese, who were studying in Taipei but were registered in other parts of the country, might not be able to cast their vote in the 14 January elections as the elections took place during exam weeks. Furthermore, the Lunar New Year holidays began one week later, meaning that these students would have to travel back home in two consecutive weeks, posing a financial and logistical burden. A number of dissident groups teamed up with the Taiwan Labor Front, the Anti-Poverty Alliance and Huang Kuo-chang to demand that these students were offered affordable transportation and that the Ministry of Education considered extending deadlines for assignments that had to be handed in during that time (02 Society et al. 2012). Ultimately, the groups were able to organise buses to be made available for at least a part of the affected students (R29).

Before we finally turn to the Anti-Media Monopoly Movement, it is necessary to discuss one episode that suggests that the radical current was gaining influence among the dissident societies between February and the 1st of May Labour Day 2012. The catalyst for this episode was indications that the KMT government reneged on its earlier assurance that tuition fees would not rise (Anti-Corporatization Front/Students Rights Survey and Evaluation Team 2012a). Two groups that were familiar with the question of tuition, the cross-campus *Student Rights Team* and the *Anti-Corporatization Front* from Tainan, then organised the "Anti-Tuition Forum: The First Left-Wing Forum on Education" on 13 February to discuss further action. At this internal meeting, the groups set out to apply and expand the radical conceptions discussed above to the question of tuition. To this end, they analysed the challenges faced by students (including rising tuition fees, the growing number of student loans and the declining wages for first-time job entrants) not separately but as aspects of class struggle on campus, which cannot, they urged, be solved by redistributive reforms (Lin 2012d; Anti-Tuition Forum 2012). They offered a systemic approach to address the role of education in capitalist social formations, including the students as workers-to-be conception discussed below (Anti-Tuition Forum 2012), but also the relation of capital, the state, education and research and development (Hsu 2012b). They concluded with the necessity to introduce notions of class and capitalism into the debate on higher education to inform the struggle on campus:

> The anti-tuition [movement] does not just demand free tuition, it is rather about anti-capitalism, because that struggle is the only way out of an educational environment that is distorted by the logic of capital.
>
> (Anti-Tuition Forum 2012)

Four weeks later, another dissident group exchange took place. In contrast to the previous meetings, the two-day event themed "'Return of the Student Wave' Action Forum" was organised at the NTU in Taipei, where dissident societies were leaning towards radical conceptions (see Table 5.4). The first day of the exchange was dedicated to discussions on the recent experiences, including the establishment of dissident societies, the role of campus magazines, the organisational aspects of the student movement and its political positioning. The second day, however, was marked by the issue of tuition, with several panels being held on neo-liberalism and the commodification of education. Even more remarkable than the conceptional and organisational efforts during these few weeks was the rapid transition from the latent to an open phase: Already on the evening of the second day of the NTU exchange, the present groups circulated a call to participate in a protest the next day, 26 March (Anti-Corporatization Front et al. 2012c). The inter-campus umbrella organisation Alliance against the Commodification of Education (ACE) was established in the immediate aftermath of that protest under the leadership of the *Student Rights Team* and the *Anti-Corporatization Front* (Anti-Corporatization Front et al. 2012b; Wei 2016: 156). In early April, the Ministry of Education announced a freeze of tuition fees, citing the maintenance of social stability as the major reason (TT 2012b).

The developments immediately prior to the AMM, therefore, do not provide a uniform picture. With regard to conceptions, the established northern dissident societies tended to adopt radical analyses, while the southern groups formed after the WSM leaned towards nationalist conceptions. The networking efforts were driven in particular by these southern groups, which sought to compensate for their lack of experience and marginalisation. Incidentally, these efforts by southern dissident societies to overcome their initially marginalised position resulted in a shift in relation of forces in their favour, as it stimulated the establishment of cross-campus organisations and events, the establishment of contacts with Taipei-based NGOs (most crucially with the TDW, TAUP, the Taipei Society and the TRF) as well as issue-based inter-campus alliances (such as the ECFA Watcher Student Alliance).

Throughout the winter and spring of 2012, however, the momentum appeared to favour the radical current, culminating in the establishment of ACE and the participation of dissident societies in the May 1st demonstration. It is conceivable that the groups constituting the nationalist current, and whose immediate goal was to ensure the defeat of the KMT during the January elections (Su and Shadow

2016), were shellshocked by the election success of Ma Ying-jeou. This coincided with the revitalisation of the radical current in response to the government's plans to raise tuition fees. Building on an established conceptual framework and well-rehearsed patterns of organisation, the radical current was able to move from refining its conceptions (Anti-Tuition Forum), organisation and mobilisation (the NTU exchange and the establishment of ACE) to action (Ministry of Education protest) and success in a short amount of time. On the eve of the AMM, a radical renaissance appeared possible. Notably, there is no evidence that student groups took note of the media issue that emerged during the same time frame. What thus remains to be explained is how the student groups got involved in the AMM and why the nationalist current ultimately prevailed.

The Anti-Media Monopoly Movement

The Emergence of the Anti-Media Monopoly Movement as a Scholar-led Media Reform Movement

Unlike the abrupt and quasi-spontaneous emergence that defined the Wild Strawberry Movement, the Anti-Media Monopoly Movement was characterised by a gradual accumulation, convergence and integration of a variety of issues. The two-year period between the first activities and the height of mobilisation was characterised by continuous shifts in the relation of forces within the movement. To appreciate these dynamics, it is beneficial to distinguish two different points of nucleation. A reformist path emerged in response to the phenomenon of embedded marketing and the increasing market concentration in Taiwan's media sector, both involving the Want Want China Times Group. This current consisted mainly of scholars and NGOs who had been involved in the media reform movement for nearly two decades and could rely on the conceptual apparatus developed during that time. A second current mobilised after Tsai Eng-meng, owner of Want Want China Times, made controversial remarks with regard to cross-Strait relations in a *Washington Post* interview. His statements alarmed human rights and democracy NGOs, whose perspective was informed not so much by media reform but by cross-Strait dynamics. Their entrance into the terrain of struggle introduced nationalist conceptions to the movement.

The multitude of trajectories into the AMM reflects the changing form of hegemony after 2008. As a consequence of the Cultural Turn, hegemonic initiatives assumed a capillary form, creating a variety of grievances across a range of sectors. As the cultural field in general and the media sector, in particular, had become the most crucial site of molecular activities, it is not surprising that resistance reflected this changing character of hegemony. While these points of nucleation are hence structurally related, it is necessary to reconstruct the trajectories that resulted in polycentric resistance, which shaped not only the various perspectives on hegemonic contestation, but also enabled or precluded forms of cooperation, integration and, ultimately, dissociation of the various currents.

The first point of nucleation arose when in September 2010, the Foundation for the Advancement of Media Excellence published a report on embedded marketing practices in Taiwanese newspapers (Hsu 2014a: 530–532). The study found 245 advertorials between January and September of that year, 108 of which had been placed by Chinese government agencies (Foundation for the Advancement of Media Excellence 2010). 69 of these were placed in the China Times, while the United Daily and the United Evening News published 30 and nine advertorials respectively. The monthly data shows a clear trend: Except for the month of September, the placing of advertorials saw a steady increase from four cases in January to 22 in August. A report published by the Control Yuan suggests that these advertorials were connected to trips of Chinese delegations to Taiwan, as these visits tended to coincide with advertorials commissioned by Chinese authorities (Control Yuan, R.O.C. 2010; Engbarth 2011). In addition to extensive news coverage of the Chinese delegation itself, the newspapers published various other unmarked advertorials depicting the respective province as a worthwhile tourist destination or highlighting its economic potential (Control Yuan, R.O.C. 2010: 5–6). Portraying the provinces and their delegations in a positive light can be seen as a reaction to the experience of the WSM, when the visit of a Chinese delegation served as a catalyst for protest. All of these advertorials were placed in publications owned by groups that were co-sponsors of the Straits Forum, namely the Want Want China Times and United Daily News groups.

Embedded marketing itself was not a new phenomenon in Taiwan. In the past, however, it were Taiwanese authorities who had placed paid but unmarked content in Taiwanese publications. In an attempt to bring advertorials in Taiwanese media to an end, media reform associations including the Association of Taiwan Journalists (ATJ), Campaign for Media Reform (CMR), and Solidarity of Communication Students Taiwan (SCS) had mobilised against both major parties in Taiwan before the 2008 elections, successfully pressuring both Ma Ying-jeou and Frank Hsieh to pledge that the practice would not be continued if they were to win (Cheng 2014: 13). The media reform movement proceeded to continuously monitor the implementation of this agreement, criticising not only the government but also the media outlets for a practice that undermined the professional autonomy of journalists (Association of Taiwan Journalists [ATJ] 2010). Due to their familiarity with the issue, the same groups also mobilised in response to the report on embedded marketing from China.

The debate became more acute when in late October 2010, Want Want China Times, the largest recipient of China-funded embedded marketing, announced that it had struck a deal with MBK to acquire the cable operator CNS through its subsidiary Want Want Broadband. The concerns of the media reform movement were twofold: On the one hand, Want Want had only recently concluded the merger with the China Times Group, already significantly increasing its share of the Taiwanese media market; on the other hand, the group's involvement in accepting embedded marketing from China was perceived as undermining journalistic autonomy, raising doubts about whether the conglomerate was qualified to own a cable operator, which would allow it to wield the power to choose which content would reach the consumer.

The National Communications Commission (NCC) initiated the process for regulatory approval of the deal, with the first hearing set for late 2011. This effectively postponed the movement for nearly a year, initiating a low-intensity phase that consisted mostly of research and the dissemination of research results through opinion pieces published in Taiwanese newspapers. As the NCC hearings approached, this process gained in intensity. The major angle advanced by critics of the merger was to prevent the emergence of a "media monster"[5], a notion coined by two NTU professors in September 2011 (Jang and Lin 2011). In its core, the "media monster" narrative is summed up by the argument that Taiwan's plurality of speech and freedom can only be safeguarded if competition in the media sector is maintained through anti-monopoly legislation. Most groups involved in the movement at that point in time subscribed to this major appeal. The major forms of practice remained on the proven ground, including the establishment of an interdisciplinary research group, regular press conferences and the lobbying of legislators (Chang 2013: 6–7), although a protest was held outside of the NCC on the first day of the hearings.

The issue of monopolisation, however, introduced a high degree of complexity into the narrative, as it necessitated a discussion on cross-media ownership structures, the institutional competence of the involved institutions in Taiwan, as well as various legal questions. Given the lack of anti-monopoly legislation for Taiwan's media sector, scholars drew on historical precedents as well as comparisons with similar legislation abroad, including the examples of Rupert Murdoch and Silvio Berlusconi, but also the recent merger and acquisition attempts involving ProSiebenSat.1 and Axel Springer AG in Germany as well as Fubon and kbro in Taiwan. The complexity arose from the question of how to attribute a relative weight to terrestrial, satellite and cable television, as well as print market and cable operations to determine the overall cross-media market share (Guo 2011). These debates necessitated specialised knowledge of economic and legal aspects, essentially limiting the movement to academics and media professionals (Ebsworth 2017: 76). As not all scholars agreed that the merger would result in a monopoly (Tsai and Lo 2016: 161), the complex arguments might have been articulated to convince other scholars before the hearings commenced as much as they were designed to inform the general public.

Before the regulatory process was completed, a second path into the movement opened up in January 2012. While the issue of China had already been touched upon in connection with the controversy regarding advertorials, it had since been relegated to a subordinate role with respect to the question of cross-media market concentration. This alternate path would instead directly politicise the media movement via the role of China-Taiwan relations. The point of nucleation for the nationalist current was an interview with Want Want China Times owner Tsai Eng-meng published by the *Washington Post* one week after Taiwan's 2012 Presidential elections. Among the more controversial parts of the interview were Tsai's blatant support for unification and his downplaying of the Tiananmen Incident of 1989. He also justified the sacking of an editor who had negatively reported on ARATS chairman Chen Yunlin, urging journalists "to think carefully before they write" (Higgins 2012).

In contrast to the media reform groups and scholars, who were careful to avoid politicisation along the blue-green spectrum, the NGOs from the nationalist current did not hesitate to put the China issue to the fore. The *Washington Post* interview had led them to the realisation that "[t]he press was a very important battle ground against the Communist Party" (R25). On 30 January, Huang Kuo-chang, then President of the independence-leaning Taipei Society, responded to the interview by co-authoring an article in the *Apple Daily*. The authors maintained that Tsai had moved dangerously close to the official CCP discourse, suggesting that he was willing to become an agent for China. They urged the Taiwanese public to defend the country's democracy, which they saw threatened by pro-unificationist "big-wigs" controlling the media (Huang and Chiu 2012). Two days later, the Taipei Society issued an open letter, inviting Tsai – who had claimed the quotes had been taken out of context – to a public debate to clarify his stance on the Tiananmen Incident and journalistic autonomy (Taipei Society 2012). The letter was signed by other pro-independence groups, including TDW and TAHR but also ATJ and CMR.

When Tsai failed to react to the invitation, the Taipei Society and TDW launched a campaign that called on Taiwan's intellectuals to refuse submitting texts to the *China Times*, which was owned by Tsai's Want Want Group. The campaign was supported by ATJ, about 60 scholars and several dozen, mostly pro-independence, associations, including TAUP, TAHR, Judicial Reform Foundation (JRF), TLF and the Taiwan Youth Anti-Communist Corps. Despite the issue of China being the major reason for the campaign (Chen 2015: 35), it resulted in a cooperation between reformist and nationalist groups, and throughout the month, representatives from both currents would integrate reformist and nationalist conceptions. A text co-authored by Huang Kuo-chang and Flora Chang can be interpreted as an attempt to reconcile both perspectives: The acquisition of CNS by Want Want China Times would not simply create a cross-media monster, but moreover one that was directed by an outspoken pro-unificationist who did not shy away from using his media power to silence critics (Huang et al. 2012).

While the complexity of the media reform narrative had precluded attempts to reach out to the wider public (R25), the emphasis on China made the issue accessible to the Taiwanese, who were familiar with the dynamics and stakes of cross-Strait relations. Taipei Society President Huang Kuo-chang was keen to reach out to activists and intellectuals beyond the realm of the media. In April, he engaged with student activists by participating in an event organised at the *Café Philo*, one of Taipei's post-WSM activist forums. In early May, he was furthermore able to secure the public support of the renowned Chinese-born American historian and Kluge Prize laureate Yu Ying-shih. In his response to a letter from Huang, Yu said:

> I feel that there are some wealthy politicians and businessmen in Taiwan who, motivated by absolute self-interest, have made up their minds to cater to the CCP's intentions and infiltrate Taiwan; buying media outlets is only one of the links … The greatest duty of Taiwanese intellectuals must be to safeguard the democratic and free system and to promote its continuous growth; the slightest weakness, and it will inevitably succumb to the CCP's 'united front' strategy.
>
> (Yu 2012)

While Yu's intervention was an achievement for the nationalist current, it risked alienating the more radical groups of the media reform movement by cementing the "united front" angle. In particular, members of CMR were hesitant to embrace the nationalist narrative, arguing that the emphasis on the person of Tsai Eng-meng obscured the acquisition of CNS had to be interpreted against the background of broader dynamics and otherwise similar cases, such as the takeover of cable operator kbro by Fubon's subsidiary Dafu Media (Chen 2015: 36).

To avoid a fragmentation of conceptions and a competition between the currents, activists moved towards clarifying the relation between the approaches. In an attempt to synthesise these positions, scholars from the two currents compiled a Q&A document, which covered all aspects that had been discussed so far. A large part of the document deals with ownership concentration, arguing that this would result in a decline in the variety and quality of news reporting (Chang et al. 2012b:: 4–8). With market share as the point of departure, the rest of the document sets out various ways of measuring cross-media market share and discusses legal and institutional models that would allow for the effective supervision and implementation. Another section discusses Tsai Eng-meng and the impact of his personal views and actions on journalistic autonomy (ibid.: 15–17).

Ultimately, this synthesis did not introduce any new conceptual elements, but instead bridged the gap between extant conceptions by offering two concrete yet relatively formal appeals that allowed groups from the various currents to rally behind them without jeopardising their particular rationale for supporting it. The first of these appeals was for anti-monopoly legislation. The media reform scholars, relying on their interdisciplinary expertise, could emphasise the structural (i.e., economic, institutional and legal) aspects and argue that excessive market concentration *per se* would negatively affect the plurality of opinions. Nationalist groups, in turn, could advance an agent-centric reading with regard to monopolisation: Against the background of the *Washington Post* interview, they could attribute Tsai's pursuit of media outlets to his personal support for unification, arguing that preventing this particular merger was even more imperative than it was in other cases. The second demand called for the establishment of an independent editorial system. For the ATJ, which represented the employee's perspective, this was a self-evident position (ATJ 2012b). Media scholars pointed to the controversy around advertorials (placed by both the KMT and DPP governments in addition to Chinese authorities) to argue that in order to avoid a further blurring of lines between journalism and marketing, mechanisms to ensure journalistic autonomy had to be implemented (Huang et al. 2012). Again, the nationalist current could present these advertorials as evidence of Tsai's close relation with the CCP, especially as they coincided with Chinese delegations visiting Taiwan.

These conceptions did not overcome the condition of "multiple elements of 'conscious leadership'" (Gramsci 1971: 196–197) in the movement. Yet, they served as a compromise that provided the ideological form in which the latent contradictions could co-exist, in particular as the controversial China issue did not become the main angle for the official appeals. The common ground was not found in the diagnostic and motivational elements of the analysis but in the fact that both currents arrived at the same conclusion from different angles. Only when articulated in the context of the whole ideological narrative of either current, these were enriched to gain their full meaning. As the subsequent months would show, the unifying potential of this equilibrium was precarious.

Actualising the Student Potential through Vertical Organisation: From the NCC Decision to the 901 Parade

On 25 July, the NCC was set to announce its decision. That morning, a group of scholars, including Huang Kuo-chang and Flora Chang, submitted a petition asking the NCC to reject the acquisition (Chang et al. 2012a), while about 200 students assembled to protest the emergence of a "media monster." The NCC tentatively approved the acquisition on the condition that Tsai Eng-meng and his family dissociated themselves from the operations of CTi TV, that the group's news channel CTV was transformed into a non-news channel, and that CTV set up an independent editorial system (Ebsworth 2017: 76). While the final condition reflected one of the movement's demands, the NCC decision limited it to only one outlet within the group. The demand for anti-monopoly legislation was not adopted. To a degree, this was blamed on the lack of wider public support that was attributed to the complex academic discussions that were thought to impede the movement's generalisation (R21).

Two days after this announcement, several media outlets of the Want Want China Times Group reported that Huang Kuo-chang had paid students to participate in the protest. Huang denied these claims during a press conference, but the coverage by Want Want China Times continued. On social media, scholars and activists rallied behind Huang. Among hundreds of others, student activist Chen Wei-ting shared a photo of a woman handing out money to protesters, stating that he believed the Want Want Group had staged the incident to discredit the movement. Want Want China Times then threatened to file a lawsuit against Chen, and the group's media outlets prominently featured Chen as they continued their extensive coverage of the incident.

The involvement of Chen Wei-ting was the catalyst that prompted the activation of student networks that had developed over the previous years (R21; R29; R31). Various student groups responded by posting messages of solidarity with Chen on their websites, while others held small protests (R29). Very quickly, however, student activists moved from individual action towards networked mobilisation. A crucial element for this form of mobilisation was the organisational sediments that were the result of cooperation between student groups and NGOs. Their cooperation on individual issues over the years had coagulated into personal and organisational ties that now only needed to be reactivated. Perhaps the most central of these was between the students and law scholar Huang Kuo-chang, whom Chen Wei-ting had invited to give a talk on student rights in his club *Radical Notes* in 2010 (R25), as this relationship represents the nucleus of the incident that involved both Huang and Chen in the aftermath of the 25 July protests. Lin Fei-fan, on the other hand, had been involved with the Cross-Strait Agreement Watch (CSAW), after his student club *02 Society* established the ECFA Watcher Student Alliance. During this time, the group cooperated not only with the Taipei Society, of which Huang Kuo-chang was the president but also other associations like TDW and TAUP. In the year 2011, Lin Fei-fan collaborated with Huang Kuo-chang on student rights and *02 Society* invited Wu Jieh-min (TDW) for a talk on social movements.

By building on these sediments, this rapid process of activating networks culminated in the formation of the YAMM within a matter of days after the Huang Kuo-chang incident, "welded together" (R21) by the pressure from the Want Want Group against one of their fellow student activists. The alliance was set up as an issue-oriented umbrella organisation, consisting of more than 30 student activist groups that were formed or reinvigorated after the WSM (see Table 5.4). This design allowed to concentrate the resources of the various campus groups and project an image of unity onto the field of hegemonic contestation.

Entering the terrain of struggle in such a rapid fashion, however, also left little time for systematic conceptual work and therefore confined the students to the ideological repertoire that was pre-structured around the two poles of reformist and nationalist narratives. While individual students, in particular Chen Wei-ting, had earlier identified themselves as "left independent" and the student group SCS had positioned itself as a strong critic of the nationalist narrative, YAMM's organisational proximity to Taipei-based NGOs contributed to their conceptual subordination during this phase. This becomes apparent from a look at the first protest organised by YAMM on 31 July, which relied on the two earlier demands to prevent Tsai Eng-meng from misusing his media outlets for personal reasons and rejecting the acquisition.

During the month of August, the rapid activation of cooperation networks allowed for an equally quick diversification of practice. From 8 to 30 August, YAMM compiled the social media-based "Anti-Want[2] TwiDaily," a digest of and commentary on news coverage of the media movement. This suggests that media was no longer seen just as the object but also as the site of contestation, as activists reviewed the ongoing coverage while simultaneously trying to transpose the complexities of the reformist arguments into comments that were more accessible to their audience. This systematic approach to managing the media gave YAMM a degree of credibility with media professionals (R25). In addition, the group launched the "Say no to Want Want during the Ghost Month" campaign (Youth Alliance against Media Monsters [YAMM] 2012c). This campaign related the tradition of the Ghost Month, where food and drinks are offered to the dead, with the cause of the movement by revealing the reach of the conglomerate in various sectors. The call to boycott snacks and drinks produced by Want Want drew on the de-centralised character of the YAMM, which made it possible to mobilise local student groups and draw attention to the campaign at convenience stores all over Taiwan.

In the meantime, the major NGOs in the movement had formed an umbrella organisation analogous to the YAMM. The Anti-Media Monster Alliance (AMMA) was established under the guidance of the ATJ, CMR and Media Watch and was joined by a large number of associations, including TDW, the Judicial Reform Foundation, the Taiwan Association for Human Rights, the Taiwan Labor Front, the Taiwan Association of University Professors, the TRF, the Taiwan Youth Anti-Communist Corps and the Taiwan branch of Amnesty International. The establishment of two umbrella organisations, each consisting of several dozen groups, facilitated the coordination between the student groups and the associations and enabled them to expand their forms of practice. In mid-August, they announced a large-scale demonstration on 1 September. This date echoes a significant historical date for the media reform movement, as the movement of 1994 had also culminated in a demonstration on 1 September. Both the ATJ and SCS had emerged from the "September 1st Task Force for Journalistic Autonomy," which had organised the demonstration 18 years earlier. The role of the ATJ and CMR in the establishment of AMMA and invoking the historical continuity between the reform movements of 1994 and 2012 to articulate a historical lineage suggests that, at least this particular point in time, media reform was still the major issue for the AMM.

To prepare for the 901 Demonstration, the two major student organisations YAMM and SCS held the "Anti-Media Monster Youth Action Camp" in late August. Supported by ATJ and hosted by NTU's Graduate Institute of Journalism, the workshop had the aim to recruit and train student cadres, and a total of 44 students from all over Taiwan were selected as participants for the three-day camp. Despite their cooperation on this issue, first tensions between YAMM and SCS emerged with regard to the character of the workshop (Cheng 2014: 50–51). SCS could draw on nearly two decades of experience on the issue of media reform. Its main interest was to disseminate its conceptions that had been systematically developed during that time, instructing students on the historical, economic and social dimensions of the media reform movement. YAMM, in contrast, lacked systematic conceptions but had a robust, capable and far-reaching apparatus for short-term mobilisation and action. Each group had different ideas of the movement, in particular with regard to the direction of a potential politicisation of the movement and whether expertise and conceptions or hands-on training were the order of the day (Wei 2016: 178–179). Ultimately, a compromise was reached, and one-half of the sessions consisted of talks by professors and activists on the media issue, while the other half was dedicated to the aspects of organisation, strategy and preparing the demonstration (Lin 2012e).

The demonstration on 1 September attracted between 9,000 and 10,000 participants. The common call issued by the co-organisers listed four demands (901 Demonstration Alliance 2012): First, the participating groups called for the preservation of journalistic standards through a series of mechanisms, including an independent editorial system, ethics committees and external oversight; second, they urged Tsai Eng-meng to apologise for the violation of professional ethics, in particular to Huang Kuo-chang and Chen Wei-ting for the abuse by the media after the Huang Kuo-chang incident; third, they demanded increased supervision of media outlets by the NCC; finally, they requested the passing of anti-monopoly legislation to prevent the emergence of excessive cross-media conglomerates.

In addition to this common call, the various groups also issued separate statements that allow us to assess the respective views held by these groups (see Table 5.5). ATJ, representing the perspective of media professionals, put journalistic standards to the

Table 5.5 Appeals by the 901 Alliance and the participating groups

Group	Official Appeals					
	Journalistic standards	*Tsai Eng-meng*	*NCC supervision*	*Anti-monopoly legislation*	*Strengthen unions*	*Public media*
ATJ	•	•	•			
Scholars		•		•		
YAMM	•	•	•	•		
CMR	•	•		○	•	•
SCS	•			○	•	•

Source: author's compilation.

Note: The ○ signifies that although SCS and CMR supported anti-monopoly legislation, their conceptualisation of markets and monopolies differed considerably from the official appeal.

fore in its 901 call. The major concern regarding Want Want was that "media obeyed the wishes of the boss" (ATJ 2012a), and in order to restore journalistic autonomy, independent editorial systems had to be established. Scholars had discussed a variety of aspects in their interventions in interviews and opinion pieces, but the demand for anti-monopoly legislation and doubts regarding Tsai Eng-meng's eligibility to control media outlets were by far the most common. Given the short lead-up of effectively one month, the student alliance YAMM was unable to articulate its own conceptions let alone assert its view within the movement, instead subscribing to the demands of the dominant current (YAMM 2012a).

The demands articulated by the radical current differed substantially. SCS's major point regards the systematic causes for the grievances, highlighting the fact that broader changes are needed to "[s]top the despot of laissez-faire capital from eating up democracy and freedom" (Solidarity of Communication Students [SCS] 2012a). Similarly, CMR justifies its demand for an independent editorial system on the grounds that it is one necessary, albeit insufficient, element "to fight for the journalists' autonomy and oppose private capital monopolising the media" (Campaign for Media Reform [CMR] 2012c). In addition, their statement demands the strengthening of unions to protect working conditions as well as public control of media and funding for all sorts of non-profit media. In a separate statement, Wei Ti of CMR raises doubts about the movement's decision to foreground the personal role of Tsai Eng-meng and his conglomerate, warning that "[i]f we now put all the focus of the fight on Want Want, it is likely there will be blind spots" (Wei 2012), the most crucial of these being the role of the market. Wei argues that competition is not the panacea but the *cause* for the defects of Taiwan's media sector. And while other activists placed their hopes on the NCC to rectify the situation, Wei points out that the logic of the market is inscribed into the institutional set-up of the NCC, arguing that the commission, since its establishment in 2006, had been an accomplice in privatisation and de-regulation, thus becoming "the main driver of shaping the media industry and the [media] market into a paradise for capitalists" (ibid.). Rather than simplifying conceptions or relying on conceptions from the authoritarian era, the AMM had "an obligation and responsibility to develop more complex movement forms and discourses" (ibid.).

The increasing variety in demands can be attributed to the conditional approval of the merger in late July. In the absence of a concrete short-term goal, the various groups shifted the emphasis on those aspects that reflected their respective historical struggles and trajectories. As the radical current's demands with regard to unions and public media were not integrated into the official list of demands, the four official appeals are therefore, at best, the common denominator among the most influential groups in the movement, showing that the radical current was not able to introduce its perspective into the broader movement. It is furthermore striking that nationalist conceptions, which emerged around the second point of nucleation, did not appear in the 901 appeals. The failure to integrate the various currents revealed the potential for tensions.

The Anti-Media Monopoly Movement at the Cross-roads: The China Factor and Its Critics

The 901 demonstration marked the culmination of public mobilisation against the media monopoly over the summer of 2012. Despite the various points of nucleation, up to this point, all groups and associations had united under a reformist approach that emphasised the need to regulate the media sector and maintain journalistic standards within media outlets. The various groups had also closely cooperated in organising events, including the preparatory Youth Action Camp and the 901 parade itself. With the conclusion of the 901 parade and without the imperative to address immediate developments, the movement entered a phase of dénouement that freed up resources for ideological and organisational discussions. This concerned, in particular, the YAMM. The group had entered the AMM when the ideological terrain had already been pre-structured by the debates on market concentration, advertorials and the Tsai remarks. Their lack of conceptions on this issue and the rather hasty entry on the terrain of struggle meant that, out of necessity, they adopted the reformist conceptions developed by media scholars and NGOs.

The dénouement provided a moment of respite that allowed for a systematic reassessment of these conceptions and forms of practice. This process was facilitated by the establishment of a student apparatus over the previous years. The WSM had mainly existed through the continuous occupation of Liberty Square, which had bound all forces and left few resources for other forms of practice. The establishment of a network of student clubs after 2008 made it possible to shift from a movement that relied on occupation to one that was based on intermittent activities. This prevented physical and mental exhaustion and freed up time for discussion, recruitment and training.

The outcome of these developments was the so-called Campus Tour (see Table 5.6) in the fall of 2012, which served as an exchange and dissemination channel between the umbrella organisation and the local groups. The tour was characterised by a horizontal and a vertical division of labour. Horizontally, three groups each organised a series of complementary and interlocking events: SCS and YAMM organised talks and debates on various campuses around Taiwan, often

Table 5.6 AMM-related public talks and debates, 2012

Date	Location	Co-organisers	Participants
8/10	Taipei	Café Philo	Lin Fei-fan, Wu Rwei-ren
8/30	NTU, Taipei	YAMM, SCS	Youth Action Camp (three days)
9/25	NYMU, Taipei	*Interesting Society*, IYF, TAUP	Chen Wei-ting
9/29	Taipei	IYF, TAUP	YAMM, SCS
10/9	NTHU, Hsinchu	*Radical Notes*, SCS	Lin Fei-fan, Wu Jieh-min, CMR
10/11	NDHU, Hualien	IYF, TAUP, *NDHU Night Salon*	YAMM, SCS
10/17	FJU, Taipei	SCS, *Black Ditch Club*	
10/18	NUK, Kaohsiung	SCS, *NUK CollectThinking*	YAMM, SCS
10/23	NCCU, Taipei	SCS, ATJ, *Club of Seeds*	Lin Fei-fan, SCS, ATJ
10/25	CCU, Chiayi	SCS, *Movement Club*	Lin Fei-fan, Chen Wei-ting, SCS, Movement Club
10/29	NTU, Taipei	SCS	Apple Daily Labor Union
11/7	CGU, Taoyuan	SCS, *CGU Talk*	Lin Fei-fan, SCS
11/8	NCKU, Tainan	YAMM, *02 Society*	Lin Fei-fan, Wu Jieh-min, 02 Society
11/10	Taichung	SCS	(film and debate)
11/13	NTPU, Taipei	SCS, *NTPUCross*	YAMM, SCS
11/28	THU, Taichung	YAMM, *People Workshop*	Chen Wei-ting, Taiwan News Media Trade Union
11/29	SCU, Taipei	SCS, *Ideology Study Club*	Apple Daily Labor Union
12/11	NCKU, Tainan	*02 Society, Anti-Corporatization*	Local Groups
12/12	AU, Taichung	*Outexpert*	YAMM
12/12	NCCU, Taipei	YAMM, IYF	Wu Rwei-ren
12/18	NCTU, Hsinchu	SCS	
12/20	Taipei	Café Philo	Lin Fei-fan, Chen Wei-ting, Wu Rwei-ren
12/21	Taipei	Café Philo	Lin Fei-fan, Chen Wei-ting
12/24	NTHU, Hsinchu	SCS	

Source: author's compilation.

Note: Participants are listed as the organisation they represented, core group members (e.g., Lin Fei-fan and Chen Wei-ting) are listed by name. Local (co-)organising groups are listed in italics.

inviting representatives of the other group as speakers, while the TAUP-affiliated Independent Youth Front (IYF) focused on the Taipei-area as well as Hualien. Vertically, these three groups relied on local campus groups as co-organisers. In close cooperation with both newer groups such as the *02 Society*, *Radical Notes*, the *Movement Club*, but also more established groups, including the *People Workshop*, the *Club of Seeds*, the *Black Ditch Club* and the *Ideology Study Club*, the Campus Tour held 13 events in a little more than seven weeks during the crucial months of October and November. This division of labour facilitated the organisation of events at short notice and allowed YAMM and SCS to maintain a constant rhythm. The Campus Tour therefore exemplifies how the apparatus established over the previous years, namely the local campus groups and networks among them, enabled and structured the movement's practice during this phase.

Bringing together scholars as well as representatives from media reform groups, dissident clubs, and the public, the tour provided the stage for a process of clarifying the ideological stance of the involved groups. The most crucial – but also most contentious – issue was the search for adequate conceptions that were able to transform the energy of the previous demonstrations into a more coherent social movement. While the 901 parade had attracted nearly 10,000 people, activists began to perceive the reformist perspective as limiting. For one, the existing frameworks failed to relate the various elements of the AMM to one another: What were the respective roles of China and the Taiwanese conglomerates, and to what extent did the personal opinions of Tsai Eng-meng matter? Neither of the groups had a systematic answer to these issues that had sufficient appeal to the broader masses.

Many activists further believed that the reformist perspective lacked affective potential, severely hampering mobilisation (R21; R25). The attempt to cover all aspects of the media issue, such as the various indicators to calculate market shares, the complex structures of ownership in the cable, TV and print media as well as the relation of media outlets to finance and industry, added up to lengthy explanations and complex policy proposals. Due to this complexity, "[m]edia monopolisation was a poorly understood issue among Taiwanese" (Wong and Wright 2018: 93). This was even acknowledged by eventual critics of the nationalist conceptions, such as Hsiao Ting-fang of SCS, who in October 2012 diagnosed a "need to turn complex questions into easy-to-understand slogans" (Hsiao 2012).

An alternative approach that could reduce this complexity already suggested itself in the person of Tsai Eng-meng, who provided a focal point that related several issues: It was his conglomerate, Want Want China Times, that sought to acquire the cable operator CNS, and his remarks earlier that year and his relationship with Chinese authorities revealed capital's interest in the cross-Strait rapprochement. Tsai, therefore, personified the relations of political and capitalist forces across the Taiwan Strait, and his portrait had been prominently featured on t-shirts and posters during the 901 parade, distilling the issue far more effectively than any complex analysis could. Nationalist conceptions had already proven their mobilisation potential in the spring of 2012 as, among others, the respected intellectual Yu Ying-shih rallied behind the cause, contributing to the issue reaching a larger audience. The media reform NGOs, however, had been hesitant to embrace the issue of China. This position was grounded in the reform movement's experience that reached back nearly two decades and took place under both KMT and DPP governments, making these groups wary of a politicisation along party lines.

While the outright adoption of the perspective was precluded in spring, the relations of forces had changed since the YAMM had entered the terrain of struggle. The YAMM activists felt the moment had come to raise the China issue as, compared to the WSM of 2008, the idea of putting the China Factor into the spotlight had gained legitimacy for two reasons: First, the Cultural Turn of the hegemonic project had reached the everyday lives of Taiwanese. Television dramas and films, either produced in China or for the Chinese market, had gained a more prominent position in Taiwanese media, as had China-related news reports (R30). Similarly, people-to-people exchanges had intensified, and students noticed an increase in Chinese tourists and had observed how Taiwan's cities and countryside were adapted to accommodate them (R29).[6] The dynamics of cross-Strait relations were therefore no longer restricted to the management of economic integration, but rather extended into the dissemination of cultural forms. Second, the recent interventions by Taiwanese tycoons, such as the open support for the 1992 consensus on the eve of the Presidential elections in January, were seen as signs that these cultural exchanges were not a "natural" phenomenon but rather a process permeated by a combination of political and capitalist interests (R22), the exact nature of which was yet to be determined. This assessment was exacerbated by the remarks of Tsai Eng-meng. His relation to the CCP, the systematic expansion of his conglomerate into the means of ideological production, and his use of media outlets in an attempt to silence critics, provided elements to articulate the interrelated roles of politics and capital in driving the rapprochement forward (R25; R29).

Taken together, these points allowed for shifting the emphasis from a question of market concentration to the media's role in cross-Strait rapprochement, but the hesitance on the part of media reform NGOs posed an obstacle to this project. The leadership of the media reform groups therefore increasingly frustrated these students, who stated during the Campus Tour that the media reform NGOs were "deliberately avoid[ing] to talk about the obvious CCP relations in the Want Want China Times issue" in an effort of "deliberate depoliticisation" (Lin 2012e). What was missing, from the perspective of student activists, was a more systematic framework.

At this juncture, the YAMM's relation to Taipei-based pro-independence NGOs would prove decisive. Just as the cooperation between SCS, CMR and other media reform groups was facilitated by their shared trajectory, YAMM and several pro-independence NGOs had been shaped by similar circumstances. But while the media reform movement attempted to avoid the blue-green spectrum, the trajectory of the latter was characterised by Taiwan's changing relation to China. While many of the NGOs emerged during the transition from authoritarianism (Taipei Society had been established in 1989, TAUP in 1990, TAHR and TLF in 1984), they had attached a pro-independence stance to their anti-authoritarian perspective. Both TDW and the leading student groups had emerged during the Wild Strawberry Movement of 2008 or its immediate aftermath, and the conceptions articulated by these independence-oriented NGOs reflected this particular trajectory. This structural common ground was subsequently actualised in various forms of cooperation between student groups and NGOs, and during the AMM, TAUP and its affiliate IYF jointly hosted events of the Campus Tour and published *The Aurora*, a web magazine that had become a platform for exchanging ideas during the Campus Tour. The cooperation with Taipei-based and like-minded NGOs had strengthened the position of pro-independence student groups within the YAMM, and the close relation to NGOs was activated during the phase of the dénouement.

It was through these networks that YAMM activists became acquainted with the ideas developed by Wu Jieh-min, a researcher at Academia Sinica and a member of TDW. At the height of the WSM, Wu not only had a central role in establishing TDW but also introduced his thoughts on the challenges Taiwan's democracy faced under the influence of the rapprochement to a wider audience via the association's blog (Wu 2008). In this piece, Wu distinguishes two prevalent views on China: China as an opportunity and China as a threat. He dismisses both as equally one-sided, attributing their shortcomings to their lack of a distinctive *social* perspective, and calls for the development of a third view on China that is founded on the civil society on both sides. In a 2009 article published in the journal *Reflexion*, Wu expands his thoughts on the character of this social perspective, coining his particular notion of the *China Factor*. According to Wu (2009: 150–151), the China Factor, conceived as the ways the Chinese Communist Party gains influence on politics and society in Taiwan through the cooperation with the KMT, by-passing democratic procedures and civic supervision, does not necessarily have to have only negative consequences for Taiwan: Under the right circumstances, he argues, social interaction across the Taiwan Strait can promote mutual understanding and thus become a resource for democratisation and reconciliation both within Taiwan and across the Taiwan Strait.

During the 901 parade, Wu Jieh-min had personally talked to individual activists, pointing out the lack of a systematic understanding of the issues at hand, and discussing both the China Factor and TDW (Wu 2012). Wu was then invited to an event of the Campus Tour in early October (see Table 5.6), where he shared his analysis. The relation of Taiwan independence, the China Factor and the role of the media in the cross-Strait rapprochement were then discussed in a series of contributions by activists to *The Aurora* (Chen 2012a; Lin 2012a, e). The publication of Wu's insights on the official YAMM website at the end of the month indicated that by then YAMM had moved towards adopting the China Factor as its ideological principle (YAMM 2012f). Coincidentally, the elaboration of Wu Jieh-min's argument was published as a book entitled "A Third View of China" on 7 November 2012, the day before he participated in another event of the Campus Tour. The conceptual convergence among pro-independence NGOs and YAMM signalled a shift in the relations of forces within the movement and allowed for subsuming the media issue under a nationalist perspective.

The China Factor narrative responded to a particular set of conceptual and organisational needs in ways that the media reform narrative could not. First, it resonated with the various experiences of student activists since 2008. Most of the groups had been established in the aftermath of the WSM, which had erupted on the occasion of a Chinese delegation to Taiwan and was therefore organically related to the dynamics of cross-Strait relations. Second, it reduced the complexity significantly. Unlike the economic and regulatory aspects of the media reform narrative, most Taiwanese were familiar with the issue of cross-Strait relations, which had been the most controversial issue in Taiwanese politics for several decades. Third, student activists were well aware that *Apple Daily* (part of the Next Media group owned by billionaire Jimmy Lai) openly sided with the movement against Want Want China Times (Lin 2012e: 79; Ebsworth 2017). From a tactical point of view, it, therefore, made sense to emphasise the differences between Next Media and Want Want China Times (i.e., their political stance) rather than focusing on their similarities (i.e., the profit-oriented operation of media outlets). Finally, the most crucial aspect in favour of the China Factor narrative was its potential to indirectly politicise the trend towards pragmatism in Taiwan. As discussed earlier, the major hegemonic effect of the rapprochement was the disaggregation of economic interactions across the Taiwan Strait on the one hand and the question of Taiwan identity on the other. Just as the Campus Tour began, Frank Hsieh had become the highest DPP official to visit China, suggesting that the DPP was open to adopting a position of "green pragmatism." As the discussion in *The Aurora* shows (Lin 2012a), the activists were well aware of these developments, and the China Factor opened up a path to re-politicising what risked becoming the "new normal."

As the Campus Tour approached its conclusion, the AMM was reinvigorated by the announcement that a consortium led by Tsai Eng-meng (Want Want China Times), Jeffrey Koo Jr. (China Trust Financial Holding) and William Wong (Formosa Plastics) was set to acquire several media outlets that were part of Jimmy Lai's Next Media group, including *Apple Daily* and *Next Magazine* (Rawnsley and Feng 2014: 114). Although the AMM is now remembered as the movement of the China Factor, up until this point, none of the AMM activities (including the 901 demonstration) had featured any substantial mention of China. But the dénouement had provided the terrain for a shift in the relations of forces within the movement, as YAMM's call for an overnight vigil on the night of 26 to 27 November shows. While the call continued to warn of a "media monopoly effect" that necessitated anti-monopoly legislation, the text goes on to say that "[t]he intervention of the 'China Factor' in Taiwan's press freedom is even more worrying" (YAMM 2012e). The call outlined Tsai Eng-meng's relationship to the CCP and its impact on editorial decisions at the China Times before explicitly referring to Wu Jieh-min (YAMM 2012e). The open shift towards the China Factor analysis was further highlighted by the fact that Wu himself was present at the protest as a speaker (Wei 2016: 180). The Executive Yuan protest was the first that featured the China Factor. This narrative was repeated at another protest at the Fair Trade Commission two days later (YAMM 2012b), and from late November onwards, the China Factor was the central ideological element in all YAMM statements and activities.

This simplification of conceptions was crucial for the efficacy of the nationalist narrative. On 28 November, a group of Taiwanese students abroad posted an appeal on Facebook, largely directed at other Taiwanese overseas students, urging supporters of the movement to post photos of themselves holding a sign with the words "Oppose the media monopoly, reject the black hands of China, defend the freedom of the press" (What's Next 2012). The wording was strikingly similar to, and in all likelihood adapted from, YAMM's 27 November press release on the protest at the Executive Yuan, the heading of which read: "Reject Black Hands, Anti-Monopoly, Freedom of Press" (YAMM 2012g). The response to this appeal was overwhelming. The campaign not only reached young Taiwanese all over the world but also secured the support of prominent figures, including Ai Weiwei and Noam Chomsky (Ebsworth 2017: 83), significantly contributing to the internationalisation of the movement. In turn, the international attention to the issue raised the awareness for the cause within Taiwan. Although only initiated at the end of November, it is this social media campaign that lastingly shaped the collective memory of the AMM as a whole. The China Factor narrative allowed for the movement's message to be condensed into a slogan that was suitable for the brief and concise style required for successful communication via social media.

However, adopting the China Factor was not an issue without contention, as it received criticism from various forces in the media reform movement, albeit with different emphases. The first response came from the radical current, when SCS criticised the emphasis of China in the immediate aftermath of the Executive Yuan protest. In a statement published on social media, the group insisted that it was necessary to oppose the media's penetration by capital in general, "regardless of whether the media boss is Chinese-, Taiwanese- or US-funded, whether he sells rice crackers or apples" (SCS 2012b), thereby refuting a substantial difference between Tsai Eng-meng, who made his fortune selling rice crackers in China, and the anti-communist media tycoon Jimmy Lai, owner of *Apple Daily*. This perspective was then developed further by SCS and the CMR, incorporating elements that had already been raised in contributions to *The Aurora* in October.

In summary, these contributions highlight three defining criticisms by the radical current. First, the radical current pointed out that politicising the media issue via the China Factor narrative ran the risk of transforming the media reform movement into a question of the blue-green political division. Emphasising the China issue was likely to result in polarisation, making the AMM vulnerable to attempts to discredit the movement as a political project by the green camp and thereby jeopardising the long battle of the media reform movement (Hsu and Tian 2012). Historical experience showed that these concerns were not unfounded, given that over the decades the media reform movement had been labelled as green (pro-independence), blue (pro-KMT) and even red (pro-China) despite efforts to be perceived as non-partisan (Cheng 2014: 65).

Second, the radical current highlighted the logic of capital as the decisive structural factor responsible for the deplorable state of Taiwan's media sector. While YAMM leaders and the reformist current proposed "free and healthy market competition" (Lin 2012e) as the cornerstone of a healthy media sector, SCS activists pointed out that despite the fierce competition among Taiwan's seven 24/7 news channels their coverage was astonishingly similar (Hsu and Tian 2012). Similar to the CMR's position during the Reject the China Times movement, SCS contended that the driving force for the dynamics in the media sector was not to be found in cross-Strait dynamics:

> If we look at the term 'Chinese capital', maybe the word 'capital' at the end is the crucial point. … Whether it is Chinese, Taiwanese, American, Korean, Japanese, or other [forms of capital], they all can monopolise Taiwan's media industry through the power of capital.
>
> (ibid.)

The radical current, therefore, highlights the structural subsumption of media reporting within the reproduction of capitalism as a whole. From the radical perspective, competition is not so much the *solution* for issues affecting Taiwan's media sector but rather their *cause* (Hsiao 2012; Wei 2012). While the anti-monopoly narrative firmly remains on the terrain of the logic of the free market (Hsiao 2012), the radical current diagnoses a fundamental incompatibility of the media's role in society and the capitalist logic of competition and market (Wei 2013: 8–9). An analysis departing from capital in general rather than Want Want in particular also results in different conclusions and appeals. Instead of reducing the struggle over the media in Taiwan to an issue about China, the radical current strives to negate the consequences of the mechanism of competition by envisioning the media as a public service guided by the general rather than private commercial interest (Hsiao 2012: 8; Hsu and Tian 2012; Wei 2013).

Third, this capital-centred analysis engendered a distinctive perspective regarding the roles of labour and students in capitalist society. This divergence in conceptions became apparent during a Campus Tour debate in which representatives of both YAMM and SCS participated. YAMM leaders conceived of students as being in a privileged epistemological position, stemming from their alleged insulation from particular social interests. Students were seen as being on "vacation from the system", and having not yet been "polluted by society" they had the capacity to be the "last conscience of society" (Chen 2012a). This stands in stark contrast to SCS's conception, where neither university nor media are independent social realms but sites of a social totality permeated and shaped by the necessities of capitalist reproduction (SCS 2007). Accordingly, resistance necessarily had to begin on campus, not because of the alleged independent or universal status of students, but rather because they are already entangled in wider social struggles due to their position as the "industrial reserve army" (SCS 2007). Instead of relying on government intervention in the media sector, the radical current insists that organising labour is necessary to resist the power of capital to achieve democratic or public control of the media (Hsu and Tian 2012; Wei 2013: 9). This perspective of students as "workers-to-be" (Chen 2012a) ties in with the personal experience of SCS members, whose status as interns in media outlets at the time of the AMM severely constrained their practice within the movement due to the actual possibility of negative repercussions on future employment chances – especially, if the movement were to be polarised along the blue-green spectrum (Lin 2012e).

Ultimately, these debates revealed irreconcilable differences between the radical and nationalist conceptions. On the one hand, the radical current did acknowledge the mobilisation potential of the China Factor narrative, which – unlike a discussion of capitalist dynamics – was rather easy to communicate (R34; R42). In particular, the "David versus Goliath" (Wei 2013: 9) narrative that pitted students against a China-funded business tycoon resonated on an affective level and became "deeply rooted in everybody's hearts", as the support by the broader population as well as public intellectuals, such as Yu Ying-shih, demonstrated (Hsu and Tian 2012). On the other hand, SCS and the CMR argued that this affective potential came at the cost of obscuring the more complex aspects of the media issue, making the China Factor a "double-edged blade" for the movement (ibid.). From the radical perspective, the nationalist analysis relied on government intervention and due to its limited diagnostic potential was unable to provide a positive counterproposal that went beyond the demand for the restoration of effective competition (Wei 2013: 8).

From the side of the reformist current, media scholars and activists Flora Chang and Lin Lih-yun came forward to emphasise the element of media concentration. Their intervention was prompted by an episode involving Noam Chomsky, who had his photo taken with a placard during the above-mentioned social media campaign. While Chomsky stated that he supported freedom of press in Taiwan, it was unclear whether he was aware that the Chinese-language text of the sign included the potentially controversial message "Reject the black hands of China". In the aftermath of this controversy, "some academics ... expressed doubts about the campaign against media monopolization in Taiwan, asking whether it is anti-Chinese in nature" (Chang and Lin 2013). The intervention by Chang and Lin can be understood as the attempt to mitigate further polarisation around the AMM's increasingly nationalist overtones by re-establishing the reformist conceptions as the dominant ideological principle. In their reaction, the two scholars argue that the central issue of the movement "is not any dispute about the Want Want Group's opinions, but the question of whether these acquisitions would lead to an excessively high concentration of media ownership" (ibid.). Chang and Lin acknowledge that, in general, Taiwan is facing the challenge of the China Factor, but argue that with regard to the events that triggered the AMM "there was no 'China factor' involved" (ibid.), urging the public to refocus the debate on the issue of cross-media concentration (ibid.).

The China Factor narrative, however, had already been adopted by the Taiwanese media and public intellectuals. In a second letter to Huang Kuo-chang, Yu Ying-shih reaffirms the "United Front" perspective, stating that the CCP had acquired media outlets in Taiwan through Taiwanese businesspeople to conduct activities aimed at disintegrating the will of the Taiwanese people. He then lauds the Taiwanese students for standing up to defend freedom and democracy: "Rise up to resist, now is the time!" (Taiwan News 2012). His intervention, widely shared on social media, both serves as an indicator of the China Factor's persuasiveness and, in turn, further accelerated its dissemination. In a Gramscian sense, the China Factor was the "language ... best understood by the masses" (Gramsci 1971: 185) as it transposed the media issue into the vocabulary of cross-Strait relations that was deeply rooted in common sense.

This analysis suggests that there were alternative paths towards contesting the media issue, namely a reformist and a radical one (see Table 5.7). The nationalist conception ultimately prevailed due to the close relationship of student groups with those organic intellectuals and NGOs that saw China as the biggest threat to Taiwan's democracy, in particular Wu Jieh-min from the TDW and Huang Kuo-chang from the Taipei Society. The China Factor therefore became the dominant principle of interpretation not because of an ideological convergence among the movement groups, but because at this point in time, it was possible for various currents to pursue different paths. This divergence in conceptions initiated a process of dissociation in practice, which would be consolidated by organisational changes.

Table 5.7 Currents of the Anti-Media Monopoly Movement

Current	Diagnosis	Proposed Measures	Proponents
Reformist	Media concentration negatively impacts the freedom and plurality of speech	Anti-monopoly legislation	Media scholars, reformist NGOs
Nationalist	China Factor adversely affects the freedom of press in Taiwan	Anti-monopoly legislation	YAMM, nationalist NGOs
Radical	Logic of capital; monopolisation as the necessary consequence of competition	Internal democracy; democratic/public control of media	SCS, CMR

The Aftermath: The Dissociation of Practice and the Silent Conclusion of the Media Movement

The unexpected success of YAMM, however, also presented new challenges. The influx of new recruits both strengthened the group and reignited debates on which organisational form was adequate to maintain this strength. Although YAMM had successfully intervened in the Anti-Media Monopoly Movement, there was no consensus on whether this participation was actually beneficial to student organisations. A cadre of YAMM-member *People Workshop* warned against misconceiving the momentary influx of recruits as a sign of the movement's success and actual strength (Luo 2012). Rather, he argued, it was merely an opportunity that needed to be seized to transform the conjunctural upswing into a foundation for future growth. According to Luo, the YAMM model, which had an alliance of several dozen local groups intervening in social movements beyond the campus, was caught in a vicious circle: In the absence of organisation, training and systematic conceptions, the student movement's only method of mobilising the broader public was through emotional appeals. While these might attract participants in the short term, these participants were likely to come and go without substantially investing themselves in movement organisations. This, in turn, would prevent the consolidation of an organisational apparatus. To escape this vicious circle, Luo (ibid.) urges dissident groups to focus on the campus as the main site of organisation. Only there could organisations recruit and train cadres in an environment that corresponded to their social position, facilitating the development and consolidation of common conceptions and skills adequate to their struggle. Prematurely intervening in movements off-campus, where students were just one group among many others, would jeopardise this process.

Chen Wei-ting agreed with Luo that the campus was the crucial site for training cadres (Chen 2012c). But he emphatically opposed the assumption that there was a contradiction between on-campus and off-campus activism. Instead, he drew on his own personal trajectory to highlight that off-campus struggles – including land struggles in Dapu and workers' struggles at Hualon – were appropriate environments to cultivate activist skills as well as conceptions. Furthermore, these movements were necessary to familiarise students with the struggle of social classes they were unlikely to encounter on campus, significantly broadening their understanding of social struggles and thus contributing to the articulation of conceptions.

Activists also reviewed the model of the inter-campus umbrella organisation. While it built on the hope that it could focus the scattered strength of various campus groups and allow students to effectively intervene in social movements, Luo (2012) suggested that the umbrella model risked absorbing organisers from the already rather weak local clubs, thus creating a more powerful centre at the expense of campus groups. The development of local groups, therefore, had to take precedence over the establishment of inter-campus alliances. Chen acknowledged the risk that came with forming unprepared ad-hoc alliances:

> In such a hurried process, the 'unorganised' situation often allows the 'strongman' [強人] in the operation or an organisation with more experience on the subject to have a greater say.
>
> (Chen 2012c)

This was the experience of YAMM, which had entered a terrain of struggle that had already been structured by media reform groups and nationalist NGOs as well as their respective conceptions. However, Chen did not follow Luo in advocating a withdrawal to the campus. Instead, he argued that the alternative would be even more detrimental to student subjectivity: Without their own group, students were destined to depend on other movement organisations to act as an intermediary in social struggle. This would impede students from developing and disseminating their particular vision, further consolidating their subordinate position (ibid.). Only by establishing their own "front-line organisations" (ibid.), could students benefit from participating in larger social movements.

A third issue concerned the decision-making process within the student alliance. Representing YAMM during demonstrations and in the media and participating in ten events during the Campus Tour had contributed – whether intentionally or not – to making Lin Fei-fan and Chen Wei-ting the "faces" of the movement. After the experience of the WSM, where the lack of decision-making and leadership structures had contributed to the movement's erosion, this was generally a welcome development among YAMM members (R21; R24). Critics countered that while YAMM had mobilised many participants, few actually sought to join organised groups (R20). Labour activist Chen Po-wei attributed this phenomenon to the lack of mechanisms that ensured participants could take a proactive role (Chen 2012b). He encouraged the movement organisations to implement democratic structures that would not simply serve to elect leaders, but rather make participants take responsibility for the movement as a whole (ibid.). Luo (2012) proposed a structural reading, arguing that strong leaders were not a solution to but rather a consequence and symptom of weak organisation. The condition of weak organisation may allow or even force individuals to assume a more central role. At the same time, the emergence of such leaders contributed to discouraging others who felt that they could not meaningfully contribute to the development of the movement. It was therefore necessary to focus on the training of cadres, whose task would then be to facilitate the transformation of movement consumers into movement organisers.

A decision on these issues was made in late December. On 20 December, the *Café Philo* hosted a podium discussion on movement organisation titled "Do social movements need heroes?" In addition to Lin Fei-fan and Chen Wei-ting, labour activist Chen Po-wei and Academia Sinica researcher Wu Rwei-ren, who had earlier stated that movements need heroes but not heroism, participated. Two days later, YAMM announced a reform of its organisational structures (YAMM 2012d). While the document reaffirms the commitment to the inter-campus model, it proposes three mechanisms as concessions to local groups. First, the umbrella organisation was to share more of its resources with the local groups. These were then, second, to largely assume the training of cadres, thereby not only becoming the central channel of recruitment but also ensuring that re-cruitment was designed in a way so as to avoid reinforcing the phenomenon of "movement consumers" and a state of passivity of supporters. Finally, the movement reaffirmed the need for leadership. In an attempt to ensure that local groups maintained control over the alliance, however, YAMM outlined a sys-tem of multi-level elections to decide which activists represent the local groups within the inter-campus alliance.

The conceptual and organisational divergence consolidated the dissociation of movement currents in practice. On their side, SCS Taiwan and the CMR initiated a series of events themed "123 Freedom of Communication Week," during which 55 teachers at communication departments held 72 classes at 17 universities (CMR 2012a). None of the publicly available sources contain any reference to the China Factor. Rather, the lectures departed from the perspective of communication stu-dents, focusing on how they could pursue a career in journalism "without being oppressed by profit-seeking capitalists" (CMR 2012b). The groups largely main-tained their stance proposed earlier that year, demanding legislation to prevent the dominance by conglomerates in the media sector, support for non-profit media and the expansion of public media, as well as the unionisation of media workers as the central instrument to ensure journalistic autonomy (ibid.).

The reformed YAMM, on the other hand, attempted to consolidate the coopera-tive relationship with the local campus groups by staging another series of events, called the "One car goes to the end of the world" tour (Wei 2016: 173). The format of this second series differed significantly from the earlier Campus Tour, which had largely taken place at universities and was first and foremost directed at stu-dents. The events of the "one car" tour pursued a different aim: Each afternoon, YAMM representatives met with local student activists and NGOs. In the even-ing, they addressed a broader audience during speeches that were staged in public spaces, including squares, night markets, parks or spaces in front of temples. Over the course of 13 days, YAMM held events in Keelung, Taoyuan, Hsinchu, Miaoli, Taichung, Changhua, Yunlin, Chiayi, Tainan, Kaohsiung and Pingtung (YAMM 2013). Lin Fei-fan likened this practice with the march of pro-democracy activist Cheng Nan-jung, who in 1988 travelled across Taiwan to campaign for a renewed national movement (Lin 2013).

The Anti-Media Monopoly Movement, however, would fade away rather than find a definite conclusion. On 20 February, the NCC announced its decision to deny Want Want's application to acquire CNS. The commission ruled that despite placing 75 per cent of its CTi TV shares in a trust, the Tsai family had not effectively divested itself from the channel and therefore failed to meet the conditions set the previous year. The acquisition of Next Media fell through the following month, after the involved parties failed to agree on the terms of the acquisition, although the television branch NextTV was eventually sold to Lien Tai-sheng, chairman of cable operator ERA Communications and vice-chairman of the Taiwan Land Development Corporation.

Although the role of the Anti-Media Monopoly Movement in the failure to conclude these deals cannot be quantified, the movement considered averting the immediate formation of a media monopoly a success. In the aftermath of these developments, activists concentrated their attention on the other major appeal, the implementation of anti-monopoly regulations. Over the years, several drafts were introduced, but none were passed into law. While the political management of the issue of anti-monopoly legislation is certainly intriguing, it represents a displacement from the realm of social contestation into the realm of parliamentary politics and therefore transcends the scope of this study.[7] The movement energy was directly diverted into the protests against the CSSTA, resulting in the formation of the Democratic Front Against the Cross-Strait Trade in Services Agreement in June 2013. YAMM joined this coalition as a founding member but was soon succeeded by the BIY which had absorbed the majority of YAMM's cadres and emerged as the leading student group. The YAMM announced its formal dissolution after the SFM, two years to the day after it had been established.

Conclusion

The Cultural Turn of the hegemonic project was a response to the challenge presented by the WSM. Intensifying the cultural cooperation across the Taiwan Strait provided a way to align the interest of capital, namely access to the Chinese market through the selective dismantlement of regulatory barriers, and the interests of political forces of projecting its narrative into everyday life via mass media and a deepening of people-to-people exchanges. The media sector therefore became the central site of hegemonic contestation.

The increasingly capillary form of hegemony resulted in a variety of particularist grievances that were refracted by the historical experiences of the involved groups. This meant that – unlike the Wild Strawberry Movement – the Anti-Media Monopoly Movement had multiple points of nucleation that resulted in polycentric patterns of mobilisation. Competing visions regarding the aims and means of the movement complicated attempts to integrate the currents. The reformist current had emerged from the struggle against the role of the state in the media sector. It could build on decades of experience and accumulated expertise but was wary of politicisation along party lines. The radical current had emerged from the same reform movement but had since adapted its conceptions to the changing media environment, identifying the logic of capitalist accumulation as the driving factor that threatened the independence of media in Taiwan.

While the student groups that formed YAMM appeared to have been on a path towards the radical current, their trajectory ultimately set them on the nationalist path of politicisation. During the latent phase after the WSM, the student groups had established networks of cooperation both among themselves and with NGOs that were also concerned by the impact of cross-Strait dynamics on Taiwan. This apparatus allowed the student groups to set up an effective umbrella organisation within one week and provided the infrastructure that facilitated the organisation of de-centralised activities, which exerted a considerable influence on the conceptual direction of YAMM. The China Factor was the conceptual principle that emerged from this cooperation. Not only was it able to mobilise through its affective dimension and its simplified analysis, which lent itself well to social media, but it also responded to the rise of pragmatism by purposefully re-politicising the intensification of cross-Strait exchanges as an issue of collective deliberation rather than individual choice. But while mobilisation based on the China Factor was a success for the nationalist current, it precluded a closer cooperation with reformist and radical groups.

The process of hegemonic contestation around the issue of media monopolisation in Taiwan had lasting effects on the conceptions, apparatus and forms of practice of the social movement in Taiwan. First, the umbrella model, that is, the establishment of a networked ad-hoc alliance of student groups all over Taiwan, had proven effective. Its success, however, initiated the progressive detachment of student groups organised on a national scale from their local roots. Only a little more than a year later, the leading student groups – such as BIY – had abandoned any organisational linkages to campus groups. This also entailed a shift from local issues to issues on a national scale. Second, the failure to integrate the various currents consolidated their organisational dissociation: As the urgency to cooperate declined, these currents pursued their own path, thus preventing a systematic process of clarifying the various positions and forging a more coherent movement. As was the case after the WSM, the hegemonic apparatus was further adjusted in an attempt to provide mechanisms of inclusion aimed at Taiwan's younger generation. During the 2013 edition of the Straits Forum, a new set of preferential policies was announced, not only highlighting the continued relevance of the media sector but suggesting a fusion between media and youth issues: The Chinese government opened professional qualification examinations in the publishing sector to Taiwanese and announced the establishment of the National Strait Copyright Trading Center, the Cross-Strait Copyright Trading Center as well as ten Cross-Strait Cultural Exchange Bases. Directed at young Taiwanese, the forum vowed to promote opportunities in the development of online and mobile games. In addition, Taiwanese students, who graduated from Chinese universities, could apply for subsidies for entrepreneurship training as well as for support in starting their own business. From 2014 onwards, the Straits Forum included the "Cross-Strait Youth New Media Cultural Innovation Forum", which resulted in the establishment of the "Cross-Strait Youth New Media Cultural and Creative Exchange Base" in Xiamen one year later, expanding the infrastructural basis to provide opportunities to Taiwan's youth. According to an interim report published by the Taiwan Affairs Office, "[i]n terms of youth entrepreneurship, 53 cross-Strait entrepreneurship bases and pilot sites nationwide had served nearly 1,900 Taiwan-funded enterprises and teams, and provided internships and jobs for nearly 9,000 Taiwanese youth as of the end of 2017" (China Daily 2018). Again, the impact of these measures is hard to assess. These initiatives do show, however, that in the aftermath of the AMM the hegemonic apparatus was further expanded to address Taiwan's youth.

Notes

1 Author's compilation based on participant lists.
2 http://www.taiwan.cn/hxlt/rwft/rw2/201006/t20100624_1425909.htm (last accessed 03/01/2020).
3 In Taiwanese, '02' is homophone with 'protest'.
4 These were: *Movement Club* at National Chung Cheng University (CCU), *Interesting Society* at National Yang-Ming University (NYMU), *CGU Talk* at Chang Gung University (CGU) and *FreeTakao* at NSYSU.
5 巨獸 can also be translated as 'behemoth' or 'giant', but with regard to the AMM is customarily given as 'monster'. Among other Mandarin terms used to refer to the same phenomenon are 'Godzilla' (酷斯拉) and empire (帝國).
6 This sentiment is supported by official statistics: In year-on-year comparison, Chinese tourism from the third quarter of 2011 to the third quarter of 2012 increased by nearly 58 per cent (Ministry of Transportation and Communication, R.O.C. 2020).
7 For a discussion of the various anti-monopoly draft bills, see Rawnsley and Feng (2014: 116-122), Ebsworth (2017: 85–87) and Huang (2020: 128–130).

Bibliography

02 Society (2009). *Change, starting now!* (In Chinese). 29th January 2009. http://tainan-02group.blogspot.com/2009/01/blog-post_28.html (last accessed on 22/07/2020).
———— (2010). *Red tape and the non-freedom of campus clubs.* (In Chinese). 26th October 2010. http://tainan02group.blogspot.com/2010/10/blog-post.html (last accessed on 22/07/2020).
———— (2011). *02 Society Consensus Camp.* (In Chinese). 26th August 2011. http://tainan02group.blogspot.com/2011/08/20110829-30.html (last accessed on 24/07/2020).
02 Society, Praxis in South, Radical Notes, Free Takao and People Workshop (2012). *I want to go home to vote!* (In Chinese). 4th January 2012. https://www.coolloud.org.tw/node/65830 (last accessed on 25/07/2020).
901 Demonstration Alliance (2012). *901 Anti-Media Monopoly Demonstration.* (In Chinese). 27th August 2012. https://www.coolloud.org.tw/node/70346 (last accessed on 16/07/2020).
Anti-Corporatization Front and Students Rights Survey and Evaluation Team (2012a). *Anti-Tuition Forum. The First Left-wing Forum on Education.* (In Chinese). 4th February 2012. https://www.coolloud.org.tw/node/66296 (last accessed on 25/07/2020).
Anti-Corporatization Front et al. (2012b). *Press Release after the protests against tuition fees at the Ministry of Education.* (In Chinese). 26th March 2012. https://www.coolloud.org.tw/node/67486 (last accessed on 25/07/2020).
———— (2012c). *Student groups to protest at the Ministry of Education.* (In Chinese). 25th March 2012. https://www.coolloud.org.tw/node/67468 (last accessed on 25/07/2020).

Anti-Tuition Forum (2012). *Anti-Tuition Q&A.* (In Chinese). 24th March 2012. https://www.coolloud.org.tw/node/67455 (last accessed on 25/07/2020).

Association of Taiwan Journalists (2010). *Press release on anti-advertorial legislation.* (In Chinese). 29th December 2010. https://www.coolloud.org.tw/node/56533 (last accessed on 09/07/2020).

———— (2012a). *901 Demonstration call.* (In Chinese). 17th August 2012. https://www.coolloud.org.tw/node/70148 (last accessed on 09/07/2020).

———— (2012b). *Association of Taiwan Journalists calls on NCC members to dismiss the Want Want acquisition case.* (In Chinese). 22nd July 2012. https://www.coolloud.org.tw/node/69711 (last accessed on 09/07/2020).

Beckershoff, André (2014). "The KMT-CCP Forum: Securing Consent for Cross-Strait Rapprochement". In: *Journal of Current Chinese Affairs* 43.1, 213–241.

Campaign for Media Reform (2012a). *123 Communication Freedom Week. Joint curriculum and joint statement from teachers in the field of communication.* (In Chinese). 17th December 2012. https://www.coolloud.org.tw/node/71968 (last accessed on 26/07/2020).

———— (2012b). *123 Communication Freedom Week. Anti-monopoly and the need for media reform.* (In Chinese). 16th December 2012. http://twmedia.org/archives/301.

———— (2012c). *901 demonstration call.* (In Chinese). 31st August 2012. http://mediawatchtaiwan.blogspot.com/2012/08/901_31.html (last accessed on 09/07/2020).

Chang, Chin-hua Flora (2013). "Big media, small democracy. The voice of the citizens on the crisis of Taiwan media". (In Chinese). In: *Annual Taiwan Press Freedom Report 2012*, 3-9. Association of Taiwan Journalists.

Chang, Flora, Hsiao-yi Chen, Kuo-chang Huang, Chung-hsiang Kuan and Lin Hui-lin (2012a). *Petition to the NCC.* (In Chinese). 25th July 2012. http://rjcts2012.blogspot.com/2012/07/0725ncc.html (last accessed on 13/07/2020).

Chang, Flora, Kuo-chang Huang, Chen-ling Hung, Show-ling Jang, Hui-lin Lin and Lihyun Lin (2012b). *Say no to the media Godzilla! Why?* (In Chinese). Association for Free Communication. 24th April 2012. https://forfreecommunication.files.wordpress.com/2012/04/e68b92e7b595e5aa92e9ab94e985b7e696afe68b89-why.pdf (last accessed on 08/07/2020).

Chang, Flora and Lih-yun Lin (2013). *Clear regulations needed for media.* Taipei Times. 9th February 2013. http://www.taipeitimes.com/News/editorials/archives/2013/02/09/2003554575 (last accessed on 08/07/2020).

Chen, Hsin-chung (2010a). *False Development, Real Destruction. Industrial Zone.* (In Chinese). People Workshop. 28th October 2010. http://asthuheadquarter.blogspot.com/2010/10/blog-post_4778.html (last accessed on 11/02/2020).

Chen, Ping-Hung (1999). "Market Concentration in Taiwan's Cable Industry. A Case Study". In: *Media Asia* 26.4, 206–215.

———— (2002). "Who Owns Cable Television? Media Ownership Concentration in Taiwan". In: *The Journal of Media Economics* 15.1, 41–55.

———— (2006). "Market Entry Modes and Determinants of Taiwanese Media Firms into Mainland China". In: *Mass Communication Research* 89, 37–80. (In Chinese).

———— (2010b). "Exploring Relationship between Media Conglomeration and Content Diversity". In: *Mass Communication Research* 104, 1–30. (In Chinese).

Chen, Shiuan-Ju (2009). "Searching for Consensus in Cross-Strait Relations". In: *Issues & Insights* 9.4, 1–38.

Chen, Ting-hao (2012a). *What the Anti-Media Monsters taught me. The Anti-Want Want movement experience from 731, 901 to 928.* (In Chinese). The Aurora. 9th October 2012. https://web.archive.org/web/20130927220716/http://blog.roodo.com/aurorahope/archives/21095134.html (last accessed on 05/12/2019).

Chen, Po-wei (2012b). *Speech at the forum 'Do Social Movements Need Heroes'*. (In Chinese). 20th December 2012. http://positionandpossession.blogspot.com/2012/12/blog-post.html (last accessed on 18/07/2020).

Chen, Wei-ting (2010c). *University as a State Apparatus*. (In Chinese). Radical Notes. 1st June 2010. http://nthuradicalpaper.medianewsonline.com/?p=118 (last accessed on 11/02/2020).

——— (2012c). *After the Tunghai exchange*. (In Chinese). 8th November 2012. http://waitingism.blogspot.com/2012/11/blog-post.html (last accessed on 17/07/2020).

Chen, Ying-Hsuan (2015). "The impact of the 'Anti-China Times Movement in the cultural field". (In Chinese). Master Thesis. National Chengchi University. http://nccur.lib.nccu.edu.tw/handle/140.119/99743 (last accessed on 14/06/2020).

Cheng, Han-Wen (2014). "Student Movement and Media Reform. A History of Solidarity of Communication Students". (In Chinese). Master thesis. National Chengchi University. http://thesis.lib.nccu.edu.tw/cgi-bin/gs32/gsweb.cgi?o=dallcdr&s=id=%22G0100451009%22. (last accessed on 14/06/2020).

Chiang, Min-Hua (2012). "Tourism Development Across the Taiwan Strait". In: *East Asia* 29.3, 235–253.

Chien, Shiuh-Shen and Chenglin Hsieh (2010). *Political Economy of Taiwan-China Transnational Interactions. A Perspective of Provincial Exchange and Procurement Delegations*. http://web.bp.ntu.edu.tw/DevelopmentStudies/Data/ACDS_2nd_B11.pdf (last accessed on 01/06/2012).

China Daily (2018). *Implementation of preferential policies for Taiwan to continue*. 16th May 2018. https://www.chinadailyhk.com/articles/9/7/6/1526471183126.html (last accessed on 19/07/2020).

China News Service (2011). *Fujian cultural exchange study group arrives in Taipei*. (In Chinese). 21st April 2011. http://www.chinanews.com/tw/2011/04-21/2988123.shtml (last accessed on 02/01/2020).

——— (2012). *Another group of business owners in Taiwan supports the '1992 consensus'*. (In Chinese). 12th January 2012. http://www.chinanews.com/tw/2012/01-12/3598710.shtml (last accessed on 28/07/2020).

China.org.cn (2012). *'1992 Consensus' beneficial to Taiwan's stability*. 14th January 2012. http://www.china.org.cn/china/2012-01/14/content_24405190.htm (last accessed on 28/07/2020).

Chung, Jin Young, Chun-chu Chen and Yueh-Hsiu Lin (2016). "Cross-Strait Tourism and Generational Cohorts". In: *Journal of Travel Research* 55.6, 813–826.

Cole, J. Michael (2019). *More than 70 participants from Taiwanese Media Industry attend 4th Cross-Strait Media Summit in Beijing*. Taiwan Sentinel. 11th May 2019. https://sentinel.tw/more-than-70-participants-from-taiwanese-media-industry-attend-4th-cross-strait-media-summit-in-beijing/ (last accessed on 18/01/2020).

Control Yuan, R.O.C. (2010). *Investigation Report 0990800421*. (In Chinese). https://cybsbox.cy.gov.tw/CYBSBoxSSL/edoc/download/15082 (last accessed on 06/12/2019).

Curtin, Michael (2007). *Playing to the World's Biggest Audience. The Globalization of Chinese Film and TV*. Berkeley and Los Angeles: University of California Press.

Ebsworth, Rowena (2017). "Not wanting Want. The anti-media monopoly movement in Taiwan". In: *Taiwan's Social Movements under Ma Ying-jeou. From the Wild Strawberries to the Sunflowers*. Ed. by Dafydd Fell. London and New York: Routledge, 71–91.

ECFA Watcher Student Alliance (2010). *ECFA Watcher Student Alliance Statement*. (In Chinese). 6th June 2010. http://ecfa-watcher.blogspot.com/2010/06/ecfa_06.html (last accessed on 24/07/2020).

Engbarth, Dennis (2011). *Media Fights Propaganda Masked as News.* Inter Press Service. 31st January 2011. https://web.archive.org/web/20110208172018/http://ipsnews.net/news.asp?idnews=54291 (last accessed on 27/12/2019).

Fell, Dafydd (2011). "More or less space for identity in Taiwan's party politics?". In: *Taiwanese Identity in the Twenty-first Century. Domestic, Regional and Global Perspectives.* Ed. by Gunter Schubert and Jens Damm. London and New York: Routledge, 95–112.

Foundation for the Advancement of Media Excellence (2010). *Report on Embedded Marketing.* (In Chinese). https://www.fame.org.tw/news_detail_51.htm (last accessed on 06/12/2019).

Ger, Yeong-kuang (2012). "The Significance of 2012 Taiwanese Elections and Its Impacts on Cross-Strait Relations". In: *American Journal of Chinese Studies* 19.2, 75–88.

Gramsci, Antonio (1971). *Selections from the Prison Notebooks.* Ed. by Quintin Hoare and Geoffrey Nowell-Smith. London: Lawrence and Wishart.

———— (2012). *Selections from Cultural Writings.* Ed. by David Forgacs and Geoffrey Nowell-Smith. Chicago: Haymarket Books.

Guo, Syu-chi (2011). *The media monster sleeps under our bed.* (In Chinese). 5th November 2011. http://mediawatchtaiwan.blogspot.com/2011/11/blog-post_7698.html (last accessed on 11/07/2020).

He, Donghong (2009). "My Taipei 'Wild Strawberry' Notes". In: *Reflexion* 11, 118–132. (In Chinese).

Higgins, Andrew (2012). *Tycoon prods Taiwan closer to China.* Washington Post. 21st January 2012. https://www.washingtonpost.com/world/asia_pacific/tycoon-prods-taiwan-closer-to-china/2012/01/20/gIQAhswmFQ_story.html (last accessed on 11/07/2020).

Ho, Ming-sho (2018). "The rise of civil society activism in the Ma Ying-jiu era. The genesis and outcome of the Sunflower Movement". In: *Assessing the Presidency of Ma Ying-jiu. Hopeful Beginning, Hopeless End?* Ed. by André Beckershoff and Gunter Schubert. London and New York: Routledge, 109–131.

Hsiao, Ting-fang (2012). *What the Anti-Media Monsters taught me. Reflections and Expectations of a Communication Student.* (In Chinese). The Aurora. 16th October 2012. https://web.archive.org/web/20130927230043/http://blog.roodo.com/aurorahope/archives/21107950.html (last accessed on 05/12/2019).

Hsieh, Meng-Yu (2012). *We have been different since childhood!* (In Chinese). Praxis in South. 4th March 2012. http://praxisinsouth.blogspot.com/2012/04/blog-post_423.html (last accessed on 20/01/2020).

Hsieh, Sheng-Yu (2010). *By accident or by necessity? Structural Limits and Opportunities of the Taipei Wild Strawberry Student Movement.* (In Chinese). Social Reform Front. 17th November 2010. http://so-front.blogspot.com/2010/11/blog-post.html (last accessed on 11/02/2020).

Hsu, Chien-Jung (2014a). "China's Influence on Taiwan's Media". In: *Asian Survey* 54.3, 515–539.

———— (2014b). *The Construction of National Identity in Taiwan's media, 1896–2012.* Leiden and Boston: Brill.

Hsu, Feng-Yuan and Yu Jhih Tian (2012). *Anti-Media Monopoly does not just mean Anti-Media Monopoly.* (In Chinese). Lihpao. 13th December 2012. https://bit.ly/2Z3HTiD (last accessed on 02/07/2020).

Hsu, Tsung Cheng (2012a). *North-South differences in educational resources in Taiwan.* (In Chinese). Praxis in South. 4th March 2012. http://praxisinsouth.blogspot.com/2012/04/blog-post_7254.html (last accessed on 20/01/2020).

Hsu, Wen-lu (2011). *When Knowledge meets Capital*. (In Chinese). Anti-Corporatization Front. 9th September 2011. http://anti-corporatization.blogspot.com/2011/09/blog-post. html (last accessed on 22/07/2020).

———— (2012b). *The four-way relationship between state, capital, university as well as research and development*. (In Chinese). 13th February 2012. https://www.coolloud.org.tw/ node/66567 (last accessed on 25/07/2020).

Hu, Yuan-Hui (2017). "Independent media, social movements, and the traditional news media in Taiwan". In: *Digital Technology and Journalism. An International Comparative Perspective*. Ed. by Jinrong Tong and Shih-Hung Lo. Basingstoke: Palgrave Macmillan, 215–235.

Huang, Jaw-Nian (2017). "The China Factor in Taiwan's Media. Outsourcing Chinese Censorship Abroad". In: *China Perspectives* (3/2017), 27–36.

———— (2020). *The Political Economy of Press Freedom. The Paradox of Taiwan versus China*. London and New York: Routledge.

Huang, Kuo-chang, Flora Chang, Hsiu-ling Cheng and Hui-lin Lin (2012). *NCC should openly investigate Tsai Eng-meng's misuse of media group resources*. (In Chinese). Taipei Society. 18th February 2012. http://taipeisociety.org/node/372 (last accessed on 11/07/2020).

Huang, Kuo-chang and Hei-yuan Chiu (2012). *Say no to Tsai, who has become a totalitarian make-up artist*. (In Chinese). Apple Daily. 30th January 2012. https://tw.appledaily. com/headline/20120130/VWVHRIQ42PC5E4S7PFWVTLWKU4/ (last accessed on 11/07/2020).

Hughes, Christopher R. (2014). "Revisiting identity politics under Ma Ying-jeou". In: *Political Changes in Taiwan under Ma Ying-jeou. Partisan Conflict, Policy Choices, External Constraints and Security Challenges*. Ed. by Jean-Pierre Cabestan and Jacques deLisle. London and New York: Routledge, 120–136.

Jang, Show-ling and Hui-lin Lin (2011). *The horrible cross-media monster*. Apple Daily. 5th September 2011. https://tw.appledaily.com/headline/20110905/EXKEHJH3NGAJR TU5EBLRPCWXNA/ (last accessed on 11/07/2020).

Kaeding, Malte Philipp (2015). "Resisting China's Influence. Social Movements in Hong Kong and Taiwan". In: *Current History* 114.773, 210–216.

Kamimura, Yasuhiro (2010). "The tripartite relationship and social policy in Taiwan. Searching for a new corporatism?. In: *Non-Standard Employment under Globalization. Flexible Work and Social Security in the Newly Industrializing Countries*. Ed. by Koichi Usami. New York and Basingstoke: Palgrave Macmillan, 142–175.

Kwong, Robin (2010). *Big interest in Taiwan cable TV stake sale*. Financial Times. 29th July 2010. https://www.ft.com/content/51e2fe98-9a68-11df-87fd-00144feab49a (last accessed on 10/01/2020).

Lee, Stanley (2015). *A historical survey of the term 'dissident society'*. (In Chinese). 27th September 2015. https://bit.ly/37vzrtr (last accessed on 17/02/2020).

———— (2017). "The Invisible Student Movement. Reflections on the History of Taiwan Student Movement and Related Issues". In: *Taiwan: A Radical Quarterly in Social Studies* 106.4, 207–224. (In Chinese).

Lee, Yen-Jhen (2012). *The relative deprivation of Southerners and Taipei-centrism*. (In Chinese). Praxis in South. 4th March 2012. http://praxisinsouth.blogspot.com/2012/04/ blog-post_2112.html (last accessed on 20/01/2020).

LePesant, Tanguy (2012). "A New Generation of Taiwanese at the Ballot Box. Young Voters and the Presidential Election of January 2012". In: *China Perspectives* (2/2012), 71–79.

Liao, Da-chi, Cheng-shan Liu and Bo-yu Chen (2018). "Taiwanese nationalism in the age of cross-Strait integration. Predominance and pragmatism in the Ma Ying-jiu era". In: *Assessing the Presidency of Ma Ying-jiu. Hopeful Beginning, Hopeless End?* Ed. by André Beckershoff and Gunter Schubert. London and New York: Routledge, 59–89.

Lin, Baohua (2012a). *How to look at Frank Hsieh's visit to China?* (In Chinese). The Aurora. 16th October 2012. http://web.archive.org/web/20130927230917/http://blog.roodo.com/aurorahope/archives/21107948.html (last accessed on 15/06/2020).

Lin, Chaoyi (2013). *Sacrificing their winter vacation, the anti-monopoly youth travels to the end of the world in a car.* (In Chinese). newtalk. 21st January 2013. https://newtalk.tw/news/view/2013-01-21/33051 (last accessed on 26/07/2020).

Lin, Fei-fan (2012b). *South and North in the current student movement.* (In Chinese). Praxis in South. 4th March 2012. http://praxisinsouth.blogspot.com/2012/04/blog-post_6737.html (last accessed on 20/01/2020).

Lin, Gang (2019). *Taiwan's Party Politics and Cross-Strait Relations in Evolution (2008–2018).* Basingstoke and New York: Palgrave Macmillan.

Lin, Hung-hsuan (2012c). *Does the Tainaner Ensemble go to Taipei?* (In Chinese). Praxis in South. 4th March 2012. http://praxisinsouth.blogspot.com/2012/04/blog-post_6706.html (last accessed on 20/01/2020).

Lin, Lihyun and Chun-Yi Lee (2017). "When Business Met Politics. The Case of Want Want, a Different Type of Media Capital in Taiwan". In: *China Perspectives* (2/2017), 37–46.

Lin, Por-Yee (2011). *How can student rights be guaranteed? A dialogue on three concepts of student rights.* (In Chinese). 22nd February 2011. https://www.coolloud.org.tw/node/57178 (last accessed on 11/02/2020).

——— (2012d). *Leftist positions against tuition.* (In Chinese). 13th February 2012. https://www.coolloud.org.tw/node/66566 (last accessed on 25/07/2020).

Lin, Yu (2012e). *The things the Anti-Media Monsters taught us this summer.* (In Chinese). The Aurora. 9th October 2012. https://web.archive.org/web/20130928001247/http://blog.roodo.com/aurorahope/archives/21095138.html (last accessed on 05/12/2019).

Luo, Shu (2012). *The crisis of organisation and direction in the student movement in recent years.* (In Chinese). 29th October 2012. https://www.coolloud.org.tw/node/71274 (last accessed on 17/07/2020).

Luxemburg, Rosa (2006). "The mass strike, the political party and the trade union". In: *Reform or Revolution and Other Writings.* Mineola, New York: Dover Publications, 101–180.

——— (2019). "The political mass strike". In: *The Complete Works of Rosa Luxemburg. Political Writings.* Vol. 1. Ed. by Peter Hudis, Axel Fair-Schulz and William A. Pelz. London and New York: Verso, 285–289.

Marx, Karl and Friedrich Engels (2010). "Manifesto of the Communist Party". In: *The Revolutions of 1848.* Ed. by David Fernbach. London: Verso, 62–98.

Ministry of Transportation and Communication, R.O.C. (2020). *Visitors arriving by residence.* https://stat.motc.gov.tw/mocdb/stmain.jsp?sys=100&funid=e7101 (last accessed on 18/06/2020).

National Policy Foundation (2009). *Fifth Cross-Strait Economic, Trade, and Cultural Forum joint recommendations.* https://www.npf.org.tw/12/6259 (last accessed on 05/12/2019).

Pan, Hsin-Hsin, Wen-Chin Wu and Yu-Tzung Chang (2020). "Does Cross-Strait Tourism Induce Peace? Evidence from Survey Data on Chinese Tourists and Non-Tourists". In: *International Relations of the Asia-Pacific* 20.1, 149–181.

Pan, Shiyin-Rung (2012). *Is there a difference between the North and the South? A civil society perspective.* (In Chinese). Praxis in South. 4th March 2012. http://praxisinsouth.blogspot.com/2012/04/blog-post_04.html (last accessed on 20/01/2020).

People Workshop (2008). *Whose Tunghai? The struggle for campus democracy*. (In Chinese). 16th September 2008. http://asthuheadquarter.blogspot.com/2008/09/blog-post_2386.html (last accessed on 12/02/2020).

———— (2011). *2011 Winter Camp*. (In Chinese). 8th January 2011. http://asthuheadquarter.blogspot.com/2011/01/2011.html (last accessed on 11/02/2020).

———— (2012). *2012 Winter Holiday Camp*. (In Chinese). 4th January 2012. http://asthuheadquarter.blogspot.com/2012/01/2012.html (last accessed on 11/02/2020).

Praxis in South (2012). *What is 'Praxis in South'?* (In Chinese). Praxis in South. 12th May 2012. http://praxisinsouth.blogspot.com/2012/05/blog-post_7600.html (last accessed on 24/01/2020).

Qiu, Shangzhi, Mimi Li, Zhuowei (Joy) Huang and Ning Dang (2015). "Impact of Tourism Openness Across the Taiwan Strait. Perspective of Mainland Chinese Tourists". In: *Asia Pacific Journal of Tourism Research* 20.1, 76–93.

Rawnsley, Gary and Qian Gong (2011). "Political Communications in Democratic Taiwan. The Relationship Between Politicians and Journalists". In: *Political Communication* 28.3, 323–340.

Rawnsley, Gary D. and Ming-yeh T. Rawnsley (2006). "The media in Taiwan. Change and continuity". In: *What has Changed? Taiwan Before and After the Change in Ruling Parties*. Ed. by Dafydd Fell, Henning Klöter and Bi-yu Chang. Wiesbaden: Harrassowitz Verlag, 225–242.

Rawnsley, Ming-yeh, James Smyth and Jonathan Sullivan (2016). "Taiwanese Media Reform". In: *Journal of the British Association for Chinese Studies* 6 (December), 66–80.

Rawnsley, Ming-yeh T. and Chien-san Feng (2014). "Anti-Media-Monopoly Policies and Further Democratisation in Taiwan". In: *Journal of Current Chinese Affairs* 43.3, 105–128.

Rigger, Shelley (2016). "The China impact on Taiwan's generational politics". In: *Taiwan and the 'China Impact'. Challenges and Opportunities*. Ed. by Gunter Schubert. London and New York: Routledge, 70–90.

Romberg, Alan D. (2008). "Cross-Strait Relations. First the Easy Steps, Then the Difficult Ones". In: *China Leadership Monitor* 26.

———— (2012a). "After the Taiwan Elections. Planning for the Future". In: *China Leadership Monitor* 37.

———— (2012b). "Following the 18th Party Congress. Moving Forward Step-by-Step". In: *China Leadership Monitor* 40.

Rowen, Ian (2014). "Tourism as a Territorial Strategy. The Case of China and Taiwan". In: *Annals of Tourism Research* 64, 62–74.

———— (2016). "The Geopolitics of Tourism. Mobility, territory, and protests in Taiwan and China". PhD thesis. University of Colorado.

Schubert, Gunter (2010). "The Political Thinking of the Mainland Taishang. Some Preliminary Observations from the Field". In: *Journal of Current Chinese Affairs* 39.1, 73–110.

———— (2018). "The DPP's China policy before and during the Ma Ying-jiu era". In: *Assessing the Presidency of Ma Ying-jiu. Hopeful Beginning, Hopeless End?* Ed. by André Beckershoff and Gunter Schubert. London and New York: Routledge, 37–58.

Siew, Vincent (2001). *Toward the Creation of a 'Cross-Strait Common Market'*. Cross-Strait Common Market Foundation. https://web.archive.org/web/20130901031240/http://crossstrait.org/version3/index.html (last accessed on 05/12/2019).

Solidarity of Communication Students (2007). *Founding declaration of the Solidarity of Communication Students*. (In Chinese). 4th May 2007. http://web.archive.org/web/20080929095830/http://blog.roodo.com/scstw/archives/3416483.html (last accessed on 06/07/2020).

———— (2012a). *901 demonstration call*. (In Chinese). 26th August 2012. http://mediawatchtaiwan.blogspot.com/2012/08/blog-post_26.html (last accessed on 09/07/2020).

———— (2012b). *Social media statement*. (In Chinese). 28th November 2012. https://www.facebook.com/scstw1994/photos/a.120208041352417.7825.108389549200933/492585884114629/?type=3&theater (last accessed on 02/10/2019).

Southern Wave Music Festival (2012). *Event Details*. (In Chinese). 23rd November 2012. https://dreamalittledream02.wordpress.com/2011/11/23/2011-%e6%bd%ae%e5%8d%97%e9%9f%b3%e6%a8%82%e7%af%80/ (last accessed on 24/01/2020).

Standing, Jonathan (2012). *Taiwan's Ma sets course for '10 golden years'*. Reuters. 5th January 2012. https://reuters.com/article/topNews/idCATRE80409L20120105 (last accessed on 28/07/2020).

State Administration of Press, Publication, Radio, Film and Television of the People's Republic of China (2008). *Supplementary Provisions #57*. (In Chinese). http://www.nrta.gov.cn/art/2008/1/30/art_1583_26308.html (last accessed on 13/01/2020).

Straits Forum (2010). *Cross-Strait publishing cooperation will be ushered in a new breakthrough*. (In Chinese). http://www.taiwan.cn/hxlt/zhuti/ztlt/lt8/zxbb/201006/t20100620_1419815.htm (last accessed on 17/01/2020).

———— (2011). *Five preferential policies issued by the General Administration of Press and Publication*. (In Chinese). http://www.taiwan.cn/hxlt/zhuti/zt3/xinwenchuban/bb057/201106/t20110612_1883950.htm (last accessed on 17/01/2020).

———— (2013). *Fujian issued five policies to promote press and publication in Taiwan*. http://www.taiwan.cn/hxlt/zhuti/ztltfour_41010/zcg/bobao/201306/t20130617_4329234.htm (last accessed on 17/01/2020).

Su, Wei and Shadow (2016). *How I understand the student and social movement (2008–2012)*. (In Chinese). Civil Media Taiwan. 13th February 2016. https://www.civilmedia.tw/archives/43264 (last accessed on 24/07/2020).

Taipei Society (2012). *Clarify the truth on a public podium*. (In Chinese). 1st February 2012. https://www.taipeisociety.org/node/361 (last accessed on 11/07/2020).

Taipei Times (2012a). *Chen Chu to take the helm at DPP*. 23rd February 2012. http://www.taipeitimes.com/News/front/archives/2012/02/23/2003526146 (last accessed on 27/07/2020).

———— (2012b). *University tuition fees to remain unchanged this year*. 3rd April 2012. http://www.taipeitimes.com/News/front/archives/2012/04/03/2003529372 (last accessed on 25/07/2020).

Taiwan News (2012). *Yu Ying-shih: Through Taiwanese businessmen, the CCP has acquired media and completely disintegrated the will of the Taiwanese people*. (In Chinese). 28th November 2012. https://www.taiwannews.com.tw/ch/news/2083755 (last accessed on 26/07/2020).

Thomas, Amos Owen (2005). *Imagi-Nations and Borderless Television. Media, Culture and Politics across Asia*. New Delhi, Thousand Oaks and London: Sage.

Tsai, Hsin-Yi Sandy and Shih-Hung Lo (2016). "Media reform movements in Taiwan". In: *Strategies for Media Reform*. Ed. by Des Freedman, Jonathan A. Obar, Cheryl Martens and W. McChesney. New York: Fordham University Press, 153–166.

Tucker, Sundeep and Tom Mitchell (2006). *Murdoch's Star TV could re-enter Taiwan*. Financial Times. 29th August 2006. https://www.ft.com/content/f13a3bb4-377f-11db-bc01-0000779e2340 (last accessed on 10/01/2020).

Wang, Jenn-hwan (2015). "Crossing borders in Greater China. A multidimensional perspective". In: *Border-Crossing in Greater China. Production, Community and Identity*. Ed. by by Jenn-hwan Wang. London and New York: Routledge, 1–18.

Wang, T. Y. and Su-feng Cheng (2017). "Taiwan Citizen's Views of China. What are the Effects of Cross-Strait Contacts?". In: *Journal of East Asian Studies* 17.2, 233–243.

Wei, Ti (2012). *Some thoughts on the Want Want China Times Group issue and the media reform movement.* (In Chinese). 29th August 2012. https://www.coolloud.org.tw/node/70416 (last accessed on 16/07/2020).

––––– (2013). "Rethinking the Anti-Monopoly Campaign. From Rhetoric to Practice". In: *AnthroVisions* 12 (3/2013), 7–9. (In Chinese).

Wei, Yang (2016). "The Restless Decade before Sunflower Movement. The Emergence and Practices of Networks of Social Movement Youth Activists (2007–2016)". (In Chinese). Unpublished Master thesis. National Tsinghua University. https://hdl.handle.net/11296/6t7myw (last accessed on 09/12/2019).

What's Next (2012). *Join 'Safeguarding Taiwan's Freedom of Press'.* (In Chinese). Social media post. 28th November 2012. https://www.facebook.com/TaiwanWhatsNext/photos/a.269052083140324/462487963796734/?type=3&theater (last accessed on 08/07/2020).

Wong, Shiau Ching and Scott Wright (2018). "Generating a Voice among 'Media Monsters'. Hybrid Media Practices of Taiwan's Anti-Media Monopoly Movement". In: *Australian Journal of Political Science* 53.1, 89–102.

World Trade Organization (2010). *Economic Cooperation Framework Agreement.* Regional Trade Agreement Database. http://rtais.wto.org/rtadocs/713/TOA/English/Combined%20ECFA%20Text.pdf (last accessed on 16/01/2020).

Wu, H. Denis and Cheryl Ann Lambert (2016). "Impediments to Journalistic Ethics. How Taiwan's Media Market Obstructs News Professional Practice". In: *Journal of Media Ethics* 31.1, 35–50.

Wu, Jieh-min (2008). *Three views of China.* (In Chinese). http://twdemocracy.blogspot.com/2008/11/blog-post_9222.html (last accessed on 05/12/2019).

––––– (2009). "The China Factor and Taiwan's Democracy". In: *Reflexion* 11 (February), 141–157. (In Chinese).

––––– (2012). *Anti-Want Want Parade Notes.* (In Chinese). Thinking Taiwan. https://www.thinkingtaiwan.com/content/78 (last accessed on 05/12/2019).

––––– (2017). "The China factor in Taiwan. Impact and response". In: *Routledge Handbook of Contemporary Taiwan.* Ed. by Gunter Schubert. London and New York: Routledge, 426–446.

Wu, Yu-Shan (2011). "The evolution of the KMT's stance on the one China principle. National identity in flux". In: *Taiwanese Identity in the Twenty-first Century. Domestic, Regional and Global Perspectives.* Ed. by Gunter Schubert and Jens Damm. London and New York: Routledge, 51–71.

Youth Alliance against Media Monsters (2012a). *901 statement.* (In Chinese). 29th August. http://idontwantwantleague.blogspot.com/2012/08/901.html (last accessed on 16/07/2020).

––––– (2012b). *Alliance Press Release.* (In Chinese). 28th November 2012. http://idontwantwantleague.blogspot.com/2012/12/blog-post_4.html (last accessed on 01/07/2020).

––––– (2012c). *August 6 statement.* (In Chinese). 6th August 2012. http://idontwantwantleague.blogspot.com/2012/12/20120806.html (last accessed on 16/07/2020).

––––– (2012d). *Become the power of change together! A vision for the organisational work of the Youth League.* (In Chinese). 22nd December 2012. http://idontwantwantleague.blogspot.com/2012/12/blog-post_22.html (last accessed on 18/07/2020).

––––– (2012e). *Call for Mobilisation.* (In Chinese). 25th November 2012. http://idontwantwantleague.blogspot.com/2012/12/20121126.html (last accessed on 01/07/2020).

———— (2012f). *Movement Blog.* (In Chinese). 31st October 2012. http://idontwant wantleague.blogspot.com/2012/10/?m=0 (last accessed on 05/12/2019).

———— (2012g). *Press Release.* (In Chinese). 27th November 2012. https://idontwant wantleague.blogspot.com/2012/11/blog-post.html (last accessed on 08/07/2020).

———— (2013). *One car goes to the end of the world event series.* (In Chinese). 18th February 2013. http://idontwantwantleague.blogspot.com/2013/02/2013012020130201.html (last accessed on 26/07/2020).

Yu, Ying-shih (2012). *Letter to Huang Kuo-chang.* (In Chinese). 4th May 2012. https://www.taipeisociety.org/node/388 (last accessed on 11/07/2020).

Yuen, Samson (2014). "Under the Shadow of China. Beijing's Policy Towards Hong Kong and Taiwan in Comparative Perspective". In: *China Perspectives* (2/2014), 69–76.

Zhang, Fucai (2012). *Fujian actively plans blueprint for digital publishing industry development.* (In Chinese). General Administration of Press and Publication of the People's Republic of China. 16th November 2012. http://www.gapp.gov.cn/contents/1672/113125.html (last accessed on 05/01/2020).

Zhang, J. J. (2013). "Borders on the Move. Cross-Strait Tourists' Material Moments on 'The Other Side' in the Midst of Rapprochement between China and Taiwan". In: *Geoforum* 48, 94–101.

Zhang, Wensheng (2010). *A People's Meeting.* Beijing Review. 19th July 2010. http://www.bjreview.com.cn/Cover_Story_Series_2010/2010-07/19/content_285997.htm (last accessed on 02/01/2020).

Zhao, Elaine Jing (2016). "Collaboration Reconfigured. The Evolving Landscape of Entertainment TV Markets between Taiwan and Mainland China". In: *Media International Australia* 159.1, 53–62.

6 The Sunflower Movement and the Contradictory Re-politicisation of Neoliberal Developmentalism in Taiwan

On the evening of 18 March 2014, about 300 students overwhelmed security forces and gained access to Taiwan's parliament, the Legislative Yuan. Despite several attempts by police forces to expel the students from the grounds during the night, the occupation of the parliament would go on to last for 24 days. The immediate trigger for what became known as the Sunflower Movement (SFM) was the rushed 30-second committee review of the Cross-Strait Service Trade Agreement (CSSTA). The CSSTA, which had been signed in June 2013 between SEF and ARATS, was the expression of a renewed push towards cross-Strait economic liberalisation: Both sides of the Taiwan Strait had agreed to open up a number of service sectors, including finance and publishing. Civic groups had criticised both the opaque negotiation process, said to have taken place in a "Black Box" shielded from the public, as well as the social, economic and political impacts of opening up Taiwan's economy to economically strong Chinese businesses that were said to pursue political goals. Under public pressure, the KMT-led government had agreed to hold a series of public hearings together with the DPP before passing the trade agreement on to the Legislative Yuan's review committee. During the committee meeting on 17 March, KMT legislator Chang Ching-chung declared the review period of 90 days over and handed the bill on to the plenary session of the Legislative Yuan, where, given the KMT's firm majority, it was expected to be passed into law within days.

Several aspects of the SFM appear remarkable in comparison to previous episodes of the protest cycle. First, compared to the WSM and the AMM, both of which were characterised by non-disruptive protests in public spaces, the occupation of the Legislative Yuan marks a striking shift in forms of practice. Second, the protest against the CSSTA was accompanied by a re-emergence of radical conceptions. The China Factor narrative appeared to move into the background as narratives centred around the questions of neoliberalism and developmentalism gained prominence. This chapter argues that this shift towards more militant protest forms did not come out of nowhere. While the SFM is today remembered for the occupation of Taiwan's parliament, the movement was preceded by a series of attempts to occupy government buildings during the 18 months prior to March 2014. These months were characterised by the intensification of local struggles over land and

DOI: 10.4324/9781003395546-6

labour issues, promoting the re-emergence of radical conceptions and forms of practice. Central to this process was the student group Black Island Nation Youth Front, the *de facto* successor group to the YAMM. Several of its key members were involved in local struggles, and the group's conceptions and forms of practice reflect the general shift Taiwan's social movements underwent at this stage.

To account for these developments, this chapter will proceed as follows. The first section is dedicated to local struggles, arguing that these are best understood as a response to the introduction of modes of living thought to correspond with Taiwan's neodevelopmentalist accumulation strategy. These struggles had a profound impact on forms of hegemonic contestation and shaped the outlook of the involved groups. Section two then discusses the SFM not simply as a protest against the CSSTA, but as a challenge to the hegemonic project of deepening Taiwan's integration into the global economy, of which the trade pact was a central initiative. Attention will be paid in particular to the attempt to integrate the various movement currents that had emerged over the previous decade.

Land, Labour and the Empty Promises of the Golden Decade

The key to understanding the dynamics that characterised the SFM lies in the particular configuration of movement currents and the management of contradictions arising from these during the occupation. The previous chapters discussed the emergence of a reformist and a nationalist current, and both would play a central role in the spring of 2014. Crucially, however, the radical current that had been marginalised during the AMM experienced a renaissance in 2013.

This renaissance can be attributed to two tendencies: On the one hand, the election victory of 2012 gave the KMT government the confidence to renew its push to transform Taiwan into what Premier Jiang Yi-huah referred to as a "free trade island" (Executive Yuan 2013), while, on the other hand, the pragmatisation of the DPP prevented the opposition parties to mount a convincing challenge to the government (Cole 2017: 20–22). This failure of representative democracy contributed to the proliferation of local struggles around three related but analytically distinct issues: urban renewal, rural revitalisation and labour. As will be discussed below, the intensification of struggles around these issues emerged in response to the government's attempt to promote economic growth, restore the economy's global competitiveness and introduce new modes of living that correspond to these structural transformations.

Urban Renewal and the Housing Crisis in the Neoliberal City

Taiwan's approach to construction and housing changed significantly during the crisis of the developmental state. From the 1980s onwards, urban renewal was seen "as the key for the development of the construction industries, which in turn were believed to be crucial for the entire economy" (Hsu and Chang 2013: 152). The promotion of the construction industry was accompanied by measures of financial deregulation during the late 1980s, which opened the real estate market to financial institutions (Chen and Li 2012: 214). Since the 1990s, "gentrification has become a major instrument of neoliberal urbanism for securing capital accumulation and attracting capital investment" (Jou et al. 2016: 563).

The trend to rely on construction and the real estate market to fuel economic growth was reinforced during subsequent economic crises (Chen 2005: 113). The global financial crisis of 2008 exposed Taiwan's dependence on the global demand for IT goods, prompting the government to reaffirm "urban renewal as a key tool of economic growth" (Hsu and Chang 2013: 154), while at the same time intensifying the flow of institutional investors into the real estate market (Wang 2010: 255). Between 2004 and 2014, Taiwan's real estate market saw a price growth of 144 per cent, with Taipei city standing out at a growth of 195 per cent (Lee 2016). Institutional investors became major agents in the real estate market, and by 2012 insurance companies accounted for 40 per cent of the turnover (ibid.).[1] To facilitate this transformation, the state became increasingly "involved in land appropriation, incentive amplification and more importantly, police containment of urban political protests" (Hsu and Chang 2013: 153).

The KMT government's "i-Taiwan 12" projects bundled several initiatives designed to revive economic growth after 2008 by increasing Taiwan's global competitiveness and facilitating the country's integration into the global economy, especially with regard to regional integration initiatives such as the Trans-Pacific Partnership (TPP). Among the 12 projects promoted by the government were the upgrading of Taiwan's transportation infrastructure, the expansion of logistics hubs – especially Taoyuan Aerotropolis, the Kaohsiung Free-Trade Zone and its harbour – rural revitalisation, the upgrading of industrial parks and urban renewal (Wang 2010: 256). The central instrument of urban renewal was a state-induced rent gap, an institutional arrangement that encouraged urban renewal as a response not to "actual physical deterioration" (in fact, land developers targeted prime locations rather than older districts) but to institutional pressures (Yang and Chang 2018: 1958). The central and local governments not only increased incentives for urban renewal by providing a bonus to the floor area ratio, the ratio of the size of a building's floor area to the size of the land it is built on, but also facilitated the implementation of these projects by reducing the number of affected households that had to consent to the project and lower the barriers for the eviction of the remaining ones (ibid.: 1950–1954). The state thus applied the principle of competitiveness to urban spaces and forms of everyday life, promoting the transformation of Taipei into a "neoliberal city" (Rogelja 2014; Wei 2018: 92).

Accordingly, Taipei saw an increase in urban renewal projects during 2010–2013. For the purposes of this section, we will here briefly discuss two representative cases that differ in the structure of land ownership. The first of these cases is the Wang family residence in Taipei's Shilin District, a case commonly referred to as *Wenlin Yuan*. The houses owned by the Wang family occupied a plot that had been selected for the construction of luxury apartments. The land developer had obtained the approval of 36 of the affected households, but the Wang family resisted eviction. Social resistance was initially organised by the Taiwan Alliance for Victims of Urban Renewal (TAVUR), an association that had been formed in response to the proliferation of urban renewal projects (Hioe 2014). The family was unable to prevent the eviction, and the houses were forcibly demolished in March 2012 after more than 1,000 policemen removed 300 protesters from the scene (Wei 2018).

Activists, however, returned the next day to occupy the site, constructing a temporary shed to continue their struggle. This occupation not only raised public awareness but served as a central hub for the recruitment of activists and fostering relations among organisations (Wei 2016: 144): Several of my respondents noted how the Wenlin Yuan case either encouraged them to become activists or helped them to establish connections to groups, thus contributing to a realisation that urban renewal was not a matter of individual hardship or fate but the expression of structural transformations (R22; R34; R37; R40; R42; R45). Young recruits also gained experience in various forms of activism by preparing press releases, holding press conferences and organising a variety of protests (Wei 2016: 139–142). Ultimately, the occupation was maintained for two years before the Wang family reached a settlement with the land developer after extensive legal disputes (Hioe 2014).

A second significant case, Huaguang community, exemplifies Taipei city's attempt to attract investments through the privatisation of publicly-owned land in a process of accumulation by dispossession (Jou et al. 2016: 571). Huaguang community originated in the immediate post-war era when the government tolerated the development of informal settlements on public land to avoid a housing crisis (Chen 2020: 628–629; Tamburo 2020: 37). For decades, occupants of Huaguang community had paid property tax and had been served by public utility companies, but they never legally owned the land (Chen 2017: 97–99). These plots of land, however, now constituted a source of revenue for the state and of profit for private land developers. The Huaguang area had first been chosen as the site for Taipei's "Wall Street." After the global financial crisis cast doubt on the viability of such a project, plans were changed to construct "Taipei Roppongi," a reference to Tokyo's nightlife district. As the occupants of the area had constructed their houses on land owned by the Ministry of Justice, they were categorised as "illegal occupants" in 2006 (Jou et al. 2016: 570). This meant that the mostly elderly residents were not entitled to rehousing or compensation and usually were asked to demolish their own houses and pay compensation for having conducted "illegal" business (Jou et al. 2016: 565; Wei 2018). The demolitions of Huaguang community took place throughout 2013 after young activists – among them Lin Fei-fan – who had rallied to Huaguang and chained themselves to the houses, were forcefully removed by the police (Chen 2017: 99–100).

Together with the Wenlin Yuan case, however, the struggle had a lasting effect on social mobilisation in Taiwan. Students were able to relate to housing struggles because they themselves felt the effects of these projects in their everyday lives as urban renewal also contributed to rising housing costs in nearby areas, and those districts of Taipei that were affected by urban renewal projects saw land values increasing by an average of 424 per cent, creating "huge pressure for the local working class residents to move out and [preventing] those of similar socio-economic status from moving in" (Hsu and Chang 2013: 156). Between the third quarter of 2010 and the first quarter of 2011 alone, housing prices in Taipei increased by 40 per cent, mostly at the cost of affordable housing (Yang and Chang 2018: 1960). This hindered the activists' own plans to move out of their parent's house and start a family (R24; R35).

Participating in the struggle against urban renewal in cases such as Wenlin Yuan, Huaguang, Shida and Shaoxing contributed to the conviction that activists were facing a deeper structural problem (R34), exposing the need for more systematic analysis centred around the common denominator of neoliberal developmentalism (Wei 2016: 139). Faced with increasingly violent police repression furthermore paved the way for the groups adopting new forms of practice: During a protest in August 2013, activists managed to enter and occupy the courtyard of the Ministry of Justice, a major agent in the privatisation of state-owned land (Chen 2017: 99).

From Land as a Resource of Inclusion to a Resource of Accumulation

The "i-Taiwan 12" projects encompassed two further initiatives that contributed to social mobilisation: rural revitalisation and the expansion of industrial parks (Chiu 2014: 19). Both of these initiatives were promoted as a restructuring necessary to "boost competitiveness of agriculture" in the face of "the changes in the global economy and industrial structure" (Council of Agriculture, Taiwan [COA] 2008a). The two ingredients to improve the competitiveness of Taiwan's agriculture, the increase in scale of farming operations and the promotion of a shift towards export orientation, however, threatened the compromise equilibrium that had been the result of the land reform during the 1950s. Once a pillar of the post-war inclusion of the subaltern, the landownership structure based on small-scale farming increasingly posed limits to accumulation. As part of its neodevelopmentalist accumulation strategy, the Taiwanese government sought to liberalise its agricultural sector to deepen the liberalisation of economic interactions across the Taiwan Strait and in preparation for Taiwan's ambition to join the US-led TPP, an agreement that sought to reduce agricultural tariffs (Schmidt Hernandez 2017: 11). The ownership structure of agricultural land, averaging roughly one hectare per household, was identified as a major obstacle to improving the international competitiveness of Taiwan's agricultural sector (COA 2008a).

Attempts to encourage land consolidation during the 1970s and 1980s failed due to restrictions on land ownership that were still in place after the land reform and continued incentives for small-scale farming (Francks et al. 1999: 200–201). Moreover, farmers were reluctant to lease out land as they feared this would eventually lead to them losing the land irrevocably (Mao 1993: 13). While the traditional commitment to landownership based on ancestry and heritage declined from the 1960s onwards as farming households tapped into additional sources of income (Gallin 1964: 316; Liao and Huang 1994: 359–360), it was complemented by a modern commitment: As land for industrial expansion became scarce, farmers chose to hold on to their land for its exchange value (Liao and Huang 1994: 360, 367). This modern commitment to landownership has since been reinforced by the introduction of welfare programs, including health insurance and retirement benefits, the eligibility of which depends on the ownership of agricultural land, even if the land is left fallow (Huang 2015: 2–3).

In an attempt to reconcile the developmentalist aims of a competitive agricultural sector with the farmers' commitment to landownership, the COA announced a scheme entitled "Small Landlords, Big Tenants" in 2008. On the one hand, this policy reaffirmed land ownership of farming households (the "small landlords") but provided incentives to lease out the land by "ensuring their continued eligibility for farmers' insurance and relevant benefits" (COA 2008c), establishing a retirement system for farmers as well as one-off payments to farmers willing to lease out their land (COA 2008a). The "big tenants", on the other hand, were eligible to applying for preferential loans, subsidies and training in the management of large farms (COA 2008a; COA 2011: 24, 61). The goal of the policy was not simply to increase the size of farming units, but rather to introduce a new mode of production, attracting not only individual tenants and cooperatives but also agri-businesses (Yang and Han 2015: 2). The policy aimed to "encourage industrialization of agricultural operations" (COA 2008c) and an "enterprise-style management" (COA 2011: 23) of farms and sought "to upgrade production and marketing equipment, lower manpower costs, and increase operational efficiency" (COA 2012: 21). "Big tenants" were furthermore incentivised to prioritise export crops "chosen based on market competitiveness" (COA 2008b; Yang and Han 2015: 3), supported by a network of expos and the establishment of special export production zones (COA 2011: 34, 42; COA 2012: 35). The scheme thus promoted not only a transformation of the mode of production but also of the mode of living, "turning a whole group of young 'farmers' into 'managers' and 'entrepreneurs'" (COA 2012: 3), reminiscent of Marx' observation that capitalism strives for "[t]he replacement of the easygoing farmer by the businessman, the farming capitalist" (Marx 1968: 110). The initiative proved more successful than previous attempts at promoting land consolidation, and by late 2014, 29,000 "small landlords" had rented their land to 1,670 "big tenants", resulting in an average farm size of nine hectares (COA 2015: 56).

These developments prompted activists and scholars to form the Taiwan Rural Front (TRF) in 2008. The aim of this group is to oppose further trade liberalisation and to promote agricultural development focused around small-scale farming, social justice, ecological sustainability and food security (R41). The TRF argues that rural revitalisation, as envisioned by the KMT, subjects agriculture to the needs of developmentalism and capitalist accumulation. Rather than allocating resources to meet the needs of the farmers, like the much-needed modernisation of irrigation systems, the KMT's plans fund "decorative" projects such as bicycle lanes and parks that are aimed at pleasing urban visitors and benefit land developers (Chen n.d.), accelerating the disappearance of rural society rather than revitalising it (Taiwan Rural Front [TRF] 2009c; TRF 2009b). The promotion of large-scale industrialised farming and the increased commodification of farmland is furthermore said to threaten the mode of living of farmers and with it "the way of thinking, the language, production activities and everyday lives of farmers" (Chen n.d.). The TRF argues that subjecting rural communities hitherto based on small-scale farming to the logic of agri-businesses, and thus global market forces, neglects their non-economic contributions, that is, their social and cultural significance (TRF 2009a). The TRF thus assumes a position that echoes arguments of scholars who see a renewed process of primitive accumulation unfolding in Taiwan (Tsai 2015: 56).

The TRF serves as a crucial hub to connect the various self-help associations that had emerged in villages affected by the new policies. In addition, a number of campus groups emerged in response to the KMT's rural revitalisation initiative in late 2008 and early 2009. These include NTU Rural Practice, the NCCU Return to the Valley Society, the National Chiao Tung University (NCTU) Agronomy Group, and the NTHU Touqian River Society. They all exhibit a similar pattern, which can be illustrated by the path of the Miaoli Youth Reading Club, of which Miaoli native Chen Wei-ting was a key member. This group was established as a reading group by students who sought to further their theoretical understanding of rural transformations taking place in their villages. The group soon established contacts with the TRF and organised lectures and debates. After enrolling at university, the members of the Miaoli Youth established the NTHU Rural Reading Club. Seeing the need to complement their theoretical enterprise with first-hand practical experience, students then transformed the Touqian River Society, a group that had been established in the aftermath of the WSM, into a group that sought to fuse the elements of theory and practice regarding rural life in Taiwan (Lu and Ye 2011; Liu 2012).

The above-mentioned groups thus evolved from reading clubs into groups that closely cooperated with the TRF to overcome the barriers between rural and urban life and between theory and practice. Two forms of practice were developed to this end. First, the "Bow to Land' farmers" markets, a monthly event organised at campuses, bring rural life into Taiwanese cities (TRF 2010a). This is meant to promote direct relations between producers and consumers and thus reveal the human relations that are normally masked by the commodity form. These farmers' markets are also the stage for festivals, lectures, workshops, concerts and similar activities to showcase the social and cultural contributions of Taiwan's countryside. Second, activists were convinced that "reflection should be able to be transformed into everyday experience" (Chen n.d.). The more theoretical activities of the reading groups were therefore complemented by hands-on forms of practice. To experience the everyday life of rural Taiwan, the TRF and the student groups began to co-organise an annual Grassroots Investigation Camp from 2009 onwards (TRF 2009b). Students participating in these camps take part in a three-day preparatory workshop that covers theoretical approaches to rural development and the training in fieldwork methods before they are embedded in the countryside to live with and study the life of peasant families in rural Taiwan over the period of a month:

> Taking part in farm labour allows those who have left their rural homes and young people who have little connection with or love for the countryside to realise that farming entails a unique set of skills and that these skills and crafts cannot be passed on by words alone. Only by learning the labour

process (yes, 'learn' to labour) will we become conscious of our position in relation to land, environment and farmers – a position that should be more humble and recognise the subjectivity of the other. Only through such a labour process will such a position be able to take root in the countryside.

(Chen n.d.)

The close-knit network of cooperation that formed after 2008 would provide the fertile soil for the more generalised mobilisation that followed the first Dapu incident. This incident was the result of another initiative that threatened to upset the post-war agricultural equilibrium. The land reform of the 1950s had put limitations on the conversion of agricultural into industrial land, but under the land shortage of the 1970s and 1980s, the government had established the model of industrial parks[2] to provide key high-tech industries with land to secure the latter's base for accumulation. Tsai (2015: 63) argues that the land grabbing that accompanied the construction of the Hsinchu Science Park in the 1970s and 1980s was an expression of the government's belief that "this farmland would be better used to improve Taiwan's competitiveness in the global market". Preferential land usage for high-tech companies was one element of the compromise with capital to root these firms in Taiwan while allowing them to set up certain manufacturing plants in China (Ngo 2005: 88). The expansion of industrial parks was on the agenda of all governments since then, and the Ma Ying-jeou government sought to continue this policy as part of its "i-Taiwan 12" initiative (Chiu 2014: 19). Among the many projected industrial expansions (see TRF 2011), the case of Dapu township in Miaoli County is the most prominent. In 2008, the InnoLux Corporation, a subsidiary of the Hon Hai Group, announced its US$16 billion plan to expand its plants in the Jhunan industrial park in Miaoli County (Chen 2017: 101). The KMT-led local government then proceeded to acquire the farmland necessary for the expansion of the industrial park, beginning with the demolition of farms in June 2010 (ibid.).

This move came as a surprise to the residents of Dapu. The forced eviction of the families from their land resulted in the suicide of a resident and sparked a public outcry and the mobilisation of local self-help associations assisted by the TRF. In a first statement, these groups declared that "the government and the conglomerates have joined forces to take away our farmland" and condemned the "spectre of developmentalism" that devastated the local communities (TRF 2010b). The mobilisation resulted in a mediation by then-Premier Wu Den-yih, who stated that the remaining houses would be spared.

The Dapu incident contributed to the deepening of cooperation networks among activists. In August 2011, the Miaoli Youth Reading Club around Chen Wei-ting organised a camp to discuss and prepare a common strategy in the face of developmentalism together with several self-help associations and campus groups, such as the NCCU Return to the Valley Society (Miaoli Youth Reading Club 2011a). By December of that year, rural-focused student groups (such as the Miaoli Youth Reading Club, the Touqian River Society and the NCTU Agronomy Group) and the local self-help associations had the support of other campus groups, including the 02 Society and Radical Notes (Miaoli Youth Reading Club 2011b).

In July 2013, the county government proceeded with the demolitions in Dapu despite earlier assurances by Premier Wu (Cole 2017: 22). After this second Dapu incident, the already-established networks of cooperation among student groups coagulated into the Defend Miaoli Youth League. This umbrella group joined the TRF and the local self-help associations in organising the "818 Protest" in Taipei in August 2013. This protest is significant for two reasons. First, participation was not limited to groups whose major concern was the rural question. Rather, they were joined by groups from other struggles that were now seen as structurally related expressions of an intensifying developmentalism. These included groups involved in urban struggles, representatives of aboriginal communities threatened by displacement, townships facing large transportation and energy infrastructure projects, as well as the autonomous labour group National Alliance for Workers of Closed Factories (TRF 2013; Chen 2017: 105–106). Together, they denounced "the tyranny of an unscrupulous government breaching contracts and monopolising interests of political and business groups" (TRF 2013). Second, the shift towards radical conceptions found its expression in the readiness to deploy more militant forms of practice. During the demonstration, protesters chanted "If you tear down Dapu today, we tear down the government tomorrow!" (R21), and a group of 2,000 activists diverted to the Ministry of the Interior, overwhelmed the security forces present at the compound and occupied it for 24 hours (R21; R28). The activists considered breaking into the building itself, but ultimately decided against it due to lack of preparation (R21).

Labour Struggles and the Convergence of Radical Groups

Another strand of mobilisation that would ultimately merge into the radical current were elements of the autonomous labour movement. Ma Ying-jeou had promised the Taiwanese, and especially Taiwan's younger generation, a "Golden Decade" (Office of the President, Republic of China (Taiwan) 2011). Reporting on the advances his government had made since 2008 to increase Taiwan's competitiveness, citing the *World Competitiveness Yearbook* and *Global Competitiveness Report*, he emphasised that his plan relied on further integrating Taiwan into the global economy (ibid.). Ma insisted that "only by [seeking closer ties with China] can we push for closer cooperation with other countries" (TT 2012), defining the cross-Strait rapprochement as a prerequisite for increasing Taiwan's competitiveness and thus for boosting economic growth and creating jobs. Opening up to China, Ma argued, was an "economic necessity" (Hu 2010: 7). His government sought to draw on the historical example of Taiwan's "economic miracle," where Taiwan's export competitiveness was said to have been the foundation for upward mobility and a relatively equal wealth distribution. The "Golden Decade" was to renew this motivating myth and legitimate the government's policies.

However, especially the younger generations no longer shared the assessment that increasing Taiwan's competitiveness by transforming Taiwan into a "free trade island" was for the benefit of all Taiwanese. While the promises of a "rapprochement dividend" might have appeared plausible in 2008, by 2013, Taiwanese felt that they had not benefited from agreements like the ECFA (R26). It was the immediate everyday experience of young Taiwanese that clashed with this narrative and undermined its legitimating power. Soaring housing prices compelled young Taiwanese to defer plans to move out of their parent's house and have children (R35). This was exacerbated by the employment situation of young Taiwanese. In mid-2012, youth unemployment in Taiwan reached 13 per cent compared to 4.3 per cent for the general population (International Labour Organization [ILO] 2013: 70). The "Golden Decade's" promise of upward mobility came in the form of the "22k" policy, a scheme that subsidised businesses that employed recent college graduates on a one-year contract for a salary of NTD 22,000 (approximately US$700) (LePesant 2012: 75). The 22k policy did not bring security but instead cemented the wage-level for college graduates at NTD 22,000 and resulted in an increased chance of young Taiwanese losing their job after the first year of employment. As such, the policy was experienced as one of many measures of labour market flexibilisation that affected Taiwanese aged between 15 and 24 in particular, who were increasingly hired as temporary or dispatched workers (Shi 2012: 86). This was exacerbated by increased competition among young graduates, as "[t]he expansion-oriented education policy has resulted in an abrupt increase in the number of new universities and colleges – and in a bulging number of college graduates" (ibid.). This put the young generation at a disadvantage in an already precarious labour market.[3] Low wages and precarious employment relations fomented the conviction that hard work no longer guaranteed rewards (R21). While the hegemonic project was further promoting cross-Strait "youth entrepreneurship"[4] as an updated imagination of "Boss Island", students came to see Taiwan's transformation into a "free trade island" not as the panacea to but the cause for their predicament.

It is therefore not surprising that many young Taiwanese cast their vote in favour of DPP candidate Tsai Ing-wen during the 2012 presidential elections to express their disappointment with the Ma government's inability to address these concerns (LePesant 2012: 75). Students, however, did not limit themselves to expressing their discontent at the ballot but also joined or formed labour groups. After the ban on labour unions in the educational sector was lifted, graduate students who worked as teaching assistants formed the NTU Labor Union to mobilise against wage cuts, while teachers in higher education formed Taiwan Higher Education Union (THEU) in 2012 (Ho 2020: 410). The cross-campus Youth Labor Union 95 (YLU), which had been established in 2005 to demand raising of the hourly minimum wage from 66 NTD to 95 NTD (Youth Labor Union 95 [YLU] 2007), was reinvigorated by the 22k policy. The YLU and the NTU Union differed from other student groups as they not only conceived of students as *future* workers but as students who had to work either on campus (as teaching assistants) or as workers off campus, where students often work on minimum wage in convenience stores to finance their studies (Shadow 2016). The YLU began organising training camps that covered organisational methods, labour laws, political and economic analyses and practical training for labour disputes, and called on fellow students to "join the ranks of resisting exploitation" (YLU 2011).

Similar groups emerged elsewhere. The *Cold-Blooded High-Tech Youth*, for instance, was established in 2010 to draw attention to the exploitation of overworked employees in the high-tech industry (Ho 2020: 411). The group denounced the destructive character of Taiwan's showcase industry, arguing that it is built on the exploitation of workers and the destruction of nature and local communities. What emerges during this time is the tendency to recognise the structural connections between the various forms of struggle that have been discussed in this chapter: "From the issue of the Yanghua Optoelectronics sweatshop to the expropriation of agricultural land in Miaoli, we have seen how beautiful high-tech brands trample labour, farmers, land and the environment in cold blood" (Cold-Blooded High-Tech Youth 2010).

The rising awareness of their precarious situation in everyday life, their own experience in labour struggles and the emergence of organisational networks sensitised students to labour disputes beyond the campus. An insightful example is the case of workers who were laid off when factories, mostly in the textile sector, were relocated to China or Southeast Asia throughout the 1990s and 2000s. In many cases, the employers left owing severance and pension payments to their former employees (R24). These payments were first covered by the Taiwanese government, which later changed its position and sued the workers for "unpaid loans" (Ho 2018b:: 122).

A prominent case is that of Hualon Textile (Chiu 2017: 207). The company relocated four of its factories abroad, maintaining one production site in Miaoli, where workers were forced to accept lower wages. In June 2012, the remaining Hualon workers went on strike. Although the National Alliance for Workers of Closed Factories (NAWCF) and the Taiwan International Workers Association (TIWA) had supported various self-help associations in labour disputes like these, their struggle received limited public attention until Chen Wei-ting, a Miaoli native whose mother had worked as a textile worker at the Hualon factory, mobilised the Defend Miaoli Youth League to block Hualon's trucks in support of the workers (Wei 2016: 164–165). In 2012 and 2013, the self-help associations together with the TIWA, the NAWCF, the NTU Union and the Defend Miaoli Youth League increased the pressure on the local and central governments, resorting to increasingly disruptive forms of practice. At one point, laid-off workers raised awareness for their cause by occupying train tracks at Taipei Railway Station, blocking train traffic for about an hour until the police was able to clear the area.

What becomes apparent here is a convergence of labour, urban and rural struggles. Not only the temporal overlap of these issues – the Wang family residence was demolished in spring 2012, the Hualon dispute intensified in the summer of 2012 and continued in parallel to the demolitions of Huaguang and Dapu that took place in the summer of 2013 – but also the systematic cooperation between the involved groups contributed to the perception that activists were not simply facing an accumulation of unrelated grievances, but rather a series of phenomena that were the expression of a push to subject an increasing number of social spheres to a logic of neoliberal developmentalism. Statements from various groups during this period document that the "spectre of developmentalism" (TRF 2010b) had become the conceptual principle, while – in stark contrast to the AMM – the motif of the China Factor had all but disappeared. What drove this shift was the immediate experience of neoliberal developmentalism in everyday life. The project to turn Taiwan into a "free-trade island" and transform students into "youth entrepreneurs" and farmers into "farming capitalists" was not experienced as a way to achieve the prosperity that the "Golden Decade" had promised but as an attempt to impose a "self-responsibilization of individuals to be entrepreneurial and competitive in the world market" (Sum and Jessop 2013: 318), permeating everyday life with insecurity and precarity. The intensification of these processes furthermore contributed to a shift in the movement's forms of practice. While the WSM and the AMM were characterised by large-scale protests and peaceful sit-ins, the convergence of local struggles increasingly saw the adoption of "'guerrilla' tactics" (Cole 2017: 21), including repeated attempts to occupy ministries, the Executive Yuan, the Legislative Yuan or other buildings of importance in Taipei.

This convergence of movements that resulted from a variety of points of nucleation found its material expression in the establishment of the 929 Alliance, a coalition of 43 labour, rural and student groups that organised a large-scale protest in September 2013 with the aim to besiege the KMT's party congress that was set to take place at the Sun Yat-sen Memorial Hall on 29 September.[5] The Alliance related the various struggles to the unleashing of capital under the "developmental hegemony" (929 Social Movement Alliance 2013), and TRF secretary-general Frida Tsai singled out capital's role in these processes: "They tore down private homes and seized private lands to benefit big corporations" (TT 2013). Given the momentum of radical struggles and the movements' willingness to resort to disruptive forms of practice, the KMT was forced to postpone the party congress. It was eventually held two months later in a remote stadium in Greater Taichung.

The renaissance of radical conceptions, however, also posed a practical problem: Many of the student groups that were involved in the local struggles had vehemently opposed radical conceptions during the AMM. While the SCS had argued that capitalism had produced the conditions that allowed for the emergence of media conglomerates, YAMM had insisted that the market mechanism and competition were the solutions to the issue of media concentration. At the time, the incompatibility of the radical and nationalist conceptions had initiated a dissociation of movement currents. This time, some of the groups that had been involved in the YAMM had themselves proposed radical analyses. Addressing this question, Chen Wei-ting stated that radical and nationalist currents were complementary, and that "nationalism is one of the tools for realising socialism" (Chen 2012).

To address these issues, several workshops and activist camps were held during the winter of 2013 and 2014 (R22). One example is a five-day training camp organised by YAMM groups, mainly Radical Notes, the 02 Society and NTPU-Cross. Around 30 groups, mostly those that constituted the YAMM, participated.[6] Reflecting the shift in the relations of forces during 2013, however, groups representing the local struggles were also invited, including the NTU Union, the Defend Miaoli Youth League as well as representatives of the TRF-organised Rural Grassroots Investigation Camp. In addition to activist training sessions and panels on organisational matters, the camp also sought "an exchange of opinions and to form a consensus" (Preparatory Committee for the Rebellion of the Common People 2014). Activities like these suggest an awareness that it was necessary to clarify these conceptual issues. We will return to the relationship of nationalist and radical conceptions below.

The Sunflower Movement

The Cross-Strait Service Trade Agreement as an Expression of Taiwan's Neoliberal Developmentalist Accumulation Strategy

It was against this background of radical convergence that the hegemonic project pressed on with its key initiative, the Cross-Strait Service Trade Agreement. A follow-up agreement to the ECFA, which had gone into force in 2010, the CSSTA was to deepen the integration of service industries across the Taiwan Strait, in particular the sectors of finance, telecommunications and publishing. As such, it was the major initiative of Ma Ying-jeou's second term. In his inaugural address after his re-election in 2012, Ma reaffirmed his vision that Taiwan's prosperity depended on trade liberalisation, and that Taiwan's integration into the global economy in turn depended on closer relations with China:

> We must step up the pace of liberalization; there can be no further delay. Only if Taiwan opens up to the world will the world embrace Taiwan. In an era when we are confronted by a restructuring of the global political and economic order and a shift in the economic center of gravity toward Asia, we must change from a protectionist mindset and revise outdated legislation. We must eliminate artificial trade and investment barriers and create a genuinely free and open economic environment for Taiwan that is more in line with international practices.
>
> We are planning to establish showcase free economic zones, one of which will be in Kaohsiung. This is a crucial step in Taiwan's move to becoming a 'free trade island.' We must speedily complete follow-up talks under the Cross-Straits Economic Cooperation Framework Agreement (ECFA) and expedite negotiations on economic cooperation agreements with important trading partners like Singapore and New Zealand. Over the next eight years, we must fully prepare to join the Trans-Pacific Partnership in order to seize the historic opportunity to become further integrated into the global trading system.
>
> (Ma 2012)

Although CSSTA negotiations involved a long list of service sectors, the financial sector was of particular significance.[7] Taiwan's bourgeoisie had long pushed for financial liberalisation between China and Taiwan. Barriers to capital flows across the Taiwan Strait, such as the lack of a clearing and settlement mechanism between the two currencies, meant that repatriating profits from China to Taiwan came with high transaction costs and additional foreign exchange risks (Chen and Yao 2017: 62). The pressure for financial liberalisation from Taiwan's China-based manufacturing enterprises increased further in the aftermath of the global financial crisis. At the height of the crisis in late 2008, the Chinese government offered US$19 billion in loans to Taiwanese businesses operating in China (Cheung 2010: 22). After the immediate crisis had been weathered, the government became concerned with bubbles in the real estate and financial sectors. To reduce excess liquidity, the access to credit was tightened again in 2010 (Han 2012: 370). Taiwanese enterprises operating in China then turned to Taiwanese banks for capital and urged the Taiwanese government to accelerate financial cooperation across the Strait (R26; R44).

This coincided with the interests of Taiwan's financial groups. Taiwan's small banking sector had suffered from overbanking since financial liberalisation in the 1990s, a situation that had not changed despite the attempts by various governments to consolidate the banking sector by encouraging mergers and allowing the establishment of financial holdings. Due to the unprofitability of the domestic market, Taiwanese banks had been longing to access the Chinese market since the 1990s. Given the limited internationalisation of China's financial sector, Taiwanese banks hoped for a first-mover – or at least early-mover – advantage.

The cooperation in the financial and other service sector industries has therefore been on the agenda of all major cross-Strait channels. The KMT-CCP Forum discussed these topics during its 4th, 6th, 7th, 8th and 9th meetings (see Table 4.2), while the Straits Forum featured a Straits Financial Forum since 2010 (see Table 5.1). Representatives of the financial industries furthermore met at the Boao Forum in 2011. Finally, the Cross-Strait CEO Summit, which is jointly organised by the TWC and the CSCMF and involves the majority of Taiwanese conglomerates (see Table 4.1), features a Financial Cooperation Promotion Group.

Throughout the years, these negotiations produced a number of agreements, which were mostly signed through the SEF-ARATS channel. The first of these was the Cross-Strait Agreement on Financial Cooperation, in which both sides agreed on the reciprocal supervision of the banking, securities and insurance sectors. Another move towards financial liberalisation was the ECFA, signed in June 2010. As per the agreement's early harvest list, Taiwanese banks were allowed to upgrade their representative offices to branches after one year and offer RMB-denominated services after two years on the condition that the operations were profitable in the second year (WTO 2010: 59). A special provision allowed Taiwanese banks to provide RMB-denominated services to Taiwanese enterprises operating in China after one year already. This put Taiwanese banks in an advantageous position compared to other foreign banks, which have to wait two years before upgrading their representative offices to branches and three years before conducting RMB-denominated services. In the months following the coming into force of ECFA, several Taiwanese banks were given the approval to open branches in China.

China and Taiwan also negotiated the inclusion of Taiwan's institutional investors in the PRC's RMB Qualified Institutional Investor scheme through which China seeks to internationalise its financial markets. The recognition as qualified foreign institutional investors would have enabled Taiwanese financial institutions to invest in the Chinese capital market, thus securing a significant competitive advantage over other foreign banks (Straits Exchange Foundation [SEF] 2013a: 47). In addition, the CSSTA would have allowed Taiwanese banks to hold 51 per cent in securities firms established in Shanghai, Shenzhen and Fujian Province (SEF 2013a: 47).

The SEF and the ARATS agreed on the text of the agreement during preparatory consultations in Taipei on 14 June 2013, announcing that the CSSTA would "elevate the complementary advantages and competitiveness of the two sides ... [and] bring about long-term and positive economic benefits for the people across the Strait" (SEF 2013b). When the agreement was officially signed by these two organisations in Shanghai one week later, it seemed as if the long-held ambition by Taiwan's bourgeoisie to turn Taiwan into an Asia-Pacific Regional Operations Center, a logistics and financial centre that could provide an entry point for the world into China's markets, was on the horizon. When the APROC plan had been devised by then-CEPD chairman Vincent Siew with the support of then Minister of Economic Affairs, Chiang Pin-kung, it failed due to political obstacles. Nearly 20 years later, the efforts by Taiwan's bourgeoisie – channelled to a considerable degree through Siew's CSCMF and Chiang's TWC – to organise the social and political conditions that allowed for a "normalisation" of cross-Strait economic relations appeared to come to fruition.

Competing Approaches to Contestation

The signing of the CSSTA initiated a process of social mobilisation around two gravitational centres, the Democratic Front Against the Cross-Strait Trade in Services Agreement (DFCSTSA), a coalition of NGOs, and the student group Black Island Nation Youth Front (BIY). Both of these built on networks that were the product of earlier episodes of hegemonic contestation, and both attempted to offer their respective synthesis of the conceptions that had emerged during the protest cycle.

The DFCSTSA emerged out of the CSAW, a coalition of about 30 NGOs, including TAHR, TDW, TLF, TAUP and the Taipei Society. It was convened by Lai Chung-chiang, a trained lawyer who had previously been the chairman of TAHR and was involved with TDW, after the ECFA had been signed in 2010. The group tasked itself with supervising cross-Strait negotiations from a perspective of democracy, human rights, the environment and labour rights, but also the procedural aspects of negotiations and the ratification of agreements (Cross-Strait Agreement Watch n.d.). As the CSAW was established as a broad coalition of NGOs from different fields, it remained firmly on the terrain of reformist conceptions based on democracy and human rights.

During the AMM, organic intellectuals related to the CSAW member TDW had articulated nationalist conceptions around the notion of the China Factor. While these had proven their potential for mobilisation, they had also stirred some controversy. In early 2013, the TDW presented the *Declaration of the Free People*, a document that attempted a synthesis of reformist conceptions, based on democracy and human rights, and the China Factor. The document, co-authored by Wu Jieh-min, sets out by defining a major distinction between China and Taiwan, with the latter having realised the hard-fought "universal values of freedom, human rights, and democracy" (Taiwan Democracy Watch [TDW] 2013). The recent negotiations between the two sides, however, brought with it the risk that "the 'China Factor' [would] erode the foundation of Taiwan's democracy" (TDW 2013). To prevent the erosion of Taiwan's democracy through the China Factor, the declaration demands the enactment of a Cross-Strait Agreement Oversight Law to ensure transparency, citizen participation and parliamentary supervision with regard to cross-Strait agreements. Cross-Strait negotiations on economic and trade issues were to include human rights clauses to guarantee press freedom and environmental protection as well as to safeguard the rights of workers and farmers, while political negotiations were to be deferred until China had become a consolidated democracy. In effect, the declaration accommodated the China Factor in the reformist conceptions, and "defending democracy" as a shorthand for "fending off the China Factor" would become a major motif during the SFM.

After the signing of the CSSTA in July 2013, the CSAW transformed itself into the DFCSTSA. Just like the CSAW, this coalition was composed of a large variety of NGOs. The different backgrounds and different views on the issues of nationalism and capitalism essentially limited the DFCSTSA to reformist conceptions (Hsu 2017: 147; R41). As a result, the DFCSTSA was not so much opposed to signing a trade agreement with the PRC *per se* as it was concerned whether such an agreement would be negotiated and ratified according to democratic procedures. The early criticism of the DFCSTSA focused on the opaque negotiation process between China and Taiwan, which they characterised as "black box negotiations." After the signing of the CSSTA, the KMT and the DPP had reached a compromise that foresaw holding 20 public hearings before the agreement was to be reviewed on an item-by-item basis (Ho 2015: 77–79). As a representative of the DFCSTSA, Lai Chung-chiang was invited to participate in these hearings, but as the KMT held four meetings over the span of two days in late July and early August, the group withdrew under protest (Democratic Front against the Cross-Strait Service Trade Agreement [DFCSTSA] 2014c).

Over the following months, the coalition closely monitored the hearings, formalising four demands (Democratic Front against the Cross-Strait Service Trade Agreement and Taiwan Democracy Watch 2014): First, a Cross-Strait Oversight Agreement was to be passed into law before the initiation of the CSSTA's review process. Second, the government was to consider and review alternatives to the agreement, including negotiating an agreement with a narrower scope. Third, the legislature was to review and vote on the agreement on an item-by-item basis. Finally, the group urged the government to first pass supporting legislation (e.g., investment regulations for Chinese companies, a Trade Liberalisation Impact Assessment and Relief Law and a Mergers and Acquisitions Law) before voting on the CSSTA. These demands would inform the positions of the NGOs during the SFM.

The second major pole of mobilisation was the Black Island Nation Youth Front. This student group was essentially a successor organisation to the Youth Alliance against Media Monsters, where many of its members had participated, and like the DFCSTSA, it emerged after a protest at the Legislative Yuan against the CSSTA in July 2013. But while the YAMM had advocated nationalist conceptions, the BIY emerged as a proponent of a radical critique of the CSSTA. It is here that we can see the "mental sediment", as Luxemburg describes it, of the radical struggles during the previous 18 months. Having confronted neoliberal developmentalism in practice and having cooperated with groups such as the TRF and NAWCF, a new perspective emerged that was described as "left independence" (Hioe 2016).

It is, therefore, helpful to briefly consider how the radical groups framed their opposition to the trade agreement. In the immediate aftermath of the signing of the CSSTA, the social movement portal *Coolloud* became a platform for developing a critique of the trade pact that differed significantly from that advanced by the DFCSTSA. As Lin Poryee and Chen Shu-han (both THEU) put it, "the right-wing pro-China and right-wing anti-China dramas that appear to be opposites are actually the same" (Lin and Chen 2013). Both frame the issue in terms of the Taiwanese nation, which is either to benefit from integration (as the pro-China groups argue) or harmed by it (as the China-sceptics argue). In both cases, this framing obscures the struggle between capital and labour *within* Taiwan, thus reproducing the subaltern status of Taiwan's working class (Chen 2013). Wang Hao-chung (Losheng) and Hu Ching-ya (Losheng and THEU) furthermore argue that both the proceduralist and the nationalist opposition to the trade agreement fail to question the interests of Taiwan's bourgeoisie, as neither objects trade liberalisation in principle (Wang and Hu 2013).

These authors did acknowledge that China is pursuing a strategy to bind Taiwan. They do emphasise, however, that many of the grievances voiced by the Taiwanese are not reducible to cross-Strait relations. Instead, the authors propose a class perspective, from which they draw two conclusions for the practice of opposing the CSSTA. First, they deem it necessary to oppose the CSSTA not because of its procedural deficits or because it is an agreement with China, but, as Sun Chiung-li, a co-founder of the Black Ditch Club, argues, because neoliberal globalisation is "a weapon of capital against labour" (Sun 2013). As "capital knows no national boundaries" (Lu 2013), not much is gained by opposing the CSSTA while simultaneously pursuing trade agreements with other countries. The grievances of Taiwan's working class, like wage stagnation, would not be mitigated but sharpened by trade liberalisation (Lin and Chen 2013). Second, instead of attributing the hardships of Taiwan's working class to external forces, such as China, the domestic class struggle in Taiwan has to be put at the centre of analysis. As Lu Chyi-horng (NAWCF) argues, "the forces that really lead to economic and political exploitation do not come from China, but from capitalists who also call themselves Taiwanese", and it is the exploitation that occurs in Taiwan every day that has to be politicised (Lu 2013).

The BIY, however, was still marked by the nationalist conceptions of its predecessor. The members generally agreed on Taiwan independence, but their views on the degree to which capitalism and free trade should be politicised differed (R23; R40). Rather than adopting a purely radical perspective, they sought to articulate a synthesis of radical and nationalist conceptions, a perspective of "left independence".

Statements that were published by the BIY during the late summer and fall of 2013 can help illustrate this perspective. The first of these is the announcement for a two-day workshop the BIY organised in late September 2013, less than two months after its establishment. As this is an announcement for the first event organised by the BIY, it is insightful to quote the following longer passage from it:

> In this era of increasing trade liberalisation, why are the people less and less free? Why is the life of ordinary people [小民] getting more and more sad? Who is 'free' under free trade? The government claims that the economic benefits brought about by trade in services are hidden behind complicated numbers … However, the fears and predicaments of the public affected by the Service Trade Agreement are extremely real. The black box of the Service Trade Agreement does not only refer to its procedural omissions. Even more, it refers to the government's deliberate deception and domestication of the people. We must dismantle this black box and crack it open. The black box signing of the Cross-Strait Service Trade Agreement in the name of 'free trade' seeks to benefit a small number of dominant companies and capitalists, crushing the right to survive of the people of Taiwan under the giant wheel of open competition.
>
> (Black Island Nation Youth Front [BIY] 2013b)

This passage illustrates that the early conceptions adopted by the BIY did not operate on an opposition of China and Taiwan but rather of "dominant capitalists" and "ordinary people". The criticism of the CSSTA is furthermore explicitly articulated as going beyond the agreement's procedural issues and is instead motivated by the detrimental effects of competition and free trade on the working people in general. The purpose of this workshop was to discuss these issues and to establish a consensus regarding the CSSTA from a youth perspective, which could then inform the development of a campaign and concrete strategies to oppose the CSSTA. The list of invited speakers – which included Huang Kuo-chang, Wu Jieh-min (TDW), Lai Chung-chiang (DFCSTSA), Frida Tsai (TRF) and Son Yu-liam (TLF) – shows that the group sought the opinion of people that were known from previous movements.

These motifs remained a cornerstone of the BIY's opposition to the trade agreement. An undated document, which can be considered the group's manifesto and was in all likelihood penned during the same period, further develops the building blocks of the workshop announcement. It repeats some passages verbatim, but specifies their grounding in the experience of exploitation and hardships:

> The people of Taiwan have become the submissive workforce of business owners. They work overtime all the time, but the meagre income from their hard work cannot keep up with soaring prices. At the same time, the government continues to provide tax cuts and tax exemptions for conglomerates. Social wealth is accumulated on one side of the balance, and distributive justice is reduced to an abstraction.
>
> (BIY n.d.)

The document does include aspects of a China Factor perspective, stating that "[t]he Chinese government and capital have penetrated and threaten Taiwan's democracy and freedom" (ibid.). The group also acknowledges that it was established in response to the CSSTA, but emphasises that it sees its mission as going beyond this "battlefield to find the common cause for the flames in Taiwan" (ibid.). This common cause, it argues, is found in the "spectre of developmentalism" – a formulation used earlier by the TRF – that brings with it the pollution and destruction of farmland, urban renewal, the expansion of industrial parks and environmental degradation: "During our continuous pursuit of the mirage of economic development, we have sacrificed mountains, forests, coasts, land, homes, and even our bodies" (ibid.). The CSSTA is thus not reduced to the political interests of the CCP, but understood as a focal point of developmentalism and trade liberalisation and as a magnifying glass that can help shed light on these processes:

> The signing of the Service Trade Agreement allows us to see the black iron box that covers the entire island. It allows us to see how we obey the neoliberal dogma under the slogans of trade liberalisation and economic globalisation, giving up our land bit by bit and sacrificing our future for short-term interests.
>
> (ibid.)

This balancing act of addressing the China Factor through a critique of developmentalism was maintained throughout the following months during a series of protests and activities. A call for a protest at Taiwan's national holiday on 10 October, for instance, states that Ma Ying-jeou signed the CSSTA "to please China and satisfy the interests of a small number of conglomerates" (BIY 2013a), but also emphasises that not only the rapprochement but also the cases of land grabbing and urban renewal are driven by the interests of Taiwanese conglomerates. And when an ARATS delegation visited the Free Economic Pilot Zone at Taoyuan airport in late November, BIY took the occasion to not only criticise the black box negotiations through the SEF-ARATS channel that resulted in the CSSTA, but also stated that "[t]he so-called 'free trade' is actually nothing but the 'freedom of capital'" (BIY 2013c), causing stagnating wages and catastrophic damage to Taiwan's agricultural sector.

Throughout the summer and fall of 2013, the BIY thus explicitly criticised the proceduralist perspective as insufficient and maintained that the China Factor analysis had to be embedded within a perspective on free trade and developmentalism (R31). The hardships of Taiwan's working class and youth, struggles over land and even the CSSTA could not be reduced to China's political ambitions, but had to take into account the increasing capacity of Taiwan's bourgeoisie to assert its interests. Having adopted radical conceptions, the tone of BIY publications is markedly different compared to YAMM statements. Both organisations were essentially composed of the same group of people, but while the YAMM had been a vocal critic of the radical conceptions advanced by SCS during the AMM, the BIY had now embraced radical conceptions itself.

With these radical conceptions came a willingness to adopt increasingly disruptive forms of practice. During the 31 July protest, which prompted the formation of the BIY, at the first public CSSTA hearing, students managed to enter the compound of the Legislative Yuan before they were tackled by police forces. The BIY then participated in the 929 Alliance that sought to blockade the KMT's national congress, resulting in the postponement of the meeting. The following day, students again protested at the Legislative Yuan, where the KMT was beginning a series of eight public CSSTA hearings in the span of eight days. This time, about 30 protesters reached the door of the parliament, before they were surrounded by police.

The reformist and radical currents maintained their latent mobilisation through the fall and winter (R22). In March 2014, they increased the intensity of their activities as the public hearings came to a close. While the KMT had concluded its last eight hearings within the span of eight days in September and October 2013, the eight DPP-chaired hearings were spread over nearly six months. After the final hearing was concluded on 10 March, the KMT scheduled four meetings of the legislative review committee, set to begin on March 17.

On the day of the first meeting of the review committee, the DFCSTSA began a marathon protest scheduled to last the entire week. Although students were convinced that such a protest would result in the expenditure of a large amount of resources for little impact, several student groups supported the event. The "120 Hours to Protect Democracy" protest reflected the reformist thinking on the issue of the CSSTA. The coalition demanded a line-by-line review in the relevant committees as well as a final line-by-line vote that "must follow democratic principles in the legislative procedures" (DFCSTSA 2017). The declaration did not question free trade as such and instead requested that "the CSSTA should undergo oversight in the legislature", arguing that "the need for oversight is very necessary to maintain the system of checks and balances in Taiwan's legislature" (ibid.). The declaration concluded with an ultimatum:

> If the Ma administration continues to ignore the demands of the majority of the Taiwanese people, this will lead to the collapse of Taiwanese democracy, trampling on the welfare of the Taiwanese people, something the Taiwanese people will not submit to and comply with, giving up their right of self-determination over their land. We will begin different forms of civil disobedience, to resist something which has not been approved by the Taiwanese people: the illegal CSSTA.
>
> (ibid.)

Originally, the review committee was scheduled to meet four times. During the first meeting on 17 March, however, verbal and physical fighting between pan-green and pan-blue legislators broke out. In an incident that is now referred to as the "30-second review", KMT legislator Chang Ching-chung, who chaired the meeting of the review committee, then declared the review complete and announced that he would send the draft bill to the Legislative Yuan. As the KMT held a firm majority in the legislature, the CSSTA was expected to pass into law within days.

Accounting for the Structure of the Sunflower Movement

The 30-second review became the point of nucleation for the SFM, and the impending ratification of the CSSTA forced the hand of the various groups. The DF-CSTSA's "120 Hours to Protect Democracy" declaration had already threatened different forms of protests if the government were to disregard democratic procedures. After the announcement by Chang Ching-chung, Hsu Wei-chun of TDW also foreshadowed an escalation of protests, stating that "[i]t is obvious to me that Ma has forced Taiwanese to search for an "outside-the-system" solution, so that is what we're going to do" (TT 2014c). From the perspective of student leaders, the 30-second review represented a blatant violation of democratic procedures and thus provided the justification for radical action (R22; R29). As discussed above, several attempts to enter the Legislative Yuan and various ministries had been undertaken over the previous months, and students argued that a more organised attempt could increase the pressure on the government to reconsider the CSSTA.

On 17 and 18 March, several meetings among activists were held to discuss the best course of action (R27; R29; R30; R31; R41). Not all NGOs in the DFCSTSA, however, supported radical forms of protest, preferring to proceed with the "120 Hours" protest (R29; R30). Students were frustrated with the hesitation, arguing that "you cannot play the same tune over and over again, you have to turn it up a notch" (R21). The students, in coordination with a select few NGOs, however, devised a plan that consisted of several stages to overwhelm the security forces at the Legislative Yuan.

On the evening of 18 March, three waves of activists approached the seat of Taiwan's parliament. While the ART caused a disturbance at the Legislative Yuan's front gate, two groups of students, equipped with the necessary tools to force their way into the Legislative Yuan, climbed over the fences at other sides of the building (R45). After entering the building, they moved furniture in front of the doors to barricade the entry points. Despite several attempts by the police to clear the parliament, the students held their position throughout the night. Legislative Speaker Wang Jin-pyng (KMT) then halted any further attempts to evict the students. Immediately after the successful occupation, the BIY published a declaration that confirms that to this point they were adhering to radical conceptions:

> We do not want to see Taiwan's youth living a 22k life ten years from now! … The opposition to the agreement is not based on [the logic of] 'everything from China must be opposed'. The biggest problem with [the CSSTA] is that under liberalisation, only big capital will benefit, allowing the large conglomerates to expand across the Strait without restrictions … The nature of the service trade agreement is that of the WTO, FTAs and the TPP. These bilateral agreements remove the protection of the people in a given country. The service trade agreement – regardless of unification or independence, regardless of blue or green – is an issue of class, where a small number of big capitalists devours small farmers, small workers and small businesses.
>
> (BIY 2014c)

This declaration, emerging out of the everyday experience of the "22k genera-tion", explicitly denies that the CSSTA is only a matter of the China Factor, equally denouncing all free trade agreements. The BIY declaration thus resonates with statements published by autonomous and student labour groups either just before or in the early days of the occupation. The NAWCF argued that the CSSTA was "draped in the cloak of trade" (National Alliance for Workers of Closed Factories [NAWCF] 2014b) but was actually designed to facilitate the export of capital. The group decries that the resistance to the CSSTA was dominated by the China issue, emphasising that labour was suffering from any move towards free trade. Similarly, the YLU said that Taiwan's working class was being exploited by the Taiwanese bourgeoisie, and that the opposition should not be limited to the CSSTA but to trade liberalisation as a whole (YLU 2014).

Nevertheless, the 318 declaration also reveals contradictions within the BIY conceptions:

> We believe that Taiwan should be a place where young people can realise their dreams of entrepreneurship by opening a coffee shop or start their own company, a paradise of entrepreneurship where anyone can become a boss [頭家] by working hard.
>
> (BIY 2014c)

Wang (2017: 180) correctly notes the tension between the opposition to neoliberal-ism and the articulation of Taiwan as a paradise for entrepreneurship. A Gramscian analysis, however, has to disagree that "[t]his sensible, yet impossible, demand gives this manifesto a utopian character" (ibid.). To the contrary, it illustrates how deeply the social forms of authoritarian developmentalism are rooted in Taiwan. Rather than exhibiting a utopian character, the demand echoes the narrative of Taiwan as a "Boss Island", where the promise of economic upward mobility – based on self-exploitation and the exploitation of unwaged family labour – was of-fered as a consolation for actual hardships and as a surrogate for political inclusion during the authoritarian era. The social forms of "Boss Island" are so deeply rooted in Taiwan's self-conception that they even imbue a declaration that is otherwise articulated as a criticism of capitalism. Crucially, the 318 declaration thus invokes the same social forms that the government appeals to when it attempts to anchor the "free trade island" narrative through hegemonic initiatives that seek to foster these desires and ambitions by encouraging "youth entrepreneurship". We will return to the implications of these contradictions at a later point.

While the first night of the movement was characterised by disorder, a distinc-tive structure emerged over the following days as the tactical situation reached a stalemate.[8] Students were in command inside of the legislative chamber. They were surrounded by the police, which still controlled other parts of the compound. The whole compound of the Legislative Yuan in turn was surrounded by a large crowd of protesters. The NGOs, which had been preparing the 120-hour protest, set up their booths and stages in the streets around the parliament building, and during the first night and the next day, a large crowd of several thousand people arrived.

From this structure derived an implicit division of labour. The students organised the occupation within the legislative chamber, while the NGOs on the outside arranged a series of events, including performances, speeches, debates, classes and concerts, in order to maintain a crowd outside of the Legislative Yuan, hoping this would prevent the police from gaining control over the whole area. The consolidation of the occupation, however, also resulted in tensions over the vision of the movement. Students had not expected that the occupation would last throughout the night, and thus the meetings prior to the occupation had focused on tactical issues rather than how to proceed after a successful attempt (R21; R29; R40). Due to the spatial situation, the students depended on the NGOs, which thus had to be included in shaping the vision of the movement.

This reignited tension over the concrete demands the movement should articulate, as these would define the broader vision of the occupation. It became clear that "the gaps between some NGOs and the students were growing bigger and bigger" (R29). The NGOs initially requested the central demand to be for an item-by-item review of the CSSTA, while the students insisted on demanding the agreement's withdrawal from the ratification process (R27; R31). At this point, the students, having shouldered the action of occupying the Legislative Yuan, were able to impose their views (R31).

On 20 March, the movement – which by then had adopted the sunflower as its symbol after a florist had donated a large number of sunflowers – announced its three demands (BIY 2014a). First, Legislative Speaker Wang Jin-pyng was to void Chang Ching-chung's announcement that the CSSTA had passed the review phase. Second, the CSSTA was to be rejected. And third, the government was to refrain from negotiating with China until a Cross-Strait Oversight bill was passed into law. With these demands, the movement issued an ultimatum, threatening further action should the government fail to respond by noon of 21 March.

What at first seems to be a specification of demands derived from the 318 statement, turns out to stand, on closer inspection, in stark contrast to the first declaration. First, it is striking that the emphatic elements are gone. The statement no longer draws on the shared experience of precarity of the "22k generation" and the framing of this experience in terms of the struggle between capital and labour. Second, we can discern a subtle but crucial shift regarding the movement's central demand concerning the withdrawal of the CSSTA. While the students were able to assert their demand for a rejection of the agreement rather than an item-by-item review, the addition of the "oversight" demand undermines this. In the early days of the occupation, the opposition to the agreement was grounded in the *categorical* opposition to free trade agreements of any kind. The demand for an oversight law now results in a *conditional* opposition based on procedural concerns. This implies, furthermore, that the opposition to other trade agreements, including the TPP, has disappeared. This suggests that despite giving in to the rejection demand, the NGOs were able to impose a proceduralist angle on the movement.

The day of 21 March passed without a government response to the ultimatum. Premier Jiang Yi-huah, however, paid a visit to the students inside the Legislative Yuan one day later (Executive Yuan 2014). He informed the protesters that the cabinet had agreed to an item-by-item review of the CSSTA. Lamenting the "disorderly behaviour" (ibid.) by students, Jiang stated that the occupation was paralysing the country's democracy and urged the students to be open to "discussing issues in a rational, peaceful, and democratic way" so that the rumours and misunderstandings about the agreement could be addressed (ibid.). Prior to the premier's visit, however, Lin Fei-fan had announced two conditions, withdrawal of the agreement and enactment of a cross-Strait oversight law, that had to be met before the protesters would talk to the premier (TT 2014b). As Jiang saw himself unable to agree to these terms, the meeting ended abruptly.

Ma Ying-jeou addressed the protesters the following day. During a press conference, he applauded the passion and the motives of the students who were occupying the Legislative Yuan but stated that the illegal occupation of the parliament jeopardised the rule of law in Taiwan and with it the country's hard-fought democracy (Ministry of Foreign Affairs, R.O.C. 2014). He asked the students to "reflect upon this calmly" and reiterated the government's justification of the agreement:

> As you know, Taiwan is a small but open economy. External trade accounts for 70 percent of our economic growth. Because of our diplomatic predicament, although many countries want to do business with Taiwan, they hesitate when it comes to signing a free trade agreement (FTA) with us. … My fellow countrymen, regional economic integration is an unstoppable global trend. If we do not face this and join in the process, it will only be a matter of time before we are eliminated from the competition. For the sake of the nation's development, we truly have no choice. We can no longer sit idly by.
>
> (ibid.)

He then framed the protests as harmful to Taiwan's prosperity:

> A high-ranking official once said that if the services agreement is not ratified, South Korea would be the happiest party. What is even more troublesome is that the services accord falls under the Cross-Straits Economic Cooperation Agreement (ECFA), so if it is not passed, it will seriously damage our international creditability and cross-strait relations, and hamper our efforts to liberalize trade. It will certainly affect our chances of joining the Trans-Pacific Partnership (TPP) and Regional Comprehensive Economic Partnership (RCEP). Taiwan's position in the international community will definitely become more difficult, and more isolated.
>
> (ibid.)

Like Jiang before him, Ma attributed the protests to "the many misunderstandings that [were] circulating regarding the services pact" and ensured that the KMT would proceed with an item-by-item review and vote after all opinions had been heard (ibid.).

These events had a paralysing effect on the movement and had the potential to drive a wedge between its various currents. Since July, the central demand of the

DFCSTSA and the DPP had been for an item-by-item review, a point that the government was now willing to concede. Only the more radical students had insisted on the withdrawal of the agreement. Shortly after Ma's statements, Lin Fei-fan addressed the press in the Legislative Yuan. He decried that Ma Ying-jeou was "willing to repeat the old and tired points in support of the CSSTA that have been used, like a broken record, by his administration over the past few days" (BIY 2014e). Dismissing Ma's characterisation of the occupation as illegal, Lin instead condemned the "autocratic and undemocratic manner" in which the agreement had been "drafted, negotiated, and signed behind closed doors" (BIY 2014e). He then announced four demands: First, he asked that the governing and opposition parties convene a "citizen's constitutional conference" that was able to include the various positions of Taiwanese society. Second, he asked the legislators to reject the CSSTA and not reconsider it before a cross-Strait oversight bill had been enacted. Third, no negotiations were to take place between China and Taiwan until an oversight bill had been enacted. Fourth, Lin asked legislators to consider the cross-Strait oversight draft bill that had been proposed by NGOs (BIY 2014e).[9] Lin Fei-fan stated that the movement would not rule out any form of resistance to ensure these demands were met.

Two aspects of this response are noteworthy. First, it confirms the changing character of the opposition to the CSSTA. Even more than the 20 March demands it undermined the students' original position, as the appeal to "not reconsider" the CSSTA until the passage of an oversight law implies that, in principle, a free trade agreement between China and Taiwan was conceivable. Second, the movement's appeals now included a demand for a "citizen's constitutional conference". The origin of this addition cannot be traced with certainty. On 24 March, however, both the TAHR and the TDW published press releases detailing their demand for such a conference (TDW 2014; Taiwan Association for Human Rights [TAHR] 2014). This confirms a statement by one of my respondents who recalls that NGOs had introduced this idea during the occupation of the Legislative Yuan (R40). Arguably, the demand for a constitutional conference weakened the movement by deferring a decision on cross-Strait agreements into the future.

The direction of the movement leadership alarmed the more radical students. As early as 20 March, the movement had threatened further action if the government failed to respond to their ultimatum, but even several days later, the movement struggled to increase the pressure on the KMT. Fearing that the government was willing to sit out the protests the way it did during the WSM, students began discussing possible ways to escalate the movement before the support outside of the Legislative Yuan would dwindle and make the group inside the parliament vulnerable to eviction (R23; R25; R27; R28; R40).

The issue was discussed among the groups leading the occupation, but a proposal made by students to increase the pressure on the government by extending the occupation to hitherto police-controlled parts of the Legislative Yuan compound was voted down, mainly due to concerns by NGOs that such a move would jeopardise public support by tarnishing the movement's non-violent image (R25; R27; R31). At this critical juncture, unclear decision-making structures, a lack of consensus on the vision of the movements' goals and the adequate means to achieve these, as well as ineffective lines of communication contributed to a semi-independent group of students conducting an attempt to occupy the Executive Yuan, the seat of Taiwan's cabinet, that is located in the immediate vicinity of the parliament (R27). On the evening of 23 March, several hundred people forced their way into the building. Premier Jiang immediately ordered the police to clear the Executive Yuan, and through the following night the protesters were forcefully evicted from the compound. During the operation, 61 arrests were made but, more crucially, the images of the police action and bleeding students would dominate the TV coverage and social media over the coming days.

Projecting Homogeneity: The Sunflower Media Strategy and Its Discontents

The 23 March (or 323) incident proved to be a turning point for the Sunflower Movement for several reasons. First, it had a lasting impact on the relation of forces within the movement. While the adjustments to the movement's demands over the previous days already suggest that the NGOs were asserting their influence, the aftermath of 23 March cemented it by substantially weakening the radical current. Ho (2018a: 195) notes how the "police manhunt drove radical activists into hiding, thus consolidating the supremacy of moderate leaders inside the legislative building unexpectedly". Several central proponents of radical conceptions were excluded and others left Taipei (R22; R30).

Second, the circumstances surrounding the 323 incident revealed the necessity to formalise the decision-making structure to ensure that all future decisions on the direction of the movement were decided unanimously (R34). Three bodies were set up to integrate the various processes into a structure designed to achieve and maintain coherence. Inside the Legislative Yuan, a *Work Congress* (工作會議) was held daily to coordinate the logistics of maintaining the occupation. During the early days of the movement, ad hoc working groups had formed on the basis of personal relationships to tackle a variety of issues that emerged (R45). These groups, which ranged from material (food, water, supplies), security, translation, medical team, lawyers to a cleaning group, were now formalised (R34). Each group sent delegates to the Work Congress to report on the state of their tasks. Whenever an initiative demanded the cooperation of several teams, this was discussed here. After each meeting, the delegates reported back to their respective teams.

The *Joint Congress* (聯席會議) served as the movement's central decision-making committee. It held ten seats for representatives of NGOs and 20 seats for student delegates and met on a daily basis outside the Legislative Yuan. While the Work Congress dealt with day-to-day matters of maintaining the occupation, the Joint Congress decided the general strategy and direction of the movement. The 30 delegates were chosen to represent the range of groups, both from the students inside the Legislative Yuan and from the NGOs that maintained the activities around it. Finally, an emergency committee consisting of five students and four NGO representatives was set up in case a pressing matter had to be decided before the Joint Congress would convene again.

This apparatus has to be understood as a reflection of the division of labour that had emerged during the first week of the occupation. This division of labour – with the students maintaining the occupation inside the Legislative Yuan[10] and NGOs organising activities outside – in turn reflects the competing imaginations and forms of practice of the movement currents, as it were the students who had conducted the occupation while the NGOs held the "120 Hours" protest outside. In recognition of the indispensable support organised by the NGOs, they were given a substantial say in the Joint Congress and the emergency committee. As a concession to the students who were controlling the parliament, they held a numerical majority in the decision-making bodies (R25).

The third consequence of the 23 March incident was the growing awareness that the movement had to project a coherent narrative into the public discourse. At this point of the occupation, the movement was facing three challenges. First, as a direct consequence of the attempt to occupy the Executive Yuan, the public narrative established a distinction between the peaceful manner of the 318 occupation and the "violent riot" of the 323 attempt (R28; R29). The movement sought to ensure that the occupation of the Legislative Yuan would continue to be considered non-violent. Second, having been confronted with the apparent contradiction of occupying a parliament and thus impeding its functioning under the justification of defending democracy, the movement set out to find ways to maintain its legitimacy. Third, opponents of the SFM attempted to construe the occupation as a plot by the DPP. To invalidate these claims, the movement had to be portrayed as non-partisan. To understand the SFM's media strategy, it is helpful to first consider the public interventions that constrained its position.

Taiwan's bourgeoisie responded to the movement in a united fashion by holding a joint press conference. Rock Hsu, chairman of the CNFI, presented a common statement by 52 business associations, among them the six largest ones[11], essentially attributing the emergence of protests to miscommunication about the CSSTA (Central News Agency 2014). The business groups expressed their concern about the social turmoil in Taipei and appealed to all parties to "seek a viable domestic consensus on various disputes through calm dialogue" (Chinese National Federation of Industries [CNFI] 2014). Students were urged to end the protests that were harmful to Taiwan's democratic system and thus allow for a return to "rational discussion" (ibid.). To avoid disputes over the expected signing of the Cross-Strait Trade in Goods Agreement as well as the TPP and similar agreements, the business groups advised the government to establish a dialogue platform with civil society and business groups to ensure a consensus would be reached in advance, reminiscent of the SFM's demand for a constitutional conference. To resolve the immediate crisis, Taiwan's bourgeoisie urged the government to essentially concede to the DFCSTSA's and the DPP's original demands by considering an item-by-item review of the CSSTA and enacting an oversight law for trade agreements as soon as possible. This suggests that the business groups sought to defuse the situation by agreeing to demands that – given the KMT's majority in the Legislative Yuan as well as the DPP's opposition on procedural grounds – appeared like concessions but ultimately were unlikely to jeopardise the hegemonic initiative.

Other representatives of business associations with stakes in the CSSTA came forward as well. Chang Chih-yuan, secretary-general of the Allied Association for Science Park Industries, stated that the protests showed that students were worried about their future, indicating that the government had failed at explaining the rationale behind the CSSTA (Taiwan News 2014). Chang continued that the students, however, had no right to destroy public property and should return to "behaving rationally". Former ROCCOC chairman and founder of the Taiwan Coalition of Service Industries, Chang Pen-Tsao, said that the protests would jeopardise Taiwan's competitiveness and urged students to "return to reading books" (Apple Daily 2014). The narrative advanced by Taiwan's bourgeoisie thus operated on similar distinctions as those that had characterised the government's response, opposing rational vs. violent action and democratic consensus vs. protests that were harmful to democracy. Another shared feature was the insistence that the protests were actually the result of a lack of understanding by the protesters or miscommunication on behalf of the government.

The students, in turn, were supported by several public figures and organisations who came forward during the early days of the occupation. On 20 March, Chinese-born American public intellectual Yu Ying-shih, who had already publicly stated his support for the AMM, published a statement on Facebook, which was reprinted by the *Apple Daily* three days later. From his vantage point in the United States, Yu essentially maintained the "United Front" argument he had advanced two years earlier. Crucially, however, he tied in with the proceduralist angle, emphasising

> that 73.6% [of the Taiwanese] say they support conducting an item-by-item review of this 'agreement.' ... The current protests are a movement to protect and heighten Taiwan's democratic system, and they are equally important to the people and the government. The people can certainly solidify their civil rights through this movement, and the government can also improve its democratic quality through 'hearing the voice of the people.' That Taiwan has permanently settled on democracy is already an unalterable fact. Under a democratic system there will often be discrepancies and controversies between the people and the government, but because under such a system there is no more space for the existence of undemocratic, non-democratic, or anti-democratic governments, it is impossible for outright hostile antagonism to exist between them.
>
> The Chinese communists have constantly been resorting to all manner of trickery and subterfuge to destroy Taiwan's democracy, and both the people and government of Taiwan need to be on the highest levels of vigilance. Democracy is the greatest guarantor of Taiwan's security.
>
> (cited in Wright 2014: 167–169)

While Yu argues from a China Factor perspective, he proposes that strengthening democracy is Taiwan's first line of defence against China and the item-by-item review is the concrete aim to be pursued by the SFM.

Students also received the backing of universities. On 21 March, the Association of National Universities of Taiwan, representing 52 institutions, stated that Taiwan's universities were "very concerned about the development of Taiwan's democracy and the safety of students" and that they were "glad to see students face problems in a rational and calm manner" (Association of National Universities of Taiwan 2014). The following day, 25 professors of the prestigious National Taiwan University published a joint statement in support of the SFM:

> Under the trend of globalisation, we are not opposed to signing the service trade agreement. But the signing and review process must be transparent and in accordance with procedures. We therefore support the demands of the students and oppose any agreement signed by the government in a "black box".
>
> (Liberty Times 2014)

Although these statements of support were welcomed by the movement, they inadvertently defined a space of legitimate protest: The first implicit condition was that the movement renounced extreme measures of escalation and conducted the protest "in a rational and calm manner". Second, these messages of support discouraged the politicisation of Taiwan's export-oriented accumulation strategy, emphasising the procedural deficiencies of the CSSTA.

In short, the story was told *about* the movement rather than *by* the movement. Telling a coherent story, however, was not an easy task as several different imaginations competed within the movement. Especially during the unclear conditions of the early days, the direction of the movement was contested. When a group of pro-independence activists wanted to put up a Taiwan independence flag in the Legislative Yuan, they were asked not to do so to avoid the movement as being seen as a "green" movement (R22). A large poster renouncing free trade met the same fate (R24). Both the WSM and the AMM were characterised by the tensions among various currents, but these were resolved by insulation (in the case of the WSM) and dissociation (in the case of the AMM) respectively. The situation during the SFM was different, as it was spatially bound to the Legislative Yuan. This confined environment acted like a pressure cooker. Precluding any paths to dissociation – at least since the failure to occupy the Executive Yuan, an action that arguably was the attempt to dissociate the radical current from the reformist one – there were only two ways to achieve a coherent leadership: either by integrating or by subordinating and excluding the various currents. Facilitated by the decision-making structure, the SFM achieved the appearance of coherence via the latter route.

The nationalist angle, which had prevailed during the AMM, was toned down significantly. On the one hand, activists were aware that the majority of Taiwanese wanted to preserve the status quo in cross-Strait relations (R30). On the other hand, Lai Chung-chiang was a key advocate of avoiding putting the China issue to the fore, as he feared the media would then frame the SFM as a DPP movement (R29). A BIY activist recalls that representatives of NGOs, including DFCSTSA's Lai Chung-chiang, instructed the students not to discuss independence (Hioe 2016).

Another activist stated that the nationalist angle was seen as problematic for both structural and tactical reasons:

> The students had a consensus [on Taiwan independence], but not the NGOs. Some of the NGO leaders were hesitant to raise this issue. We also feared a government propaganda attack. We did not voice it [the issue of Taiwan independence], because we did not want to risk the movement by giving [the government] an excuse.
>
> (R32)

The attempt to limit the influence of pro-independence forces was reflected in the composition of the decision-making structure. While the NGOs that were involved in the planning stages of the 318 action were given seats in the two decision-making groups, the pro-independence ART, which had launched the distraction that allowed the students to enter the Legislative Yuan, was not invited to join, as leaders "were afraid that the image [of Taiwan independence] might be problematic" (R22). A representative of ART confirms that the group's openly political stance was seen as controversial by those NGOs that preferred to deal with the CSSTA on purely procedural terms (R36).

Although the NGOs conceded a numerical majority in the decision-making bodies to the students, several of my respondents argued that these numbers were deceiving, and that the organisational structure had a taming effect on the movement: "Some of the students were freshmen, for many it was their first [movement] experience – how could young students stand against professors?" (R22).[12] Furthermore, the commitment to unanimity meant that proposals could effectively be vetoed by those NGOs that were uncomfortable with going beyond the proceduralist demands. As a consequence, the rather moderate concerns of the NGOs tended to prevail over the more radical views held by the students despite the latters' majority.

Nevertheless, while activists "chose not to make it [the movement] about independence on the surface" (R31), the nationalist perspective resonated implicitly in the reformist conceptions: The TDW's *Declaration of the Free People* had already proposed a synthesis of the reformist narrative, based on democracy and human rights, and the nationalist narrative. Yu Ying-shih had argued along similar lines. Proponents of the China Factor perspective could thus pursue their demands within the ideological confines of proceduralist demands. As the nationalist perspective thus remained influential on an implicit level, it can be argued that the nationalist angle was *subordinated* to the proceduralist angle preferred by the reformist current.

The radical perspective, which had not only informed many of the struggles that led up to the SFM but also dominated its early hours, faced a different fate. Unlike the nationalist perspective, the radical current was *excluded* rather than subordinated due to several factors. One of the reasons for this outcome was the relative weakness of Taiwan's labour movement, which is still suffering from the repression and corporatism of the authoritarian era. While the occupation had prompted a variety of social groups to position themselves publicly, Taiwan's traditional labour unions had remained silent (R26).[13] And while the Taiwan Labor Front was an active participant in the movement and its decision-making bodies, it has to be considered a pro-independence labour movement organisation rather than a union (Hsu 2017: 142). The TRF, in turn, had been absorbed into the larger bloc of NGOs. Similarly, those radical leaders of the BIY that remained after the 323 incident – such as Chen Wei-ting, who had participated in the Dapu land struggles and the Hualon labour disputes – had been integrated into the leadership structure that precluded radical forms of practice and conceptions.

A second factor, which also provides context to the first, is the dominant ideology in Taiwan, which draws on the historical experience of the "Taiwan Miracle" and is continuously reproduced in education, the media and political discourse. This deep-seated belief that export competitiveness and thus long working hours and labour flexibilisation are necessary so that Taiwan can maintain its level of prosperity goes largely unquestioned: "We are educated to be pro-free trade, so many people may not oppose it" (R35).[14] According to Ho and Lin (2019: 304), "Taiwanese do not in general reject free trade with other countries" (ibid.), and in fact, Sunflower activists worked from the assumption that "the large majority of Taiwanese [was] convinced that opening up trade [would] result in increasing levels of income" (R26). In fact, even after the SFM, two-thirds of Taiwanese supported free trade with China (Ho and Lin 2019: 291).

This meant that the radical and reformist conceptions were irreconcilable. Positions such as

> It is not just the China Factor, it is capital. Even if we resist the China Factor, what about the US and the WTO killing our agriculture?
>
> (R34)

or the demand to emphasise class struggle against the bourgeoisie in Taiwan (R24) stood in contradiction to the nationalist position that saw free trade agreements with other countries as desirable to strengthen Taiwan's position vis-à-vis China.[15] Faced with the obstacle of the developmentalist elements anchored in the common sense and the contradictions of the "left independence" position, even BIY core group members that opposed free trade acknowledged that "most people come [to the occupation] for a different reason" (R40). A BIY spokesperson illustrates that this position ultimately prevailed within the student group:

> We think that Taiwan is an island nation. You can't break off all free trade. So our position was that we felt that free trade was necessary, but there needs to be a framework to avoid danger. Or to avoid things going wrong. This is not just regarding China, although one may need to be more careful regarding China, but also includes with [sic] other countries. Nonetheless, we didn't oppose all free trade.
>
> (cited in Hioe 2016)

In summary, the proceduralist narrative prevailed for the following reasons. First, the conjunctural element of the blatant disregard for procedures during the 30-second review of the CSSTA nucleation favoured proceduralist critiques (R21; R22; R24). Second, the 323 incident weakened the radical current and shifted the relation of forces in favour of the reformist current. Third, this shift was consolidated by the design of the decision-making structure, which restrained radical conceptions and forms of action, conforming with outside expectations of "orderly and non-violent" protest. Fourth, the proceduralist perspective was able to accommodate an implicit form of nationalist demands. Finally, the dominant ideology impeded the effectiveness of radical critiques. The proceduralist angle was therefore not simply the common denominator of the groups involved in the movement. A Gramscian perspective shows that this outcome is rather a reflection of structural and conjunctural constraints, which were internalised by a series of compromises (with NGOs) as well as processes of subordination (with regard to the nationalist current) and exclusion (with regard to the radical current).

Having achieved a certain degree of coherence, albeit a precarious one, this self-conception could now be projected into the public discourse. The SFM's media strategy was conditioned by the experience during the Anti-Media Monopoly Movement, when media outlets of the Want Want China Times Group "tried to discredit the movement and make it fail" (R45). Building on this past experience and relying on an organised media group in the Legislative Yuan, the SFM pursued what Liao et al. (2020: 277) call an "[e]motion-generated communitive consciousness":

> Media need a focus. If we don't give them a focus, they will chase it. We discussed it, and they [Sunflower leaders] said: We don't work for the media, but for the movement! But I knew from [my working experience at a media outlet] that media need a story!"
>
> (R35)

The relative importance of the media group is demonstrated by the fact that it had a delegate in the nine-person emergency committee (R45). Together with the separately organised international media group, it was tasked with monitoring, analysing and digesting the media coverage of the SFM around the clock. These summaries and analyses served to brief group leaders who then shared it within their working groups (R34). The decision-making group would then decide on a response to the coverage, and this decision became the basis on which the media group would prepare press conferences and speeches for Lin Fei-fan and Chen Wei-ting (R45). Overwhelmed by inquiries from television channels, the media group also trained young and inexperienced students to represent the SFM on television. To ensure that readers and viewers across all television channels, newspapers and online media encountered a coherent narrative, all of these spokespersons were meticulously briefed. As a result, the movement's message was condensed into a message that was far less complex than the movement itself:

> When the government or the KMT said something, we needed to find the best story we were going to tell among all the possible routes. ... Each day we had three to four people go to TV shows, and we had to react to events or stories in the same way. Producing the common story was our main task. ... Different

groups had different agendas: democracy, free trade, independence. We took the strategy to focus on procedures, because this was the one everybody could accept. But it was highly criticised. ... Our response to criticism: We have to be concerned with the reality of the Taiwanese people. We are either successful or not, and this is measured by the support: We have to mobilise as many people as possible, then this is a sacrifice we have to make.

(R45)

The media strategy was not restricted to the Taiwanese press. The experience of the AMM had shown that the virtual internationalisation of a movement could also help to shape the domestic context. The international media group therefore translated the movement's press releases into 14 languages. Major US and European newspapers and television channels used these for their coverage. Activists furthermore crowdfunded the publication of a full-page advertisement in the *New York Times*. The advertisement, funded by 3,621 donations, showed images of the police action against the protesters at the Executive Yuan during the night of 23 to 24 March. These images were accompanied by a brief text that focused on the procedural deficiencies of the CSSTA's negotiation and ratification process and decried the police violence against peaceful protesters.

The activists furthermore provided live transcripts of the events in and around the Legislative Yuan in both Chinese and English. One respondent set up live streaming from inside the parliament:

I wanted to live stream because of concerns about how the event would be represented in the media. Social movements rely on mass media to spread the images, but one cannot trust the Taiwanese media, so we wanted to control the public images by doing it ourselves.

(R43)

After the first days of the occupation, my respondent trained further activists to use the equipment, and after a week, about ten live streams were running continuously. As Lee (2015: 33) observes, the constant live broadcast from within the Legislative Yuan provided a material expression of the movement's demand for transparency, a critique *in praxi* of the "black box's" opacity. The movement presented itself not as a mob of violent rioters, but as an orderly group of activists who cleaned up after themselves. But the constant media presence also acted as surveillance, the counterpart to transparency, and limited the movement. One of my respondents stated that whenever Chen Wei-ting went to the toilet, 20 cameras followed him (R34). This tongue-in-cheek comment illustrates that every single moment of the occupation took place under the eyes of the public. Soon, the question of how a statement or action would appear on the media mattered more than the substantial vision and purpose of the movement (R29). As Lee aptly put it:

While resistance is intended to break rules and challenge order to make change possible, the resistance of the Sunflower Movement turned into guarding rules and maintaining order. Drinking in the chamber was criticized; recycling was praised. The public gaze confined the occupation to social norms, and therefore constrained resistance.

(Lee 2015: 38)

During the second week of the occupation, the proceduralist narrative that criticised the CSSTA on the grounds that it undermined Taiwan's democracy became dominant. On 27 March, the movement announced a large-scale protest to take place on 30 March in front of the Presidential Palace under the motto "Defend Democracy". The withdrawal of the CSSTA was still the first demand listed in the announcement, but the demand for supervision of cross-Strait agreements now clearly allowed for another review of the agreement after the legislation had been enacted (DFCSTSA 2014a). On the day of the large demonstration, all ambiguity regarding whether the movement insisted on the categorical rejection of the agreement or whether the agreement allowed for another review after the oversight legislation had been passed was removed, as the central demand had now become: "Withdraw the CSSTA, legislate before review" (BIY 2014b).

The 30 March demonstration itself was another indication of how the proceduralist framing precluded radical forms of practice that had not only characterised the months before the SFM but had also made possible the occupation in the first place. The event was framed by the opposition between state violence and peaceful protesters, and the organisers asked the participants to follow a published list of principles of non-violence (DFCSTSA 2014b). Channelling the movement's energy into this demonstration had been contested within the movement (R27; R30), but according to the organisers, the event attracted 500,000 people.[16]

This streamlining of the movement's outward appearance, however, came at a cost. To voice their dissatisfaction with the direction of the movement, several groups openly criticised the movement leadership. We can gauge the character of the discontent by looking at two forums that were established outside the Legislative Yuan. The *Dalit Liberation Zone* emerged out of a forum that had been convened by autonomous labour groups already during the first week of the movement (R24). As the dissatisfaction with the movement leadership grew, the forum reconstituted itself in a more organised form and named itself after the Dalit, the caste of "untouchables" in Indian society, to refer to both the exclusion of dissenting voices within the movement and the political exclusion of the working class under capitalism. The organisers hailed mainly from radical groups, such as NAWCF, TIWA, the Losheng Youth Alliance or the Huaguang Community Self-Help Association. These groups shared the perception that radical conceptions and forms of practice were being excluded from the movement.

The organisers sought to include social groups that were not represented in a movement that had been portrayed as a "student movement" in the media, such as workers. Debates, which often took between six and seven hours, were centred on the growing dissatisfaction with the movement's decision-making, but from April onward, the attention shifted to issues of capital and labour, the class-character of the CSSTA and the shortcomings of the China Factor analysis. The debates not only openly criticised the mainstream narrative of procedural justice but also raised concerns about the nationalist theme, which in their view fostered chauvinistic resentments rather than providing a clear analysis of cross-Strait relations (R24).[17]

While the Dalit Liberation Zone represented the radical current, the *Large Intestine Flower Forum* tended to represent those who were dissatisfied with the subordination of nationalist conceptions.[18] The forum is often dismissed as a curiosity among the activities outside the Legislative Yuan, as its events were often marked by profanity and sporadically by nudity. But the form of the Large Intestine Flower Forum is actually quite telling. In a certain way, the "carnivalistic obscenities" (Bakhtin 1984: 123) sought to counter and criticise the movement's self-restraint as well as the coercive imperative to behave in a rational and orderly manner, as one of the forum's initiators remarked:

> The movement tried a lot to avoid stigmatisation through the media, because the media would stick a negative image on the movement. At the Forum, you [were] able say what you really think without being afraid.
>
> (R43)

But not only the form represented a critique of the way the movement attempted to shape the way it was perceived. A major topic that emerged was the issue of Taiwan independence, and people who took the microphone began introducing themselves by saying: "My name is … I stand for Taiwan independence", quoting a famous statement by Cheng Nan-jung, a Taiwanese democracy activist and publisher who on 7 April 1989, 25 years to the day before the forum was initiated, committed suicide by self-immolation to avoid arrest by the police. Both of these forums thus bear witness to the growing dissatisfaction of the positions that were marginalised during the occupation of the Legislative Yuan and illustrate that the movement leadership did not represent the views of all participants.

The growing difficulties of reconciling the various interests within the movement was only one of the reasons why the search for an exit strategy became the dominant issue from early April onwards (R32). To everybody involved, it was apparent that the 30 March demonstration was the high point of mobilisation, and that a failure to capitalise on it could result in the movement's failure (R23). All participants, both inside and outside the Legislative Yuan, were physically and mentally exhausted, and the number of supporters gathering outside the Legislative Yuan dropped to 1,000 on 1 April (R31). Furthermore, public opinion shifted after the large-scale demonstration, and the majority of respondents to a poll stated that protesters should end the occupation (Wu 2019: 296). Crucially, the booths and stages set up by NGOs outside of the parliament posed a significant financial burden. While these activities had been partly financed through donations, these also dropped after 30 March, leading some NGOs to press for a conclusion of the occupation (R26; R40).

On the eve of the 30 March demonstration, Ma Ying-jeou and Jiang Yi-huah reiterated their position that they would not accept the movement's demands. The SFM leaders shifted their attention to Wang Jin-pyng, the speaker of the Legislative

Yuan, seeking to exploit a conflict between Wang and Ma, which went back nearly a decade when both competed for the chairmanship of the KMT (R23; R31). The struggle between Ma and Wang had intensified when in September 2013, the KMT's Central Evaluation and Discipline Committee revoked Wang's party membership at the request of Ma Ying-jeou, accusing Wang of influencing the outcome of a legal procedure against DPP caucus whip Ker Chien-ming. A court overturned the decision of the KMT committee on 19 March 2014, the second day of the occupation. Wang then failed to appear at a high-level meeting that had been called by Ma Ying-jeou in response to the occupation of the Legislative Yuan the same day, and on the evening of 20 March, he stated that the students' voices had been heard and he would use every possible channel to negotiate a solution. These developments convinced the movement leadership that they could exploit the rivalry between Ma Ying-jeou and Wang Jin-pyng, who, as the speaker of the Legislative Yuan, also had the final say on a potential police action on the parliamentary compound, and the Sunflower leadership.

On 6 April, Wang visited the Legislative Yuan and promised that he would ensure that an oversight bill was enacted before the parliament would review the CSSTA, thus fulfilling the movement's central demand. He also appealed to the activists to end their occupation to allow the democratic process to resume. Despite dissenting voices within the movement leadership, a general consensus emerged that this was the opportunity that had to be seized to conclude the movement before it would meet the same fate as the WSM (R45). It took the Joint Congress ten hours to come to a decision (R34), but on 7 April, student leaders announced that they would leave the parliament three days later.

The majority of Sunflower activists left the Legislative Yuan on 10 April. Protesting the leadership's inability to integrate dissenting views, the organisers of the Dalit Liberation Zone left one day early (Dalit Liberation Zone 2014). For the same reason, the newly formed Free Taiwan Front, consisting of more than a dozen pro-independence groups, including ART, the Radical Wings (or *Le Flanc Radical*) as well as remnants of the Youth Alliance against Media Monsters, vowed to stay longer (Free Taiwan Front 2014; TT 2014a).

Whether the Sunflower Movement can be considered a success depends on the criteria. In the most concrete terms, the movement succeeded in obstructing the ratification of the Cross-Strait Service Trade Agreement, which was never submitted to the Legislative Yuan's general assembly. In 2019, legislators also amended the Act Governing Relations between the People of the Taiwan Area and the Mainland Area to impose high thresholds for future negotiations between both sides. The most substantial consequence of the Sunflower Movement, however, was the cessation of the cross-Strait rapprochement: In the local elections of November 2014, the KMT, which previously held 14 out of 22 municipalities and counties, suffered considerable losses. The DPP gained control of another seven municipalities and counties, while the Taipei mayoral election was won by independent candidate Ko Wen-je. The KMT did not recover from the lack of public trust during the remainder of Ma Ying-jeou's term as president, and in January 2016, DPP candidate Tsai Ing-wen won the presidential elections with 56.12 per cent of the vote (compared to KMT candidate Eric Chu's 31.04 per cent), while the DPP secured 68 out of 113 seats in the legislative election, winning a parliamentary majority for the first time.

Conclusion

The Sunflower Movement was thus the decisive episode in the cycle of hegemonic contestation in Taiwan. The ratification of the CSSTA, which had been conceived as the major initiative of the hegemonic project, had been successfully prevented by a coalition of student groups and NGOs, actualising a network of cooperation that was a product of the struggle over the previous years. Social contestation also drew on conceptions that had been developed since the groups and activists first protested in late 2008.

What deserves a brief discussion is the role of the radical critique of the service trade agreement. The months leading up to the occupation of the Legislative Yuan had been characterised by the convergence of radical struggles, the increasing cooperation among radical groups and the continuous refinement of radical conceptions. These struggles had been rooted in and put to the fore the immediate experiences that resulted from the attempt to impose new modes of living and production that corresponded with Taiwan's developmentalist accumulation strategy: the precarious situation of Taiwan's "22k" youth, stagnating wages and the flexibilisation of labour relations, rising housing prices and forced evictions, as well as land grabbing, the commodification of farmland and the creation of "farming capitalists". In short, these groups sought to exorcise the "spectre of developmentalism".

Even during the early hours of the SFM, the leading youth organisation BIY insisted that it opposed the trade agreement not only because it served the political goals of the Chinese Communist Party, but also because it was an expression of the KMT's project to turn Taiwan into a "free trade island," which would benefit Taiwan's capitalist class at the expense of workers, farmers and the young generation. And yet, these radical voices fell silent as the movement progressed. This chapter has demonstrated that the outward appearance of a homogeneous movement was not simply the result of activists converging towards a common denominator. Rather, it has to be understood as the outcome of processes of subordination and exclusion that were deemed necessary to forge a "collective political will" (Gramsci 1971: 228). Cracking open the "black box" of internal struggles within the Sunflower Movement brings to light that the movement was animated by concerns not only about China but also about Taiwan. This insight puts into perspective the China Factor analysis of the SFM and has significant implications for our understanding of post-Sunflower political dynamics in Taiwan.

The exclusion of radical conceptions within the SFM was not only favoured by the immediate circumstances of the occupation, including the violation of democratic procedures that favoured the proceduralist narrative or the weakening of the radical current in the aftermath of the 23 March attempt to occupy the Executive Yuan. Rather, deeper-rooted factors were at play. Activists of all currents suggested that the radical critique of the CSSTA was "too complex" to grasp the imagination of the general public (R42), that it would have been unable to arouse emotions (R24), or that it would have struggled reaching the Taiwanese who are educated to support free trade (R35). Activists thus felt that developmentalism was firmly anchored in the common sense, drawing on the collective experience of the Taiwan Miracle and nurturing the ambitions of "'Boss Island'".

Chen Wei-ting had suggested during the Anti-Media Monopoly Movement that the lack of organisation and the failure to clarify conceptions were factors that resulted in the YAMM's subordination in the early stages of the movement. Arguably, the BIY found itself in a similar position during the Sunflower Movement. The "left independence" position appealed to young activists, but the relationship between radical and nationalist conceptions had never been systematically clarified. The tensions that resulted from the attempted synthesis of these two views weakened the group's ideological position vis-à-vis the NGOs. Furthermore, the YAMM had never fulfilled its promise of implementing an apparatus that involved and empowered the campus groups organisationally. In fact, compared to the YAMM, the BIY was less anchored in the various dissident societies. While it *recruited* its members from various student groups, there were no mechanisms in place to ensure that it *represented* them by integrating the various local positions systematically.[19] The student groups did establish connections between radical student groups and autonomous labour organisations during that time, but these forms of cooperation were mostly on an *ad hoc* basis and there is no evidence that a more formalised coalition was attempted to strengthen the organisational links among the radical groups. In the absence of such links, in the days after 18 March the BIY defaulted to the relations its activists had established with the more moderate NGOs since the post-WSM phase.

Without the straitjacket that was the Legislative Yuan occupation, however, the Black Island Nation Youth Front returned to the positions it had held before the SFM. The group participated in the Labour Day parade on 1 May 2014 together with campus groups that cooperated during the AMM (Black Ditch Club, NTPUCross, NTU Continent, Taiwan Humanities Society, Club of Seeds, Anti-Corporatization Front), student groups that emerged after the SFM (Democracy Kuroshio, Second Floor Slaves) and the youth labour groups YLU and NTU Union. In a lengthy statement that does not mention China even a single time, this coalition asserted that "transnational capital has achieved unprecedented economic and political dominance", which was responsible for the young generation's hardships like the "22k generation" phenomenon, wage stagnation, labour flexibilisation and rising tuition fees (Youth Labour Brigade 2014). The groups urged all Taiwanese to oppose not only the CSSTA but also the Trans-Pacific Partnership and the Regional Comprehensive Economic Partnership.

The BIY also held a series of three-day workshops in Taipei, Kaohsiung and Hsinchu during the months of May and June under the motto "Getting out of Free Trade Island: The CSSTA and its free trade companions". These workshops were to serve a double purpose:

> On the one hand, we will implement the original declaration of 'go out to sow, bloom everywhere'. On the other hand, we also hope to elevate the level of this movement from 'criticism of the black box procedures' to 'an alternative imagination of economic life.'
>
> (BIY 2014d)

The group thus sought to address the two major issues that contributed to the failure to generalise the radical narrative during the SFM radical current, the lack organisation among radical groups and the need to clarify radical conceptions on the basis of everyday life experience. Committed to criticising "the developmentalist myth of 'growth first'" (ibid.), the workshop announcement again singled out the Trans-Pacific Partnership and the Regional Comprehensive Economic Partnership as a continuation to turn Taiwan into a "free trade island". These developments suggest that there was a potential to revive the radical critique of developmentalism in Taiwan. The following chapter will discuss why these attempts had limited results.

The hegemonic project reacted to the SFM by adjusting its apparatus considerably. After the shock of the SFM, the KMT-CCP Forum originally planned for May 2014 was postponed "due to various factors" (NPF 2015). When the CSCMF and the TWC co-organised the second Cross-Strait CEO Summit in December 2014, Vincent Siew stated that young people feeling left out of the benefits of cross-Strait cooperation had weakened public support for the cross-Strait rapprochement (Cross-Strait CEO Summit 2015). Speaking at the Forum, Jack Ma, founder of the Chinese e-commerce company Alibaba, outlined his plans to establish a foundation to support young Taiwanese entrepreneurs, leading to the Taiwan Entrepreneurs Fund being established the following year. The renewed focus on youth was reaffirmed when the KMT-CCP Forum met in Shanghai in May 2015 for a shortened one-day event. Among the meeting's central topics were the creation of youth employment and entrepreneurial opportunities as well as the intensification of student and vocational training exchanges (NPF 2015). The Forum also suggested a strengthening of exchanges on the city and township levels.

The event in Shanghai was the final meeting of the KMT-CCP Forum. Following an investigation into the reasons for the KMT's defeat in the 2016 presidential and legislative elections, a report recommended the discontinuation of the forum (TT 2016). This spelled the end of the monolithic elements of the hegemonic apparatus that had been crucial in organising the rapprochement but ultimately revealed the particular interests behind it. Equally aware of these contradictions, the CCP increasingly co-operated with local forces in Taiwan, by-passing the KMT (Romberg 2014: 2). These direct contacts had been cultivated over the years, when Chinese officials visited farmers' associations and similar groups even without the involvement of the SEF or the MAC (R4), but now increased in relative importance. The Chinese approach was informed by the slogans "three middles and one youth" (三中一青), the "three middles" being central and southern Taiwan, middle and low-income families and small and medium enterprises, and "one generation and one stratum" (一代一線), referring to the youth and the grassroots. One of the manifold initiatives was the expansion of cooperation on a city-to-city basis such as the Taipei-Shanghai Twin-City Forum (Qiang 2020: 548–549).

The hegemonic apparatus thus further embraced capillary forms of intervention. One month after the final KMT-CCP Forum, the Straits Forum was held under the motto "Focusing on the Youth and Serving the Community", and nearly half of the forum's events were related to Taiwan's younger generation (CCTV 2015). The following years saw a proliferation of youth-focused entrepreneurship events, such as the Shanghai Cross-Strait Youth Entrepreneurship Competition or the An-hui-Taiwan Youth Innovation and Entrepreneurship Exchange. These are aimed directly at the Sunflower generation and attempt to draw on Taiwan's deep-seated admiration for entrepreneurship to make the young generation active participants in cross-Strait relations. The focus on young Taiwanese led to the establishment of the Cross-Strait Youth Development Forum in 2018, which has since been held an-nually. Then-KMT chairwoman Hung Hsiu-chu, who led the Taiwanese delegation of 200 young people, stated that "[t]he achievement of the Chinese Dream cannot be detached from Taiwan compatriots' integration and involvement, and it cannot be detached from the mutual participation and sincere cooperation between youths among the two sides of the Straits" (China Daily 2018).

The Cross-Strait Youth Development Forum became the stage for the announce-ment of preferential policies specifically aimed at Taiwan's youth, with Zhejiang Province unveiling 76 such measures at the 2018 edition, which included, among others, support in accessing youth entrepreneur bases. Similar measures aimed to provide tangible benefits to young Taiwanese by giving them equal treatment with Chinese in education, employment and the establishment of business start-ups (Qiang 2020: 542) and by further expanding employment bases and internship programs (Wang and Lee 2020: 77–79). Studies suggest that nurturing this form of pragmatism might be paying off: Even after the Sunflower Movement, a third of young Taiwanese strive to work in China despite their commitment to a Taiwanese identity (Clark and Tan 2016: 339). It remains to be seen how the continuation of capillary forms of molecular intervention will affect the political dimension of cross-Strait relations.

Notes

1 A common narrative in Taiwan, at times also invoked by my respondents, is that the opening of the real estate market to Chinese buyers in 2002 is a major factor behind this development (R35). There is, however, little data to support this argument. By 2018, only 463 housing unit sales by Chinese buyers had been approved, suggesting that the return of Taiwanese overseas capital as a result of global financial uncertainty rather than Chinese investors accounts for the dynamics in the real estate market (Chen 2020: 632–633).

2 Although these parks are officially referred to as 'Science and Industrial Parks', 'Sci-ence-based Industrial Parks' or even simply 'Science Parks' to create a "smokestack free" (Tu 2005: 294) image of Taiwan's IT industry, this section will generally refer to them as 'industrial parks' to emphasise that despite the technology-intensive character of the industries, these parks host manufacturing plants that put the parks into competi-tion over resources (such as water) with surrounding communities and cause various forms of pollution (see, for example, Tu 2005; Chiu 2011; 2014; Tsai 2015).

3 According to the International Labour Organization (ILO), real wages in Taiwan saw negative growth in four out of six years between 2008 and 2013 (ILO 2014: 14). Real wages in 2012 were lower than in 2000, and the labour share of national income de-clined from 54.6 per cent in 1995 to 47.8 per cent in 2011 (Pirie 2018: 144–145).

4 E.g., at the 2011 KMT-CCP Forum; see table 4.2.

5 The 929 Alliance consisted of groups representing labour, urban struggles, rural struggles, various campus groups and NGOs. For a full list, see 929 Social Movement Alliance (2013).

6 For a full list, see Preparatory Committee for the Rebellion of the Common People (2014).

7 Taiwan was to open 64 service sectors, including computer-related services, advertisement, marketing of films, construction, retail, hospitals, tourism, transportation, laundry and hairdressing. China committed to opening 80 sectors, including accounting, computer-related services, real estate, telecommunication, film production, construction, retail, hospitals, travel agencies and transportation. For a complete list, see SEF (2013a: 47).

8 Rather than providing a detailed depiction of the movement's chronology, the emphasis here lies on understanding how the previous years of hegemonic contestation shaped the process. For studies focusing on the chronology of the Sunflower Movement, see Wright (2014), Rowen (2015), Ho (2015) and Beckershoff (2017).

9 The statement by the BIY has been published in a Chinese and an English version. As the English translation differs slightly from the Chinese version, I have here relied on the latter.

10 According to surveys, two-thirds of the activists inside the Legislative Yuan were students (Hsieh/Skelton 2018: 108).

11 These are the CNFI, the CNAIC, the ROCCOC, the NASME, the TFI, and TEEMA.

12 Similarly, (R29 and R34).

13 If these factors lead Ho (2020: 411) to the conclusion that "[o]rganized labour was conspicuously absent during this political crisis", this is only partly true. While none of the traditional labour unions were active, autonomous groups such as TIWA, NAWCF and members of Federations of Industrial Unions as well as YLU participated.

14 Similarly (R24 and R37). Another respondent states: "The only 'left' contact we have here is with China, so people are afraid these ideas ... and if you say that the Sunflower Movement is not only about the China Factor, then it becomes very complex. ... 'Anti-China' is very easy to communicate, but anti-capitalism is not. Free trade is so natural to people" (R42).

15 For example: "If Taiwan can have a choice, we should have free trade with democratic countries, not with dictatorships like China" (R36).

16 According to the police, 116,000 people participated.

17 See also (NAWCF 2014a; Dalit Liberation Zone 2014).

18 The forum's name is based on a pun, as the Chinese characters for 'large intestine flower' (大腸花) resemble those for 'sunflower' (太陽花).

19 The high frequency of struggles after the AMM is likely to have prevented the consolidation of the apparatus during the 'busy' year of 2013.

Bibliography

929 Social Movement Alliance (2013). *929 Protest Announcement*. (In Chinese). 23rd September 2013. https://www.coolloud.org.tw/node/75688 (last accessed on 30/12/2020).

Apple Daily (2014). *Resistance against the Service Trade Agreement. Chang Pen-Tsao: everybody will lose.* (In Chinese). 26th March 2014. https://tw.appledaily.com/property/20140326/ZE3PMQSPLYCTJNXGH2BBIHGVXU/ (last accessed on 04/11/2020).

Association of National Universities of Taiwan (2014). *Joint Statement by the Executive Directors of the Association.* (In Chinese). 21st March 2014. http://anutw.org.tw/announce/ann20140321.html (last accessed on 04/11/2020).

Bakhtin, Mikhail (1984). *Problems of Dostoevsky's Poetics*. Minneapolis: University of Minnesota Press.

Beckershoff, André (2017). "The sunflower movement. Origins, structures, and strategies of Taiwan's resistance against the 'Black Box'". In: *Taiwan's Social Movements Under Ma Ying-jeou. From the Wild Strawberries to the Sunflowers*. Ed. by Dafydd Fell. London and New York: Routledge, 113–133.

Black Island Nation Youth Front (2013a). *Retake the country, the People are dying*. (In Chinese). 8th October 2013. https://www.coolloud.org.tw/node/75867 (last accessed on 14/12/2020).

——— (2013b). *The Free Age of Unfreedom. Cracking open the Service Trade Black Box*. (In Chinese). https://www.facebook.com/events/575238662523112/ (last accessed on 14/12/2020).

——— (2013c). *The protests of the people are like a shadow*. (In Chinese). 25th November 2013. https://www.coolloud.org.tw/node/76433 (last accessed on 14/12/2020).

——— (2014a). *20 March Demands*. (In Chinese). 20th March 2014. https://www.facebook.com/lslandnationyouth/posts/10203327450175366/ (last accessed on 14/12/2020).

——— (2014b). *330 Demonstration Statement*. (In Chinese). 30th March 2014. https://www.facebook.com/lslandnationyouth/posts/245963695586884/ (last accessed on 19/12/2020).

——— (2014c). *Declaration of the 318 Occupation of the Legislative Yuan*. (In Chinese). 18th March 2014. https://www.facebook.com/lslandnationyouth/photos/a.178388802344374.1073741829.177308745785713/241331436050110/ (last accessed on 19/12/2020).

——— (2014d). *Post-Sunflower Workshop Announcement*. (In Chinese). 4th May 2014. https://bit.ly/3plMt6i (last accessed on 19/12/2020).

——— (2014e). *Statement in Response to President Ma Ying-jeou*. (In Chinese). 23rd March 2014. https://www.facebook.com/lslandnationyouth/posts/242992019217385/ (last accessed on 19/12/2020).

——— (n.d.). *Self-description on Facebook*. (In Chinese). https://www.facebook.com/lslandnationyouth/info (last accessed on 16/10/2014).

CCTV (2015). *7-day Straits Forum opens focusing on youth and communities*. 13th June 2015. http://web.archive.org/web/20160102080258/http://english.cntv.cn/2015/06/13/VIDE1434190441706213.shtml (last accessed on 19/10/2020).

Central News Agency (2014). *Business Community calls for a national conference*. (In Chinese). 25th March 2014. https://www.cna.com.tw/news/firstnews/201403250149.aspx (last accessed on 04/11/2020).

Chen, Po-chien (2013). *Reflecting the Cross-Strait Service Trade Agreement through the history of Taiwanese capital*. (In Chinese). 29th August 2013. https://www.coolloud.org.tw/node/75216 (last accessed on 12/07/2019).

Chen, Ketty W. (2017). "This land is your land? This land is MY land. Land expropriation during the Ma Ying-jeou administration and implications for social movements". In: *Taiwan's Social Movements Under Ma Ying-jeou. From the Wild Strawberries to the Sunflowers*. Ed. by Dafydd Fell. London and New York: Routledge, 92–112.

Chen, Yi-Ling (2005). "Provision for collective consumption. Housing production under neoliberalism". In: *Globalizing Taipei. The Political Economy of Spatial Development*. Ed. by Reginald Yin-Wang Kwok. London and New York: Routledge, 99–119.

——— (2020). "'Housing Prices Never Fall'. The Development of Housing Finance in Taiwan". In: *Housing Policy Debate* 30.4, 623–639.

Chen, Yi-Ling and William Derhsing Li (2012). "Neoliberalism, the developmental state, and housing policy in Taiwan". In: *Locating Neoliberalism in East Asia. Neoliberalizing Spaces in Developmental States*. Ed. by Bae-Gyoon Park, Richard Child Hill and Asato Saito. Oxford: Blackwell Publishing, 196–224.

Chen, Qin and Yan-Yan Yao (2017). "Strategic Conception About Impelling the Financial Integration between Taiwan and Mainland". In: *Advances in Social Science, Education and Humanities Research* 99, 61–63.

Chen, Vickie Ying-en (n.d.). *Cross-Sectoral Participation, Youth Solidarity. Practice and Reflection on Taiwan Rural Front*. Partnership for Community Development. https://www.pcd.org.hk/en/newsletter/practice-and-reflection-taiwan-rural-front (last accessed on 28/12/2020).

Chen, Wei-ting (2012). *After the Tunghai exchange*. (In Chinese). 8th November 2012. http://waitingism.blogspot.com/2012/11/blog-post.html (last accessed on 17/07/2020).

Cheung, Gordon C.K. (2010). "New Approaches to Cross-Strait Integration and Its Impacts on Taiwan's Domestic Economy. An Emerging 'Chaiwan'?". In: *Journal of Current Chinese Affairs* 39.1, 11–36.

China Daily (2018). *Cross-Straits youth forum boosts Chinese Dream of reunification*. 13th July 2018. http://www.chinadaily.com.cn/a/201807/13/WS5b480ddaa310796df4df6463.html (last accessed on 20/12/2020).

Chinese National Federation of Industries (2014). *Statement on the Sunflower Movement*. (In Chinese). 3rd April 2014. http://dns1.cnfi.org.tw/kmportal/front/bin/ptdetail.phtml?Category=100554&Part=magazine10304-529-1 (last accessed on 04/11/2020).

Chiu, Yu-bin (2017). "Rising from the ashes? The trade union movement under Ma Ying-jeou's regime". In: *Taiwan's Social Movements under Ma Ying-jeou. From the Wild Strawberries to the Sunflowers*. Ed. by Dafydd Fell. London and New York: Routledge, 199–218.

Chiu, Hua-mei (2011). "The Dark Side of Silicon Island. High-Tech Pollution and the Environmental Movement in Taiwan". In: *Capitalism Nature Socialism* 22.1, 40–57.

——— (2014). "The Movement Against Science Park Expansion and Electronics Hazards in Taiwan. A Review from an Environmental Justice Perspective". In: *China Perspectives* (3/2014), 15–22.

Clark, Cal and Alexander C. Tan (2016). "Identity and Integration as Conflicting Forces Stimulating the Sunflower Movement and the Kuomintang's Loss in the 2014 Elections". In: *Contemporary Chinese Political Economy and Strategic Relations. An International Journal* 2.1, 313–349.

Cold-Blooded High-Tech Youth (2010). *About the Cold-Blooded High-Tech Youth*. (In Chinese). https://sites.google.com/site/coldtech2010/06-guan-yu-wo-men (last accessed on 30/12/2020).

Cole, J. Michael (2017). "Civic activism and protests in Taiwan. Why size doesn't (always) matter". In: *Taiwan's Social Movements Under Ma Ying-jeou. From the Wild Strawberries to the Sunflowers*. Ed. by Dafydd Fell. London and New York: Routledge, 18–33.

Council of Agriculture, Taiwan (2008a). *COA Promotes Small Landlords and Big Tenant-Farmers Project To Improve the Farm Land Use as well as Adjust Production Structure the Agricultural Production*. 19th November 2008. https://eng.coa.gov.tw/theme_data.php?theme=eng_news&id=192 (last accessed on 31/12/2020).

——— (2008b). *Enhancing international cooperation and expanding agricultural exports*. https://eng.coa.gov.tw/ws.php?id=2502383 (last accessed on 31/12/2020).

——— (2008c). *Promoting farmland reform and expanding the scale of farming*. https://eng.coa.gov.tw/ws.php?id=2502380 (last accessed on 31/12/2020).

———— (2011). *2010 Annual Report of the Council of Agriculture, Executive Yuan.*

———— (2012). *2011 Annual Report of the Council of Agriculture, Executive Yuan.*

———— (2015). *2014 Annual Report of the Council of Agriculture, Executive Yuan.*

Cross-Strait Agreement Watch (n.d.). *Purpose and Members of the Alliance.* (In Chinese). https://web.archive.org/web/20140326151029/http://www.csawa.org/home/guan-yu-liang-du-meng/lian-meng-zong-zhi-yu-cheng-yuan (last accessed on 15/12/2020).

Cross-Strait CEO Summit (2015). *Opening Speech by Vincent Siew.* http://www.ceosummit.org.tw/summit/?K=56 (last accessed on 19/10/2020).

Dalit Liberation Zone (2014). *9 April Statement.* (In Chinese). 9th April 2014. https://newtalk.tw/news/view/2014-04-09/46176 (last accessed on 31/12/2020).

Democratic Front against the Cross-Strait Service Trade Agreement (2014a). *330 Demonstration Announcement.* (In Chinese). 27th March 2014. https://dfactsa.wordpress.com/2014/03/27/267/ (last accessed on 21/12/2020).

———— (2014b). *330 Press Release.* (In Chinese). 30th March 2014. https://bit.ly/3iKnSWo (last accessed on 21/12/2020).

———— (2014c). *The public hearings should practice democracy rather than trample on democracy.* 30th July 2014. https://bit.ly/3paBeh4 (last accessed on 15/12/2020).

———— (2017). *120 Hours to Protect Democracy.* 21st July 2017. https://daybreak.newbloommag.net/2017/07/21/120-hours-democracy-declaration/ (last accessed on 21/12/2020).

Democratic Front against the Cross-Strait Service Trade Agreement and Taiwan Democracy Watch (2014). *Four Principles of Legislative Review of the Service Trade Agreement.* (In Chinese). 2nd March 2014. https://www.twdem.org/2014/03/blog-post.html (last accessed on 21/12/2020).

Executive Yuan (2013). *Free economic zones to aid Taiwan's integration into regional economy.* http://www.ey.gov.tw/en/News_Content.aspx?n=1C6028CA080A27B3&s=425598E0103CED94 (last accessed on 31/10/2014).

———— (2014). *Premier Jiang went to the Legislative Yuan to talk to the students.* (In Chinese). 22nd March 2014. http://web.archive.org/web/20140328223730/http://www.ey.gov.tw/News_Content2.aspx?n=F8BAEBE9491FC830&sms=99606AC2FCD53A3A&s=22E648C6AD29461C (last accessed on 04/11/2020).

Francks, Penelope, Johanna Boestel and Choo Hyop Kim (1999). *Agriculture and Economic Development in East Asia. From Growth to Protectionism in Japan, Korea and Taiwan.* London and New York: Routledge.

Free Taiwan Front (2014). *Press conference on the establishment of the Free Taiwan Front.* (In Chinese). 8th April 2014. https://www.coolloud.org.tw/node/78139 (last accessed on 30/12/2020).

Gallin, Bernard (1964). "Rural Development in Taiwan. The Role of the Government". In: *Rural Sociology* 29.3, 313–323.

Gramsci, Antonio (1971). *Selections from the Prison Notebooks.* Ed. by Quintin Hoare and Geoffrey Nowell-Smith. London: Lawrence and Wishart.

Han, Miao (2012). "The People's Bank of China During the Global Financial Crisis. Policy Responses and Beyond". In: *Journal of Chinese Economic and Business Studies* 10.4, 361–390.

Hioe, Brian (2014). *Taiwan Alliance for Victims of Urban Renewal.* New Bloom. 23rd November 2014. https://newbloommag.net/2014/11/23/profile-taiwan-alliance-for-victims-of-urban-renewal/ (last accessed on 22/12/2020).

———— (2016). *Interview: Lai Yu-Fen.* New Bloom. 8th December 2016. https://daybreak.newbloommag.net/2016/12/08/interview-lai-yu-fen/ (last accessed on 22/12/2020).

Ho, Ming-sho (2015). "Occupy Congress in Taiwan. Political Opportunity, Threat, and the Sunflower Movement". In: *Journal of East Asian Studies* 15.1, 69–97.

——— (2018a). "From Mobilization to Improvisation. The Lessons from Taiwan's 2014 Sunflower Movement". In: *Social Movement Studies* 17.2, 189–202.

——— (2018b). "The rise of civil society activism in the Ma Ying-jiu era. The genesis and outcome of the Sunflower movement". In: *Assessing the Presidency of Ma Ying-jiu. Hopeful Beginning, Hopeless End?* Ed. by André Beckershoff and Gunter Schubert. London and New York: Routledge, 109–131.

——— (2020). "From Unionism to Youth Activism. Taiwan's Politics of Working Hours". In: In: *China Information* 34.3, 406–426.

Ho, Ming-sho and Thung-hong Lin (2019). "The power of sunflower. The origin and the impact of Taiwan's protest against free trade with China". In: *The Umbrella Movement. Civil Resistance and Contentious Space in Hong Kong.* Ed. by Ngok Ma and Edmund W. Cheng. Amsterdam: Amsterdam University Press, 279–309.

Hsieh, Yu-Chieh and Tracey Skelton (2018). "Sunflowers, Youthful Protestors and Political Achievements. Lessons from Taiwan". In: *Children's Geographies* 16.1, 105–113.

Hsu, Jinn-yuh and Wei-hsiu Chang (2013). "From state-led to developer-led? The dynamics of urban renewal policies in Taiwan". In: *The Routledge Companion to Urban Regeneration.* Ed. by Michael E. Leary and John McCarthy. London and New York: Routledge, 148–158.

Hsu, Szu-chien (2017). "The China factor and Taiwan's civil society organizations in the Sunflower Movement. The case of the Democratic Front Against the Cross-Strait Service Trade Agreement". In: *Taiwan's Social Movements Under Ma Ying-jeou. From the Wild Strawberries to the Sunflowers.* Ed. by Dafydd Fell. London and New York: Routledge, 134–153.

Hu, Lingwei (2010). "The Basic Features and Challenges of Cross-Strait Relations in the New Era". In: *American Foreign Policy Interests* 32.1, 5–12.

Huang, Chen-Te (2015). *The Restructuring Policy of Agro-Manpower and Farmland in Taiwan, R.O.C.* FFTC Agricultural Policy Platform. 9th June 2015. https://ap.fftc.org.tw/article/884 (last accessed on 31/12/2020).

International Labour Organization (2013). *Global Employment Trends 2013*. Geneva.

——— (2014). *Global Wage Report 201/15*. Asia and the Pacific Supplement. Bangkok.

Shadow (2016). *The emergence of the 'student labourer' perspective*. (In Chinese). Civilmedia Taiwan. 8th August 2016. https://www.civilmedia.tw/archives/51865 (last accessed on 31/12/2020).

Jou, Sue-Ching, Eric Clark and Hsiao-Wei Chen (2016). "Gentrification and Revanchist Urbanism in Taipei?". In: *Urban Studies* 53.3, 560–576.

Lee, Mei-chun (2015). "Occupy on Air. Transparency and Surveillance in Taiwan's Sunflower Movement". In: *Anthropology Now* 7.3, 32–41.

Lee, Ping (2016). *Trends in the Taiwan Property Market*. Taiwan Business TOPICS. 24th October 2016. https://topics.amcham.com.tw/2016/10/trends-taiwan-property-market/ (last accessed on 25/01/2017).

LePesant, Tanguy (2012). "A New Generation of Taiwanese at the Ballot Box. Young Voters and the Presidential Election of January 2012". In: *China Perspectives* (2/2012), 71–79.

Liao, Cheng-hung and Chun-chieh Huang (1994). "Attitudinal changes of farmers in Taiwan". In: *The Role of the State in Taiwan's Development.* Ed. by Joel D. Aberbach, David Dollar and Kenneth L. Sokoloff. Armonk: M.E. Sharpe, 354–369.

Liao, Da-chi, Hsin-Che Wu and Boyu Chen (2020). "Social Movements in Taiwan and Hong Kong. The Logic of Communitive Action". In: *Asian Survey* 60.2, 265–289.

Liberty Times (2014). *The National Taiwan University's Department of Mathematics Supports the Student Movement*. (In Chinese). 22nd March 2014. https://news.ltn.com.tw/index.php/news/politics/breakingnews/973031 (last accessed on 04/11/2020).

Lin, Poryee and Shu-han Chen (2013). *A look at the policy of 'profit distribution' under the Cross-Strait Service Trade Agreement*. (In Chinese). 31st August 2013. https://www.coolloud.org.tw/node/75215 (last accessed on 12/07/2019).

Liu, Guancheng (2012). *Grassroots practice connecting rural areas and campuses*. (In Chinese). 12th January 2012. https://www.newsmarket.com.tw/blog/2465/ (last accessed on 28/12/2020).

Lu, Chyi-horng (2013). *Evoking Identity through opposition to the CSSTA*. (In Chinese). 2nd September 2013. https://www.coolloud.org.tw/node/75213 (last accessed on 12/07/2019).

Lu, Xuanhao and Zonghua Ye (2011). *Defend Land Justice, Visit the Touqian River Society*. (In Chinese). Radical Notes. 19th May 2011. http://nthuradicalpaper.medianewsonline.com/?p=49 (last accessed on 26/12/2020).

Ma, Ying-jeou (2012). *Full text of President Ma Ying-jeou's inaugural address on May 20*. Taiwan News. 20th May 2012. https://www.taiwannews.com.tw/en/news/1925248 (last accessed on 19/12/2020).

Mao, Yu-kang (1993). "Structure and change in the agriculture of Taiwan". In: *Agricultural Policy and U.S.-Taiwan Trade*. Ed. by D. Gale Johnson and Chi-ming Hou. Washington, D.C: The AEI Press, 11–53.

Marx, Karl (1968). *Theories of Surplus-Value*. Vol. 2. Moscow: Progress Publishers.

Miaoli Youth Reading Club (2011a). *2011 Miaoli Consensus Camp*. (In Chinese). 11th August 2011. https://web.archive.org/web/20130927164406/http://www.wretch.cc/blog/miaoliyouth/22973191 (last accessed on 28/12/2020).

———— (2011b). *Protest Announcement*. (In Chinese). 23rd December 2011. https://www.coolloud.org.tw/node/65621 (last accessed on 28/12/2020).

Ministry of Foreign Affairs, R.O.C. (2014). *President Ma News Briefing on the Cross-Strait Trade in Services Agreement*. 23rd March 2014. https://en.mofa.gov.tw/News_Content.aspx?n=1328&s=33108 (last accessed on 11/11/2022).

National Alliance for Workers of Closed Factories (2014a). *Statement from the National Alliance for Workers of Closed Factories*. (In Chinese). 1st April 2014. https://www.coolloud.org.tw/node/78014 (last accessed on 31/12/2020).

———— (2014b). *Unscrupulous Capitalists and Shameful Government*. (In Chinese). 17th March 2014. https://www.coolloud.org.tw/node/77783 (last accessed on 31/12/2020).

National Policy Foundation (2015). *Report on the 10th Cross-Strait Economic, Trade and Cultural Forum*. (In Chinese) https://www.npf.org.tw/3/15019 12th May 2015. (last accessed on 05/12/2019).

Ngo, Tak-Wing (2005). "The political bases of episodic agency in the Taiwan state". In: *Asian States. Beyond the Developmental Perspective*. Ed. by Richard Boyd and Tak-Wing Ngo. Oxon: RoutledgeCurzon, 83–109.

Office of the President, Republic of China (Taiwan) (2011). *President Ma holds press conference to explain his vision for a 'golden decade'*. 29th September 2011. https://english.president.gov.tw/NEWS/3746 (last accessed on 29/12/2020).

Pirie, Iain (2018). "Korea and Taiwan. The Crisis of Investment-Led Growth and the End of the Developmental State". In: *Journal of Contemporary Asia* 48.1, 133–158.

Preparatory Committee for the Rebellion of the Common People (2014). *2014 'Rebellion of the Common People' Youth Activist Training Camp*. (In Chinese). http://goo.gl/ygTrnT (last accessed on 31/12/2021).

Qiang, Xin (2020). "Selective Engagement. Mainland China's Dual-Track Taiwan Policy".
In: *Journal of Contemporary China* 29.124, 535–552.

Rogelja, Igor (2014). "The Production of Creative Space in Taiwan and China". PhD Thesis.
School of Oriental and African Studies. https://eprints.soas.ac.uk/20323/1/Rogelja_3765.
pdf (last accessed on 22/12/2020).

Romberg, Alan D. (2014). "Cross-Strait Relations: Portrayals of Consistency. Calm on the
Surface, Paddling Like Hell Underneath". In: *China Leadership Monitor* 45.

Rowen, Ian (2015). "Inside Taiwan's Sunflower Movement: Twenty-Four Days in a Student-
Occupied Parliament, and the Future of the Region". In: *The Journal of Asian Studies* 74
(01 Feb.), 5–21.

Schmidt Hernandez, Fernando Mariano (2017). "The Causal Role of Ideas in Taiwan's
Protectionist Agricultural Trade Policy". In: *Issues & Studies* 53.3, 1–29.

Shi, Shih-Jiunn (2012). "Shifting Dynamics of the Welfare Politics in Taiwan. From Income
Maintenance to Labour Protection". In: *Journal of Asian Public Policy* 5.1, 82–96.

Straits Exchange Foundation (2013a). *Cross-Strait Service Trade Agreement. Appendix 1
Specific Commitment Table of Service Trade.*

——— (2013b). *Ninth Round of Cross-Strait High-Level Talks to be Held from June 20
to 22 in Shanghai of the Mainland. Straits Exchange Foundation Press Release No. 19,
2013.* 14th June 2013. https://ws.mac.gov.tw/001/Upload/OldWeb/www.mac.gov.tw/
ct8b30.html?xItem=105023&ctNode=7461&mp=191 (last accessed on 26/12/2020).

Sum, Ngai-Ling and Bob Jessop (2013). *Towards a Cultural Political Economy. Putting Culture in Its Place in Political Economy.* Cheltenham and Northampton: Edward
Elgar.

Sun, Chiung-li (2013). *The paradox of legalization, occupation and democracy.* (In
Chinese). 27th August 2013. https://www.coolloud.org.tw/node/75102 (last accessed on
12/07/2019).

Taipei Times (2012). *Ma defends record on seeking foreign trade agreements.* 9th February
2012. https://taipeitimes.com/News/taiwan/archives/2012/02/09/2003525048 (last accessed on 29/12/2020).

——— (2013). *Tens of thousands rally against Ma.* 30th September 2013. https://taipeitimes.
com/News/front/archives/2013/09/30/2003573331 (last accessed on 29/12/2020).

——— (2014a). *Hawks' coalition to stay outside Legislative Yuan.* 9th April 2014. http://
www.taipeitimes.com/News/front/archives/2014/04/09/2003587609 (last accessed on
02/04/2015).

——— (2014b). *Jiang-protester talks fail before they start.* 23rd March 2014. http://
www.taipeitimes.com/News/front/archives/2014/03/23/2003586322 (last accessed on
29/03/2015).

——— (2014c). *Protesters slam KMT over pact.* 18th March 2014. https://taipeitimes.com/
News/taiwan/archives/2014/03/18/2003585948 (last accessed on 30/03/2015).

——— (2016). *KMT report tackles CCP forum, assets.* 4th April 2016. https://taipeitimes.
com/News/front/archives/2016/04/04/2003643136 (last accessed on 15/05/2020).

Taiwan Association for Human Rights (2014). *Emergency Statement.* (In Chinese).
24th March 2014. https://www.tahr.org.tw/news/1366 (last accessed on 19/12/2020).

Taiwan Democracy Watch (2013). *Declaration of the Free People.* (In Chinese). https://
www.twdem.org/p/blog-page_4.html (last accessed on 19/12/2020).

——— (2014). *Democracy must be reborn. Support the convening of a Citizens' Constitutional Conference.* (In Chinese). 24th March 2014. https://www.twdem.org/2014/03/
blog-post_27.html (last accessed on 19/12/2020).

Taiwan News (2014). *Hsinchu Science Park: Return to rationality and explain the Service Trade Agreement*. (In Chinese). 23rd March 2014. https://www.taiwannews.com.tw/ch/news/2442376 (last accessed on 04/11/2020).

Taiwan Rural Front (2009a). *Protect the Countryside 123*. (In Chinese). 23rd March 2009. https://www.coolloud.org.tw/node/37212 (last accessed on 28/12/2020).

——— (2009b). *Rural Grassroots Investigation Camp*. (In Chinese). 2nd July 2009. https://www.coolloud.org.tw/node/42670 (last accessed on 28/12/2020).

——— (2009c). *The critical moment for the survival of Taiwan's agriculture has arrived!* (In Chinese). 16th March 2009. https://www.coolloud.org.tw/node/36758 (last accessed on 28/12/2020).

——— (2010a). *2010 Bow to Land*. (In Chinese). 15th October 2010. https://www.coolloud.org.tw/node/55051 (last accessed on 28/12/2020).

——— (2010b). *Peasants' Joint Declaration on Combating Expropriation*. (In Chinese). 20th June 2010. https://www.coolloud.org.tw/node/52790 (last accessed on 28/12/2020).

——— (2011). *Call for due procedure in rectifying the Land Expropriation Act*. 12th December 2011. https://www.farmlandgrab.org/post/view/19772-call-for-due-procedure-in-rectifying-the-land-expropriation-act (last accessed on 28/12/2020).

——— (2013). *818 Protest Announcement*. (In Chinese). 17th August 2013. https://www.coolloud.org.tw/node/75317 (last accessed on 28/12/2020).

Tamburo, Elisa (2020). "High-Rise Social Failures. Regulating Technologies, Authority, and Aesthetics in the Resettlement of Taipei Military Villages". In: *Focaal. Journal of Global and Historical Anthropology* 86, 36–52.

Tsai, You-Lin (2015). "Behind the Economic Success of Taiwan's Hsinchu Science Industrial Park. Zoning Technologies Under Neo-Liberal Governmentality, Ongoing Primitive Accumulation, and Local's Resistance". In: *Journal of Comparative Asian Development* 14.1, 47–75.

Tu, Wen-Ling (2005). "Challenges of Environmental Governance in the Face of IT Industrial Dominance. A Study of Hsinchu Science-Based Industrial Park in Taiwan". In: *International Journal of Environment and Sustainable Development* 4.3, 290–309.

Wang, Chia-Chou and Liang-Cheng Lee (2020). "Analysis of Factors Influencing the Willingness of Taiwanese Students to Work on Mainland China. An Example of '31 Preferential Policies for Taiwan'". In: *Pacific Focus. Inha Journal of International Studies* 35.1, 76–108.

Wang, Chih-ming (2017). "'The Future That Belongs to us'. Affective Politics, Neoliberalism and the Sunflower Movement". In: *International Journal of Cultural Studies* 20.2, 177–192.

Wang, Hao-chung and Ching-ya Hu (2013). *Overcoming the Economic System of the Cold War. Reconsidering the Anti-Service Trade Discourse*. (In Chinese). 4th September 2013. https://www.coolloud.org.tw/node/75212 (last accessed on 12/07/2019).

Wang, Jiann-Chyuan (2010). "The Strategies Adopted by Taiwan in Response to the Global Financial Crisis, and Taiwan's Role in Asia-Pacific Economic Integration". In: *Japan and the World Economy* 22, 254–263.

Wei, Lily (2018). "Art as Protest, Cooking as Resistance. Everyday Life in Taipei's Housing Rights Movement". In: *Lateral. Journal of the Cultural Studies Association* 7.2.

Wei, Yang (2016). "The Restless Decade before Sunflower Movement. The Emergence and Practices of Networks of Social Movement Youth Activists (2007-2016)". (In Chinese). Unpublished Master Thesis. National Tsinghua University. https://hdl.handle.net/11296/6t7myw (last accessed on 09/12/2019).

World Trade Organization (2010). *Economic Cooperation Framework Agreement*. Regional Trade Agreement Database. http://rtais.wto.org/rtadocs/713/TOA/English/Combined%20 ECFA%20Text.pdf (last accessed on 16/01/2020).

Wright, David Curtis (2014). "Chasing Sunflowers. Personal Firsthand Observations of the Student Occupation of the Legislative Yuan and Popular Protests in Taiwan, 18 March-10 April 2014". In: *Journal of Military and Strategic Studies* 15.4, 134–200.

Wu, Charles K.S. (2019). "How Public Opinion Shapes Taiwan's Sunflower Movement". In: *Journal of East Asian Studies* 19, 289–307.

Yang, Daniel You-Ren and Jung-Che Chang (2018). "Financialising Space Through Transferable Development Rights. Urban Renewal, Taipei Style". In: *Urban Studies* 55.9, 1943–1966.

Yang, Min-Hsien and I Han (2015). *Policy Analysis of Implementation on 'Small Landlord Big Tenant' in Taiwan*. FFTC Agricultural Policy Platform. 4th May 2015. https://ap.fftc. org.tw/article/854 (last accessed on 31/12/2020).

Youth Labour Brigade (2014). *Labour Day Announcement*. (In Chinese). 30th April 2014. https://www.coolloud.org.tw/node/78486 (last accessed on 19/12/2020).

Youth Labor Union 95 (2007). *History of the Youth Labor Union 95*. (In Chinese). 9th March 2007. https://web.archive.org/web/20080818230239/http://blog.roodo.com/ youthlabor95/archives/2841791.html (last accessed on 30/12/2020).

——— (2011). *2011 Training Camp*. (In Chinese). 3rd March 2011. https://web.archive.org/ web/20130720223653/http://blog.roodo.com/youthlabor95/archives/15279229.html (last accessed on 30/12/2020).

——— (2014). *The Youth Labor Union opposes the Trade in Services Agreement*. (In Chinese). 24th March 2014. https://www.coolloud.org.tw/node/77901 (last accessed on 30/12/2020).

7 Conclusion

Hegemony and Resistance in Taiwan

This study has argued that the cross-Strait rapprochement was not a natural or inevitable process as claimed by the Kuomintang. Nor can it be reduced to the political ambition by the Chinese Communist Party to integrate Taiwan economically and politically, a thesis advanced by proponents of the China Factor analysis. While the CCP has long pursued a strategy of exploiting the growing economic interdependence between Taiwan and China politically, this cannot account for the particular ways in which Taiwan has dealt with these pressures. In particular, a more nuanced explanation is necessary to explain why the state of cross-Strait relations has swung from one of confrontation to one of rapprochement within a few years.

The present study proposes that the key to understanding these dynamics lies in examining the role of social forces. It has found that Taiwan's bourgeoisie was the major driving force behind a project that sought to improve the conditions for capital's own development by organising the consent of Taiwan's subaltern groups for a normalisation of economic relations across the Taiwan Strait. In order to universalise its particular interests, Taiwan's bourgeoisie supported the establishment of organisations such as the Cross-Strait Common Market Foundation and the Third Wednesday Club, which served not only to articulate a common ideological narrative but also to erect a network of forums and channels that were able to disseminate this ideology and coordinate the provision of material concessions to Taiwan's subaltern classes.

The hegemonic project attempted to broaden the social base for a rapprochement between China and Taiwan through a wide array of molecular transformations. These induced a form of pragmatism within Taiwan's society by ensuring that Taiwanese no longer perceived Taiwan's relation to China through a lens of national identity or political affiliations, but *qua* apolitical personal interests in sports, art, literature, religion, tourism and, above all, education and employment opportunities in China. Cross-Strait channels such as the Straits Forum not only served to coordinate the interests of the elites but also to deepen the inclusion of hitherto neglected groups, including the youth, women and the working class. These initiatives aimed to transform Taiwanese into active participants of the rapprochement, thus anchoring the project in their everyday lives.

DOI: 10.4324/9781003395546-7

But everyday life was also a source of grievances for Taiwanese. Taiwan's working population decried stagnating wages, a high level of youth unemployment as well as rising tuition fees and housing prices. While social movements emerging from these grievances failed to lastingly politicise these developments, the hegemonic project's "Cultural Turn" revealed the very particular interests it sought to obscure: The cooperation between Taiwan's bourgeoisie, the KMT and the CCP suggested that the rapprochement was not to the benefit of all Taiwanese, but rather based on the particular interests of political and economic elites. Instead of the successful articulation of a historical bloc, the rapprochement resulted in "a rift between popular masses and ruling ideologies" (Gramsci 1971: 276).

The analysis of the cross-Strait rapprochement as a hegemonic project contributes to our understanding of social and political dynamics in Taiwan. The investigation sheds light on the role of Taiwan's bourgeoisie in "fixing the limits," to use Gramsci's words, of political imaginations. We also arrive at a more adequate analysis of resistance, which no longer appears as a homogeneous reflex to "top-down" initiatives but is characterised by creative praxis and attempts to forge a collective political will out of competing visions. If the Sunflower Movement appears as homogeneous, this is the result of complex processes of integration, subordination and exclusion, the analysis of which enriches our understanding of the movement.

Hegemonic contestation, however, did not cease with the conclusion of the Sunflower Movement, and the framework laid out here lends itself to studying the social, economic and political dynamics in Taiwan since the DPP came into power. Following the cooling of cross-Strait relations in the aftermath of the change in government, the DPP proposed an alternative way of deepening Taiwan's integration into the global economy. At first glance, the New Southbound Policy (NSBP) resembles previous attempts by the governments of Lee Teng-hui and Chen Shui-bian to reduce Taiwan's economic dependence on China by promoting economic exchanges with Southeast Asian countries. What sets the NSBP apart from its predecessors is not simply the geographical extension (to include South Asia as well Australia and New Zealand) but more crucially its systematic and comprehensive approach. The policy not only promotes economic exchanges but also pursues a deepening of cooperation in the fields of education, culture, agriculture and tourism. At least on a superficial level, it adopts methods similar to those of the cross-Strait rapprochement by relying on "private-sector organizations such as academic, research, religious, cultural, artistic, industrial and commercial groups as well as associations of Taiwan-invested enterprises and NGOs" so that "private-sector firms can bring their energy fully into play and play a vanguard role in implementation of the New Southbound Policy" (Office of the President, Republic of China (Taiwan) 2016). In other words, the initiative seeks to simultaneously improve the conditions of accumulation for Taiwan's bourgeoisie and secure the consent of subaltern groups by creating tangible opportunities for broader strata of Taiwan's society.

The support of Taiwan's bourgeoisie for the NSBP can be at least partly explained by the fact that the implementation of the policy coincided with profound structural transformations. Labour disputes in the coastal regions of China had resulted in rising wages that made the country less attractive for Taiwanese manufacturing companies. As early as 2015, a year before Tsai Ing-wen was elected, Foxconn had announced that it would set up 12 factories, conceived to eventually employ one million workers, in India (Financial Times 2015). The interest of Taiwan's bourgeoisie in moving production facilities to South and Southeast Asia or to return to Taiwan was further amplified by trade tensions between the United States and China. In 2018, then-Premier William Lai thus announced that the government would support Taiwanese companies which sought repatriation to mitigate the fallout of these tensions. The following year, Lai's successor, Su Tseng-chang, approved the "Action Plan for Welcoming Overseas Taiwanese Businesses to Return to Invest in Taiwan" (Ministry of Economic Affairs [MoEA] 2019). The plan made available US$16 billion in preferential loans to companies that had been invested in China for a duration of at least two years and were now seeking to return to Taiwan (MoEA 2020). The ministry also promised "to help companies deal with land acquisition, water and electricity usage, and taxation issues" (MoEA 2019). To avoid labour shortages, companies that returned to Taiwan were allowed to increase their percentage of foreign employees up to a maximum of 40 per cent (MoEA 2020). A further US$2.6 billion in loans were made available to strengthen the "roots" of large businesses that had never invested in China before, while a similar programme was implemented for SMEs. As of November 2022, the applications of 276 enterprises that had invested China and 152 large enterprises that did not had been approved, resulting in investments amounting to approximately US$58 billion (MoEA 2022).

What becomes apparent from this brief characterisation is that the DPP government is not pursuing a *counter*-hegemonic project as much as an *alter*-hegemonic project that is committed to adjusting Taiwan's neoliberal developmentalist accumulation strategy to the new political conditions. This raises the question of social contestation. A future study would need to address the absence of radical mobilisation, which had accompanied comparable initiatives of the Ma government. A Gramscian analysis could focus on the absorption of movement leaders by political parties, which contributed to the disorganisation of activist groups in the aftermath of the Sunflower Movement, a process that Gramsci refers to as *transformism*.

The social conditions that facilitated this process of transformism were the fragmentation of social resistance after the Sunflower Movement. While often dismissed as the pursuit of complementary paths to achieving the same goal, a careful analysis of the documents from various groups as well as interviews with their representatives brought to light the contradictions between approaches to the re-politicisation of cross-Strait relations. These contradictions resurfaced after the movement and contributed to the fragmentation and atomisation of organisational structures that had taken nearly a decade to set up and consolidate. The attempt to dissolve the polarisation of Taiwan's political spectrum by establishing a "third force" beyond the pan-green and pan-blue camps failed as the initiators of the Taiwan Citizen Union split into the pro-independence New Power Party (NPP) and the Social Democratic Party (SDP), which sought to pursue a path of economic redistribution, effectively subordinating the former to the pan-green camp and marginalising the latter. This demonstrates the necessity to further investigate the fragmentary pressures resulting from the ideological superstructure of the blue-green division. From a Gramscian perspective, the key to understanding the resilience of Taiwan's bipolar political spectrum cannot be found in the structure of political society alone. Rather, such an investigation needs to include the structures of civil society that reinforce the blue-green spectrum, and as we have seen over the previous chapters, the polarisation of *political* society is cemented by the analogous polarisation of *civil* society institutions, including television channels, newspapers, labour unions and religious groups, which in Taiwan can usually be attributed to one camp or the other.

The beneficiary of these fragmentary pressures was the DPP. Tsai Ing-wen's Thinking Taiwan Foundation began systematically recruiting Sunflower activists in the immediate aftermath of the movement, and for the 2014 local elections, the DPP launched its "Democracy Grass" initiative, sponsoring 37 young candidates, nine of whom were elected (Ho 2018: 98). Before the 2016 elections, Tsai had recruited 11 core Sunflower activists to executive or secretarial positions in the party apparatus and her campaign office (Ho 2018: 98). Lin Fei-fan, who had played a crucial role in the cycle of hegemonic contestation, became deputy secretary-general of the DPP prior to the 2020 elections, while other activists ran as candidates for the party in the legislative election (Hioe 2019; Ho 2019).

This "green harvest" weakened resistance and simultaneously increased the DPP's legitimacy without significantly affecting the party's course. While campaigning ahead of the DPP's primaries for the 2020 presidential elections, William Lai declared in May 2019 that his goal was to transform Taiwan into a "Free Economic Island" (Taiwan News 2019). Although Lai was defeated by Tsai Ing-wen during the primaries, he became vice president on a common ticket with Tsai in 2020. Lai's statement is certainly representative of the DPP's policies that seek to deepen Taiwan's integration into the global economy. Although now firmly on the ground of China-scepticism, the DPP thus faces socio-economic challenges that are not too dissimilar to those faced by the KMT government, and a latent potential for social contestation exists. Contradictions that might resurface include the land question, which essentially remains unresolved (Fu 2019: 2; Huang 2019), and which might be sharpened by the government's plan to make 1,470 hectares of land available for the expansion of industrial parks (MoEA 2018).[1] The years 2017-2018 also saw the controversy over changes to the Labor Standards Act that raised the limit for monthly overtime hours from 46 to 54 (Ho 2020: 415). Finally, President Tsai announced in August 2020 that Taiwan would ease its restrictions on beef and pork imports from the United States "based on national economic interests and … future comprehensive strategic objectives" (Taipei Times 2020). The move, designed to pave the way for a bilateral free-trade agreement with the United States and the support to join regional trade areas, sparked protests in Taipei later that year.

The "spectre of developmentalism" thus still haunts Taiwan, and the potential for social contestation remains. The fate of the DPP's project to further deepen Taiwan's trade liberalisation through the NSBP and similar initiatives rests not only on the project's capacity to accommodate the interests of capital but also on its potential to incite a period of hope and expectation within Taiwan's society. Against the background of persisting and newly emerging contradictions, it is therefore imperative to study the mechanisms through which the hegemony of capital is reproduced in Taiwan and how it is challenged.

Note

1 For comparison, Taiwan's three largest industrial parks covered 4,663 hectares in the year 2014 (Chiu 2014: 16).

Bibliography

Chiu, Hua-mei (2014). "The Movement against Science Park Expansion and Electronics Hazards in Taiwan. A Review from an Environmental Justice Perspective". In: *China Perspectives* (3/2014), 15–22.

Financial Times (2015). *Foxconn to build up to 12 factories and employ 1m in India*. 13th July 2015. https://www.ft.com/content/1ef06826-2952-11e5-8613-e7aedbb7bdb7 (last accessed on 19/10/2020).

Fu, Wei-Che (2019). *Land and Democracy. Land Expropriations, Protests, and Votes in Taiwan Democracy Transiting Process*. ERCCT Online Paper Series.

Gramsci, Antonio (1971). *Selections from the Prison Notebooks*. Ed. by Quintin Hoare and Geoffrey Nowell-Smith. London: Lawrence and Wishart.

Hioe, Brian (2019). *As the NPP's internal crisis continues, the DPP takes steps to promote young people within the party*. New Bloom. 13th September 2019. https://newbloommag. net/2019/09/13/npp-crisis-dpp/ (last accessed on 22/12/2020).

Ho, Ming-sho (2018). "From protest to electioneering. Electoral and party politics after the Sunflower Movement". In: *A New Era in Democratic Taiwan. Trajectories and Turning Points in Politics and Cross-Strait Relations*. Ed. by Jonathan Sullivan and Chun-Yi Lee. London and New York: Routledge, 83–103.

——— (2019). "The road to mainstream politics. How Taiwan's Sunflower Movement activists became politicians". In: *After Protest. Pathways Beyond Mass Mobilisation*. Ed. by Richard Youngs. Washington, DC: Carnegie Endowment for International Peace, 61–67.

——— (2020). "From Unionism to Youth Activism. Taiwan's Politics of Working Hours". In: *China Information* 34.3, 406–426.

Huang, Wei-Ju (2019). "The New Spatial Planning Act in Taiwan. A Messy Shift from Economic Development-Oriented Planning to Environmental Conservation-Oriented Planning?". In: *Planning Practice & Research* 34.1, 120–130.

Ministry of Economic Affairs (2018). *Government removing investment obstacles to help Taiwanese firms in China return home*. https://investtaiwan.nat.gov.tw/newsPage?lang= eng&search=31466 (last accessed on 22/12/2020).

——— (2019). *Three major programs to give businesses greater confidence to invest in Taiwan*. https://investtaiwan.nat.gov.tw/newsPage?lang=eng&search=31574 (last accessed on 22/12/2020).

——— (2020). *Three Major Programs for Investing in Taiwan*. https://web.archive.org/ web/20211117074426/https://investtaiwan.nat.gov.tw/showPageeng1135?lang=eng& search=1135&menuNum=47 (last accessed on 22/12/2020).

——— (2022). *Three Major Programs for Investing in Taiwan*. https://investtaiwan.nat.gov. tw/showPageeng1135?lang=eng&search=1135 (last accessed on 23/11/2022).

Office of the President, Republic of China (Taiwan) (2016). *President Tsai convenes meeting on international economic and trade strategy, adopts guidelines for 'New Southbound Policy'*. 16th August 2016. https://english.president.gov.tw/NEWS/4955 (last accessed on 14/07/2020).

Taipei Times (2020). *Taiwan to ease rules on US pork, beef*. 29th August 2020. https://www.taipeitimes.com/News/front/archives/2020/08/29/2003742461 (last accessed on 29/08/2020).

Taiwan News (2019). *William Lai: Taiwan should strive to be 'Free Economic Island'*. 7th May 2019. https://www.taiwannews.com.tw/en/news/3696280 (last accessed on 05/12/2020).

List of Interviews

Table A.1 Interviews 2011–2012

No.	Interviewee	Date
1	Expert on cross-Strait relations	14/06/2011
2	Expert on cross-Strait relations	08/12/2011
3	Member of the KMT delegation during Lien Chan's trip to China in 2005	17/02/2012
4	New Frontier Foundation (Research Fellow)	06/03/2012
5	Mainland Affairs Council (Former senior official under Chen Shui-bian, first term)	09/03/2012
6	Expert on cross-Strait relations	09/03/2012
7	Mainland Affairs Council (Former senior official under Chen Shui-bian, first and second term)	12/03/2012
8	Taiwan Institute of Economic Research (Associate Research Fellow)	13/03/2012
9	Former DPP legislator	20/03/2012
10	Taiwan Foundation for Democracy (Senior official)	21/03/2012
11	Taiwan Thinktank (Senior official)	22/03/2012
12	Chung-hua Institution for Economic Research (Senior official)	22/03/2012
13	Cross-Strait Common Market Foundation (Senior official)	26/03/2012
14	Taiwan Competitiveness Forum (Convenor for Cross-Strait Affairs)	26/03/2012
15	Monte Jade Science and Technology Association (Senior member)	27/03/2012
16	Straits Exchange Foundation (Senior official)	28/03/2012
17	KMT-CCP Forum (Organiser and delegation member); National Policy Foundation	28/03/2012
18	National Security Council (Former member under Ma Ying-jeou, first term)	02/04/2012
19	Expert on the Democratic Progressive Party's China policy	15/05/2012

Table A.2 Interviews 2014

No.	Affiliation	Date	WSM	AMM	SFM	Notes
20	University Professor	17/09/14			∘	Held class at Legislative Yuan
21	Student activist	25/09/14	•		•	Dalawasao
22	YAMM, SFM spokesperson	25/09/14		•	•	Huaguang movement
23	BIY spokesperson	26/09/14		∘	•	University Student Rights Investigation and Evaluation Team
24	National Alliance for Workers of Closed Factories; Dalit Liberation Zone	29/09/14			•	Losheng movement
25	Taipei Society	30/09/14		•	•	SFM core decision group
26	Taiwan Labor Front	01/10/14			•	SFM core decision group
27	YAMM	02/10/14	•	•	•	Formoshock
28	Student activist	04/10/14			∘	MoI occupation
29	YAMM	06/10/14		•	∘	02 Society, Praxis in South
30	YAMM	07/10/14	•	•	•	Consciousness Paper, Formoshock
31	YAMM, BIY, Sunflower student leader	07/10/14	•	•	•	02 Society
32	Taiwan Association of University Professors	08/10/14		•	•	SFM core decision group
33	Radical Wings	10/10/14			∘	
34	SFM group coordinator	12/10/14			•	Ideology Study Club, Losheng, Youth Labor Union 95, Democracy Tautin
35	SFM International Media coordinator	13/10/14			•	Kuokuang protests, Democracy Tautin
36	Alliance of Referendum for Taiwan	13/10/14			∘	
37	DPP Social Movement Department	14/10/14		∘	∘	
38	Appendectomy Project	15/10/14			∘	
39	Expert on social movements	16/10/14				
40	BIY core group	16/10/14		∘	•	Radical Notes, Defend Miaoli Youth League
41	Taiwan Rural Front	18/10/14			•	SFM core decision group
42	Co-founder of an activist magazine	19/10/14			∘	Interesting Society, Shilin and Huaguang movements
43	Large Intestine Flower Forum organiser	20/10/14			∘	
44	Taiwan Democracy Watch	21/10/14		•	•	
45	BIY	21/10/14		∘	•	SFM media group

Notes

All interviews conducted in Taipei, Taiwan, with the exception of interviews No. 19 (Tübingen, Germany) and No. 21 (Keelung, Taiwan).

For abbreviations used, see List of Abbreviations.

Symbols used:
• Movement leader or core participant with organisational functions
∘ Participant.

Index